THE RISE AND FALL OF METER

The Rise and Fall of Meter

Poetry and English National Culture, 1860–1930

MEREDITH MARTIN

Princeton University Press

Princeton & Oxford

Copyright © 2012 by Princeton University Press

Published by Princeton University Press, 41 William Street,
Princeton, New Jersey 08540

In the United Kingdom: Princeton University Press,
6 Oxford Street, Woodstock, Oxfordshire OX20 1TW

press.princeton.edu

LIBRARY OF CONGRESS CATALOGING-IN-PUBLICATION DATA

Martin, Meredith, 1976–

The rise and fall of meter : poetry and English national culture,
1860-1930 / Meredith Martin.—1st ed.

p. cm.

Includes bibliographical references and index.

ISBN 978-0-691-15273-8 (hc. : alk. paper) ISBN 978-0-691-15512-8
(pbk. : alk. paper) 1. English poetry—19th century—History and criticism.
2. English poetry—20th century—History and criticism. 3. English language—
Versification. 4. National characteristics, English, in literature. 5. Poetics—
History—19th century.
6. Poetics—History—20th century. I. Title. II. Title: Poetry
and English national culture, 1860–1930.

PR595.V4M37 2012

821'.809–dc23   2011026832

British Library Cataloging-in-Publication Data is available

This book has been composed in Garamond Premier Pro

Printed on acid-free paper. ∞

Printed in the United States of America

1 3 5 7 9 10 8 6 4 2

FOR MY BROTHER

First of all it is expedient to get rid of the word Poetry.

—Robert Bridges, 1922

Contents

ACKNOWLEDGMENTS

❦

This book is the result of years of conversation, consultation, and collaboration with many friends and scholars. The first and foremost among these is my brother, Robert Martin, whose intellectual investment, editorial acumen, and unconditional love is woven into every word of this project. This book would not have been possible without him, for so many reasons.

The support, kindness, and perspective of Zahid Chaudhary has been both constant and invaluable; I am so thankful to have him as a friend and colleague.

I have been privileged to think about historical poetics with a dream group of scholars over the past five years: Max Cavitch, Michael Cohen, Virginia Jackson, Meredith McGill, Yopie Prins, Eliza Richards, Jason Rudy, and Carolyn Williams. I am in awe of each of you and thank you for your contributions to this project. Many of the arguments and ideas I make here were first rehearsed in our meetings. This book is for all of us.

Yopie Prins deserves special recognition for nurturing this project in its nascent stages, for encouraging my research and writing, for teaching and training me, and for being my constant champion. She has been beside me every step of the way.

I am grateful for the support (over the years and across the globe) of my many dear friends, colleagues, teachers, and students: Gayle Salamon, Jess Roberts, Bonnie Smith, Martin Harries, Tricia McElroy, James McNaughton, Anne Reader, Eric Geile, Martha Carlson Mazur, Amy Young, Graham Smith, Miriam Allersma, Dana Linnane, Lani Kawamoto, Kathleen Brodhag, Janine Konkel, Mary Thiel, Trish York, Mary-Ellen Hoffman-Dono, Tina Fink, Vlad Preoteasa, Vicki Chen, Alex Lester, Matt Hopkins, Margot Wylie, Steve Heard, Peter Miller, Liz Alfred, Allen Grimm, Justin Read, Ania Woloszynska-Read, Ben Conisbee-Baer, Siona Wilson, Eve Sorum, Vivica Williams, Susan and Scott Hyman-Blumenthal, Forrest Perry, Laura Shingleton, Stewart Coleman, Rob Karl, Beth Rabbitt, Evan Johnston, Laura Halperin, Indra Mukhopadhahy, Charles Sabatos, Sylwia Ejmont, Michael Dickman, Peggy Carr, Stan Barrett, Kristen Syrett, Sean Cotter, Meg Cotter-Lynch, Cathy Crane, Alia Ayub, Gary Lloyd, Ben Crick, Jonathan Butt, Bryony Hall, James Hammersly, Lena Hull, Bill Howe, A. B. Huber, Mike Laffan, Charles LaPorte, Jason Hall, Kirstie Blair, Catherine Robson, Anne Jamison, Jim Richardson, John Whittier-Ferguson, Marjorie Levinson, Paulann Petersen, Ken Pallack, Ward Lewis, Karl Kirchwey, Mia Fineman, Joel Smith, Devin Fore, Simon

Gikandi, Jeremy Braddock, Caroline Levine, Veronica Alfano, Evan Kindley, Gregory Londe, Amelia Worsley, Jacky Shin, Sara Grossman, Bea Sanford-Russell, Matt Steding, Donald Dietz, Jeff Strabone, Ben Glaser, Matthew Campbell, Simon Jarvis, Herbert Tucker, and Derek Attridge.

I am grateful for my dream research assistant Grant Wythoff, whose work with the Princeton Prosody Archive has helped construct the scaffolding on which this book was built as well as provided the platform for future historically poetic pursuits.

Immeasurable thanks are due to Terry Brogan, whose original archival work made this book possible.

Special thanks to Sarah Cole and Julia Saville for reading early versions of chapters, and to Anne Jamison, Jason Rudy, and Jim Richardson for comments on the final stages. I am grateful to the anonymous readers at Oxford University Press and Princeton University Press for their intelligent and engaging suggestions.

Thank you to my Swiss family: Raphael Vangelista and Gino, Michèle, and David Vangelista.

My editors at Princeton University Press, Hanne Winarsky and Christopher Chung, have expertly coaxed this book into its current form. I would also like to acknowledge the encouragement, intelligence, and good humor of Brendan O'Neill at Oxford University Press.

I am grateful for all of my supportive, engaging, and helpful colleagues at Princeton University, especially Daphne Brooks, Eduardo Cadava, Anne Cheng, Jeff Dolven, Sophie Gee, Pat Gugliemi, Claudia Johnson, Karen Mink, Deborah Nord, Jeff Nunokawa, Sarah Rivett, Marcia Rosh, Esther Schor, Nancy Shillingford, Nigel Smith, Valerie Smith, Susan Stewart, Benj Widiss, Tamsen Wolff, Susan Wolfson, Michael Wood, and Alexandra Vasquez.

For assistance with archives I am grateful to Helen Gilio, Sue Usher, Jon Stallworthy, Phillip Endean, and the staff of the Harry Ransom Research Center, Bodleian Library, English Faculty Library, Scottish National Library, British Library, Durham University Library, University of Michigan Library, and Princeton University Library.

Parts of chapter 5 were previously published in the article "Therapeutic Measures: The Hydra and Wilfred Owen at Craiglockhart War Hospital," in *Modernism* 14:1 (2007), 35–54. © The Johns Hopkins University Press. Reprinted with permission of The Johns Hopkins University Press. Thank you also to Indiana University Press for permission to reprint a version of "Gerard Manley Hopkins and the Stigma of Meter," from *Victorian Studies* 50.2 (Winter 2008): 243–53. A version of "Prosody Wars" was first published in the book *Meter Matters: Verse Cultures of the Long Nineteenth Century*, edited by Jason Hall. Reprinted with the permission of Ohio University Press, Athens, Ohio (www.ohioswallow.com).

I am, as always, strengthened by and grateful for the love and support of my wonderful parents, Robert and Mary Martin.

❧ THE RISE AND FALL OF METER ❧

Introduction: The Failure of Meter

When he walked over the meadows
He was stifled and soothed by his own rhythm.
—T. S. Eliot, from "The Death of Saint Narcissus,"
The Waste Land (facsimile)

It is certain now (thanks in part to Mr. Saintsbury), as it has long been obvious, that
the foot is immensely important in English prosody.
—Rupert Brooke, reviewing Ezra Pound's *Personae* in *The Cambridge Review*

Modern Instability

I don't believe in iambs. I am keenly interested in why people do or do not believe in iambs and why the proper way of measuring a verse is such a defensive issue for critics. Why have critics still not agreed upon one system of prosody for English verse? Why do most contemporary poets think that metrical poems are conservative or "old-fashioned"? Why is such a stigma attached to the word "meter"? And how, and why, has this suppressed narrative of metrical disagreement been crucial for both the formation and advance of English literary study in the twentieth century?

The Rise and Fall of Meter questions our assumption that "English meter" was and is a stable category. Metrical discourse flourished in the nineteenth century but it intensified toward the 1880s and into the early twentieth century. Why was there such an interest in defining English meter at the turn of the century? What was so important about establishing the history and meaning of English meter at that particular historical moment? Usually read as a transition between the Victorian and Modernist eras, the period between 1860 and 1930 is a crucial epoch in its own right, a moment in which the *New English Dictionary* and state-funded education defined and promoted ideas of Englishness through the use and measure of English language and literature. Within a changing religious and political climate, poets and prosodists turned to meter as an organizing principle—a possible means to order and stabilize

1

their relationship to the changing nation-state. But English meter presented the poet with an array of choices and associations that could be destabilizing as well; the myriad hybrid and new poetic forms (the verse-novel, the dramatic monologue) of the nineteenth century provide by virtue of their very existence clear evidence that poets saw poetic form as malleable and culturally contingent. At once bound to and always questioning literary tradition, poets brought their revisions and questions, experiments and conversations to bear on the shifting category that was called "Poetry" or "Verse" in the nineteenth century. Though I focus on the historical moment when our concept of "English meter" seems to stabilize, the main intervention of this book is to alter our assumptions about English meter as a stable concept, to ask what else "English" and "meter" meant, and might mean.

In 2006, I typed the word "versification" into the British Library's online catalog. Amid the various records—over a hundred—were four citations for a journal titled *Versification*. I had found more evidence, I thought, of late nineteenth- and early twentieth-century debates about prosody, meter, and versification—what I call the "prosody wars." I waited the rest of the afternoon for the librarian to pull up the library's four issues. Unapologetic, the librarian replied that, of the four, two were "lost" and one was listed as "destroyed by the war." She asked me to come back the next day, as they were still trying to track down the fourth issue. When I returned the following day another librarian kindly told me that the final issue of *Versification* in the online catalog had also been "destroyed by the war." I don't know why I was surprised; I was discovering, first-hand, that the war had materially erased bits of the archival record on which my research must rely, but such losses are, in fact, central to my argument. *The Rise and Fall of Meter* reveals the lost history of metrical debate and, via metrical debate, national definition, a history obscured both by war and by the narratives about meter that modernists invented in roughly the same period.[1] The minor poets editor Alfred Nutting published in his short-lived journal *Versification* (1891–92)[2] were no doubt judged according to some standard of "style and quality of composition," but I argue in the following pages that the standards for English meter were different in different communities, and that the concept of English meter measured not only English poetry but English history and national identity as well.

The story of English poetry between 1860 and 1930 is one we know very well and not at all. The familiar series of pat narratives includes, in roughly chronological order, an individualist and decadent poetics, politicized and then derided after the Oscar Wilde trial; the reactionary jingoism of turn-of-the-century poets like Alfred Austin and Rudyard Kipling; and a pastoral neo-Romantic mode characterized by the now nearly forgotten but then best-selling Georgian poetry anthologies published between 1910 and 1922. Fin-de-siècle poetry was weak and whiny, patriotic verses were loud and brassy, and Georgian poets were a yawn. The movements associated with the experimental avant-garde, retroactively named "Modernism," arrived as if to jolt, shock, and shake up old-fashioned, post-Tennysonian, post-Victorian poetry into something that could "respond to the scenario of . . . chaos."[3] Ezra Pound, in particular, challenged what Ira Nadel calls "the entrapment of poets by iambic pentameter."[4] In content but more importantly in form, the movements associated with the experimental avant-garde in the period before, during, and after the First World War changed the course of contemporary Anglophone poetry, loosening the "shackles of meter,"[5] the ticktock of its regular metronome, unleashing freedom of expression and experimentation, while creating new polyphonic, polyglossial, polyrhythmic poems. This is the narrative we have been taught. Rebecca Beasley writes that T. S. Eliot, T. E. Hulme, and Ezra Pound "revolutionized Anglo-American poetry, arguing that traditional poetic forms and themes could no longer encapsulate the experience of the modern world."[6] Pericles Lewis writes that "the victory of free verse over traditional meters" was "decisively won in English by Ezra Pound and his friends" and that "free verse abandoned traditional versification methods including meter, rhyme, and stanza forms; it often also violated standard syntax."[7] Even early historians of Modernism describe the break with tradition as cataclysmic, a "Great War"–sized upheaval of literary convention and tradition in the early twentieth century.[8]

These examples from Nadel, Beasley, and Lewis all promote the received view: modernists violated an established and stable tradition of English versification itself little concerned with experiment. I have culled these examples from teaching texts—pedagogical introductions written for beginning literature students. They provide clear narratives, but they leave out whole stories that, therefore, are never told, can never be brought to bear on either early free verse and its relation to forgotten metrical experiments, or on, say, the rhythmic intricacy and formal dexterity of poems written before the twentieth century in relation to metrical tradition. It is time for a more nuanced understanding of the history of form in English poetry. Even the language used to describe these traditional forms—"entrapment" and "encapsulate"—betrays the teleological attraction toward freedom and away from the repressive past. Indeed, the use of the word "standard" in "standard syntax" suggests that scholars think poets writing in the early twentieth century were reacting to ideas that had been fixed for so long as to become obsolete.

The narrative that Malcolm Bradbury and James McFarlane would call the "Great Divide" ("between past and present, art before and art now"[9]) is easy to teach and easy to understand[10]; it encourages students to think of poetry in terms of expression and persona, which is an inheritance from German romanticism and aesthetic theory and provides an abstract idea of literary genius. The version of twentieth-century English poetry in the literary history we teach is that modernist poetry is difficult; that difficulty, in content rather than mere form, is what makes it interesting; that expression and allusion are key; and that meter is old-fashioned, outdated, and a marker of the past.[11] The narrative implicit in the "great divide" assumes that prior to the modernist break, meter had been a stable, constraining, and limiting institution in poetics.

The conventional narrative of English meter's evolution from "regular" to "free" maps usefully onto ideas of progress and expansion, of empire as well as of social democracy; that is, the idea of breaking free from the "shackles" of meter is often understood in terms of the inevitable rise of the welfare state in England. It is also a narrative that was created and promoted in the nineteenth century—despite a diversity of metrical approaches prior to and during the period I discuss—in order to provide a unified concept of English meter for the quickly expanding literate masses and, later in the century, the expanding voting public in the new national school system. Though my focus is the late nineteenth century, I am in no way suggesting that this is the only moment in which metrical forms were called upon to do the work of the nation. However, I want to argue that our misconceptions about "English meters"—that is, reading English meter as a narrative of progress and evolution rather than a collection of competing metrical forms—emerge in the period between 1860 and 1930.

Most accounts of literary Modernism take Ezra Pound's salvo in 1945, "to break the pentameter, that was the first heave" (1.55),[12] as a reaction against the formal strictures of the Victorian era. But what if our understanding of the pentameter depends inaccurately on the modernist's simplified narrative of the nineteenth century? *The Rise and Fall of Meter* follows a neglected but major narrative about poetry, education, and national identity in a time when concepts of meter took on significant cultural weight: I begin just before the Reform Act of 1867, a key moment in Britain's history that established English literary education in grammar (and eventually secondary) schools, and I end with the beginnings of New Criticism in 1930. I read metrical experiments from this formative period in terms of a series of revised ideas about poetic education: what poetry means privately and publicly in the national imagination, and how meter is at once intrinsic and extrinsic to a formal reading of a poem. The result is a conception of meter that stands for a host of evolving cultural concerns, including class mobility, imperialism, masculinity, labor, education, the role of classical and philological institutions, freedom, patriotism, national identification, and high art versus low art.

I want to reiterate that "meter" in the nineteenth century meant different things to different communities, as well as to different poets, and that a poet's use of meter almost always implied a concept of the community and the nation. By stabilizing, attempting to define, or grappling with their use of meter, poets and prosodists were often attempting to define, transform, or intervene in an aspect of national culture. Throughout the book, the concept of "meter" emerges as a way for poets to mediate between various publics, broadly conceived. For instance, a poet could use a new metrical system to teach an audience to read differently: Gerard Manley Hopkins's sprung rhythm hearkened back to what he understood to be an Anglo-Saxon strong-stress meter more accurately representative of the speech dialects he wanted to preserve—even as he was equally committed to preserving another history of English only visible in written text. Matthew Arnold's obsession with translations of Homer in dactylic hexameter attempted to create a "new national meter"[13] that, as Yopie Prins has argued, could graft classical ideals onto English society through metrical translation. Poets in the late nineteenth and early twentieth centuries understood the nuances and possibilities of English meter in relation to broader cultural forms.[14] And yet, just as poets and prosodists were invested in these attempts to create new or adequate meters for England, so too were they aware of the increasing anxiety over meter's failure to provide an accessible form of national identification.

The proliferation of prosodic theories in the nineteenth and twentieth centuries reflects a similar anxiety on the part of prosodists and pedagogues to establish a system of meter that could reflect the greatness of English poetry and adequately measure the English language. On the one hand, pedagogic necessity solidified one idea of meter as a stable, readable pattern that moves, sometimes unchangingly, through the periods of English literature; within this tradition we read formal ruptures as expressive and quibble over metrical feet. On the other hand, our fixed attention to this established, foot-based scansion has obscured a vast body of writing about other possibilities for English prosody concurrent with the institutionalization of English studies. We should not take meter's meaning for granted as merely the measure of the line; rather, it operates as a powerful discourse that interacts with and influences discourses about national culture. This book reveals a variety of interrelated metrical cultures at the turn of the twentieth century that have shaped our current understandings, and misunderstandings, about the aesthetics and politics of poetic form.

Metrical Communities

It is the premise of this book that the literary movements around the time of the First World War, along with the national, pedagogical, and political movements in the period leading up to it, essentially erased a vast history of debates about versification in English. These debates, for which evidence exists despite their long tenure in the shadows of history, are the grounds for my claim that poets did not always approach meter as a stable category. Poets and prosodists grappled with, argued over, and attempted to standardize, alter, or disrupt concepts of "English meter" throughout the nineteenth and early twentieth centuries: the same era during which English meter became irrevocably associated with English national culture. The proliferation of metrical discourse from the late eighteenth to the early twentieth century is vast and nuanced, and teasing out all of the various approaches to meter and their historical contingencies cannot be the main task of this project. Controversies about English metrical form involved many of the major poets of the period. These controversies (evident in reviews and in histories of the period) included but were not limited to the resurgent interest in Anglo-Saxon meters (the accentual experiments of Samuel Taylor Coleridge) and revivals of Scottish meters (the Habbie stanza of Allan Ramsay and Robert Burns); the importance and influence of elocutionary science (William Wordsworth); the rise of the Spasmodic poets (Alexander Smith and Sydney Dobell), the perceived threat to English poetry from the Spasmodics, and the consequent renationalization of the ballad meter (W. H. Aytoun); the increased interest in translating metrical forms from other languages (Gerard Manley Hopkins, Robert Bridges, Thomas Hardy, etc.); the use of syntax and dramatic monologue to modulate rhythm (Robert Browning); the translation of metrical forms from classical verses (Elizabeth Barrett Browning, Robert Browning, A. Mary F. Robinson, Lord Alfred Tennyson, Algernon Swinburne, Matthew Arnold); arguments about the propriety of rhyme's role and the possibility of slant rhyme (Elizabeth Barrett Browning); arguments over the proper way to understand meters of the canonical poets (Chaucer, Shakespeare, Milton); the revision and reclassification of the sonnet sequence (Christina and Dante Gabriel Rossetti, George Meredith); the revival of Skeltonic meters and hybrid metrical forms (Christina Rossetti, Elizabeth Barrett Browning); the attempt to replicate classical quantities in English verse which, in many ways, resulted in the great hexameter debate; the emergence of and confusion over Walt Whitman's free verse; the ballad revival; the idea of musical notation to scan poetry repopularized by Sidney Lanier; the proliferation of and attempts to standardize hymn meters; the scientific study of phonology and its effects on metrical theory; the list goes on and on. Treatises, handbooks, introductions to writing poetry, and linguistic accounts of meter increased so much by the end of the nineteenth century that T. S. Omond, George Saintsbury, and Jakob Schipper all published competing histories of metrical theory in an attempt to account for the surge in interest. This book is not an attempt to account for all of these prosodic discourses, but I am aware, as the poets and prosodists I discuss were aware, that this vast field is the background of the prosody wars I will describe.

This book charts three interconnected and concurrent narratives that run from roughly the end of the eighteenth century to just after the First World War. The first narrative arc takes up English pedagogy's dream of English literature as a civilizing force. English literature, and the rhythms and meters of English poetry in particular, could, according to this narrative, civilize the newly enfranchised English masses and elevate the vernacular, infusing it with the same status as the classical languages. This pedagogical narrative is inextricably bound to the rise of the working classes and to the English empire, as is legible in Macaulay's 1835 "Minute on Education", which directly concerned the teaching of English in India but was obliquely involved with the development of local educational authorities in Ireland. The idea that English prosody could civilize the masses, both at home and abroad, is articulated again and again, from rhetorical treatises and grammar books in the eighteenth century to Matthew Arnold's writing about education and civilization in school reports and essays to Henry Newbolt's work in the English Association as the editor of the 1921 report, *The Teaching of English in England*.

I am interested not only in the inherent patriotism of these educational discourses, but in the way the discourse moves from a dream of pedagogical practice to an increasing insistence on the naturalness of the English language and meter. Nineteenth-century scholars who were trained in the classics wanted to translate the prestige- and character-building discipline of the classical languages into English poetics. As the century progressed and as the realities of state-funded education set in, the discourse of character-building discipline shifted toward a naturalized concept of English rhythm: the belief that the mechanics of English prosody (as a poetic reading practice, and not, in the late nineteenth century, as pronunciation) was inherent and common to all English speakers, irrespective of what or how they had been taught. Increasingly, these corporeal and phenomenological aspects of English meter displaced the goal that the school system could instill a kind of English national character in the pupil. Rather, school texts and curricular reform toward the beginning of the twentieth century increasingly insisted that the teaching of English poetry should bring out characteristics the English pupil already possessed, inherently, in his or her body.[15]

The belief that English meter was somehow inherent in English bodies surfaced in the rhetoric of eighteenth-century prosodic treatises (as well as even earlier treatises). But this concept of English meter's innateness—along with an increasing investment in the innateness of English accent, in particular, as opposed to the measured time of a line in either syllables or quantity—was far more characteristic of the late nineteenth century, when standards for English pronunciation had been more widely adopted. This investment in the innate ability to feel English rhythm, furthermore, persists in scholarship today, continuing to disguise and distort the complexity of meter and rhythm. And despite their consolidation and wide dissemination in popular English grammar books toward the end of the nineteenth century, these ideas about the "nature" of English rhythm were widely contested, debated, and called into question outside of the state-funded classroom.

The second overarching narrative of this book more specifically concerns the discourses of "the learned," and both influences and complicates the idealization and naturalization of innate rhythm as "English" meter I outline above. Even before the late nineteenth century, when state educational institutions were "expected to inculcate in the nation's children a proper sense of patriotic moral responsibility,"[16] I argue, the uneven and contested development of standards for English as a discipline created varied possibilities for collective English national identities with relation to English history, English language teaching, and histories of English literature. As we know from the work of scholars like Gillian Beer, Linda Dowling, and Lynda Mugglestone, the nineteenth-century rise of the discipline of phonology and the compilation of the *New English Dictionary* generated conflicting discourses about fixing standards to spoken English sounds (a debate I take up further in the following chapters).[17] Eighteenth-century rhetoricians and elocutionists were already concerned with the standardization of the English language, and Samuel Johnson's 1755 *Dictionary* promoted and popularized the potentially civilizing powers of the English language a century before the *New English Dictionary*. The epigraph to the sixteenth English edition of Lindley Murray's *English Grammar* (1809) is taken from Hugh Blair's *Lectures on Rhetoric* and demonstrates the civilizing importance of ordered language: "they who are learning to compose and arrange their sentences with accuracy and order, are learning, at the same time, to think with accuracy and order."[18] This dream of an ordered language and an ordered mind expanded into a dream of ordered meters and an ordered nation in the nineteenth century, and it was this hope, I claim, that generated many of the disagreements and debates about the grammatical study of prosody, versification, and meter within nineteenth-century teaching texts and among prosodists and poets. That is, although one system for English meter was ideologically popularized in the early twentieth century, the anxiety about the "rise of English" and the rise of the English working classes who required civilizing both stirred up the need for a stable system for English meter and generated the educational conditions to impose it. If the terrain of English language study was already uncertain, it follows that the study of English prosody, particularly the rules for versification and meter, was on uncertain ground as well. Even the most educated critics are tempted to gloss over the difficulty of defining meter in order to present a unified English meter for the twentieth-century English student-subject.

Broadly speaking, my study's second narrative traces the way that concepts of "native" and "foreign," or "inside" and "outside," are written and rewritten into the various attempts to establish English versification among the discourses of the learned. As Paul Fussell explains, "the association of verse structure with the political ideas of its makers"[19] has been at work since the very first definitions of meter in English. For instance, Fussell explains that

> [t]he idea of progress, a notion implicit in many of the most characteristic intellectual tendencies of the Renaissance, is intimately connected with the development and codification of what the Restoration hailed as the New Prosody. The outcome of the civil war had represented, to

most of the literate, a triumph of the forces of irregularity, and the wits who returned from France upon the restoration of Charles II were not slow to infuse poetic and prosodic theory with the political-social concept of progressive refinement and to exhibit a consciousness of a very recent victory over barbarity, disharmony, and regularity.[20]

According to Fussell, the Augustan verse line measured strictly by quantity and not by accent rose to prevalence through the influence of both ancient and French prosody. Though I do not propose to agree or disagree with Fussell's theory of quantity and verse origins here, I am interested in his alignment of prosodic order with national order—that is, strict prosodic rules meant a smoothly functioning, civilized literary and national culture. Likewise, just as the eighteenth century turned away from these meters, he argues, "a literary generation terrified by the French Revolution and its repercussions on the British political scene instinctively saw in the rise of a more free and varied prosody a lurking and sinister Jacobism."[21] For Fussell, metrical innovations could and should be read as culturally contingent. But Fussell missteps when he claims "the study of versification gradually came to seem of less importance" at the end of the eighteenth century as it "took refuge in the university and learned society." On the contrary, the idea that "prosody," as both pronunciation of the language and as the study of versification, could stabilize and define English national identity so permeated nineteenth-century English culture that it became almost illegible in its ubiquity. The project of "naturalizing" certain concepts of English prosody succeeded so thoroughly by the early twentieth century that we, like Fussell, understand these issues as resolved before the rise of Modernism, rather than splitting, as in fact they did, into a series of related discourses, each of them dynamic and historically contingent.

For example, the discourses surrounding the development of linguistic science and the project of national definition through historical narrative both influence the way we now understand prosody as both pronunciation and versification. These more complicated discourses of the learned were in turn re-translated toward the end of the nineteenth century back into the school system, framed (somewhat inversely) as a battle between the foreignness of classical, or "other" meters and the indigenousness of Anglo Saxon. Whereas at the beginning of the nineteenth century, Anglo-Saxon was associated with working-class regionalism, by the end of the century it stood for a somewhat sweepingly unified concept of English national character that permeated even the classically educated upper classes. The dream of the schools (the civilizing aspects of English education) and the discourses of the learned (meter and prosody as part of a larger historical narrative for England) combined by necessity after the passage of the late nineteenth-century Education Acts. Meant to civilize the working classes in much the same way that Macaulay wanted to civilize Indian subjects earlier in the century, the "Poor Man's classics" of English literature were called upon as forces for social good, and English meter played a surprisingly prominent role in the debates about the quality of English literary education as a replacement for the classics.

Indeed, the way English meter would be taught in schools or would be readable or understandable to a reading public informs this entire project, but especially the third narrative, which could be called "metrical communities." The most popular form of English meter borrowed its terminology (iambs and trochees, spondees and dactyls) from the classical languages, so it had a cachet, elite knowledge—the terms for metrical feet were Greek but had become English via Latin; like Latin grammars, the prestige of classical education might have clung to these words. On the other hand, despite their familiar associations, these terms were also suspect—Why use foreign names for something English? Why scan verses according to the classical system at all? Many of the debates toward the end of the century were staged somehow as a battle between those who clung to the conventions of classical foot-scansion versus those who wanted to reform English meter for the new English students. Though some of this discourse never made it into the schools, many of the most revolutionary systems for English meter were proposed with school use in mind. Robert Bridges's best-selling *Milton's Prosody*, despite its highly technical nature, was in its original form an introductory preface to a school edition of *Paradise Lost*. Many of the tensions surrounding linguistic nationalism and the metrical history of England—where it should begin, whether it should be accentual (natural) or scanned according to a classical system and therefore by "feet" (learned, associated with the classical languages and a classical idea of England)—were thrown into stark relief with the rise of the English education system. What new English reading community would form in the place of the classically educated elite? I claim that poets, especially, believed that poems—and their forms—could not only speak to different communities, but could also help create, shape, and sustain them. But we, today, have lost the sense that the decision to define, promote, or defend a certain system of English meter in English literary study was, and is, akin to other forms of dogma. That is, we accept the naturalness of the iamb as a fact, whereas linguistic scholarship has never supported the pedagogical practice of taking the "iamb" (or "trochee," etc.) for granted as accurate and stable in English. When we accept the "Englishness" of the iamb we forget to acknowledge or question the national and class ideologies that made it so.

Meter as Culture

The misreading of multiple metrical cultures as a homogenous, stable whole haunts the linguistic and literary critical climate to this day, creating an artificial division between aesthetics and politics that this book hopes to repair. The book's argument is presented in three parts, made up of two chapters each. Each part includes a discussion of the poet and prosodist Robert Bridges, whose life (1844–1930) and work spans the time period I cover; he is in many ways the book's protagonist. In the first two chapters I describe the multiple, competing models of English meter in the nineteenth century. Chapter 1, "The History of Meter," provides the book's historical and methodological framework. Despite the modernist characterization of Victorian tradition as unified and steadfast, the various approaches to Victorian meter in English histories, grammars, and metrical studies reveal ideologically charged histories of English culture, often presented as Roman or Anglo-Saxon. Gerard Manley Hopkins was himself a mediator between various metrical discourses and theories. As a Catholic priest who taught the classics and an English poet who attempted to valorize the material history of the English language in his syntax and through his use of sprung rhythm, Hopkins is a test case for the personal and national ideologies of English meter. Chapter 2, "The Stigma of Meter," resituates Hopkins, whose name has become synonymous with metrical experiment, within the prosodic, philological, and theological debates of his time. Hopkins's commitment to defining accent and stress in English was a critical turning point in his thinking about his identity as a Catholic and as an Englishman; in 1887 he wrote to Robert Bridges and Coventry Patmore that "a great poem in English is like a great battle won for England."[22] Rather than read Hopkins's experiments as anachronistic, I argue that his attempt to create a new English meter was a particularly Victorian engagement with poetic form, national identity, and the English language. Broader movements in comparative philology (particularly those associated with scholars such as Max Müller and Richard Chevenix Trench) influenced Hopkins's attempts to reconcile the history of English and the materiality of meter with his Catholic beliefs. Alongside Coventry Patmore's "Essay on English Metrical Law," Hopkins's attempt to find the "true" meaning of accent in English shows how metrical questions were a matter of both personal and national salvation. I thus use Hopkins to prove that even the most obscure and alienated-seeming poet must be read as part of the broader debate about what meter can do for the quickly changing nation. Hopkins's successes and failures, I conclude, anticipate later attempts to examine the constituent parts of meter and the English language.

Chapters 3 and 4 describe the institutionalization of "English meter" in both elite and mass cultural contexts, showing how and why one model for English meter emerged as representative for early twentieth-century national culture through the work of Hopkins, Bridges, George Saintsbury, Matthew Arnold, and Henry Newbolt. Many aspects of the popular concept of "meter" that emerged in the prewar period had little to do with "meter" (as the measure of a verse-line) at all. The patriotic representation of poetry in the state-funded schools promoted a distinction between "Verse" and "Poetry" that mirrored the earlier distinction between English and classical poetry. Chapter 3, "The Institution of Meter," begins with a discussion of metrical mastery, outlining the way that Bridges's intervention in his best-selling treatise *Milton's Prosody* expanded and popularized the theories that he and Hopkins discussed together. I show how Bridges and Saintsbury were jostling for position during the height of the prosody wars between 1900 and 1910 and how their successes and failures characterize, for better or for worse, much of our contemporary thinking about early twentieth-century prosody. Author of the three-volume *History of English Prosody* (1906–10), Saintsbury was a prime mover in both the foundation of English literary study and the institutionalization of the "foot" as the primary measure of English poetry. Infused with Edwardian-era military rhetoric, Sainstbury's foot marched to a particularly English rhythm, which he traced through the ages with wit and martial vigor. Chapter 4, "The Discipline of Meter," looks closely at the rise of state-funded English education to uncover the disciplinary role that poetry, in particular, played. Matthew Arnold and other educational theorists tried to replicate the character-building aspects of classical education in the state-funded classroom, employing pedagogical models that relied on rote memorization. I show how the naturalization of English "meter" was a crucial part of the English literary curriculum. I put "meter" in quotation marks, because the "meter" that emerges in the state-funded classroom has little to do with the prosody wars going on outside its walls. Arnold's cultural metrics, in which poetry by Shakespeare, for instance, will subtly and intimately transform a student into a good citizen, is replaced by a patriotic pedagogy wherein verses written in rousing rhythms are taught as a naturally felt English "beat." By 1907, half of the state-funded schools recited patriotic poems en masse for "Empire Day," and the students were encouraged to feel the rhythms of verses in their bodies. I suggest that poet and educational theorist Henry Newbolt's figure of the "drum" performed a naturalized rhythm that brought England together as a collective. The collective mass identification with (and proliferation of) patriotic verses created an even sharper divide between the high and low, elite and mass, private and public cultures of poetry in the early twentieth century.

This divide deepened during the soldier poetry boom of the First World War. The final two chapters, 5 and 6, show how the pressure to conform to one model of English meter and English national identification produced fractures in the poetic-national identity of soldier poets in particular and, more broadly, reactionary misunderstandings about English metrical cultures for poets associated with the modernist avant-garde. In this final section, I examine poems and prose by Robert Graves, Siegfried Sassoon, Wilfred Owen, W. B. Yeats, T. S. Eliot, Ezra Pound, Robert Bridges, and Alice Meynell. Building on my argument in previous chapters that Victorian meters were dynamic and not at all stable, I argue in chapter 5 that the modernist account of meter at the turn of the twentieth century was a selective history, conflating the militaristic meters that had taken hold of English national culture with "English meter" tout court. The thousands of soldiers and women poets on the home front who wrote poems during the First World War were engaged in a larger national metrical project, and yet the merit and meaning of these poems has been largely ignored. Chapter 5, "The Trauma of Meter," shows how metrical poetry was used as an allegory for order, and examines in particular the metrical cultures of the Craiglockhart War Hospital. Reading early psychological and sociological theories by W.H.R. Rivers and Arthur Brock, I relate how treatments for shell shock included writing metrical poetry. Poems written in or inspired by time in the hospital, as well as the letters and articles published in the hospital magazine *The Hydra,* show how soldiers turned to writing as therapy. My readings illustrate how poets reconfigured metrical form as an artificial yet necessary order, one to which their identities as English soldiers and subjects were bound. Unlike the formal ruptures of experimental Modernism, these poems bitterly accept the arbitrary nature of all forms of order, be they mental, military, or metrical. I recontextualize First World War poets as the products of Edwardian and Georgian metrical culture and as sites for reinterpreting the nuances of meter's narrative in the early twentieth century. The fact that these poems occupy a middle ground between the aesthetic and the political, bridging the divide that the school system helped foster between "poetry" and "verse," complicates the stability of each category.

Chapter 6, "The Before- and After-life of Meter," turns once more to Robert Bridges, whose death in 1930 marks the end of the book. He did not believe that English meter could be adequately represented by only one system, nor did he believe that the four systems he mastered exhausted its possibilities. He struggled with the pedagogic necessities of his time, founding the Society for Pure English, participating as poet laureate in the national metrical project during the First World War by writing for the war office, and editing the popular anthology of verse, *The Spirit of Man.* Bridges's late career poem "Poor Poll" engages with the modernist polyglossia and the rise of free verse (particularly Eliot's *The Waste Land*) by presenting an English prosody accessible to both high and popular audiences. It was Pound's eventual dismissal of Bridges that guaranteed his obsolescence: I argue that Pound's changing reactions to Robert Bridges over the course of Pound's career betray an anxiety about meter's role in poetic mastery, as well as an attempt to control the narrative of English meter. Along with the English men of letters that are prominent in my argument, women poets played an important role in shaping English metrical culture at the turn of the century and before. A thorough examination of women's education, poetess poetry, and the gendering of classical meters and classicism must lie beyond the scope of this study. I nonetheless end with a reading of

Alice Meynell's poems, "The English Metres" and "The Laws of Verse," calling for a reexamination of metrical cultures that have been effaced from our literary history.

A Note on Historical Prosody

Since the late 1990s, scholars like Isobel Armstrong, Joseph Bristow, Max Cavitch, Linda K. Hughes, and Anne Jamison, to name a few, have shown the ways that the poetics of Victorian poetry, in particular, were engaged with many of the same concerns as twentieth-century poetry: recuperations of history and abandonment of tradition, engagement with both elitist and populist forms of literature, and attempts to make sense of the chaos of modernity.[23] Part of the impetus behind this reevaluation and recontextualization of meter as a mediating cultural category and as a contested discourse is to think through the ways that "meter" becomes a nexus between two very similar sets of concerns for two very dissimilar sets of poets. To one set of poets, meter represents a standard that could and should be broken; to another, meter needs to become a standard, but isn't quite. What if meter "moved," not only with its pathos, but also changed as a dynamic cultural category and a generative discourse rather than a static, ahistorical form into which content might be molded, or emotion fixed and calmed?

In addition to these questions, I ask why and how our contemporary associations with the word "meter" became fixed in the nineteenth century. How did meter permeate discussions of religion, education, psychology, and disciplinary formation in general? What does "meter" mean if we refuse to take for granted that our traditional understanding of iambs and trochees is an artificial, cultural construct? Scholars have been reading metrical form as an allegory of order or, as Caroline Levine has demonstrated, as a collision of incompatible forms.[24] Form, then, becomes a kind of trope and this troping of form has become a staple of much neoformalist criticism, with exciting and interesting results that have taught us much about the various contexts for poetry in the nineteenth century. Though work on English meter by critics such as Derek Attridge (*The Rhythms of English Poetry*, 1982) and Timothy Steele (*Missing Measures: Modern Poetry and the Revolt Against Meter*, 1990) has been invaluable, I am not attempting to replicate their work by putting forth a new theory of meter, nor am I attempting to explain why or how certain theories may have failed. Moving beyond Fussell's *Theory of Prosody in Eighteenth-Century England* (1954) or O. B. Hardison's *Prosody and Purpose in the English Renaissance* (1989), *The Rise and Fall of Meter* focuses on multiple theories of prosody and their purpose in late nineteenth-century England, asking why and how meter was on the minds of so many poets in a time of national insecurity, and how this insecurity and instability are inherent, now, in any definition or discussion of meter in English. Single author studies, like

Dennis Taylor's *Hardy's Metres and Victorian Prosody* (1988), A. A. Markley's *Stateliest Measures: Tennyson and the Literature of Greece and Rome* (2004),[25] as well as much work on Gerard Manley Hopkins, show how metrical theory may have been dynamic over time for a particular writer; however, few of these works are concerned with the way that meter, as a discourse, was deeply imbedded in cultural politics and the institutions of the state.

The politics of poetic form have been key to many reconsiderations of nineteenth-century poetry, including Isobel Armstrong's foundational *Victorian Poetry: Poetry, Poetics, Politics* (1993); over the past decade critics such as Susan Wolfson, Herbert Tucker, Yopie Prins, Simon Jarvis, and Angela Leighton have each, in very different ways, called for a historical reexamination of nineteenth-century English meter. Recent books by Jason Rudy (*Electric Meters: Victorian Physiological Poetics*, 2009) and Kirstie Blair (*Victorian Poetry and the Culture of the Heart*, 2006) argue that rhythm was imagined as physically expressive for Victorians, and Catherine Robson's *Heart Beats: Everyday Life and the Memorized Poem* (2012) presents a cultural history of memorization in arguing that we have lost a physical connection to poetry as pedagogic methodologies have changed. To add to these fine contributions and to encourage a historically responsible reading of a crucial and yet overlooked period, this book makes several interlinking claims about the concept of meter, its rise and fall, and the way that meter as a cultural category is inextricably tied to ideas of national identity in England in the nineteenth and early twentieth centuries.

The History of Meter

When this, this little group their country calls
From academic shades and learned halls,
To fix her laws, her spirit to sustain,
And light up glory through her wide domain;
Their various tastes in different arts display'd
Like temper'd harmony of light and shade,
With friendly union in one mass shall blend,
And thus adorn the state, and that defend.
— Anna Laetitia Barbauld, "The Invitation: To Miss B*****"

Upon few other subjects has so much been written with so little tangible result.
—Coventry Patmore, "Prefatory Study on English Metrical Law"

When you are at school and learn grammar grammar is very exciting.
— Gertrude Stein, *Poetry and Grammar*

A Metrical History of England

With the above lines from "The Invitation" by "Our Poetess" (Anna Laetitia Barbauld), William Enfield begins his 1774 *The Speaker,* an elocutionary handbook that was intended for use in classrooms at the moment when vernacular literature was beginning to displace classical literature in private grammar schools.[1] Enfield was a schoolmaster at the dissenting Warrington Academy, and both he and Anna Laetitia Barbauld (daughter of schoolmaster John Aiken, also of Warrington Academy, and author of *The Female Speaker* [1811]) were invested in the cultural capital of English literature. As John Guillory describes it, "by the time Thomas Sheridan published *British Education: Or the Source of the Disorders of Great Britain* (1756), the connection between vernacular linguistic refinement and a progressive political agenda was firmly entrenched."[2] Urging English literature as "models of style," Sheridan expressed "anxiety . . . that in the absence of an institutional form of dissemination, literary culture [could] not be entrusted to preserve English works of the past.[3] It is in this climate that Barbauld imagines a collective classroom community in which (as the epigraph to this chapter states) "academic shades and learned halls" will "fix the laws" of the English language and do their duty: "with friendly union in one mass shall blend / And thus adorn the state, and that defend." Barbauld hints at the act of friendly union between England and Scotland in 1707 in her imagined classroom, a classroom in which the potential differences in English pronunciation might blend into an English language that "adorns" England with its greatness. By bringing together students to practice reciting English literature and learning English grammar, education would inspire all students subject to the English language to defend Britain.

In the late eighteenth century, this classroom community was limited. Dissenting academies (schools, colleges, and nonconforming seminaries) like Warrington provided an education for those who did not agree with the tenants of the Church of England,[4] which had a stronghold at Oxbridge. Those who could pass the entrance exams to the old universities (Oxford and Cambridge) were educated in grammar schools or by schoolmasters or schoolmistresses in the ancient languages. Elocutionary guides, grammar books, and other pedagogical literature rushed to fill the void created by England's express desire, after the publication of Johnson's *Dictionary* in 1755, for a unified linguistic and literary culture at a time when it lacked any organized national school system to support it. Intended to provide a "proper course of instruction," Enfield's *Speaker* and John Walker's *Elements of Elocution* (1781) were two of the most popular guides to the proper performance of speech for those aspiring to the upper classes as well as for those already in the upper classes who wanted to supplement their classical educations with a working knowledge of English literature. "By a steady attention to discipline," Enfield's speaker promised the literate, who were willing to practice, the ability to pass as aristocracy. Here was no course of study for the mere hedge school or church school, though that was exactly the sort of community that would find these lessons useful. For both Enfield and Walker, "accent" should follow the abstract "laws of harmony," "general custom," and "a good ear."[5] Though the Scots dialect was everywhere present in eighteenth-century discussions of "proper" English speech accent, the hope of these and other late eighteenth-century textbooks was for a national unity that could be achieved through linguistic unity. But linguistic unity, for these popular elocutionists, also meant a unified approach to the measure of English speech in *poems* (ever popular for recitation) and therefore a unified approach to English meter.

Though Fussell has argued that the idea of classical quantity in English was practically irrelevant in eighteenth-century English verse, supplanted by "conservative" syllabic and stress regularity (the number of syllables and stresses per line), the dream of establishing universal and standard pronunciation was nonetheless evident in discussions of versification. Prior to phonetic science, authors like Enfield and Walker often took for granted the ideal of sameness in "English" quantity (the short "e" versus the long "e" for instance) and therefore in pronunciation. Because their idea of proper speech was so ingrained, Enfield and Walker eschewed a system for measuring meter through quantity at all, as a student of the classics would have, precisely because "quantity" would have been associated with classical languages and literature, on the one hand and, on the other, actually providing rules for quantity in English would mean securing, standardizing, and fixing pronunciation in a concrete way that neither Enfield nor Walker was yet able to imagine. That is, the abstract notion of "speech accent" (or emphasis, or just "accent") is paramount to the proper measure of an English verse line, quite beyond the rules for pronunciation that nineteenth-century grammar books would establish. In fact, as if to preclude any disagreement, Walker writes "it is accent, or emphasis, and these only, and not any length of openness of the vowels, that forms English metre,"[6] Both writers are invested in speech accent as the only ruling constituent of the English verse line. By erasing questions of English quantity, Enfield and Walker effaced the very differentiation of speakers from different regions of the country. If accent is the only measure of English meter (rather than the time it would take to pronounce the words, or the different ways the vowels might sound), then all Englishmen (irrespective of their Scottish origin) can access it. An idealized and yet-still-unestablished "English" accent, when properly learned and performed, would not, according to these rules, differentiate speakers; rather it would blend them into the "one mass" of the English nation.

With the expansion of the franchise, the growth of the linguistic sciences, and the rise of a state-controlled and somewhat regulated education system, English would haltingly replace the classics as the language and literature of the educated elite in Victorian England. But before the anxieties later in the century about the adequacy of English literature's role as a civilizing force, the study and attainment of "proper" English pronunciation and usage was already associated with upward mobility and national stability. Within the narrative of the "rise of English," (which begins even before the eighteenth century) we also find the "rise of meter" in popular pedagogical textbooks in English history and grammar. English "meter" emerges as an important yet still hotly contested and unstable medium for the transmission of English values.[7] Despite what Fussell argues are the widely held beliefs of the eighteenth century, that "prosodic regularity forces the ordering of the perceiver's mind so that it may be in a condition to receive the ordered moral matter of the poem," the desire for a stable and regular prosody was often complicated by the unstable ways that these terms ("prosody," "meter," "versification") circulated. The apparently specialized terms "prosody," "meter," and "versification" enjoyed a surprising prominence in English national life, in unexpected arenas. "Syntax" and "prosody" circulated not only in grammar books, but also as cartoon characters, even popular racehorse names. School stories (popular "boy's tales from school," such as *Tom Brown's School Days* [1857]) often included stories about Latin exercises as punishment and bemoaned the rigors of scansion, yet the *bout-rimé* was a popular pastime throughout the Victorian era. Mnemonic jingles were used to teach a variety of different school subjects. From the middle of the eighteenth century onward, the terms "prosody" and "meter" mediated between elite and mass cultures, Latin and English, speech and text, classical and "native" pasts, "England" and its others.

Nineteenth-century poetics developed via a vast, unruly array of handbooks, manuals, periodical articles and reviews, memoirs, grammar books, philological tracts, essays, letters, and histories, all with something to say about English meter. Prosodic discourse extended into multiple disciplines, each with different disciplinary practices, expectations and, importantly, different audiences. These diverse methodologies and disciplines, however, came together to lay the groundwork for English literary studies as we now know it—a product of this cross-disciplinary project of nation making. To illustrate the centrality of meter to this nation-making project, the first part of this chapter studies nineteenth-century English history teaching, which employed various concepts of English "meter" to solidify a stable concept of England's regal past. I then turn to eighteenth- and nineteenth-century grammar books to show how, despite the hopes of grammarians to stabilize all aspects of "English grammar," English meter continued to evolve and change, playing a liminal and shifting role in the evolution of English grammatical study. The delineation of English meter in Victorian grammar books exposes many facets of the controversies that erupted in the later nineteenth-century "prosody wars." Grounded in Latin grammatical and metrical theory (about which scholars disagreed), but grappling with broadening cultural and historical contexts, grammar books reveal an oft-neglected ambivalence about English meter as grammar. Late nineteenth-century conflicts about meter are rooted in the disciplines of rhetoric and elocution, and even a subtle tension between classical and Anglo-Saxon meters. Through the study and investigation of both Anglo-Saxon and classical meters—and also of Anglo-Saxonism and classicism—historians, grammarians, and prosodists attempted to define concepts of English national identity that were often redefined radically by the century's end. The final section of this chapter broadly outlines the contours of prosody debates throughout the century, arguing that prosodic discourse was founded on disagreement and discord, and that the dream of a system for English prosody was also a dream of a stable national identity that was, perhaps, unattainable.

Though the use of versification to teach history might not seem all that different from using versification to teach other subjects, "metricality" in history teaching sometimes called upon a "natural" and emphatic rhythm that was distinct from subtly modulated rhythms of more "refined" poetry and the technical vocabularies that were being developed for these. Simple rhythms, called "meter," made it easier for the student-subject to memorize historical chronology. Hundreds of "metrical histories" appeared in the nineteenth century. These "metrical histories"were associated with progress in two respects: first, this somehow more natural "meter" was seen to aid the natural development of mental order and discipline; second, the periodicity and seeming inevitability of the succession of regents aligned meter with the development of the English nation. The pedagogic use of versification in teaching history promoted an understanding of English verse form as an emblem of order itself, applied to, but also derived from, a progressive and dynastic English past. English metricality, rather than English poetry or versification, was a popular vehicle for knowledge that skirted aesthetic questions and raised ideological questions instead. The "metrical histories" of England, then, can be read as the union of a particular idea about English meter with a particular idea of English national culture—orderly and falling into a natural line that should be easy to remember. At the same time, while this kind of "meter" may be easy for some to remember, the idea that "meter" could create mental discipline was derived from the traditions of memorization in classical education. Some metrical histories included an ironic subtext for more educated readers, employing subtler metrical systems but marketing their texts to the lay reader, who may not have any idea of what metrical forms were being employed. In that way some "metrical histories" spoke to more than one metrical community. Others were careful to separate their method of "versification" from a perceived aesthetic category of higher "poetry" with standards against which they did not wish to be judged. In all of these texts, however, even those that promote ease and pleasure in memorizing verses, there is a hint of the inherent difficulty and artificiality of meter—a meter that is not natural, that is not, in fact *rhythm*, which is what these texts mean when they say "metrical" in the first place. That is, while the ideologies of history pedagogy and mental ordering for the masses relied on metrical order, we find, especially toward the end of the nineteenth century, a suspicion about a form that could control you without your knowledge, an issue that was central to the teaching of poetry and the approaches to poetic education promoted by scholars like Matthew Arnold and Henry Newbolt at the end of the nineteenth and beginning of the twentieth centuries.

Reading these histories in meter, and the meters of these histories, shows the tangled metrical and historical genealogy of England's classical and Anglo-Saxon pasts. For instance, we find what may be an entirely accidental line of dactylic hexameter (a meter associated with England's history only explicitly through translations) in the subtitle of Seymour Burt's 1852 *Metrical Epitome of the History of England*: "A **Met**rical **List** of the **Sov**ereigns of **Eng**land: // The **Ang**les and **Sax**ons." These hexameter lines reveal that English metrical history is more complicated than even the most straightforward-seeming metrical list of the earliest leaders of England. Though Burt writes the text of his metrical history in the more accepted Anglo-Saxon four-beat line (complete with alliteration on either side of the caesura), the dactyls of the subtitle regulate the following alliterated lines:

Egbert and Ethelwolf, Ethelbald, Ethelbert
Ethelred, Alfred, and Edward and Athelston
Edmund and Edrid, and Edwy and Edgar
Edward and Ethelred, "Ironside" Edmund.[8]

Though these alliterative four-beat lines hint toward the dactylic pattern of the title, they seem to Anglo-Saxonize the possibility of dactylic hexameter, so that the subtitle reads, in retrospect, as a preview of the list to come—"A Metrical List of the Sovereigns of England" and then another subtitle: "The Angles and Saxons." Rather than civilize the Anglo-Saxon names into classical feet, the accents of the subtitle stand out prominently. But Burt does not attempt to make his metrical list imitate Anglo-Saxon meter so much as he uses the naturally alliterating names of the sovereigns to hint at the common Anglo-Saxon metrical patterns of two beats on either side of the caesura. At the same time, Burt was conforming to a classical standard; dactylic hexameter was widely known as the heroic classical meter of both Homer's *Iliad* and Virgil's *Aeneid*. Though the title is certainly not signaling the classical nature of England's history, the gesture to an epic meter with the Anglo-Saxon beats inside it makes the names of England's earliest leaders seem appropriately epic themselves. That is, the only appropriate meter for naming the founders of the English nation might be this hybrid of classical and ancient English patterning. Burt adds the word "and" to make the verse even more dactylic when a regent's name comes up one unstressed syllable short: "Edward and Athelston," the "and" a conjunction that ties the rulers to one another, echoing the "d" ends of their names, and filling the dactylic line.

Despite Burt's metrical performance, joining the alliterative Anglo-Saxon, four-beat line to the dactylic pattern, he states early on that his primary goal is a proficiency in pedagogical transmission of historical fact. In the preface, Burt offers his *Metrical Epitome* to the British public with "extreme diffidence" and "fears . . . of [his] skill in versification" (iii). Yet he has assurance, despite these fears, that the details and facts of the *Epitome* "may be looked upon with all confidence." From diffidence in versification to confidence in the presented facts, Burt prefers to bolster the historical accuracy of his account as the most valuable feature of his *Epitome* and downplay the potential faults in the verse form. He assures the reader that he has included all "leading features" of England's history but purposefully excluded any reference to the "more poetical incidents" (iii) in the record, thus protecting the reader from unnecessary (and potentially un-heroic) distraction. The "students of our History" (iii) who are his hoped-for audience should not be concerned with aesthetics, but should find the verses in which the facts are delivered to be simply the most effective vessels for transmission. With pedagogic simplicity at the forefront, Burt advertises that in a mere hour, his metrical epitome can provide the amount of information that a week's reading "in the ordinary [prose] manner" (iv) would require. Burt's use of the term "metrical" here means "narrative" or "vehicle for transmission and retention of a narrative pertaining to England" particularly. We can also read, in his reluctance to claim responsibility for his meter, that "meter" was also associated with a kind of potentially measurable accuracy, which his "epitome" would like to sidestep, or perhaps replace with the measurable accuracy of its historical account. What Burt takes for granted is that the regularity and familiarity of a dactylic tetrameter will only help the foreign-sounding Saxon names to become part of the English historical record.

Why would Burt need to fix these Anglo-Saxon names into the more familiar dactylic meter rather than into an Anglo-Saxon meter? The "metrical" of Burt's *Metrical Epitome* is distinct from the varieties of English meters with which Victorian poets were experimenting and to which he himself alludes; it is also distinct from the rigorous classical meters of the public school and Oxbridge,[9] not participating in any of the discord about translations into English from classical meters that took place at midcentury (translating the quantitative dactylic hexameter into a six-beat line.)[10] Burt avoids explicit discussion of versification and begins his history with only these names, which call attention to their own, seemingly inherent strong-stresses—through the very Anglo-Saxon alliteration and mid-line caesura—while at the same time making them conform to a familiar dactylic pattern. Burt begins English history here, in a subtly hybrid past in which alliterative, stressed Englishness seems to overtake the familiar conventional dactylic tetrameter. As we will see, linguistic and metrical forms are often conceived as part of a series of narratives of conquest and submission, and even in this proclaimed non-poetic English history, we may read subtle tensions between national and metrical pasts.

In addition to these relatively inconspicuous details, however, Burt's "metricality" was meant to counterbalance the supposed dryness of historical facts, to dress them up, organize, and stabilize them so that they could be more easily retained by the memory. "Versified" history organized the facts of England's past so that the younger generation could remember it; just as the regents themselves provide an "order" to the epochs of history, so too did nineteenth-century meter, broadly conceived as part of English history, provide an "order" for the overwhelmed mind of the young student. This "metricality," therefore, did not allude to the more complicated dactyls of the public schoolboy's exercise in translating from Greek and Latin hexameters, though that exercise was intended to provide a similar kind of mental discipline. The intended audience for metrical histories needed historical knowledge first, with the verse forms, never named or discussed, securing that knowledge in a student's memory. Like Macaulay's *Lays of Ancient Rome*, published ten years earlier in 1842 to astonishing success,[11] these were histories first, and poems second, if at all. The very fact of *historical* fact absolved the verses of any poetic responsibility. Though the exact choice of meter in the metrical histories may not have carried a specific message, they were nonetheless influenced by the way that each author wanted his or her "English history" to be received. The fact that the often unnamed meters were simple, emphatic, and recognizable—ballad meters, double dactyls (common in nursery rhymes), and pentameters—nonetheless expressed a sense of community and connection. English meter in its various unnamed forms was familiar enough to make English history easier, and English history, in turn, joined English meter (or at least the adjective "metrical") to a progressive national narrative.

The late nineteenth century saw the growth of "History" and "English" as disciplines that would eventually rival the classical curriculum, and both amateur and specialized metrical histories of England circulated widely in the period. The phenomenon of the metrical history, however, was not unique to the nineteenth century; many of the earliest histories of England were metrical, and many of the earliest poems in English were about the history of England. Layamon's *Brut*, (or "A Chronicle of Britain, a poetical Semi-Saxon paraphrase") written in the first part of the thirteenth century, tells the history of the Britons from the fall of Troy to the fall of King Arthur, and was published by the Society of Antiquaries of London in 1847. In the sixteenth and early seventeenth centuries, the six editions of the progressive, cumulative, and multiauthor collection of poems *The Mirror for Magistrates*[12] told verse stories of the lives of ancient Romans, ancient Britons, and even Queen Elizabeth and her immediate predecessors.[13] Part ghost story, part national history, the *Mirror for Magistrates* participated in a pattern that continued in Spenser and throughout the eighteenth century of tacking ancient and contemporary English history onto the history of ancient Rome. The *Mirror for Magistrates* was a poem that told a story, or many stories, but seemed less concerned with whether or not the story was going to be repeated verbatim. In the eighteenth century, the metrical history begins to concern specifically *English* history and eschews the common myth of Roman origins, no longer recruiting these in the service of legitimizing a succession. Rather, the "metrical histories" become explicitly concerned with the successful transmission of English history and English values into the minds of its readers in a time of nation building and imperial expansion.

Scholars who wanted to teach a more "native" ancient English history in the eighteenth century turned to "artificial memory" methods, of which Richard Grey's 1737 *Memoria Technica* is the predecessor. His "new method of artificial memory" was, as stated on the title page, "applied to and exemplified in chronology, history, geography, astronomy, and also Jewish, Grecian and Roman Coins, Weights, and Measures" and its methodology consisted of assigning sections of made-up words to events in history, so that syllables, or rather, phonemes, stand for numbers which, in turn, make up dates in a historical chronology. Grey's *Memoria Technica* was written in barely perceptible hexameters, which are only evident if you read his preface, since the "memorial lines" read as a kind of Latinate gibberish, complete with entirely useless accent marks in superscript (see figure 1).

Despite their surreal quality, the metrics of Grey's memorial lines nonetheless inspired later histories in so-called "mnemonic hexameters."[14] But beyond the epic nature of its rough meter, Grey's *Memoria Technica* was concerned with measure to such a degree that the epochs of history, cycles of the moon, and ancient weights and measures all appeared reduced into one, albeit extremely complicated, system of assigning each historical figure his own letter—a mnemonic cipher. He admits that the verse structure is not as important as the cipher, writing,

> to make this even easier to be remember'd, the *Technical* words are thrown into the Form of common *Latin* Verse, or at least of something like it. For as there was no Necessity to confine my self to any Rules of *Quantity* or *Position*, I hope I need make no Apology for the Liberty I have taken in having, without Regard to either, and perhaps now and then without so much as a Regard to the just Number of Feet, only placed the Words in such Order as to make them run most easily off the Tongue, and succeed each other in the most natural Manner.[15]

Since Gray's "Technical Words" consist of such inventions as "Casibe*lud* Bóad*aup* Vortig*fos* Heng*sul* & Arth*laf*" (14), it is quite astonishing that he would be concerned with the "natural" manner that these words would be pronounced out loud. Bringing a whole new level of pedagogical and cultural meaning to the idea of poetic "numbers," which usually refer, as above, to the number of feet, syllables per a line of verse, or the quantity of time it might take to pronounce a line of verse, Grey's "artificial memory" valued arithmetic over language and, indeed, subdued the idea of a dactylic hexameter to that arithmetic, shrugging off the obligations of Latin hexameter while at the same time admitting it may be helpful.

Despite its various contradictions and complications, the "artificial memory" system took hold and Grey's odd volume went into eight editions. Richard Valpy took up the idea of Grey's "artificial memory" but lamented that Grey's verses were too difficult to memorize. In his *A Poetic Chronology of Ancient and English History* (1794), Valpy discards the complicated mnemonic cipher and happily hopes that a poetic form will simplify the method of memorizing history: "if the knowledge of dates, which is happily connected with that of facts, could be reduced to a poetical form, to a series of English verses, which might be learnt on account of their simplicity, and remembered with-

Henry the third [Hethdas]	*Oct.*	19.	1216
Edward I. [Eddoid]	*Nov.*	16.	1272
Edvardus secundus [Edfetyp]	*July*	7.	1307
Edvardus tertius [Edtertes]	*Jan.*	25.	1326
Richardus secundus [Rifetóip]	*June*	21.	1377
Henry the fourth [Hefotoun.]	*Sept.*	20.	1399
Henry the fifth [Hefifád]	*Mar.*	20.	1412
Henry the sixth [Hénfifed.]	*Aug.*	31.	1422
Edvardus quartus [Edquarfauz]	*March*	4.	1460
Edward the fifth } [Efi-Rokt]{	*April*	9.	1483
Richard III. } {	*June*	22.	1483
Henricus septimus [Henfépfeil]	*Aug.*	22.	1485
Henricus octav. [Henoclyn]	*April*	22.	1509
Edvardus sextus [Edfexlos]	*Jan.*	28.	1546
Mary [Marylut]	*July*	6.	1553
Elisabeth [Elsluk]	*Nov.*	17.	1558
James I. [Jamfyd]	*March*	24.	1602
Carolus primus [Caroprimfel]	*March*	27.	1625
Carolus secundus [Carfecfok]	*Jan.*	30.	1648
James II. [Jamfeif]	*Feb.*	6.	1684
William and Mary [Wilfeik]	*Feb.*	13.	1688
Anne [Anpyb]	*March*	8.	1701
George I. [Gëobo]	*Aug.*	1.	1714
George II. [Gëofecdoi].	*June*	11.	1727

The Memorial Lines.

Cafibelud Bóadaup Vortig*fos* Heng*ful.* & Arth*laf.*
Egbe*kek* Alfré*kpe* Canbau Confés*fe.*

Wil-con*fau* Ruf*koi* Henr*ag.* ——
Steph*bil* & Henfec*buf* Ricbein Jann Het*hdas* & Ed*doid.*
Ed*fatyp* Edtert*es* Rifetóip Hefotoun Hefifád*que.*
Hénfifed Edquarfauz Efi-Rokt Henfépfeil Henoclyn:
Edfexlos Marylut Elsluk Jamfyd Caroprimfel.
Carfecfok Jamfeif Wilfeik Anpyb Gëobe —— doi.

N. B.

Figure 1. Illustration of the "artificial memory" method, applied to the regents of England. Richard Grey. *Memoria Technica; or, a new method of artificial memory, applied to, and exemplified in chronology, history, geography, astronomy. Also Jewish, Grecian, and Roman coins, weights, and measures, &c. With tables proper to the respective sciences, and memorial lines adapted to each table.* London: Printed for John Stagg in Westminster Hall, 1737, p. 15.

out disgust, a benefit of some importance would be conferred on the rising age."[16]

Rather than rely on artificial memory, the English verses (as opposed to Grey's hexameters of invented Latinesque words) are memorable for their simplicity:

> When years one thousand and threescore and six
> Had pass'd, since Christ in Bethlem's manger lay,
> Then the stern Norman, red from Hastings' field,
> Bruis'd Anglia's realm beneath his iron sway.   (26)

Though these lines are syllabic (each containing ten syllables with the aid of elision) they are neither regularly nor emphatically accentual; they seem, rather, to be syllabic on the French model. There are, throughout, more emphatically regular lines, as the final stanza shows:

> In sev'nteen hundred sixty, George the Third,
> In Britain born, his people's dear delight,
> Receiv'd the scepter twin'd with laurel round,
> And with fresh force renew'd the thicken'd fight.   (52)

Just as we move closer to the present day, so too does Valpy grow more confident in his pentameters. But the pentameters were not really his; Valpy admits that his chronology was inspired by an anonymous *Poetical Chronology of the Kings of England* that appeared in *The Gentleman's Magazine*[17] over several months in late 1793 and early 1794, and that he had to perform "alterations . . . from a sense of moral and political propriety" on his source text. He explains:

> It is the duty of a teacher to instill into the minds of youth the purest constitutional principles. He must have the care to reconcile the lofty sentiments of Republican liberty which occur in the perusal of the Greek and Latin writers, with a loyal submission to that form of Monarchy, which the experience of ages has proved to be the best calculated to insure private security, and to promote public happiness, in this country. (5–6)

Valpy admits that he rewrote lines from the prior chronology so as to save England's princes from "unmerited obloquy" and "cruel invective."[18] It is no surprise that history writing is ideological and political; here, the loyal submission to the ten-syllable lines, often (but not always) rhymed *abab*, is also, explicitly, submission to that form of monarchy to which the "rising age" should pledge unequivocal allegiance (both accounts are written in pentameter, and Valpy only makes subtle changes to the original text). Valpy was a schoolmaster (he had already attempted to simplify Latin grammar and would later go on to simplify Greek grammar) and he intended his work to be used primarily in his own school, but the book went through sixteen reprints and was absorbed as the appendix to Putnam's more historical, non-poetic chronology in 1833. If facts can be reduced to a simple poetic form, then the student might easily recall them, without the "harshness of measure" (4) to which we are subjected in Grey's *Memoria Technica*.

Metrical histories that abandoned the "artificial memory" method, and abandoned "ancient history," (meaning Roman history) began to appear in 1812, along with a revival of ancient ballads and translations from Alfred.[19] Rather than focus on learning a new system, the majority of nineteenth-century metrical histories emphasized the ease with which verses could be remembered and the connective tissue to a metrical and national community that the meter provided.[20] The wider historical context of a revived interest in all things Anglo-Saxon is important as a possible reason why many of the nineteenth-century histories, though they tended to be shorter and easier to memorize, began before 1066, returning to a pre-Norman past, rewriting the Battle of Hastings as "the Norman yoke," as well as appealing to vernacular and less complicated verse structures, mostly ballads and tetrameters. Pedagogically, these metrical histories tended to emphasize that poetic learning could be pleasurable and, just as Anglo-Saxon was being rewritten as a native and natural form in English, so too did the nineteenth-century metrical histories tend to emphasize ease and instinct in memorizing verses. For instance, we can immediately sense the appeal of the popular late eighteenth-century song, the "Chapter of Kings": "The Romans in England they once did sway, / And the Saxons they after them led the way, / And they tugg'd with the Danes 'til an Overthrow, / They both of them got by the Norman Bow. / Yet barring all Pother, / the one and the other / Were all of them kings in their turn." The song, by Irish schoolmaster John Collins,[21] was printed in a slightly less vernacular form in 1818, changing "butchering Dick" back to "Richard" (but keeping the line that calls Henry the Eighth "fat as a pig"). Reducing the complexities of English history to a schoolroom song created communities of subjects who could easily imagine becoming "kings in their turn," no matter their background. The refrain of "the one and the other" is particularly evocative at a moment when grammarians and rhetoricians, as scholars like Strabone and Elfenbein have noted, were attempting to suppress the internal "others" of Saxon-derived dialects in the process of standardizing English grammar.[22] The fact that the song was originally composed by an Irish schoolmaster gestures to the way that nineteenth-century England often derived its native "authenticity" from linguistic communities that it had attempted to erase or eradicate.

The wide circulation of popular songs and ballads about English history promoted and sustained the perceived connection between England's regal

rulers, its folk communities, and vernacular poetic forms. But the trend to ver-
sify England's history appealed to authors who were cannily aware of the way
that the idea of "meter" would speak differently to differently educated readers
and relied, therefore, on a common "history" to unify them. The popularity of
the "Chapter of Kings" inspired Thomas Dibdin to "attempt versifying . . . the
leading points of our history" in 1813.[23] Though Dibdin wanted his verses to
be entertaining, he also wanted them to be historically and poetically accurate.
That is, rather than provide a history connected by the sameness of meter, he
varies the form of the verse, or "the style of the narrative" as he calls it, "as the
colour of circumstances to be depicted in each Reign might seem to require"
(vi). He tries to make his account more historically accurate—and more entertaining—by matching different poetic genres such as "a Comic Song, a Tragic
Tale, or an irregular Poem" to different eras of English history. The very variety
of poetic genres within the already versified narrative might provide "relief"
from the imagined rigor of so much history but, more importantly, might "im-
press on some juvenile memories a species of Index to the voluminous labours
of genuine Historians" (vi–vii). In Dibdin's index, then, the shifting style of
meter signals a historical shift—the changing meters providing yet another
level of organization.[24] In Dibdin's index, among other instances, a "history of
meter" and a "metrical history" are one and the same.

Dibdin sought to appeal to two audiences with his versified histories: first,
the readers trained at "Cam and Isis" (Cambridge and Oxford) who might
still find his "insignificant" poem entertaining, and second, the younger generation of scholars who needed to get their history right. Dibdin plays on a
theme that continued throughout the nineteenth and twentieth centuries:
meter was both a way to convey information to a specialized class of people
and a way to help people learn and organize information, and thus help them
advance through life.

Though the author confesses that he himself was not privileged to attend
Oxford or Cambridge, he appeals to the first audience by admiring their col-
lections of comic verse, the Oxford *Sausage* and the Cambridge *Butter*, and
therefore signals that his verses are humorous and should not be judged by
regular critical standards:

> Yet deem not CAM, that ig'rance quite pervades
> My brain, tho'never in thy halls refined;
> Nor Isis, think thine academic shades,
> Tho'out of sight, were always out of mind;
> Thoughts of ye both, to neither tho'consigned,   5
> Wou'd put my infant bosom in a flutter;
> For oft my taste was seriously inclined,
> With how much goût I'm half ashamed to utter,
> To Oxford sausage rich; and curious Cambridge butter. (xiv)

The humorous magazines of Cambridge and Oxford provided Dibdin with the early training necessary to compose his own humorous verses, and as such to bridge the gap between high and low audiences. He provides a list of imaginary critical commentaries from such invented publications as "The Pedantic Exterminator" and "The Scalping Knife" to emphasize that his position as a "vociferous ballad singer" is not supposed to be taken seriously. But at the same time, he is careful to portray himself as highly educated, acknowledging his debt to no fewer than five authoritative histories. This claim to erudition also aids his appeal to the second audience, which needs assistance in receiving the correct history; he insists that "the dates of every incident occurring in the History, were correctly and progressively placed opposite the relation of them" (16). He proves his literary interest and expertise by his "miniature attempts to point out, by abridged examples, the progress of English Poetry," which "necessarily cease at the period of Charles the Second's Restoration, the Works of most Authors of that and subsequent periods being generally known." Dibdin's second audience, therefore, is a society that was beginning to believe in the value of English literature and the importance of English history, the "juvenile" mind that, increasingly toward the end of the century, required historical facts to be impressed upon it efficiently, naturally, and easily, by the pressures of the fledgling national school system. Though many of these texts were responses to the midcentury national obsession with history that Catherine Hall has noted,[25] most of the late nineteenth-century histories described the necessity of memorizing facts for eventual examination.[26]

But if verses are meant to take the place of more difficult lessons, what does that imply for the study of metrical form itself? These histories purvey a metrical language that is natural and simple, but also insidiously easy. George Raymond's 1842 *Chronicles of England: A Metrical History* believed that "no fact in the world is better known than that metre, or rhythmical construction, is that form of language which is the first beloved of memory in its dawn, and the latest which attends it in its journey in decline" (viii). But Raymond warns that versified language, "[l]ike bearded grass . . . has crept up the sleeve of fancy, whence no power can dislodge it—it has attained its place with but little solicitation, and holds it with obstinacy—indeed, such is the nature of metrical language . . . no effort in acquisition; and almost appearing of spontaneous existence" (viii). With a gesture to Robert of Gloucester, Raymond recommended that his book be used as a study guide, not as a replacement "for such a study in its ampler and more venerable garb." The student must first digest the "sober prose narration" and, "by means of this thread of rhyme," "tie up the bulk of the weighty historic yarn, which laborious hands have wove, that the fibres may not unravel, and its continuity and purpose perish together" (xii).[27] Like Dibdin's hope that the varied metrical forms might provide an index to the various epochs in English history, Raymond wants the sameness of his verse form, a rather choppy pentameter that is held together mostly by its couplets, to connect the phases of England's history to one another: "Thus Smithfield flames, as equal victims mix, / Both martyred Lutherans and Catholics. / Now sacrificed is Anna Boleyn's life, / That Seymour may become the tyrant's wife" (78) to the broader imperial history "[a]gainst the convoys of Columbian Spain, / The British projects terminate in vain; / But in a brighter expedition, foil / Her native efforts on Gibraltar's soil" (195), and connect the student to the bounded whole. But the connective tissue of the poem's meter doesn't lodge itself into the student's memory like a flowering plant—it is a weed, and it is an obstinate one. The verse form itself, then, emblematizes the history's inevitable forward movement, and the rhyme's chime at the end reminds the reader that it all, eventually, holds together. But the thread of rhyme is also the *threat* of rhyme; if rhyme is holding together the ample and venerable garb of prose narration, where the real history lies, then we also must take pains to not notice it, to have it work on us rather than have us work on it. The phases of England's history and its progression must appear seamless just as the student citizen must be seamlessly absorbed into the larger nation—lest the nation's continuity and purpose perish together. The measured verses in which Raymond delivers his history should help the student remember with little regard for his or her will. He ends his *Chronicle* with the hope that it will succeed in being "felt, own'd, and understood":

Thus in our record we have nearly ran
Through half the era of the Christian span;
Attested kings and kingdoms in their range—
Dearth, in the proudest—in the happiest, change;
Have watched their rise, the progress, and the wane—
        The "Imperial," trodden—and th' "Eternal" vain:

Vain for that cause which still shall overthrow
Systems to come, as those already low;
Till it be felt, and own'd and understood,
The "Social Contract" is the Common Good. (270)

And so, too, is the kind of metrical contract that Raymond imagines, binding together his history in rhyme in the text of the long metrical history, while his more extensive prose notes populate the bottom of the manuscript.

And perhaps this insidious, spontaneous, obstinate metrical form might need an even more powerful method of securing its place in the student's mind. Perhaps, as Rossendale writes in his 1846 *History of the Kings and Queens of England in Verse: from King Egbert to Queen Victoria*, the student might need "a kind of walking-stick for the memory; and if sung, (which may easily be managed) a musical one!"[28] Rossendale describes his history as a series of invasions—from "Julius Caesar's invasion, down to the period of the invasion of England by Railroads in the nineteenth century," the "Roman yoke" and the railways both invading a more natural England, one that would require a walking stick. Like Collins's song "Chapter of Kings," Rossendale provides the musical score for Robert Burns's "Auld Lang Syne," whose original lyrics are, of course, all about remembering and forgetting:

> About two thousand years ago,
> Came Julius Caesar here;
> And brought with him the Roman foe
> With bright and glitt'ring spear
> The natives that in England dwelt,
> Were wild and cruel too;
> And they—the pow'r of Druids felt, —
> A tyrannizing crew.

These stanzas, and the book as a whole, are easily sung; and, like the lyrics of "Auld Lang Syne," they adhere easily to the pattern of ballad meter. I imagine students sitting in public examinations and humming under their breath the entirety of English history as we might hum our ABCs. But whose ABCs are these? The familiar form of this popular schoolroom history was written by the Scottish National poet Robert Burns, who gets no mention here—he is forgotten, like the original words of "Auld Lang Syne"—just as the revised "Chapter of Kings" makes no mention of the Irish schoolmaster John Collins. The history of England and the shapes through which it is transmitted are composed and carved by writers from communities whose dialects complicate the dream of "standard" English, and whose imaginary "native" origins have been co-opted as England's own.

The "metrical" in English metrical histories refers at various times to simple and pleasurable pedagogical methods, to artificial memory, to nation building, and to nature itself (as in the case of Raymond), and touches on issues of education, racial origins, national identification, and class. Following the Revised Code of 1861–62 and the examinations that these imposed on a new generation of schoolchildren, shorter metrical histories appeared so that they could be "learned completely by heart by any student of ordinary capacity,"[29] as Montefiore's 1876 *The History of England in Verse* promises. Catherine Robson usefully summarizes the implications of the Revised Code (and its "payment by results" scheme) on pedagogical methods: "[i]n consequence of the financial pressure [The Revised Code] exerted on over-extended educators, the code . . . plays a significant role in the history of memorization: because schools and teachers were subject to monetary penalties if their pupils did not satisfy visiting examiners, rote learning, particularly in reading, became the norm."[30] Though there was a revival in the artificial memory method around this time, with Lewis Carroll as a famous experimenter,[31] mnemonic systems were largely outnumbered by the more approachable and teachable metrical histories in the late nineteenth century. One popular short version was called *Granny's History of England in Rhyme* (1871), which began with a dedication that encapsulates the use of versification (as well as the generic shifts by late century between poetry and the novel) in many late Victorian classrooms: "A rhyme may glide into the mind / Like wedge into the oak, / Op'ning a broad, marked path for prose."[32] By 1896, educational theorists were assessing the success of versified histories. Charles Wesley Mann explained in "School Recreations and Amusements," "without orderly arrangement in the mind, history becomes a chaos of heterogeneous and isolated facts. For this reason, various mnemonic jingles have been utilized as a means of fixing in the minds of pupils, in regular order, the names of dynasties and sovereigns."[33] What was "metrical" at midcentury changed, significantly, after the Revised Code: no longer "metrical," these histories were now "in verse" or "in rhyme," "versification" or "versifying," as we shall see, replacing "meter" or "metrical" as the purely technical, non-poetic aspect of poem making. Just as poets, educators, and prosodists were defining and redefining "verse" and "poetry" in the late nineteenth century, so too were they defining and redefining, with a great deal of fervor, "meter," "prosody," and "versification."

The history of English language and literature as a discipline is bound to the way that "history" was taught through these metrically mnemonic methodologies. English history, language study, and literary study all relied on the possibility that meter could help students remember—could be a signifier for—their role as subjects of the nation. "Meter" for the nation was orderly, regal, and signified a long line of battles won; "meter" for the growing middle class could be accessible and an easy to remember layperson's tool—"meter" could also hint at a level of technicality that would only be perceptible to someone properly trained. "Meter," in the histories, was not referring to the shifting terms of cadence, accent, and tone discussed in grammar books and prosodic treatises. A popular concept of "meter" and "English national identity" emerged in these metrical histories: progressive, chronological, and tied to a glorious past of either classical or ancient English origin. "Meter" for these histories, except in the case of Dibdin, had more to do with memorization and rhythm than with what became known as the study of verse-measure. But despite the way that "verse" and "rhyme" began to replace "meter" as signifiers of mental and national order and accessible, even vernacular knowledge, "meter" as a term is still haunted by its simplification in the service of English history teaching. At the same time, there is, even within the discourse of memorization and rhythm, a hint of a more complicated knowledge—an erudite, elite knowledge of verse form to which these histories do not aspire, as if to approach the frightening study of verse form might alienate the student altogether and undermine the more important English history lesson. "English meter" is at once used in the service of a vernacular, popular tradition and also connected to higher learning, even if many of the histories go to great pains to avoid the judgment that they imagine an "actual" poem about history would attract.

A Grammatical History of England

In the same classrooms where history teaching was changing, the teaching of English grammar also shifted radically over the course of the nineteenth century. Though I focus on the period after the second reform bill in 1867, I want to turn for a moment to the one hundred preceding years to briefly outline the ways that the expansion of the franchise and the empire of English letters were intertwined. When, in 1833, the Factory Act limited child labor and prevented children under age nine from legally working, two hours of schooling became compulsory for all children up until the age of nine. This minimal educational standard followed on the heels of the Reform Bill of 1832, which extended the franchise to one in every five voters in England. Passed only with considerable controversy, the 1832 Bill resulted in insecurity about the prevalence of church-run schools as the sole basis of education among the newly empowered voting classes. Concurrent with the subsequent increase in grammar schools, Christopher Stray and Gillian Sutherland note that the first of two "surges" in book publishing began in 1830 and continued until roughly midcentury. Called the "distribution revolution," and underpinned by the impact of the Fourtinier paper-making machine, steam-driven presses, case binding, and the progressive abolition of the taxes on knowledge, these market developments corresponded with the rise of formal schooling and the rise of public examinations in England. Formal schooling had begun to play a more central role in the socialization of children from the latter half of the eighteenth century. The expansion of the franchise in 1832 only accelerated the push toward national education. Stray and Sutherland note that "the sons of elite families and those whose parents had aspired to gentility were increasingly being sent to school," and "the idea of a textbook in the modern sense of the word solidified around 1830."[34] The elocution handbooks of Enfield and Walker were just two examples of a number of new English schoolbooks that were printed and circulated informally in the scattershot early days of compulsory education. Education was conducted in various church schools (which mostly relied on the Bible and the Book of Common Prayer), hedge schools, charity schools, dame schools, grammar schools for the upper classes, and by schoolmasters and schoolmistresses in addition to the traditional "public" schools and each of these may have used different grammar books, standards, or anthologies. The English grammar book attempted to provide a unifying linguistic authority in the subject of the English language for a nation that had no centralized educational authority over its young subjects. Just as the school histories consolidated England's past in the service of nation building, so too did the English grammar book attempt to consolidate English usage in order to organize an idea of the English empire of letters.[35]

"Meter," as we have seen, carried connotations of national and mental order, hinting at a more technical and elite classical knowledge that might distract some students from the process of becoming proper English subjects through memorizing the historical facts of England's origin. But what was this erudite, elite knowledge of English verse form, and where could the non–classically educated but still literate English person, looking to better him or herself, find out about it? Prosody, as a subset of the evolving field of "English grammar" at the turn of the nineteenth century, registered the broader expectations of "grammar" as a prescriptive, unchanging system of rules at the same time that it registered the resistance to these rules by approaching the study of versification differently from one grammar book to the next.[36] The metrical discourses one finds in early grammar books are haunted by the same aspirations toward standard English pronunciation as the elocution manual, as well as the desire for a stable system of grammar based on the authority of Latin. However much English grammar books wanted to provide prescriptive rules, the "prosody" sections of these books heralded the advent of a more descriptive linguistic model. While providing external rules and conventional models for verse form, many grammar books also hinted at the inherent freedoms of English meter, so that English meter used what it wanted from the Latin model but also surpassed it.

Even before the critical events of the 1830s and 1860s expanded the franchise and slowly nationalized the education system, before the conception and execution of the *New English Dictionary*, the idea of "standards" for English usage was already influencing the study and understanding of English meter. Looking at the late eighteenth century and Victorian grammar books reveals the ways that the debates about accent, quantity, and the terms that make up verse study were simplified or abstracted for the sake of an imagined grammar student, a student whose need for a stable system of English prosody (as standardized pronunciation) and a stable explanation of English meter (as the representation of English literature's parallel greatness to the classics) expanded with each expansion of the franchise.

In grammar books, "prosody" referred to both pronunciation and the study of English versification. Over the course of the nineteenth century, uncertainty about prosody and versification often mapped onto uncertainty about standards for pronunciation and ideas about poetic form. For both standardized pronunciation and poetic form, at stake was an appeal to a unified, broad national public as well as an appeal to the preservation of individuality and personal freedoms in dialect and metrical (or artistic) choice. While there seemed to be a move to standardize both English meter and English grammar, there was an equally strong desire to preserve the freedom of poetry to be individual—at once appealing to the collective but also intensely personal.

Some of this uncertainty was evident in the construction of grammar books and the place of prosody, meter, and versification within them. Commonly, historical grammars were divided into four sections: orthography, etymology, syntax, and prosody (perhaps moving down the scale of most easily standardized to least). In many nineteenth-century grammars, "prosody" was further divided into "pronunciation, utterance, figures, and versification." Doubly marginalized, "prosody" was the last part of the traditional grammar book, and "versification," which literary scholars often (and some would argue confusedly[37]) equate with "prosody," was the fourth and final definition of that word.[38] The relegation of "prosody" to the end of grammar books from the late eighteenth century through the beginning of the nineteenth shows that, despite, or perhaps because of, the nervousness about standard pronunciation that accelerated toward the end of the century, the study of spelling, history, and ordering of words took precedence over their pronunciation. Or rather, "grammar books" were prescriptive, whereas the quite distinct guides to elocution and rhetoric were meant as aids to individual performance, and "prosody" bore traces of both of those fields, as well as the quite distinct model of the "poet's handbook."[39] This tension between allowing or eliminating individuation in performance often lurked behind the prosody wars in the late nineteenth century, and is the root of our contemporary inability to decide whether meter is essentially a textual form or a guide to vocal performance.

Within the section "prosody," the subsection "versification" is nearly an appendix, evidence of the way that versification, as a field, was either so simplified as to provide only the rudiments of verse form (and even these were different from book to book) or so technical that it required a treatise or manual all to itself.[40] The uncertain and marginalized status of meter and versification in the study of grammar is an important reason why so many scholars of poetics found themselves with differing opinions on the matter—the simple fact is that the authors of grammar books not only did not know what to do with versification as a subsection of grammar, but that in attempting to find a way to turn the study of versification *into* a kind of grammar, and thus provide it with rules and standards, they presented the topic *as if it were* a discipline. Though prosody and versification appeared as an afterthought in these books and eventually disappeared entirely, the tensions and disagreements over their aims and uses were evident in the way that a single grammar book changed its approach to them over the course of the nineteenth century.[41] In attempting to standardize and simplify the rules of English versification and meter, these grammar books prove the desire for a stable system at the same time that their constant revisions belie the instability of "prosody" as a subject. Could "prosody" at once provide a certain amount of discipline (like a grammar and within the grammar book), while at the same time reaching the status of a "grammar" with standards all its own?

The standardizing projects of the eighteenth century and the conservatism and classicism that we associate with the century in general do not apply neatly in the case of prosody. Jeff Strabone has recently outlined the way that Samuel Johnson's standardizing project in *The Dictionary* (1755) was ambivalent about its own cultural-imperialist aims,[42] and Paul Fussell has noted that Johnson's own revisions to the fourth edition of *The Dictionary* (1773) added to the generalization, "every line considered by itself is more harmonious, as this rule is more strictly observed," the warning, "[t]he variations necessary to pleasure belong to the art of poetry, not the rules of grammar."[43] As Strabone argues elsewhere, the national myths of England's classical origins were being revised long before the study of language in England was crucially influenced by Danish and German philological study. Dialect poems, a renewed interest in ballads, and the collection of folk forms from rural Scotland competed with the standardization and Latinization of English language and grammar. Strabone suggests that *Reliques of Ancient Poetry: Consisting of Old Heroic Ballads, Songs, and other Pieces of our earlier Poets*[44] contained a kind of metrical discourse that rivaled the standardizing impulses of the prescriptive grammars, especially in Percy's long headnote, "On the Metre of Pierce Plowman's Visions."[45] Part of a general interest in pre-Chaucerian meters as unifying, folk-meters of the people, Percy notes the division of Langland's meter into lines of two parts, or "distichs" each, measured by alliteration. Percy writes, "the author of this poem will not be found to have invented any new mode of versification, as some have supposed, but only to have retained that of the old Saxon and Gothic poets."[46] A resurgent interest in "folk" forms, more purely "English" in some ways than the Latin forms imposed on English verse, both anticipated and was concurrent with the renewed interest in Anglo-Saxon at the turn of the nineteenth century.

In an 1835 review in *The Gentleman's Magazine* of Rev. Samuel Fox's *King Alfred's Anglo-Saxon Version of the Metres of Boethius, with an English translation and notes* (translator of the poetical calendar of the Anglo-Saxons), the reviewer notes that "A taste for Anglo-Saxon literature is still increasing. The most unequivocal proof of this is, the constant demand for standard Anglo-Saxon books."[47] The reviewer notes "Mr. Fox properly states that '[i]t is now ascertained beyond all doubt that alliteration is the chief characteristic of Anglo-Saxon verse; and this is also accompanied with a rhythm which clearly distinguishes it from prose.'" The histories of England and the history of English meter are intertwined into one volume. England's history is given a different kind of authority because it is not only about King Alfred but is actually written *by* him; the Reverend Samuel Fox has also translated the "poetical calendar" of the Anglo-Saxons and has clearly distinguished alliteration as the principle by which Anglo-Saxon meters are distinguished from prose. By 1807, Sharon Turner's *History of England: The History of Anglo-Saxons from the Earliest Period to the Norman Conquest*, alludes to the already extant controversies over Anglo-Saxon meter and also foreshadows the ways that Anglo-Saxon "rhythm" would be revived institutionally at the turn of the twentieth century in the name of stable English national culture. Turner explains (quoting liberally from Bede):

> The style of their poetry was as peculiar. It has been much disputed by what rules or laws the Saxons arranged their poetical phrases. I have observed a passage in the general works of Bede which may end the controversy, by showing that they used no rules at all, but adopted the simpler principle of consulting only the natural love of melody, of which the human organs of hearing have been made susceptible; and of using that easy allocation of syllables which pleased the musical ear. In defining rhythmus Bede says, "It is a modulated composition of words, not according to the laws of metre, but *adapted in the number of its syllables to the judgment of the ear*, as are the verses of our vulgar (or native) poets. Rhythm may exist without metre, but there cannot be metre without rhythm, which is thus more clearly defined. Metre is an artificial rule with modulation; rhythmus is the modulation without the rule. Yet, for the most part, you may find, by a sort of chance, some rule in rhythm; but this is not from an artificial government of syllables. It arises because the sound and the modulation lead to it. The vulgar poets effect this rustically; the skilful attain it by their skill." From this passage it is obvious that Bede's poetical countrymen wrote their vernacular verses without any other rule than that of pleasing the ear.[48]

The first thing to observe here is that the definition of Anglo-Saxon meter was already a controversy. The rules of even the most native rhythms were not easily definable, and despite attempts to turn "meter" into a grammar, scholars disagreed about the best way to read, teach, and analyze English meter. Though Turner concludes that "pleasing the ear" (Bede's "musical" ear) was the only rule, the surge of interest in Anglo-Saxon poetry and grammar in the early nineteenth century meant that more readers would have been listening to and perhaps accustoming their own ears to the particular imagined sounds of Anglo-Saxon accentual-alliterative meters.[49]

Though the status of prosody in the grammar book seems far afield of our more traditional concept of poetics, it has, nonetheless, influenced how we think about the authority of English versification in the nineteenth century. The simplification of prosodic discourse and the limitation of complex discussions of prosodic controversies tended to collapse the concept of English prosody into its two most basic parts: an ordering system that had certain laws, and a system of English laws that are better than classical meter because they give the poet more freedom and are therefore proudly and identifiably English. Though most of the prominent English grammarians, or "New Rhetoricians"—Joseph Priestley, William Ward, Charles Coote, and Lindley Murray—adopt the Latin model for grammar, their disagreement about how to graphically represent accent anticipates broader disagreements in the nineteenth-century about scansion but also about the representation of sound in text. Priestley and Murray used the Latin macron (¯) and breve (˘), which correspond to the measure of quantities (the macron for a long vowel and the breve for a short), when they discuss versification. These signs would be familiar to students of Latin who would use them to translate into a metrical grid; they signified the imagined pronunciation of a dead language based on a system of rules of position. Murray, however, used the acute accent when discussing emphasis in pronunciation. He thus distinguished the vocal performance of English from its arrangement in the metrical grid and implied that accent was linked to pronunciation in English more than to a metrical system. Though the substitution of "accent" for "quantity" in English verse was not new, the move away from the older macron and breve does indicate that English meter, at least for Murray, would follow a more accentual model. Murray, Priestley, and Ward also characterized the metrical feet according to the classical names, and Murray went so far as to give the measures particular characters (on "trochaic" meter: "[t]his measure is defective in dignity, and can seldom be used on serious occasions"[50]). Though Thomas Sheridan was aware of the disagreements about the various models for English prosody and said as much in his *Rhetorical Grammar* (printed with the *A Course of Lectures on Elocution* in 1762 and the *Dictionary* in 1780),[51] popular grammars nonetheless continued to print their various approaches to the measure of English verse, more or less modeled on Latin grammars, with an increasing emphasis on examples from English poetry as descriptive proof of their seemingly prescriptive models.

And as English versification became more descriptive it also, at times, departed from the Latin model and gestured to alternative histories. In 1788, Charles Coote introduced the "Anglo-Saxon" along with the "Old English" alphabet in his grammar (the "Old English" alphabet actually referring to a font style), which, significantly, contained "notes critical and etymological." Coote's grammar foreshadowed the inadequacy of the Latin model to account for English versification, even in a simplified grammar. In a subtle move away from classical meter, Coote used the acute accent to indicate stress rather than resorting to the classical macron and breve; pronunciation and *not* the classical rubric thus subtly appeared as the proper way to scan a line of English verse. Though Coote wrote, "a *foot* is a particular division of a line, consisting (in English verse) of two or three syllables,"[52] he did not name those feet according to any Latin model but rather explained verse forms or "species of metre" by the placement of accent only. For instance, "[t]he *heroic* metre, so called from its being principally used in heroic poetry, is composed of lines of ten syllables, the accent being placed on the second, fourth, sixth, eighth, and tenth." After describing "heroic metre," "blank verse" ("destitute of rhyme"), "Alexandrine

verse" ("usually used in heroic poetry intermixed with lines of ten syllables"),
and "elegiac" (which could be "appropriate for elegies" but is also "a common
metre for poems of a lighter cast"), Coote seems to throw up his hands at
"lyric": "[i]n *lyric* poetry, or that which comprehends odes, sonnets, songs, &c.
various measures are adopted." Though he goes on to name a few possibilities
for rhyme schemes and accents, he ends his discussion by admitting "the measure of odes is so variable and irregular, that no determinate rules can be given
for them." Coote's "Laws of Verse" only followed the Latin model by using the
word "feet," but he departed from the standard set forth by the other grammars in favor of attempting to describe English meters based on English poems
themselves. There is a hint, here, with his inclusion of the Anglo-Saxon alphabet and his avoidance of the classical names for the metrical feet that Coote
was leaning toward a potentially more autonomous possibility for English
versification.

Grammatical Instability

Though the emergent interest in Anglo-Saxon verse forms subtly influenced
the versification sections of English grammar books, the authority of classical
metrical feet remained prominent in standard grammars until the end of the
nineteenth century. Despite the ascendancy of the classical model, however,
the terms for prosody, meter, and versification were still unstable even in the
most widely circulating and popular grammar textbooks. Lindley Murray's
best-selling *English Grammar* sold a staggering sixteen million copies in the
United States and four million in Great Britain. William Woods asserts that
it was Murray's *Grammar* that "brought the eighteenth-century emphasis on
correctness and rules into the nineteenth century and established it as the
reigning tradition."[53] This was, perhaps, the case for the elements of grammar
except prosody. In the case of the metrical aspects of prosody, Murray's *Grammar* shows both how the poetics of prosody anticipates the descriptive model
for grammar adopted later in the nineteenth century and how, despite the
descriptive model, the specific terms we use for English meter are historically
contingent.[54] In 1795, the year of Murray's first edition, "prosody" had two
simple definitions: "the former teaches the true pronunciation of words, com-
prising accent, quantity, emphasis, and cadence, and the latter the laws of versification."[55] We can sense, already, how these two definitions are intertwined,
for the laws of versification depend on the very definitions of accent, quantity,
emphasis, and cadence. To give just one example of the volatility of "prosody,"
in the 1810, 1828, and 1839 editions of Murray's *Grammar*, pronunciation is
comprised of "accent, quantity, emphasis, pause, and tone."[56] "Cadence" has
been replaced by "pause" and "tone." In elocutionary terms, emphasis meant
raising the voice while cadence meant lowering the voice, but in the later editions the falling voice is replaced by "pause," which has a spatial counterpart in

the caesura, and "tone," which is increasingly associated with affect. By 1867, the fifty-sixth edition of the *Grammar,* the editors erase "tone," leaving only "pause."[57] As the science of linguistics was growing—indeed developing the science of phonetics—the perceived "problems" of pronunciation in prosody that may have required "tone" were, perhaps, no longer necessary.

The section "versification" that follows these revisions to "prosody" may, we might expect, shift away from performance, voice, and affect and, like "prosody" begin to sound more and more like a grammar with applicable and clear rules. And yet if the student must master the proper pronunciation of words (the former definition of prosody) before moving onto their measure (the latter definition, the laws), and if these rules of proper pronunciation are in flux, it follows that the "laws" of versification are also malleable. But though editors did revise the rules of versification from one edition to the next, they did not do so in order to reflect disagreements and dynamism; rather, the history of English versification in the grammar book is a history of repetition and reiteration—often without giving credit where credit is due. For instance, the non-abridged versions of Murray's *Grammar* gave a detailed definition of "versification" that reads, in many ways, identically to contemporary accounts of English verse form. Yet Murray borrowed liberally from Thomas Sheridan's popular eighteenth-century elocutionary manual, *The Art of Reading* (1775).[58] Sheridan's section, "Of Poetical Feet," appeared first in the fourth edition (1798) of Murray's grammar and bore the traces of turn-of-the-century elocutionary and prosodic discourse that was concerned with the rhetorical function of verse, specifically its performance. As if to anticipate a more advanced pupil's question ("why do we call these line divisions 'feet?'"), the text explains: "they are called <u>feet</u> because it is by their aid that the voice, as it were, steps along, through the verse, in a measured pace; and it is necessary that the syllables which mark this regular movement of the voice, should, in some manner, be distinguished from the others."[59]

In a statement that could as easily refer to quantity (understood here as the length of time it takes to say a syllable) as accent (often understood in the grammars as emphasis), Sheridan's definition in Murray's popular grammar allowed the student to believe that by vocal right-reading, the "poetical feet" would distinguish themselves "in some manner." Or, rather, the poetical feet would be distinguished on or in the syllables by either quantity or accent or both, and the voice would be able to "step along" toward a right reading.[60] The voice, here, already displaced onto the feet, is not certain; only "in some manner," not at all uniform, might the voice distinguish each syllable (a wobbly stone in a river), feeling shakily for the right way to get across the line. Rather than providing his own definition, Murray reprints Sheridan's abstract definition, a practice I want to highlight as integral to the way that the idea of "English feet" (both in opposition to, and as a natural progression from, classical feet) circulates in the nineteenth century: that is, via the repetition and reprinting of formulations that stress instinct in performance, holding onto the shadow of elocution and projecting forward to Pound's desire for a "natural rhythm." The abstraction of "feet" in the English grammar book elided controversies over what went into their composition (accent, quantity, emphasis) and the particular interpretive problems that each of these issues presented.

In another example, Murray's *Grammar* included Sheridan's now familiar definition of English versification translated from Latin quantities into accents: "In English, syllables are divided into accented and unaccented; and the accented syllables being as strongly distinguished from the unaccented, by the peculiar stress of the voice upon them, are equally capable of marking the movement, and pointing out the regular paces of the voice, as the long syllables were, by their quantity, among the Romans."[61] Murray stops there, but Sheridan continues, complaining that "the whole modern theory of quantity will be found a mere chimera."[62] By leaving out what his predecessor knew, that the "theory" of quantity would obscure a student's eventual understanding of accent, Murray gestures to the Roman genealogy of English verse as if to give it a high-cultural precedent, but does not reprint Sheridan's warning that a deeper investigation into quantity would produce a "mere chimera." In fact, Sheridan's choice of words was incredibly apt for the study of English prosody more generally: the myth of the chimera involved, of course, a monster put together from various animal parts, much the same as late nineteenth-century prosodic historians would argue that English prosody was made up of various linguistic influences. Likewise, a chimera is a something hoped for and dreamed of, but seldom achieved. The hope for and dream of a stable system for English prosody, and the buried fear that it might not be achievable was, as I argue specifically in the following chapters, the engine that drove the study of prosody into a kind of obsolescence.

While Lindley Murray certainly helped popularize and circulate (though he did not originate) the idea that English poetic feet had both accent and quantity, he failed to define either. Versification must follow pronunciation both literally (students must get through accent, quantity, and emphasis in the basic pronunciation of words before they get to "versification" at the end) and metaphorically. The "quantity" of a syllable is defined simply as "the time which is occupied in pronouncing it."[63] Rather than admit that English speakers had no system for quantity, Murray made it seem as if what we did have was far better than what the ancients had. That is, he turned a complicated chimera into a statement of linguistic superiority: the English had "all that the ancients had, and something which they had not."[64] This additional component, Murray asserted, was that we had duplicate feet to match the ancient meters, but "with such a difference, as to fit them for different purposes, to be applied at our pleasure." Our accent allowed English feet pleasure and freedom, as opposed to those fixed Greek and Latin feet. Further, Murray continued, "[e]very [English] foot has, from nature, powers peculiar to itself; and it is upon the knowledge and right application of these powers, that the pleasure and effect of numbers chiefly depend." Whereas the terms "cadence," "pause," and "tone" are part of the debate, the problem of metrical feet in English concerns those three seemingly nonvariable terms of versification: "accent," "quantity," and "emphasis." The terms themselves appear again and again but, as we can see in Sheridan and Murray, the ways that prosodists and poets defined and used these terms varied widely, and the various ways that English readers and poets understood these prosodic terms was what identified them as English. The English feet, then, to the average student coming across Murray's best-selling grammar book, had authority from classical meters (not exactly defined, but there nonetheless). Mastery of the peculiar and particular powers of these "feet" would allow us to understand a more specialized kind of "English meter." We can see how the obfuscating tendency of these constantly revised textbooks created the market for the definitive guide to English meter that emerged toward the end of the nineteenth century.

In addition to the revision and repetition of metrical terms, another of my concerns here is how certain ideas about prosodic form are stabilized by the contingencies of pedagogy. That is, the simplification, for pedagogical purposes, of the historical disagreements about certain aspects of English meter masks the ideologies of improvement within the Latin grammar and presents English meter as a self-evident truth. The self-evidence of English meter's classical roots took on an even broader ideological meaning at the turn of the twentieth century, as we will see in chapter three. In one early example of what will be promoted as a metrical dogma toward the end of the century, we can see even Murray's abridged grammar efface and simplify the complex history of English meter. When Murray's grammar was abridged, as it often was, the "versification" section of "prosody" states the following: "versification is the arrangement of a certain number and variety of syllables, according to certain laws."[65] There was no reference to problematic accent, quantity, or emphasis here; versification was simply "arrangement" according to law. This was from an 1816 edition, intended for a "younger class of learners" who should be protected from the more technical aspects of English versification, a pedagogical impulse that would take root in the late nineteenth century.[66] The "certain laws" of versification and meter are English laws, which should be justification enough for following them.

Metrical Instability

In addition to the political changes and social changes I outlined above, scholars questioned the widely held belief that Greek and Latin should be the only languages studied in earnest by the educated elite. Though the true devaluation of Greek and Latin did not begin until the end of the nineteenth century (and even then it was a slow fade), the discoveries and revivals of eighteenth-century comparative philology on the continent had a profound impact on the study of the English language and the perception that the English language, with a genealogy that was perhaps different from that of the ancient languages, should and could reflect the greatness of the nation. Formed in response to this new comparative philology, a group of scholars under the name of the "Philological Society" met in London in 1830 with the aim of combining the old classical philology with the new comparative philology. By 1842, Edwin Guest founded the English Philological Society, whose published intentions were to "investigate the Philological Illustration of the Classical Writers of Greece and Rome" and to investigate the "Structure, Affinities, and the History of Languages" both in England and in other countries. This is, of course, the society that eventually created the *New English Dictionary* (*NED*) and its members included, at one time or another, *NED* editors James Henry Murray and Richard Chevenix Trench, as well as Alexander Ellis and Henry Sweet, both late-century pioneers in the study of English phonology. In addition to establishing the English Philological Society, Guest—archeologist and self-taught Anglo-Saxonist—was the author of *Origines Celticae: A History of Britain in two volumes,* in 1883 (published posthumously), and the monumental *History of English Rhythms,* in 1838, which reflected his interest in philology and Old English by asserting, quite controversially, that the accent was "the sole principle"[67] that regulated English rhythm. This assertion, though it did not gain as much traction in 1838 as it did when it was reprinted in 1882, is important not only because it shows how differently—even abstractly —the problem of pronunciation is taken up by prosodic theorists, but also because it shows the deep-seated influence of the revived interest in Anglo-Saxon literatures on the study of English meter in the twentieth century.

Along with the new philology,[68] new histories of English literature,[69] and the rise of English education, historical interpretations of prosody flourished in the nineteenth century. Yopie Prins writes, "English Prosody becomes a national heritage, with a political as well as poetical purpose."[70] As Prins asserts in her ground-breaking essay "Victorian Meters," following John Hollander's claim that "prosodical analysis is a form of literature in itself,"[71] Victorian prosody as "a literary genre . . . raises important historical and theoretical questions about the interpretation of poetry, beyond a merely technical, seemingly ahistorical approach to the scansion of a particular text."[72] The main prosodic theorists in this book—Hopkins, Bridges, Patmore, Saintsbury, Guest, Newbolt, Meynell, Pound—did not emerge in a vacuum. Even by midcentury, prosodic discourse was already known as a complicated and unresolved subject. In 1858, Goold Brown wrote on page 827 of the over 1,000 page *Grammar of English Grammars*[73] a two-page definition of "versification" (but then appended to this definition two additional pages of smaller text "observations," including the following: "If to settle the theory of English verse on true and consistent principles, is as difficult a matter, as the manifold controversies of doctrine among our prosodists would indicate, there can be no great hope of any scheme entirely satisfactory to the intelligent examiner. The very elements of the subject are much perplexed by the incompatible dogmas of authors deemed skillful to elucidate it" (828).

Brown then goes on to enumerate (a favorite practice of those interested in grammar and prosody) the many issues over which prosodists quarreled at midcentury about versification.

> The existence of quantity in our language; the dependence of our rhythms on the division of syllables into long and short; the concurrence of our accent, (except in some rare and questionable instances) with long quantity only; the constant effect of emphasis to lengthen quantity; the limitation of quantity to mere duration of sound; the doctrine that quantity pertains to all syllables as such, and not merely to vowel sounds; the recognition of the same general principles of syllabification in poetry as in prose; the supposition that accent pertains not to certain letters in particular, but to certain syllables as such; the limitations of accent to stress, or percussion, only; the conversion of short syllables into long, and long into short, by a change of accent; our frequent formation of long syllables with what are called short vowels; the necessity of some order in the succession of feet or syllables to form a rhythm; the need of framing each line to correspond with some other line or lines in length; the propriety of always making each line susceptible of scansion by itself; all these points, so essential to a true explanation of the nature of English verse, though, for the most part, well maintained by some prosodists, are nevertheless denied by some, so that opposite opinions may be cited concerning them all. (828)

This list is, sadly, not at all exhaustive.[74] The disagreements he cites here are a common trope of the prosodic handbook, so that Coventry Patmore began his 1857 essay, "English Metrical Critics,"[75] with the claim that, since the establishment of blank verse just after Surrey, "the nature of modern verse has been a favourite problem of enthusiasts who love to dive in deep waters for diving's sake. A vast mass of nondescript matter has been brought up from the recesses visited, but no one has succeeded in rendering any sufficient account of this secret of the intellectual deep."[76] Patmore ostensibly begins his own theory by reviewing Guest's *History of English Rhythms* (1838), William O'Brien's *The Ancient Rhythmical Art Recovered* (1843), and *The Art of Elocution* (1855) by George Vandenhoff. To show the diversity of approaches, Guest's volume was concerned with accent as the basis for English verse, O'Brien's was a study of Greek alcaic choruses, and Vandenhoff's presented a system of rising and falling meters complete with a new system of marking the rise and fall of the voice. New marking systems, new names for metrical feet, and new definitions of and arguments over the definitions of terms were all part of prosodic discourse in the nineteenth century. Each writer presented a different definition, term, or even marking system for English verse form, and scholars would do well to examine the vast and nearly unexplored archives of the thousands of other schoolmasters and mistresses, linguists, prosodists, and poets who weighed in on the question of English meter.

In this way, prosodists created the field of prosody, counting and accounting for each other's theories, disagreeing with them, and putting forth their corrections, adjustments, and improvements, both of each other and, in a series of revised and reprinted editions, of themselves.

Prosodic discussions were also transatlantic. Lindley Murray and Goold Brown were American by birth. Vandenhoff was born in England but moved to the United States in 1842, where he met Edgar Allan Poe, with whom he co-wrote *A Plain System of Elocution.*[77] Poe himself published the "Rationale of Verse" in the *Southern Literary Messenger* in 1848, and Emerson's essay "The Poet" was published in his collected essays in 1844. The desire to define English national culture against various competing communities or nations— Scottish, Irish, Indian, American, German—influenced and determined certain aspects of the global circulation of meters at end of the nineteenth century in England; the establishment of English literature as a discipline of study at Oxford and Cambridge created an even greater need to provide an answer to the perceived conflicts and controversies about English meter. If the metrical histories of England used meter to order England's past, then histories of meter emerged toward the late nineteenth century that attempted to justify their systems by presenting evolutionary narratives of England's progress, histories of the English language, and metrical systems that could adequately teach younger generations about English poetry in the new century.

The discourse was often patriotic and bombastic. Robert Bridges's book *Milton's Prosody,* published alongside a reprint of the late William Johnson Stone's treatise *On the Use of Classical Metres in English,*[78] sold out its first print run and *Milton's Prosody* was revised and reprinted in 1921.[79] The German, Jakob Schipper, who not only wrote about the form of English meter but had also written a three-volume history of versification, published *Englische Metrik*[80] in 1888 and the much-called-for abridged edition appeared in 1895 as *Grundriss der englischen metrik* (Wein, 1895). The classicist Joseph Mayor published the first edition of *Chapters on English Metre* in 1886 and the revised, second edition in 1901. Thomas Stewart Omond published *English Hexameter Verse* and *English Verse-Structure* in 1897, and in 1903 brought out *English Metrists* and *A Study of Metre.*[81] This is only a small example of the field that prosodists and poets were carving out for English poetics in the late nineteenth century. In each of these, the history of prosody is bound to the history of England, and prosodic discourse becomes a contentious battlefield.

In the late twentieth century, Dennis Taylor brought attention to the explosion of scholarship about meter in the late nineteenth century; the remainder of this book explores the ways that the accelerated concerns of English national culture intensified debates about English poetry at the turn of the twentieth century. Due in part to Taylor's work, scholars of nineteenth-century poetry have paid much attention to the metrical theories of Coventry Patmore, first published in the *North British Review* in 1857 as a review of "English Metrical Critics," and revised and reprinted as *Prefatory Study on English Metrical Law* in 1878 as an appendix to his volume of poems *Amelia, Tamerton Church Tower*.[82] Patmore's essay seems the harbinger of this explosion of interest in metrical form in the late nineteenth century, reevaluating the philosophical implications of and abstract models for English prosodic form.[83] The conflicts over defining English meter are bound to the problems of the development of English linguistic and literary study as a discipline, and the desperation to provide rules for English meter is often powerfully allegorized, for poets and prosodists, as akin to providing rules for civilizing and educating the unruly masses of the quickly developing welfare state. For poets like Patmore and Gerard Manley Hopkins, however, metrical rules could also provide powerful allegories for religious and moral order in a spiritual sense.

Though there are many ways to read the dynamic history of prosody and its impact on poetics, the idea that the measure of the nation's language could somehow represent the measure of the nation's greatness—and that in turn could be related to the nation's spiritual health—gained momentum in the Victorian era. Philologist R. Chevenix Trench published *On the Study of Words* in 1851 (nine years after the formation of the English Philological Society in 1842, which would eventually hire him as an editor of the *New English Dictionary*). Both Guest's *History of English Rhythms* and Trench's *On The Study of Words* were reprinted in 1882 (the former in a highly anticipated second edition, edited by Cambridge philologist Walter Skeat, and the latter in its nineteenth edition, attesting to the book's popularity). Trench writes that the English language contains "[a] faithful record of the good and of the evil . . . in the minds and hearts of men. [It is] a moral barometer, which indicates and permanently marks the rise or fall of a nation's life. To study a people's language is to study them."[84] Indeed, the rise and fall of the nation's life—through its language, literature, and its definitions of meter (and definitions of itself in metrical and allegorical terms)—were issues at the forefront of the national imagination in the formative period between 1860 and 1930. It is in this climate that the poet Gerard Manley Hopkins experimented with sprung rhythm (rivaled only by the long lines of Walt Whitman in nineteenth-century poetic nation making). Hopkins, Patmore, and Bridges, as the next chapter argues, were participating in a much larger discourse about poetry and national culture, the distances between poet and reader, citizen and country, speaker and hearer, and the seen and unseen presence of Christ, readable both in the marks of Christ's nature and in the marks that man makes on his poems. Poets like Hopkins and Bridges mediated between and at times tried to merge classical and Anglo-Saxon meters, incorporating linguistic and metrical histories into their attempts at new metrical systems. Their aim was to teach the reading public something about their national past, even if that past was a classical one. In the case of Hopkins, these attempts at new systems were meant to ensure a kind of salvation for the nation's future; in the case of Bridges, new metrical systems were intended to preserve and protect the freedom and variety of English meter in a new century that might not have the education to understand it.

❧ 2 ❧

The Stigma of Meter

It is quite plain that writing is but an external and necessarily
imperfect vesture, while the true and natural and real form of language
is that which is made of sound, and addressed to the ear.
—John Earle, "Of Prosody," *The Philology of the English Tongue*

A word exists as truly for the eye as for the ear, and in a highly advanced state
of society, where reading is almost as universal as speaking . . . in the *written* word
moreover is the permanence and continuity of language and of learning.
—Richard Chevenix Trench, *On the Study of Words*

Oh which one? Is it each one?
—Gerard Manley Hopkins, "Carrion Comfort"

And is it to the eye only that the metre is to be marked? The eye, which,
of itself, can form no judgment of measure in sounds, nor take any pleasure
in such arrangements of words; and shall the ear, the sole judge of numbers,
to which nature herself has annexed a delight, in the perception of metre,
be left without any mark, to point out the completion of the measure?
—Thomas Sheridan, "Rhetorical Grammar,"
A General Dictionary of The English Language[1]

Metrical Irrelevance

Meter in late nineteenth- and early twentieth-century England was indelibly
marked by the culture around it; those who wished to transform or redefine
meter were also attempting to transform or redefine aspects of English culture.
There is no better test case for the oppositions inherent in English metrical
form (private vs. public, spiritual vs. national, visual vs. aural, native vs. foreign) than the poetry, journals, and letters of Gerard Manley Hopkins. Despite the disappointment that he had published only a few poems in his lifetime (a few early poems, three comic triolets, Latin versions of an epigram by
Dryden, and two songs by Shakespeare),[2] Hopkins remained hopeful about
the place of poetry in public culture, writing to his friend Robert Bridges in

1886: "A great work by an Englishman is like a great battle won by England."[3] After Hopkins's death three years later, Bridges was reluctant to publish Hopkins's poems despite the fact that he had a fair copy of a manuscript. Hopkins's experiments in "sprung rhythm," a new meter for English and England, necessitated marks for meter or, as Bridges explained in his introduction to Hopkins's poems in Alfred A. Miles's *Poets and Poetry of the Century* (1893): "Some syllables have been accented in the text, as a guide to the reader, where it seemed that the boldness of the rhythm might otherwise cause him to doubt the intended stress."[4] Bridges facilitated the publication of at least nineteen of Hopkins's poems between 1893 and 1902 before including six extracts and poems in his self-edited and immensely popular wartime anthology, *The Spirit of Man*, in 1916; here, he reproduced some but not all of the metrical markings for which Hopkins is now well known.[5] But what did these marks mean? Did Hopkins always intend to guide an imaginary, idealized performer toward one kind of reading, or did his metrical marks and their material manifestation on the page indicate the possibility of different readings, or the struggle to read accurately at all? Hopkins's struggles with his meters reflect and intersect with struggles about his role as a poet, investigations into philology, interest in the visual world, and his hope that reading could lead to salvation. Reading Hopkins's meter as a crucial part of his conception of the visual world and therefore of his theology, we can understand more fully his desperate, hopeless, and frustrated desire to transmit this particular visual and spiritual theology to his few readers and, ideally, to the rest of England. The developments of linguistic science and Hopkins's position both as a Jesuit priest and as a student and teacher of the classics position him uniquely to mediate between the Anglo-Saxon and the classical and the public and private worlds of Victorian poetry and prosody.

Writers and critics associated with the modernist avant-garde have relied on the "great divide" narrative so much that any seemingly anachronistic experiments of the nineteenth century are reinterpreted as anticipating the experiments of the twentieth century. When Hopkins's *Poems* were published in 1918, critics like I. A. Richards heralded him as a "proto-modernist" rather than a Victorian poet whose concept of "standard" prosody and syntax may have been wildly different from what the modernists would have us believe. Hopkins's poems seem "modern," that is, because of a misreading or ignorance of the proliferation of metrical experiments in the nineteenth century. Bridges, who was Hopkins's close friend, interlocutor, and his editor published Hopkins's poems in book form in 1918.[6] At that time, Bridges had the prestige of the poet laureateship, and the poems fit perfectly into the context of "difficult" modernist works emerging in the postwar moment—poems that reconsidered form in all its guises. Construed by critics as "always obscure"[7] and "music too difficult,"[8] the first edition of Hopkins's poems baffled more readers than it converted. In September 1926, Richards published an essay in *The Dial* titled simply "Gerard Hopkins." The piece begins: "[m]odern verse is perhaps more often too lucid than too obscure," and makes a case for "some slight obscurity in its own right,"[9] using Hopkins as an example for the "practical criticism" that Richards would set forth in 1929. It is not surprising, then, when one considers the antiphilological and antihistorical approaches to literature that Richards espoused, that he would praise Hopkins for his mastery. Despite this respect for Hopkins's "mastery," the early history of his publication is one of truncation and erasure: just as Bridges was reluctant to reproduce all of Hopkins's metrical marks, Richards included none of them in *Practical Criticism*. Hopkins's obscurity, according to Richards, repelled the "light-footed reader" who had been conditioned to expect clarity in metric and narrative not only by English education but also by the inundation of metrically simplistic Edwardian and Georgian poetry—the conventional backdrop for the rise of experimental Modernism.

Though Richards was comfortable with the way that Hopkins's metrical form helped to create a kind of modern-seeming obscurity, he was uncomfortable with the metrical marks indicating Hopkins's rhythm.[10] In Richards's 1929 textbook, *Practical Criticism*, he eliminated the accent mark over the word "will" in a line from the poem "Spring and Fall." I'll quote the poem in full, including the marks that Richards erased:

SPRING AND FALL

to a young child

Márgarét, áre you grieving
Over Goldengrove unleaving?
Leáves, like the things of man, you
With your fresh thoughts care for, can you?
Áh! ás the heart grows older   5
It will come to such sights colder
By and by, nor spare a sigh
Though worlds of wanwood leafmeal lie;
And yet you wíll weep and know why.
Now no matter, child, the name: 10
Sórrow's spríngs áre the same.
Nor mouth had, no nor mind, expressed
What heart heard of, ghost guessed:
It ís the blight man was born for,
It is Margaret you mourn for.   15

Richards eliminated all metrical marks on the poem, but he discussed in detail his decision to erase the mark in line 9: "And yet you wíll weep and know why." Using the unmarked and truncated text from Bridges's *The Spirit of Man*, Richards acknowledged that Hopkins was aware of the "possible alternative readings of the seventh (sic) line" because of the "accent-mark he originally placed on 'will.'" In the 1918 edition of Hopkins's poems, also edited by Bridges, accent marks appeared in lines 1, 3, 5, 9, 11, and 14 (Bridges's 1918 version also includes lines 3 and 4, omitted from both *The Spirit of Man* and *Practical Criticism*, and no other published versions of "Spring and Fall" published prior to this moment retained Hopkins's marks).[11] Richards's excuse for the erasure "to avoid a likely temptation to irrelevant discussions"—demonstrates a critical unwillingness to engage with meter's material, historical, and spiritual presence. Indeed, it explicitly deems any such discussion "irrelevant." Richards writes, "[w]hen 'will' is accentuated it ceases to be an auxiliary verb and becomes the present tense of the verb 'to will.'"[12] His criticism of the word is that even without the accent mark, the hint that it gives toward the meaning of the poem "ought to be retained."[13] As Richards's reading of Hopkins shows, because of and despite its erasure of the mark, meter's meaning is seldom secure.

This line, if we reinsert the mark, gestures to its own possible reception. The alliterative "will," "weep," and "why," demote the stress on "know," so that the line defers any stable knowledge of why the reader *will* weep. Hopkins inscribes the critical pathos into the poem's falling rhythm, bolstered by the words "worlds" and "wanwood" in line 8: "Though worlds of wanwood leafmeal lie." In this way, the poem commands us to recognize the "sights" (l. 6: "such sights colder") that bend our critical will to react, "by and by" (l. 7). Richards effaces this reading, refusing even to recognize the metrical pun of the poem's title—"Spring and Fall," as Hopkins called his most famous poetic experiment "sprung rhythm"—and this poem, using that rhythm, springs and falls in and out of a more traditional alternating pattern. By removing the mark, Richards, in effect, erases his own willingness to engage with meter on Hopkins's specific historical terms, preferring to make meter a constant, and therefore immaterial, issue.

Richards's early assessment has haunted critical accounts of Hopkins. Along Richards's lines, a critical tendency has arisen to read the sound effects in Hopkins's poetry as either magically clarifying or obfuscating, without considering the fact that the very concept of sound was changing as Hopkins composed his poems and theories. Indeed, late twentieth-century critics followed the same well-trodden paths as nineteenth-century prosodists like Hopkins, idealizing the possibility of meter as a constant system that could be replicated by more than one speaker in more than one historical moment. Eric Griffiths's landmark book, *The Printed Voice of Victorian Poetry* (1989), so vividly imagines scenes of hearing and so carefully shows instances and tropes of voice and silence in Victorian poetry that poetic meter becomes merely voice's vehicle without an expressive capacity of its own. Poetic meter, in particular, becomes a predicament of speech. Griffiths's work has been instrumental in continuing the tendency to read meter purely as an instruction to a voice, one that makes "claims" on it that are sometimes contradictory.[14] When complicated meter renders accurate voicing impossible—perhaps even silent—Griffiths posits that Hopkins is allegorizing Christ's silence. But Griffiths and Richards are all subject to a naturalized idea of "hearing" that derives from the nineteenth-century dream of universal pronunciation, (a dream to which Richards devoted much of his late career).[15] If were we all able to hear alike, then we would be able to retroactively "hear," or more accurately perform, and therefore imagine, the precise sounds that Hopkins intended. Philologist John Earle provides a convenient example: in his 1873 chapter "Of Prosody," which I quoted in the epigraph, Earle called voice "the necessary vehicle of the meaning"; sound alone was the "illustrative agency" and meter was mere modulation of emphasis.[16] But the material form of metrical marking was proof, in itself, that all ears do not hear alike, nor do all voices emphasize in the right way, despite convention. If these scholars perceived metrical marks materially, it was only as an instruction for an imagined, idealized voice that would, even with the marks, be able to speak and hear the same way. Despite good intentions toward historicism, critical focus on the oral recitation and aural reception of Hopkins's poems in this way has shifted our focus away from the material form of Hopkins's metrical marks.

The British Empire of Letters

During the last decades of the nineteenth century, a number of English poets and prosodists were concerned with the greatness of the English language and the role poetry played in preserving that greatness. For Hopkins, Robert Bridges, and Coventry Patmore, the forms of English meter were not only implicated in measuring English poetry, but in measuring England's character as well. In 1886, three years before his death, Hopkins wrote to Patmore, praising his poems as the kind that might be best suited to save England from the spiritual dismay that was now spreading into the empire. "Your poems," Hopkins wrote, "are a good deed done for the Catholic Church and another for England, for the British Empire." He then asked, "What marked and striking excellence has England to shew or make her civilization attractive? ... I hold that fine works of art ... are really a great power in the world, an element of strength even to an empire."[17] Hopkins's use of the phrase, "marked and striking," carries more import than mere indication. By 1886, when he wrote this phrase, meter was a crucial site for resolving his spiritual dilemmas, as well as dilemmas about what he perceived, as an "exiled" Catholic, to be England's wavering Christianity. Hopkins's idea of the marked and striking power of English poetry evolved over his lifetime into a philosophy influenced by his work in the classics, his intense reading in philology, and his spiritual struggles. And his concern with meter as a spiritual and national form was more markedly visual than his own instructions, and his critical legacy, have led us to believe.

As Linda Dowling and Cary Plotkin[18] have argued, the visual nature of the English language was hotly debated in the late nineteenth century (a philological discourse that any reader of his Oxford notebooks, available in Lesley Higgins's new edition, will see interested Hopkins intensely). The *New English Dictionary* began to codify the representation of speech with visual signs in its first fascicle (A–Ant) in 1884, but as much as twenty years earlier Hopkins had attended lectures by linguist Max Müller on the science of language at Oxford (1863–67) and had been recording his own etymologies in his notebooks. Plotkin argues that both Müller and Richard Chevenix Trench studied language as "a means of investigating and penetrating human history and human nature" along the lines of Grimm, Schlegel, and Humboldt.[19] From Müller, it is widely accepted that Hopkins gleaned his understanding that "numerically limited roots that are uncovered as the primary elements of language groups are *phonetic types* produced by a power inherent in human nature."[20] This concept was increasingly important to Hopkins toward the end of his life, but in his earliest notebooks and poems at Oxford—as he considered his conversion to Catholicism—he was more concerned with language, and in particular with the English language, as the highest form of a nation's civilization and the preservation of language as a form of national salvation. This was the subject of work by Trench, an early editor of the *New English Dictionary*, who had done a great deal to establish English's superiority through his moral and spiritual explanations of English etymology. His two texts, *On the Study of Words* and *English Past and Present,* argued that the written history of English, inscribed in its letters, should in no way be subordinated to the mere sounds of words; the important ancestry of English words could only be represented in script:

> A word exists as truly for the eye as for the ear, and in a highly advanced state of society, where reading is almost as universal as speaking, as much perhaps as the first as for the last, that in the *written* word moreover is the permanence and continuity of language and of learning, and that the connection is most intimate of a true *orthography* with all this, is affirmed in our words "letters," "literature," "unlettered," even as in other languages by words entirely corresponding to these.[21]

Trench made a case for textual philology as opposed to the new science of English phonology. In text, the English language presented traceable etymological paths to the roots of a particularly English morality and character. In *On the Study of Words*, he wrote that language is a testament, a "faithful . . . record of the good and of the evil which in time past have been working in the minds and hearts of men," and that English may be considered "a moral barometer, which indicates and permanently marks the rise or fall of a nation's life. To study a people's language will be to study *them*" (40). Words "indicate or permanently mark" the rise and fall of a nation's life, just as Patmore's poetry benefits the nation's life because of its marked and striking excellences.

Hopkins's reading in philology reinforced his thinking that the moral life of a culture could be allegorized in the written word. In 1878, two years before Hopkins read Trench, he considered the physical material of words in terms of sprung rhythm. In his essay, "Rhythm and Other Structural Parts," which he wrote as a novitiate at St. Bueno's in Wales, Hopkins wrote, "we may think of words as heavy bodies . . . every visible palpable body has a centre of gravity round which it is in balance and a centre of illumination . . . up to which it is lighted and down from which it is shaded . . . English is of this kind, the accent of stress strong."[22] The importance of perceiving words visually, as bodies, directly corresponds to Hopkins's metaphysical theories of inscape and instress. "Instress" is crucially related to the metrical mark for stress—the actual, physical mark for accent that Hopkins scored above words in his poems—and that stress measured his spiritual hopes for the nation throughout his career. Examining how Hopkins made these marks *onto* and *above* the word-bodies of his poetry, I argue that the "stigma" of meter is a crucial figure for the mark on language that makes this national and spiritual reading visible. Meter, rather than abstracting, clarifies and brings into focus Hopkins's linguistic intentions. Material marks and patterns in nature and on poems figure into Hopkins's understanding of the imaginary, idealized realms of England and of heaven.

Marking Instress

In Hopkins's early diaries, his observation of patterns in the natural world precipitated the theory of inscape and instress. These terms were not merely tools for the definition and manipulation of meter, but inevitably dealt with the fundamentals of perception, reality, and existence. Put simply, "inscape" is the unified complex of characteristics that gives each thing its uniqueness and thereby differentiates it from other things, and "instress" is the force of being that holds inscape together—the impulse or force of a pattern that carries the inscape into the mind of the perceiver or beholder. In his 1868 "notebook on the history of Greek philosophy, etc." Hopkins began to define the instress of language, of words. He wrote: "A word then had three terms belonging to it, 3 *opoi*, {terms} or moments—its prepossession of feeling; its definition, abstraction, vocal expression or other utterance; and its application, 'extension,' the concrete things coming under it."[23] Essentially, as he sees it, a word possesses a subjective state, is a thing itself, and names something in the objective world. A few essays later in the same notebook, in an essay on Parmenides, Hopkins further defined language as the very "stress" or force that carried the mind over into things, and things over into the mind. "Stress" is crucially related to the copula "to be."[24] He writes that without it "there would be no bridge, no stem of stress between us and things to bear us out and carry the mind over: without stress we might not and could not say / Blood is red . . ."[25] He continues: "Being and thought are the same. The truth in thought is Being, stress, and each word is one way of acknowledging Being and each sentence by its copula *is* (or its equivalent) the utterance and assertion of it." When "stress" is "uttered," a word becomes "being."[26] By emphasizing the word *stress* as a particular assertion of being, Hopkins implies that language, uttered in a certain way and perceived in a certain way, becomes an assertion of being. But how might we understand metrical stress as a measure of being? And how might those beings then make up a nation?

Hopkins first began to define the instress of words in his notes on Greek philosophy in 1868; he also began working toward connecting the "thisness" or "markedness" of words with that of people, natural things, and metrical stress. Reading Greek philosophy through an idea of an essential "thisness" of language (also an influence from Anglo-Saxonist movements), Hopkins mediated between the classical and nativist views of language, which he used equally to form his theories of language. Furthermore, all of this patterned energy needed to be reconciled with the universal truths of the church. Through a consideration of the Scottish Franciscan philosopher Duns Scotus (1265–1308), who also attended Oxford, "Hopkins coined the word 'inscape' for every natural pattern he apprehended." Harold Bloom defines "Instress" as "the effect of each pattern upon [Hopkins's] own imagination."[27] The "stress" of the "scaped" patterns on and in things in the external world meant that meaning was elaborated, doubled, when it entered Hopkins's philosophical and spiritual domain. The application and graphic marking of prosodic stress evolved, for Hopkins, into an indication of that elaborated significance in nature and in "things." The mark, itself, also evolved into its own elaborated significance as not only the marker of verbal or philological proliferations of meaning, but as a part of larger patterns of graphic stresses with inscape, and eventually with transformative powers themselves. Tracing the mark through Hopkins's letters as he develops his theory of instress, we see the way that the philosophical idea of "instress" often follows Hopkins's apprehension of a visual mark in nature or, inversely, how considering instress makes him more aware of visual patterns that resemble ordering marks. Passages in his journals and papers that consider marks, strokes, and graphic signs show how their growing significance, over and above "letters," parallels his decision to use these signs as superimposed indications of his new metrical stresses.

Hopkins was received into the Roman Catholic Church in 1866. It was the year before he graduated with First Class in "Greats" from Balliol College at Oxford. He had met Bridges (an Anglican) at Oxford three years earlier.

Hopkins's many journals recorded his daily observations about the weather, his activities, his reading notes, and questions about his various intellectual pursuits. A sample of this detailed writing reveals his close attention to the physical patterns in nature:

> Was happily able to see composition of the crowd in the area of the theatre, all the heads looking one way thrown up by their black coats relieved only by white shirt-fronts etc.: the short strokes of eyes, nose, mouth, repeated hundreds of times I believe it is which gives the visible law: looked at in any one instance it flies. I could find a sort of beauty in this, certainly character—but in fact that is almost synonymous with finding order, anywhere. The short parallel strokes spoken of are like those something in effect on the cusp-ends of six-foils in the iron tracery of the choir gates in our chapel.[28]

Hopkins transforms the theater crowd into an impression, noticing the "strokes of eyes, nose, mouth" as if they had been painted onto a blank canvas. He immediately likens these ordered strokes to the architecture of the choir gates, bringing a theater crowd into the forged gates of the church. In the year of his conversion, Hopkins's remarks subtly trace a path toward his spiritual beliefs about the nature of things and begin to tie his theory of patterns to his theory of religion. While considering a move toward Catholicism, Hopkins subtly allegorizes the discipline of meter (the ordered stroke of the mark) into the discipline of spiritual devotion, thus connecting himself to the broader field of the English language and English poetry; he thus remains bound to an important—and spiritualized—aspect of the English language. He continued to explore and deepen this fraught connection to the holiness in the English language and the particular power of metrical instress to convert readers for the remainder of his career.

Two years later, in 1868, Hopkins's poetic, linguistic, and metaphysical consideration of stress comes together. The year Hopkins first defines instress is when he first employed diacritical marks for metrical stress on a syllable, in the poem "St Dorothea."[29] He visually marks the page with acute accents to help his reader, Robert Bridges, navigate the "new rhythm." He writes, with some trepidation, to Bridges: "I hope you will master the peculiar beat I have introduced in 'St. Dorothea.'"[30] Hopkins's revisions of "St. Dorothea" outline an early struggle over how to represent stress graphically—believing in something seen and determining the visual proof necessary for a true conversion. In version A[31] of the poem, there are only "grave" accents, which appear on many of his early poems ("quenchèd not" l. 16), but in version C, subtitled "lines for a picture" (as if to emphasize the visual aspect of his rhythm), he uses diacritical marks in lines 2, 4, 8, 13, 16, 18, 19, 40, and 47. Her "básket" is made of "white rods," similar to those he observes two years earlier on Ascension Day:

"Children with white rods beating bounds of St. Michael's Parish."[32] In version D, Hopkins moves the diacritical marks to the side of the syllable "I´ am so´ light´ and fair / Men are amazed to watch me pass / With´ the bas´ket I bear.´"[33] He has added beats and diacritical marks to indicate those beats, carving up the words "Quinc´es look´, when´not one´/ Is set in any orchard" and forcing us to look at the effect these marks have on the rhythm of the poem. These detached diacritical marks seem to require adding a beat, so one is tempted to read an accented pause after the syllable intended to carry that beat. They also more closely resemble the children's rods—though here they are beating the words themselves. The "St. Dorothea" manuscript is one of the only drafts in which Hopkins places accent marks to the side of the syllables— imitating popular pronouncing dictionaries but also signaling his ambivalence over whether or not the mark should occupy the space above the letter. The mark, here, is not *of* or above the letter, but seems to send our eyes darting backward toward the stressed syllable we should have pronounced.

But recall that Hopkins's devotion to marking the instress and inscape is not limited to the performance or pronunciation of the poem; it is also a commentary on the perception of and connection to the realms of the natural and spiritual. The poem concerns the conversion of the pagan lawyer, Theophilus, who jeered at Dorothea on her way to a winter execution: "Bride of Christ, send me some fruits from your bridegroom's garden." The poem names quinces, dewbells, and mallow-row as the fruits and flowers brought by the angel commanded by St. Dorothea to prove to Theophilus that she is the bride of Christ, and yet the poem's central question and exclamation is, "How to name it, blessed it!" in line 25. The "stressed" words become "being" of a different sort here: the quince transforms into "the sizing moon" and the dewbells into stars; the mallow-row becomes "tufts of evening sky." Theophilus, witnessing this transformation, cries, "My eyes hold yet the rinds and bright / Remainder of a miracle," concluding that "wordy warrants are flawed through" since they can only be heard and not witnessed. Theophilus has to see with his own eyes the transformation of one named thing into another; the answer to "how to name it," in the poem, is by *seeing* the visual proof, in nature, of the miracle of Christ's existence. The "remainder" of that miracle hovers over the stressed words in the poem: we are asked to look at what the messenger brings with differently trained eyes, eyes that might perceive the multiple meanings of a thing outside the shaky authority of "wordy warrants" and through the authority of Christ's word.

It seems no accident that the only other occasion in which Hopkins used diacritical marks for accent on his poems before "The Wreck of the Deutschland" was a translation titled, "O Deus, ego amo te," in which he proclaims: "O God, I love thee, Í love thée — / Not out of hope of heaven for me / Nor fearing nót to love and be / In the everlasting burning." Here, the words "I," "thee," and "not" are stressed, showing the intimate proximity to and insecure distance from the Lord between which the poet wavers. In "O Deus," Hopkins writes that Jesus, "for my sake sufferedst nails and lance." The strokes of diacritical marks emphasize Christ's suffering even more corporeally, the word-as-God bearing the stigmata of Christ's suffering. In 1882, Hopkins notes John 1:14, "and the Word was made Flesh." "God's utterance of himself in himself is God the Word, outside himself is this world. This world then is word, expression, news of God. Therefore its end, its purpose, its purport, its meaning, is God and its life or work to name and praise him."[34] The flesh and thingness of words is one main theme of "The Wreck of the Deutschland"; the diacritical marks on "I" and "thee," referring to Hopkins and Christ, then, might fasten the two together—binding them but also symbolizing the marks on Christ's body that he withstood when fastened to the cross before ascending into heaven. "St Dorothea" and "O Deus, ego amo te" demonstrate how, even in his earliest use of a diacritical mark for accent, Hopkins indicates not only his intended rhythm but his hopes that stress can indicate a kind of "being" *in* the word.

As he begins increasingly to incorporate marks for meter on his poems in the years following 1868, excerpts from Hopkins's journal show that he was also considering words, beings, and stress in complex ways. In his journal writings, both the word itself and the mark above the word might become a kind of "being," possessing the possibility of inscape. From a December 23, 1869 entry, Hopkins notes:

> As we went down a field near Caesar's Camp I noticed it before me *squalentem* [from the Latin "squaleo": to be stiff, to be rigid, to be rough] coat below coat, sketched in intersecting edges beating 'idiom', all down the slope: — I have no other word yet for that which takes the eye or mind in a bold hand or effective sketching or in marked figures or again in graphic writing, which not being beauty nor true inscape yet gives interest and makes ugliness even better than meaninglessness.[35]

Hopkins makes evident here the importance of graphic representation, of marking, and of a "bold hand" making visible something close to beauty or inscape but that, in effect, only draws our attention to other possible meanings of the marks. A famous journal passage written in late March, 1871 describes how the power of this interest goes both ways: "What you look hard at seems to look hard at you, hence the true and the false instress of nature." Perhaps the desire for recognition—to be seen as well as to see—is a distracting potential power of instress—a false instress. What "looks hard at you" has power and might bend you to its will. He continues:

> . . . one large flake loop-shaped, not a streamer but belonging to the string, moving too slowly to be seen, seemed to cap and fill the zenith

with a white shire of cloud. I looked up long at it till the tall height and the beauty of the scaping — regularly curled knots springing if I remember from fine stems, like foliation in wood or stone — had strongly grown on me. It changed beautiful changes, growing more into ribs and one stretch running into branching like coral. Unless you refresh the mind from time to time you cannot always remember or believe how deep the inscape in things is. (*JP*, 204)

The ribbing and branching and the lines of the string are motifs that appear again and again in his writing, replicating graphic signs. He writes, a few days later, that a flash of lightning resembles "a straight stroke, broad like a stroke with chalk and liquid, as if the blade of an oar just stripped open a ribbon scar in smooth water and it caught the light." [36] These lines that Hopkins describes grow on him and have power; though the "stroke" here refers to an oar in water, the chalk brings us back to the graphic sign, and the "ribbon scar" to the potential violence of that graphic sign. In another entry, Hopkins shows explicitly the power that "looking" or taking interest in the mark can have on a body—it is not beautiful, but is nonetheless powerful:

Mesmerised a duck with chalk lines drawn from her beak sometimes level and sometimes forwards on a black table. They explain that the bird keeping the abiding offscape of the hand grasping her neck fancies she is still held down and cannot lift her head as long as she looks at the chalk line, which she associates with the power that holds her. This duck lifted her head at once when I put it down on the table without chalk. But this seems inadequate. It is most likely the fascinating instress of the straight white stroke. (*JP*, 207)

The fascination of the chalk line creates the effect of stress in the bird—the instress of a "straight white stroke" has power over the being that perceives it. Hopkins marked his meter with a blue chalk stroke, so this attention to the "white stroke" of the white chalk shows his concern with the power of metrical signs—here a power that holds as long as it is being visually perceived.

"St. Dorothea" was one of the few poems Hopkins sent to Bridges during the seven years in which he refrained from writing poetry in order to focus on his spiritual development as a priest. However, Hopkins's journals through the 1870s continue to record his fascination with the markedness of nature. Indeed, his definitions of inscape and instress seem to move more solidly toward an idea of "markedness" or "muchness" relevant to his investigation of the graphic mark for accent. In 1871 he wrote: "End of March and beginning of April—This is the time to study inscape in the spraying trees, for the

swelling buds carry them to a pitch which the eye could not else gather—
for out of much much more, out of little not much, out of nothing nothing: in these sprays at all events there is a new world of inscape"(*JP,* 205).
And in 1872:

> Stepped into a barn of ours, a great shadowy barn, where the hay had
> been stacked on either side, and looking at the great rudely arched tim-
> berframes—principals (?) and tie-beams, which make them look like
> bold big *A*s with the cross-bar high up—I thought how sadly beauty of
> inscape was unknown and buried away from simple people and yet how
> near at hand it was if they had eyes to see it and it could be called out
> everywhere again. (*JP,* 221)

Hopkins wishes that everyone "had eyes to see" the patterns of inscape all
around, and especially the patterns of inscape in or on *letters* ("big bold *A*s") so
that they could perhaps perceive the patterns in the natural world as well—
patterns that would lead to spiritual and national awareness and salvation. In
1874 he writes of the "single sonnet-like inscape—between which the sun sent
straight bright slenderish panes of silvery sunbeams down the slant toward the
eye"(259). The slant of the sunbeams, like the slant of a metrical ictus, seems to
reach toward the eye, so that what we visually apprehend also gestures or
reaches towards us: "what you look hard at seems to look hard at you." His
growing awareness that marks in nature that form inscape beckon to be perceived, interpreted, and transformed into instress increases in proportion to
his development of sprung rhythm, in which the accent is meant to "make
much" of the word or syllable, and through which the reader is encouraged to
"let the stress be made to fetch out both the strength of the syllables and the
meaning and feeling of the words."[37] Hopkins's ideas about visual marks and
patterns germinated in his journals through the 1870s: the mark as an indication of elaborated significance; the mark as an allegory of Christ's "word" and
visible law, as well as Christ as Word or Logos; the power of marks and lines on
a body and on a reader's eye; the way multidimensional meanings of words
and things becomes defined as "markedness." When Hopkins wrote to his
friend Digby Mackworth Dolben that he composed "The Wreck of the
Deutschland" in sprung rhythm, he mentioned that during a hiatus from writing the idea of sprung rhythm had "haunted his ear." It is clear from his journals that the markedness of visual as well as aural patterns was on his mind.
Because his writing about visual marks parallels his "haunting" thoughts about
metrical accent, we must also remember to read the composition in 1875 of
"The Wreck of the Deutschland" on a visual level. Rather than trying to hear
sprung rhythm properly, we can read the marks that Hopkins employs beyond
their rhythmic notation and on their own terms, as indications of deeper philosophical and spiritual struggles.

Acute Stress in "The Wreck of the Deutschland"

In October 1878, Hopkins wrote a clear definition of sprung rhythm for his colleague, former teacher and admirer Reverend Richard Watson Dixon, in which he bemoaned the necessity of marking metrical stress with blue chalk:

> [Sprung rhythm] consists in scanning by accents or stresses alone, without any account of the number of syllables, so that a foot may be one strong syllable or it may be many light and one strong. . . . I do not say the idea is altogether new; there are hints of it in music, in nursery rhymes and popular jingles, and in the poets themselves, and, since then, I have seen it talked about as a thing possible in critics . . . to me it appears, I own, to be a better and more natural principle than the ordinary system, much more flexible, and capable of greater effects. However I had to mark the stresses in blue chalk, and this and my rhymes carried on from one line to another and certain chimes suggested by the Welsh poetry I had been reading (what they call *cynghanedd*) and a great many more oddnesses could not but dismay an editor's eye, so that when I offered it to our magazine *The Month*, though at first they accepted it, after a time they withdrew and dared not to print it.[38]

The offended eye is to blame for "The Wreck"'s eventual rejection—a reaction that Hopkins tried to prevent when he sent the poem to Bridges.[39] He instructs Bridges in May 1878 to "not slovenly read it with the eyes but with the ears, as if the paper were declaiming it at you."[40] With blue chalk marks, the "eye" is dismayed at the patterns of the verse, held under the yoke of a visible rhythm. Without diacritical marks, the unmarked poem is "quite a different thing. Stress is the life of it," but only if it is read aloud properly. The power of the visual mark to hold the reader's eye and, at the same time, dismay is part of the instress of that blue chalk line. Hopkins, too, is at once fascinated and frustrated by this perceived power.

Both thematically and metrically, wavering between that which is heard and that which is visually perceived but *not* heard, serves as another level of narrative in the poem. The poem's story details the shipwreck of "The Deutschland," as derived from newspaper reports.[41] The epigraph reads: "to the happy memory of the five Franciscan nuns, exiles by the Falk Laws, drowned between midnight and morning of Dec. 7th, 1875." The first stanzas of the poem (st. 1–10), which comprise "part the first," are a meditation on emotional stress and what it means for God and man. The second part of the poem moves from narration of the events on "The Deutschland" (st. 11–21) to a series of questions about language, measure, marking, words, hearing, seeing, and finally concludes with the possibilities of belief—that is, imagining the salvation of England through God's grace. Though the poem is too long to discuss in its entirety, a few representative stanzas will show how Hopkins "makes much" of his "marked" words and how, in his consideration of stress, we can see him marking the body of English and England for salvation.

The poem begins, daring us to master its new meter—sprung rhythm:[42]

> Thou mastering me
> God! giver of breath and bread;
> Wórld's stránd, swáy of the séa;
> Lord of living and dead;
> Thou has bóund bónes and véins in me, fástened me flésh,   5
> And áfter it álmost únmade, what with dréad,
> Thy doing: and dost thou touch me afresh?
> Óver agáin I féel thy fínger and fínd thée.

Here, as we can see, Hopkins physically marks the stresses in lines 3, 5, 6, and 8, but gives no hints as to where to place the two stresses on the first line's "Thou mastering me." Hopkins thus causes generations of critics to wonder: Does he sees himself as equal to the Lord (if "thou" and "me" both carry stress)?; Is he attempting to alliterate and allude to Anglo-Saxon strong-stress meter ("mast" and "me" carry stress)?; Or, is he punning on other meanings in the syllables with his stresses ("Thou" and "mast") to show that the Lord is both the master of the poet, as well as the "mast" of the ship? The stresses are interpretive unless Hopkins marks them for us, and our possible interpretations have both philological and theological consequences.

In the 2nd stanza, Hopkins asserts that all things are "laced with the fire of stress." The 4th and 5th stanzas connect Christ's mystery with instress and the patterns of metrical stress. This is in the penultimate line of stanza 4: "Chríst's gíft" is stressed, as are the words that lead to it: "a préssure, a prínciple." The stress of Christ's gift, the pressing burden of it, is a theme of the entire poem. The stress of the word "prince" in "prínciple" hints at the multidimensionality of language that Hopkins often exploits—Christ is the prince. Stanza 5 goes on: "Since, thóugh he is únder the wórld's spléndour and wónder, / His mystery múst be instréssed, stressed; / For I greet him the days I meet him, and bless when I understand." The second to last line of stanza 5 is missing Hopkins's fourth marked emphasized stress; it is as if Hopkins knew that the reader would know to stress "stressed" of all words, and he chose to leave off the blue chalk mark. Hopkins suggests, with diacritical stress marks, that the mystery of Christ is potentially readable. By "meteing" or measuring Christ in verse with the appropriate stress, Hopkins is able to greet Christ.

Indeed, Christ's measure and judgment and the inverse, "measuring" Christ, take a violent turn in stanza 6:

> Not out of his bliss
> Springs the stress felt

> Nor first from heaven (and few know this)
>   Swings the stroke dealt —
> Stroke and a stress that stars and storms deliver,   45
>   That guilt is hushed by, hearts are flushed by and melt —
>   But it rídes tíme like ríding a river
> (And here the faithful waver, the faithless fable and miss)

Even Christ's anger, his stress and strokes, are cyclical, metrical: his anger rides time like riding a river. The second to last line of the stanza carries the only indicated stresses, as if to emphasize the marked regularity of Christ's eventual rage. "The stroke dealt" is not only a blow from the Lord but also the "strike" of stress above the line, particularly noticeable in this primarily monosyllabic stanza. The parenthetical final line of the stanza: "and here the faithful waver: the faithless fable and miss" might indicate the true and false readers of Hopkins's meter—the faithless might miss the beats he intends, whereas the faithful will catch them, though they will be forced to "waver." The line also refers to the process of marking the "strokes of stress" on a poem about divine transformation, itself a process in which the poet wavers.

Uncertainty (wavering) over whether or not to mark, indeed, *how* to mark the "divine" word is writ large in the example of the nun's death. In stanza 17, "the women" are "wailing" (l. 134). The dissolution of spoken words becomes evident in the accusation of stanza 18: "make words break from me here all alone, / Do you!" (l. 139), and in the desperation of stanza 19: "Sister, a sister calling / A master, her master and mine!" (l. 145). Hopkins likens himself to the nun, here, serving the same master. Nature blinds her, but she "sees" figuratively how its "smart" blows will transform her and how, despite the "brawling" of the storm, her call will be heard:

>   The rash smart sloggering brine
> Blínds her; but shé that wéather sees óne thing, óne:
> Has óne fetch ín her: she réars hersélf to divíne   150
>   E'ars, and the cáll of the táll nún
> To the mén in the tóps and the táckle rode óver the stórms brawling.

Though she wants her voice to be heard by divine "E'ars," it is the men "in the tops of the tackle" who hear her. Hopkins plays on the repetition of "ear" in "rears" and marks that her "self" is what she is sending up with her voice. But the word "Ear" is broken—the metrical mark to the side again. By isolating the "E" of "Ears," Hopkins introduces a pun on "ars," on arsis, the Greek name for the metrical mark on a stressed syllable.[43] By emphasizing the marked, stressed syllables in the stanza, we see through Hopkins's marked words "one," "one," "one" that the nun's self knows precisely what she is about to become (one with God). She is both "nun" and "none," one part of a larger pattern of inscape that marks her for transformation into the divine. Julia Saville calls this a celebration of "ultimate sublimity" and hints that perhaps Hopkins envies the nun's ability to become absorbed, erotically, anonymously, into Christ as her "chivalric savior."[44] Hopkins, with his metrical mark, transforms the word "nun" into both "none" and "one," just as Christ will transform the nuns into martyrs.[45] Like his marks on "I," "thee," and "not" in "O deus amo te," here the marks indicate that the nun, who has already lost her identity as a Bride of Christ, will be even more subsumed into God.

Christ is the "mártyr-master" in whose "sight" the "flákes" of the storm become marks or words—scroll—on the "leaves" or blank text of the nun's bodies. The nun's salvation is "spelt" on the "leaves" of their bodies as in Hopkins's later poem, "Spelt from Sybil's Leaves"; they have been already marked for salvation by Christ.[46] Hopkins emphasizes that the nuns have already been "marked" before they are physically and visually marked. He allegorizes the five nuns who perish in the wreck, just as there are five wounds of Christ and five marks of the stigmata.[47] With Christ watching, the poem narrates the transformation of the nuns' bodies into text: "in thý síght / Storm flákes were scróll-leaved flówers" (ll. 167–68). Flakes, for Hopkins, mean sea-flint but, as we see elsewhere in the poem, "flesh." It is the nuns' flesh that is "scroll-leaved," inscribed by their own salvation.

> Five! The finding and sake
>   And cipher of suffering Christ   170
>   Márk, the márk is of mán's máke
>   And the word of it Sacrificed,
>   But he scores it in scarlet himself on his own bespoken
>   Before-time-taken, dearest prizèd and priced —
>   Stigma, signal, cinquefoil token   175
> For léttering of the lámb's fléece, rúddying of the róse-fláke.

The poet must mark the word, both sacrificing and guaranteeing its sanctity by doing so. Hopkins used blue chalk to "score" the poem, his own "bespoken" verses, knowing that the marks both litter and "letter" the purity of any poem he writes. By this point, two-thirds of the way into the poem, we might begin to see the stressed words in the 5th and 6th lines of the stanza—the two lines which the rule of Hopkins's stanza form requires to carry five stressed syllables: "score," "scar," "self," "own," "spoke," and "fore," "take," "dear," "prized," "priced." These two sets of five words spell out the mark of sacrifice and salvation. All of the words in the second to last line—stigma, signal, cinquefoil, token—are synonyms for the chalked-in mark, the arsis. The chalk mark hovers over "man" whose "mark" must "let" the "lamb's" "fleece," must turn "ruddy," so that he, the man, mankind, might be saved. Like the shepherd branding his flock, the nuns are owned by and have been claimed by Christ, just as Hopkins hopes that all mankind will be marked for salvation. The marked stress on the "let" of lettering emphasizes the bloodletting that comes from "scoring the scarlet," a metaphor linking metrical form to sacrifice and the crucifixion.

The "róse-fláke" of Christ's flesh also hearkens back to the poems Hopkins was writing just before "The Wreck of the Deutschland." The rose is connected to the number five not only through the flake of Christ's flesh but also through the emblem of the Virgin Mary, the mystical rose. In "Rosa Mystica," a poem that Hopkins may have written in the early 1870s or as late as 1874 or 1875, Hopkins specifically connects the number five with the wounds of Christ and the Virgin Mary (ll. 31–42):

> What was the colour of that Blossom bright?
> White to begin with, immaculate white.
> But what a wild flush on the flakes of it stood,
> When the Rose ran in crimsonings down the Cross-wood.[48]
> > *In the Gardens of God, in the daylight divine* 35
> > *I shall worship the Wounds with thee, Mother of mine.*
> How many leaves had it? Five they were then,
> Five like the senses, and members of men;
> Five is the number by nature, but now
> They multiply, multiply, who can tell how. 40
> > *In the Gardens of God, in the daylight divine*
> > *Make me a leaf in thee, Mother of mine.*[49]

From the manuscript of this poem, Hopkins asks of the Rosa Mystica, "is it more than a word"?

The "róse-fláke" of Christ's flesh is more than a mere "ruddying" of the figure of Christ. In the word "flake" we can read deeper understanding of Hopkins's philological joining of the word "flesh" with the word "cut." The word "flesh" cannot be separated from the mark, the stigmata of meter, above it. Hopkins knew that "acute" meant "sharp" in Latin (*acutus*) as well as "intense."[50] In his early diaries he considers the words "flesh," or "flake" and "strike," or "cut," to be related.

> *Flick* means to touch or strike lightly as with the end of a whip, a finger, etc. To fleck is the next tone above flick, still meaning to touch or strike lightly (and leave a mark of the touch or stroke) but in a broader less slight manner. Hence substantively a fleck is a piece of light, color, substance, etcetera, looking as though shaped or produced by such touches . . . Key to meaning of *flick*, *fleck*, and *flake* is that of striking or cutting of the surface of the thing.[51]

After reading this passage and seeing the strokes of metrical marks on the poem, the last line of the 1st stanza bears new significance: "Óver agáin I féel thy fínger and find thée." Over the letters is the whip, the punishing spiritual devotion between Christ and the poet, between the word and its stress. The poem has been "shaped or produced by such touches" as the poet's hand applies.[52]

As if to justify his practice, Hopkins turns to the necessity of measure in the last part of the poem. The "five-livèd and leavèd" daughters will "bathe in his fall-gold mercies," but Hopkins is in Wales, far away from the judgment and acceptance he envies in the characters of his poem. Hopkins asks: "What bý your méasure is the héaven of desíre, / The tréasure never éyesight gót, nor was éver guessed whát for the héaring?" The heaven of desire can be measured, though it cannot be seen or heard, much the way that the true word of God can never be spoken. Hopkins dramatizes this impossibility in his stammering in stanza 28: "But how shall I . . . Make me room there; / Reach me a . . . Fancy, come faster — / Strike you the sight of it?" In order to be named, the material needs to be seen. In order for the material, the body or the word, to be seen and saved, it needs to be *struck*. The bell of being in each person can only ring when it is struck by the external application of Christ—his "finger" or the blow of nature. (In stanza 31, Hopkins wavers between his happiness that the nuns have found salvation in Christ and pity for the "comfortless unconfessed of them" who also perished. The nun was already marked for salvation: "maiden could obey so, be a bell to, ring óf it, and / Stártle the poor sheep back!") Some critics see Hopkins's project in this poem as a gesture of differentiation. J. Hillis Miller, in *The Linguistic Moment*, summarizes Geoffrey Hartman's interpretation of Hopkins's basic poetic strategy (in *Unmediated Vision*) as "a differentiation of language that attempts to say the Word by dividing the word";[53] Miller counters that "the tragic limitation of poetic language lies in the fact that the Word itself cannot be said . . . a word by the very fact that it is just that pattern of vowels and consonants which it is, cannot be the Word . . . Words have therefore a tendency to proliferate endlessly their transformations by changes of vowel and consonant, as if they were in search for the magic word that would be the Word."[54]

Rather, the line in which Hopkins names the variations on Christ's name is not admitting failure to unify letters into the divine Word as in the Gospel of John, but affirms and acknowledges that each word, even Word, contains its own multiples. The accent mark "makes much" of these dimensions, showing that even when the names are spelled out for us to read, there are many levels of definition and variegated meaning beneath the particular form (or flesh) of each word. "The Master, / Ípse, the ónly one, Chríst, Kíng, Héad" (st. 28, l. 221)—the five stresses fall on the "three-numberèd form" (st. 9, l. 66) of God, marking his inscape in the world. "Wording it how but by him that present and past, / Heaven and earth are word of, worded by?—" (st. 29, ll. 229–30). Words themselves are beacons, marks of God; accents that emphasize and make much of words both do violence to His word by the ugly striking or scoring that pollutes them, but also allegorize the violence that God visits upon his subjects, especially his son, in the five marks of the crucifixion that signal both Christ's death and the salvation of all of God's subjects.[55]

The final stanza of the poem addresses and emphasizes an imagined community in thirty-three stressed syllables, more marks than in any other stanza (ll. 275–80):

> Remémber us in the róads, the heaven-háven of the rewárd
>   Our kíng back, Oh upon Énglish sóuls!
> Let him éaster in us, be a dáyspring to the dímness of us,
>   be a crímson-cresseted east,
> More bríghtening her, ráre-dear Brítain, as his réign rólls,
>   Príde, rose, prínce, hero of us, hígh-príest
> Oür héart's charity's héarth's fíre, oür thóught's chivalry's thróng's Lórd.

Here, the religious and national are reconnected. If the word is flesh, then this stanza imagines an English word, the flesh of English citizens whose salvation must be marked. The "king" is not upon English "soil," but *upon* English *souls*.[56] Reading Hopkins's marks here, we see that both the metaphysical transformation of the English language and the religious conversion of England are bound by the discipline of this new meter. The process that the poem performs, of wavering into faith, is bound to hopes for a national meter—and a deeper understanding of the English language through the road map of his meter—that Hopkins tries to bring back to England. By performing the process of reckoning with the words as flesh—and that flesh as scored and scarred—the poem is riddled with its own anxiety about the necessary wavering that "reading" those marks requires.

Mistrusting the Ear

"The Wreck of the Deutschland"'s first three Victorian readers—Fr. Henry Coleridge, Robert Bridges, and Coventry Patmore—all rejected it. Coleridge, who was planning to publish it in the Catholic magazine, *The Month*, first asked Hopkins to "do away with the accents which mark the scanning."[57] Hopkins protested: "I would gladly have done without them if I had thought my readers would scan right unaided but I am afraid they will not, and if the lines are not rightly scanned they are ruined . . . some lines at all events will have to be marked" (138). Bridges responded to the poem that he would not "for any money read [the] poem again."[58] In August 1877, Hopkins wrote to Bridges: "I cannot think of altering anything. Why should I? I do not write for the public. You are my public and I hope to convert you."[59] As the first non-Catholic reader of the poem, Bridges was subject to Hopkins's poignant "hopes" to convert him. Likewise, Hopkins's Welsh pseudonym at the end of the poem, "Brân Maenefa," is a bittersweet example of how Hopkins hoped that his verses could convert the whole of Britain—Bran ("crow" in Welsh) the Blessed was reputed to have brought Christianity to Britain.[60] When, in 1879, Hopkins shared "The Wreck of the Deutschland" with Canon R. W. Dixon, he found his most sympathetic reader. Dixon wrote, "I have your Poems and have read them I cannot say with what delight, astonishment, & admiration. They are the most extraordinary I ever read & amazingly original."[61] In December 1880, Hopkins explained his new prosody, sprung rhythm, to Dixon in some detail (quoted above); Dixon responded supportively, that the remarks on meter were "very curious original & valuable." Hopkins agreed to share his poems with Dixon so as to illustrate the rhythm he described: "all that I have said is of course shewing you the skeleton or flayed anatomy, you will understand more simply and pleasantly by verses in the flesh" (23). After reading poems by Hopkins and Bridges, Dixon asks Hopkins if he might be able to draw out a "system of rules" for it or if it "must be a matter of ear, rather than of formal rule" (35). Through the "marked and striking excellence" of the English language and by the stigmata of metrical marking, Hopkins recognized that perhaps a more universally accepted definition of stress in English was needed in order to accomplish the national salvation he sought—a definition in which the mark for meter could somehow enter all ears, if eyes could not be properly taught to perceive the instress of the meter.

It was with this hope that Hopkins reached out to his fellow Catholic poet and metrist, Coventry Patmore. Patmore visited Stonyhurst College in August 1883, where Hopkins was a classics instructor. The two began corresponding almost immediately, beginning with Patmore's publisher sending Hopkins the four-volume 1879 edition of his *Collected Poems*. Hopkins returned the favor by sending Patmore copies of published poems by Bridges and Dixon, with no indication that he himself wrote poetry. Their correspondence was both cordial and critical, with Hopkins including insightful yet stringent comments on Patmore's poems. In November of 1883, Hopkins turned to Patmore's *Essay on English Metrical Law*, which had been included as part of the 1879 edition of Patmore's poems, reprinted from the earlier essay "English Metrical Critics."[62] This was not Hopkins's first encounter with Patmore's law; in a January 1881 letter to Bridges, Hopkins commented at length on the 1878 reprint of "Metrical Critics," which was then titled *Prefatory Study on English Metrical Law* (and appeared in Patmore's edition of poems *Amelia, Tamerton Church Tower, etc.* . . .). As if to clarify Patmore's theory to Bridges and to himself, Hopkins writes: "Patmore pushes the likeness of musical and metrical time too far—or, what comes to the same thing, not far enough: if he had gone quite to the bottom of the matter his views would have been juster . . ."[63] But for Hopkins, the "bottom of the matter" is the strict definition of accent in English; it is no accident that his long discourse on Patmore's avoidance of accent winds back around to Hopkins's problems with how to signal the accent in his own poems. He complains: "Italics do look very bad in verse. But people will *not* understand where the right emphasis is" (120). In the manuscript versions of his letters, Hopkins underscores for emphasis (a kind of reverse metrical bar below the poem), which was changed to italics in all modern editions. But accent and emphasis must be marked somehow, whether for the eye or for the ear, and it is precisely this issue that Hopkins raises with Patmore two years later, in 1883.[64]

The correspondence between the two in 1883 shows the trajectory of Hopkins's prosodic thinking, beginning with his doubts about Patmore's portrayal of accent in English. Like Bridges, Hopkins is excited about reform in verse practice, and hopes that Patmore's theories will usher in a kind of "stricter verse prosody." As he explains his ideas to Patmore about how accent works in English, he moves toward a definition of what those accentuated syllables and words might indicate and how a writer like Patmore could explain these concepts clearly. But Patmore does not adopt this view despite Hopkins's clear expertise, and the poems Hopkins writes after 1883 reflect his attempts to demonstrate figuratively and prosodically the way that stress may be grounds for spiritual communication and national community building, as well as a growing despair that this communication is impossible.

Hopkins had every reason to hope that Patmore would be open to feedback on the metrical law; after all, he had paid careful attention to Hopkins's comments on *The Angel in the House* only a few months earlier.[65] On the manuscript of Patmore's letter from Hopkins (in which Hopkins gives numbered feedback), there are large "X" marks over comments with which Patmore disagrees, and the word "Done" scrawled across those suggestions he does honor.[66] On Patmore's copy of the letters in which Hopkins criticizes *The Essay on English Metrical Law*, there are no such marks. Hopkins is pedagogical as he moves through the essay, telling Patmore plainly that "the stress, *the ictus* of our verse is founded on and in the beginning the very same as the stress which is our accent" and "it is a radically bad principle to call English feet iambs and trochees. . . . Names ought to be invented for rhythmic feet."[67] After "The Wreck of the Deutschland," Hopkins was still concerned with the way meter might join the nation in a kind of spiritual understanding, though these concerns shifted from a broad hope for spiritual salvation for the entire metrical community of the nation to a smaller, more individual communication between the poem and the reader.

Patmore writes that the two indispensable conditions of meter are first that "the sequence of vocal utterance, represented by written verse, shall be divided into equal or proportionate spaces"[68] or "a simple series of isochronous intervals" (10). Second, "the fact of that division shall be made manifest by an 'ictus' or 'beat' actual or mental, which, like a post in a chain railing, shall mark the end of one space and the commencement of another" (15); this beat, he says elsewhere, shall be "marked by accent" (10); however, Patmore's mark for accent was not material—his metrical grid was abstract—and it was sometimes supplemented by an "imaginary beat." This abstraction was unsatisfactory to Hopkins; how would the reader know that accent is stress? He asserts that "the English accent is *emphatic accent*, is stress: it commonly includes clear pitch, but essentially it is stress. Pitch totally disappears in whispering, but our accent is perfectly given when we whisper."[69] His letter continues, revealing Hopkins's larger philosophical investments in the idea of stress:

> But perhaps one ought further to explain what stress is. Stress appears so elementary an idea as does not need and scarcely allows of definition; still, this may be said of it, that it is the making of a thing more, or making it markedly, what it already is; it is the bringing out of its nature. Accordingly, stress on a syllable (which is English accent proper) is the making much of that syllable, more than of the others; stress on a word or sentence (which is emphasis) is the making much of that word or sentence, more than the others.[70]

Hopkins joins accent and stress conclusively here, and he seems also to join metrical stress with his theory of instress: "the accented syllable then is one of which the nature is well brought out, whatever may become of the others." Syllables and words, then, are marked outwardly and bring out the nature of the syllable or word—a nature that actually exists within the syllable or word, not as an abstraction of it. Hopkins's objection to Patmore shows us how greatly Hopkins invests in the materiality of English accent, the marking of stress, so that we might "catch first" or "lose last" the nature of a sound, made material in the ear. As Hopkins narrows his definition of accent and stress here, he tries to enlist Patmore's support for a concept of the English language that mimics Hopkins's metaphysical definitions of nature and inscape. The "thingness" of language, manifest in marked stress, has the same potential for transformative power, for instress, as nature itself, beckoning to be seen in a certain way. Just as we might see inscape in the natural world or in the graphically marked metrical stress, Hopkins seems to be grasping at a definition of concrete accent that might go beyond the visual realm. If he cannot teach eyes to see in instress the visual patterning in nature but can hope to teach or train his readers to recognize the flashes of meaning in a metrical mark or a visual sign, perhaps a heard "accent" can become a universal way of communicating meaning from poem to reader. Just as he saw that the wavering apprehension of the stigma's visual marks were a necessary part of faith in his consideration of instress, here, too in his consideration of accent we see Hopkins hoping, as he does in his many explanations of how to "perform" his poetry, that all ears might hear alike.

For Hopkins, then, the "markedness" of stress is not only to be read literally, as a graphic mark; the inscape might also be "marked" for the ear, but unlike the perceivable patterns in nature, the markedness of sound is particular to each individual ear. Hopkins was aware that not all eyes would read his marks correctly—indeed, his marks were not always intended to give a right or uniform reading, but rather to alert the reader to the fine similarities and differences that constitute the inscape of the English language. For Hopkins, if readers could appreciate these nuances, then they might be more aware of divine immanence (and therefore enriched,). Throughout the composition of "The Wreck of the Deutschland," Hopkins was considering the relative stability of graphic signs to indicate or mark where he hoped syllables would receive emphasis. In his arguments with Patmore over accent, Hopkins was engaged with the inadequacies of situating the interpretation of accent solely in oral and aural performance. Hopkins anticipated what twentieth-century linguists now know: if we perceive English accent aurally we are still not guaranteed to hear the same stresses as the person next to us. This element of visual perception versus aural perception, and how the two are intimately related, is brought out in Patmore's and Hopkins's exchange about the alliteration of vowels.

In Patmore's *English Metrical Law*, he writes, "[t]here could scarcely have been devised a worse illustration of alliteration than Pope's oft-quoted example 'apt alliteration's artful aid.'" For Pope and Patmore, alliteration is "essentially consonantal" whereas rhyme is the resonance of vowels. Patmore also asserts that in Anglo-Saxon "there is properly no such thing as alliteration of vowels," even though three vowels that differ enough from one another are allowed to take the place of alliterating consonants in special cases. Hopkins writes: "I should like you to reconsider the alliteration of vowels. To my ear no alliteration is more marked or more beautiful, and I used to take it for granted as an obvious fact that every initial vowel lettered to every other before ever I knew that anything of the sort was practised in Anglo-Saxon verse."[71]

Hopkins tries to explain to Patmore that Pope blundered by assuming that the "a" sounds in "apt alliteration's artful aid" produced the same sound ("[t]he *a* in *apt* is the common English short *a*. The *a* in *artful* is the English broad *a*, a very different thing" (184) and so on). An ear, perhaps aided by the reader's visual apprehension of the identical letters, may hear them as sufficiently similar to alliterate, but sufficiently different from each other to be heightened in beauty. Hopkins contends that "[Pope] was nothing *ultra crepidam* and here he seems to have gone *ultra crepidam*," the Latin here suggesting that in Hopkins's view, Pope was a fine shoemaker, but he should keep his eye on the shoe (poetry) and not theorize about his craft. Whether the ear does or does not hear alliteration is secondary to the fact that the eye must see those lined-up "a"s even to imagine the line as alliterative. Without the visual apprehension of the line, the alliterative modulation of any metrical stress might not work. Despite Patmore's later point that the alliteration in Anglo-Saxon verse was so regular that the dot normally used to mark the caesura became "unessential," Hopkins is arguing here that Pope must have heard one kind of alliteration in the line, Patmore another, and Hopkins still another. Though Hopkins understands this dilemma, Patmore replies along the lines of generations of scholars —as if confounding the senses is the only way to properly see and hear English poetry: "I must try to teach my ear to adopt your view of alliterative vowels. I do not see the way to do it at present" (186). But this is precisely the problem: Patmore wants to hear the alliterative vowels without seeing them first—without the visual aid of the letters lined up. Patmore wants all ears to hear alike and this reply shows how, like Bridges, he is a product of Victorian education —demonstrating the common conception that we might "teach our ear" to hear correctly. Though teaching the ear to see and the eyes to hear might seem the only way to understand accent in English, Hopkins backs away from this abstract and absolute notion, and in his next letter comforts Patmore: "As for vowel alliteration, it is clearly not for you to accommodate your ear to mine. Besides, if you do not agree with me now, it is likely there is some fundamental difference and *we do not hear alike*" (187, italics mine). Patmore, looking for a metrical law, would like for all ears to hear "alike" so that a metrical rule might follow; Hopkins, recognizing that neither visual nor aural markedness is entirely stable, believes that variation invariably heightens beauty but is also fascinated and frightened by the fact that there might not be one law to which all eyes and ears adhere concordantly. This admission, that two English prosodists simply do not hear alike, refers back to a letter that Hopkins wrote to Patmore over a month earlier, in which he states: "I shall be more careful about making metrical objections. I used to object to things which satisfied Bridges and we came to the conclusion that our own pronunciation, by which everyone instinctively judges, might be at the bottom of the matter" (165). Whereas many prosodists and pedagogues, especially toward the end of the nineteenth century, relied on concepts of an "English Ear" that could instinctively hear English meter, Hopkins asserts that instinct is what makes listeners hear different prosodic effects. What is "marked" for the eye graphically might guide readers toward a deeper understanding of the poem, but what is "marked" for the voice and for the ear is an indeterminate science, one that Hopkins emphatically refuses to falsely determine.

Hopkins grants this same freedom to the ear in the "Author's Note" preceding "The Wreck of the Deutschland," which he reluctantly sent to Patmore soon after this correspondence occurred,[72] along with the rest of his poetic manuscript (put into fair copy by Bridges) in March of 1884.[73] On April 1, 1885 he again wrote to Bridges, insisting, "[t]his is my difficulty, what marks to use and when to use them: they are so much needed and yet so objectionable" (215). His "Author's Note" is in dialogue with his commentary on Patmore's *English Metrical Law*: "Which syllables . . . are strong and which light is better told by the ear than by any instruction that could be in short space given," but a later line from the note reveals the complexity of meanings available to the reader who understands Hopkins's multifaceted "stress." Rather than empowering the reader's ear, stress is distinct from the poem in the final line: "And so throughout let the stress be made to fetch out both the strength of the syllables and the meaning and feeling of the words." Though the stress needs someone to activate it—to make it fetch out and perform its metrical, semantic, and pathetic labor—Hopkins shows that it is there, ready to be perceived and to flow, as instress, into the mind of the beholder who must "allow" it to do its work.

The idea of a word "fetched out" by its stress is crucial to Hopkins's moral and poetic philosophy as well as to his conception of how a poem relates to its reader. In Hopkins's 1880 writings on Duns Scotus, he describes his relationship between the self and the "object-world" as both intrinsic and overlapping:

> Part of this world of objects, this object world, is also part of the very self in question, as in man's case his own body, which each man not only feels in and acts with but feels and acts on. If the centre of reference spoken of has concentric circles round it, one of these, the inmost say, is its own, is óf it, the rest are tó it only. Within a certain bounding line all will be self, outside of it nothing: with it self begins from one side and ends from the other. . . . A self then will consist of a centre *and* a surrounding area or circumference, a point of reference *and* a belonging field.[74]

Hence, Hopkins concludes that the self of the universal is not the self of anything else: "In shewing there is no universal true self which is 'fetched' or 'pitched' or 'selved' in every other self, I do not deny that there is a universal really, and not only logically, thus fetched in the universals" (402–03). In both his use of the word "fetched" with "pitched" and "selved," as well as his use of diacritical marks above the prepositions "of" and "to" the center of reference, we see that for Hopkins the idea of "stress" is bound to an idea of self that extends into the object world. The mark, then, is the connection that fetches out one possible meaning in the poem to the reader and he marks the prepositions "óf" and "tó" to indicate how stress might mark that bounding line of self. Hopkins is only one remove from stating that language is part of that object world as well, and by "stressing" syllables or words we see/hear the object-history of that particular sound. Metrical marks on their own could not convey instress and therefore could not affect spiritual understanding of conversion. If the English ear was unstable, never guaranteed to hear the same way twice, the voice was unlikely to perform the poem as intended.

Only two years after Hopkins was thinking about the concurrent failure of voices to sound the same and searching for marks that would assure a right-reading, Hopkins encountered the work of Dorset poet and Anglo-Saxon grammarian William Barnes, whose *An Outline of English Speech-Craft* (1878) also considers the power of the mark. There were a number of texts that tied the perceived "purity" of nineteenth-century English speech specifically back to its Anglo-Saxon origins and emphasized the importance of "accent" in a purely English prosody, in addition to Guest's *A History of English Rhythms*

(1838, 1882). This interest was stirred by Benjamin Thorpe's translation into English of R. K. Rask's *Grammar of the Anglo-Saxon Tongue,* first published in 1830 but reprinted and more widely circulated in 1865. Rask's section "Of Versification" appeared as no mere speculation: "The Anglo-Saxon versification, like the Icelandic, and that of other ancient Gothic nations, has a peculiar construction, the chief characteristic of which does not consist in syllabic quantity, but in *Alliterative Rime* or *Alliteration.*"[75] Anglo-Saxon prosody, although linked to other cultural practices, distinguished itself by its "peculiarity"; indeed, with this statement, we sense the origins of the English prosodic camp that associate English meter with a national past disassociated from the classical languages rather than in relation to them. The prosodic concerns that tie Anglo-Saxon to late nineteenth-century English were bound by a national border—any variation therein should still be accountable to a common English origin.[76] Though Hopkins does not refer to Guest directly in his letters, we know that he first read Barnes in 1870 ("I was almost a great admirer of Barnes' Dorset (not Devon) poems."[77] Around the same time that he read Barnes's *An Outline of Speech-Craft* in 1882, Hopkins began to study Old English and to consider the ways that current English could not only bear, but also reveal, the marks of its history.

Scholars have discussed Hopkins's interest in the Anglo-Saxon history of words and often mention Barnes's writings.[78] Barnes's Anglo-Saxon theories joined "breath" to the page and brought English back to a primal "purity." In the same letter in which Hopkins attests that Patmore's poems "are a great battle won by England," he says that he has been meaning to return Patmore's volume of Barnes's poems to him. Barnes represented a new way of thinking about preserving and representing dialect in English—a kind of representation of the "common" speech of the common man. The influence of *Piers Ploughman* and strong-stress verse has been widely documented in Hopkins criticism, but the history of the mark in Anglo-Saxon poetry is particularly useful for our understanding of Hopkins's fusion of etymological, spiritual, and national concerns, stressed all at once.[79] From its first appearance in English translation, the question of marks for meter in Anglo-Saxon verse was contested; Anglo-Saxon marks for accent were deliberately suppressed in order to make the verses appear more readable. Hopkins's fascination with Anglo-Saxon fused his refusal to give up the mark in later poems to his fascination with the way a language could portray the instress of an entire people. To Hopkins, William Barnes wrote "true poetry" and was "the soul of poetry" because he composed not only in Dorset "dialect" (transcribed into text),[80] but because he used Anglo-Saxon words: "an unknown tongue, a sort of modern Anglo-Saxon."[81] This "unknown tongue" preserved the Anglo-Saxon history of English words and also expanded the boundaries of English syntax. Hopkins wrote to Bridges that Barnes's use of dialect was "the instress of Westcountry," and to Patmore "it is his naturalness that strikes me most; he is like an embodiment or incarnation or manmuse of the country, of Dorset, of rustic life and humanity. . . . His rhythms . . . smack of the soil."[82] Barnes defines accent as "word-strain, a strain of the voice, higher or lower, on a breath-sound." A "high word-strain" is accent, whereas a "high speech-strain" is emphasis. Accent is differentiated from emphasis when it is not spoken. That is, the word contains accent, its *strain*, but as soon as it is spoken that *strain* might be misinterpreted as mere emphasis on the sound of speech and not of the word itself. The strain is on the "root or stem-word." Words are defined as "breathsounds"—evidence of a now lost, oral Anglo-Saxon ancestry: "Speech was shapen of the breath-sounds of speakers, for the ears of hearers, and not from speech-tokens (letters) in books, for men's eyes, though it is a great happiness that the words of man can be long holden and given men to the sight; therefore I have shapen my teaching as that of a speech of breath-sounded words and not lettered ones . . . "[83]

The monosyllable is the original "breath-sound" for Barnes, and each compound word is a combination of breath-sounds. Barnes writes that "*Mark* is here taken in its old Saxon meaning, *mearc*—what bounds, defines, describes, distinguishes. The Welsh call the adjective the *weak name* or noun." Hopkins lamented to Bridges, in 1882: "It makes one weep to think what English might have been; for in spite of all that Shakspere [*sic*] and Milton have done with the compound I cannot doubt that no beauty in a language can make up for want of purity. In fact I am learning Anglo Saxon and it is a vastly superior thing to what we have now . . . [Barnes] calls degrees of comparison pitches of suchness; we *ought* to call them so, but alas!"[84]

Like Hopkins's understanding of "fetch" and "self," Barnes associates "suchness" with "mark." Nouns are renamed "thing-names" and these can be "marked" as having "much" of something. "Mearc" or Mark, then, is a descriptive word, an adjective. Numerical mark-words are "tale mark-words," because they "tell" or count. Suchness is the particular kind of adjective that describes a thing in relation to another thing. "Pitch-mark words" describe these degrees of comparison, so that "things are marked as having much of something." For Hopkins, words that were "marked" were "made much of," and language was "heightened," but English was also defined and distinguished by Hopkins's marks, describing the acceptable boundary of current speech in Hopkins's ideal form of poetry. To see how this marking changed his later poetry, one need only glance at the manuscript version of "Harry Ploughman" or "Spelt from Sybil's Leaves."

Rather than pointing to one stable meaning, as many scholars have attempted to prove, Hopkins's marks on the page ask the eyes to work more intensely than the ears to maximize potential meanings. In an oft-quoted letter to Bridges, Hopkins eternally frames "Spelt from Sybil's Leaves" by its correct recitation: "On this long sonnet above all, remember what applies to all my verse, that it is, as living art should be, made for performance and that its performance is not reading with the eye but loud, leisurely, poetical (not rhetorical) recitation, with long rests, long dwells on the rhyme and other marked syllables, and so on. This sonnet should be almost sung."[85]

But by assuming that a proper recitation is possible, readers overlook the visual aspect of reading, and therefore miss the connection between the development of Hopkins's meters as a crucial aspect of his particular vision, as well as how these poems exemplify the ways in which "meter" extends beyond the poem itself and into the public domain of national salvation and the very private domain of spiritual identity. My reading of Hopkins's metrical marks implies that any idealized or fetishized vocal performance of Hopkins's poems— indeed, of any poem—is a distorted (or selective) reading of nineteenth-century prosodic practice. I'll end this chapter, then, with a particularly stunning display of Hopkins's simultaneous celebration of and dismay about the stigma of meter (the marks from manuscripts A and B); a kind of frantic stressing and marking that, nonetheless, we read with the hope that we will understand.

Spelt from Sybil's Leaves

Earnest, earthless, equal, attuneable, ' vaulty, voluminous, . . . stupendous
Evening strains to be tíme's vást, ' womb-of-all, home-of-all, hearse-
    of-all night.
Her fond yellow hornlight wound to the west, ' her wild hollow
    hoarlight hung to the height
Waste; her earliest stars, earl-stars, ' stárs principal, overbend us,
Fíre-féaturing heaven. For earth ' her being has unbound, her dapple
    is at an end, as-   5
tray or aswarm, all throughther, in throngs; self ín self steedèd and
    páshed—qúite
Disremembering, dísmémbering ' áll now. Heart, you round me
    right
With: Óur évening is over us; óur night ' whélms, whélms, ánd will
    end us.
Only the beak-leaved boughs dragonish ' damask the tool-smooth
    bleak light; black,
Ever so black on it. Óur tale, O óur oracle! ' Lét life, wáned, ah lét life
    wind   10
Off hér once skéined stained véined variety ' upon, áll on twó
    spools; párt, pen, páck
Now her áll in twó flocks, twó folds—black, white; ' right, wrong;
    reckon but, reck but, mind
But thése two; wáre of a wórld where bút these ' twó tell, each off
    the óther; of a rack
Where, selfwrung, selfstrung, sheathe- and shelterless, ' thóughts
    agaínst thoughts ín groans grínd.

If we read Hopkins's metrical practice as a wavering between seeing the mark's meaning immediately (Christ's presence) and trusting that it will come back when we do not see the mark infused with this meaning, then this late poem, written and revised in the mid-1880s, is at once a more personal and more public negotiation of a broader wavering between the light (the revelation of Christ's presence) and dark (darkness configured as an absence of Christ or the despair over Christ's return)—over which he equivocates in many of his poems, both thematically and formally—than has yet been recognized. The mark in "Spelt from Sybil's Leaves," then, is the culmination of his early desire to connect with a reader and have that reader connect to Christ, therefore conditioning and reeducating a community of English readers to see and hear as he saw and heard the world; but it is also a later, more mature consideration of the failure to connect—the yearning for a connection that may never happen with a reader, a nation, or with Christ, and the realization that the metrical system he professes to have mastered will never become a universal metrical system, visible or audible to all. Indeed, at this point, Hopkins was well aware that his system would be available only to a precious few. The mark, then, is also a response to Hopkins's failure and frustration, a wavering, a hope, but also, at times an acknowledgment that despite all of our intentions to see or hear in common, we are ultimately isolated in the inherently subjective process of fetching out the meaning and feeling of words.

While Bridges wanted to move toward even greater transparency in English—reforming spelling so that there could be no doubt about pronunciation and thus no variation in metrical reading—Hopkins was committed to preserving and exploiting the dense variety available in the written record of English, and at the same time, urging readers to read above and beyond the language even though they might waver and fail. It is through this lens that we must look again at Hopkins's metrical marks and his equivocation about stress as a spiritual and national concern. This wavering marks the bodies of his poems and their surrounding fields, and colored his reception—and the reception of a great deal of experimental metrical writing—in the twentieth century.

In the poems and theories I have discussed, meter is an unstable, political, and external mediator that Hopkins, Bridges, and Patmore attempted, variously, to stabilize into systems with spiritual and national meaning. Hopkins's isolation as a Catholic perhaps only increased the fervor with which he coded his writings with marks and signs, instructions for the reader who would someday come across his verses. His project shifted significantly over time, as did his own definition of meter and how it could or should be mastered. Encountering his poems is an exercise in instability and failure: all of the poems waver between the inside and outside, the unseen and seen, the absence and presence, the dark and the light, understanding and not understanding. When in "Carrion Comfort," he asks, "Which one? Is it each one?" so, I argue, should we.

Hopkins's metrical experiments were not ahead of his time; on the contrary, they place him firmly amid the Victorian concerns about the standards and character of the English language, issues that demarcated a kind of boundary against threats from without and disagreements within the ground of English letters. This metrical imaginary was shifting along with the idea of a British Empire, and Hopkins, who was writing concurrently with that linguistic imperialist project, the *New English Dictionary*, was invested in the way that poetry served the nation's greatness. In 1886, Hopkins writes that "to be active in writing poetry" is "even a patriotic duty."[86] Imagined by modernist readers as an isolated maverick and absorbed into literary history as a poet of individual and misunderstood genius, Hopkins's legacy deserves to be understood through the public and private cultures of English meter that his writing negotiated. Rather than the frustrated and secluded priest struggling privately with his own faith, his fraught attraction to and repulsion from visual temptation, perhaps we can read Hopkins's considerations about the visual field—in his development of inscape, in his wavering about the metrical mark, in his understanding of accent, and in his indication of phonemic depth—as a way to enrich our own understanding of his evolution as a poet deeply connected to the spiritual health of the nation. By seeing Hopkins as a product of and respondent to Victorian insecurities about its empire of letters, we might not become an ideal imagined reader, converted by his verses, the stigma transferred to us, but if we read his marks carefully and recognize the struggles that those marks indicate, we take a step toward seeing the larger, national landscape against which those struggles occurred.

❦ 3 ❦

The Institution of Meter

It has been said that our English rhythms are governed by accent; I, moreover, believe this to be the *sole* principle that regulates them.
—Edwin Guest, *A History of English Rhythms*

What, then, is the upshot of the whole matter? This, for certain: that we have as yet no established system of prosody.
—T. S. Omond, *English Metrists*

The reader will already have discovered that I am writing under a conviction that the musical and metrical expression of emotion is an instinct, and not an artifice.
—Coventry Patmore, *Essay on English Metrical Law*

Metrical Mastery

Robert Bridges's experimental and dynamic poetic forms (and his discussions of these forms) were central to the changing perception of English meter from the late Victorian to the postwar period. Bridges's role in the prosody wars, in particular, complicates the accepted narrative of the rise of free verse, and shows how the consolidated concept of traditional meters was challenged not only from the modernist avant-garde but also from poets who had been expanding the concept of English meter throughout the late nineteenth century. The dynamism of meter in English and Bridges's deep commitment, not unlike that of Ezra Pound's, to mastering various English traditions and to creating an English verse form that could accommodate foreign languages is evident in his innovations in multiple metrical forms. Whereas Hopkins receives most of the attention from scholars eager to find a "protomodernist" in the late nineteenth century, in many ways Bridges, whose late career spanned the heyday of high Modernism, has been overlooked as a poet whose experimental approaches to English meter were in conversation with the experiments of the avant-garde. But also important is the fact that Bridges was in conversation with the institutions of the English school system. For Bridges, English meter in its multiple forms was a mediating force to be mastered, a symbol of difficulty overcome, and a changing yet traditional representative of an idea of

79

English literature that challenged the sciences and displaced the classics as the proper discipline of study for an English gentleman. Contrasting Bridges with his influential competitor, George Saintsbury, reveals the contested landscape of the Edwardian and Georgian prosody wars, which have been largely ignored or suppressed in favor of the more convenient narrative of the rise of free verse. The personal, institutional, and national stakes of these prosody wars are clear in Bridges's poems but, most especially, in the prosodic writing of these two important, and generally overlooked, figures.

This chapter begins with a sustained look at the relationship between Hopkins's and Bridges's approach to prosodic practice and, especially, poetic mastery. I then turn to an examination of Bridges's dynamic thinking about English and classical prosody over the course of his long career, before arguing that despite the multiple and competing theories with which Hopkins and Bridges experimented, the prosodic work of historian and journalist Saintsbury, whose career runs parallel to Bridges, necessarily simplifies the story of English prosody for institutional and ideological reasons. Sainstbury's promotion and institutionalization of the foot-based system of scansion (a system that made little or no sense to many practicing poets of the time) is just one of the reasons that the meter of English poetry seemed as if it had one history and one overarching form to those poets devoted to rebelling against it. It was, I suggest, less the meter itself and more the ideological associations to which Saintsbury was committed that inspired many poets to think that meter was inexorably associated with a certain kind of Englishness. In chapter 4, I continue along these lines, showing how the institutionalization of a differently ideological, but still nationalistic, brand of Englishness was prevalent in the state-funded school system and developed into a fetishizing of a native English "beat."

Bridges's privileged classical education at Eton and Oxford influenced his reception as a poet and critic. For instance, literary historian David Perkins writes in 1976 that Bridges's "emphasis on tradition, consciousness, and criticisms as essential elements in the creative process were fostered more by the classics than by current excitements,"[1] and a review in 1889 foreshadowed his reception in the early twentieth century and beyond, naming his work (and character) "austere, classical, precise, reticent."[2] The term "classical" refers here not only to his education but also to his careful approach to poetic process. It is tempting to read Bridges as a static figure that provides both a traditional and aristocratic backdrop against which the modernists outlined their own distinctive art. Indeed, from Bridges's Victorian education to his seemingly detached wartime anthology, *The Spirit of Man* (1916), we see a figure whose public persona is committed to ideas of poetic and civic order, seemingly untouched by the poetic cultures of the 1910s. But Bridges's attempts to reform the way students studied English poetry and his frustration that he could not affect change were deepened and redirected once he became poet laureate in

1913. Though he failed to influence a large reading public with his new approaches to poetic form until just before his death, his revisions of the influential and controversial book, *Milton's Prosody*, as well as his own commitment to publishing poems in a number of new and experimental forms—along with the apparatus of footnotes and explanatory prefaces—shows that, although he did not succeed in changing the way poetry was taught, he seldom succumbed to any expectation that there was only one tradition through which poetic form should be read. What sets Bridges apart from other Victorian poets who were experimenting with poetic form is that he was innovating in order to standardize, in many ways, a more complex model for English meter. He, like the modernists, believed that the old forms were "worn out," but thought that they could still be refreshed, properly understood, and reshaped to accommodate the dynamic and polyglossial future of poetry that was being imagined in the early twentieth century. Perkins notes that, though Bridges's poems seem "curiously empty," his popular *Shorter Poems* in 1884 contained no two poems in the same verse form, and Edmund Gosse assigns to Bridges the first specimens of the triolet printed in English.[3] But it was not only his command of foreign verse forms in English that demonstrates Bridges's importance as a metrical experimenter: it was his insistence that the English language itself was a treasure house of unrealized metrical and poetic potential that had been misunderstood and, more importantly, mistaught. His poetic career and the fate of that career today illustrates how the rise of English as a discipline both shaped and reshaped the character of English prosody by suppressing the various English metrical histories that Bridges hoped to restore, remake, and make available to poets in the twentieth century.

Around the same time that Hopkins sent Bridges "Spelt from Sybil's Leaves" (1886), Hopkins also sent Bridges a translation, in Latin, of a poem from Bridges's own sonnet sequence, *The Growth of Love*, which Bridges began ten years earlier in 1876 (the year after Hopkins composed "The Wreck of the Deutschland"). Bridges's sonnet is, like many of the poems in the collection, about his love for his wife and about the tradition and perceived constraints of writing a sonnet sequence. He writes in sonnet one, "Behold me, now that I have cast my chains, / Master of the art which for thy sake I serve" (l. 14).[4] This poem was a leitmotif in their letters; a poem to which Hopkins suggested revisions multiple times. Perhaps perfecting it, somewhat, by translating it into Latin in 1886 (from the original 1876 edition which, MacKenzie notes, Hopkins had imperfectly memorized for his translation),[5] Hopkins's gesture (as well as his final poem, "To R.B.") shows Bridges's importance as the one reader who might still master a new metrical system for England and who could, Hopkins hoped, read his verses with a kindred eye.

In Bridges's sonnet, the beloved's passionate voice can penetrate the ear like the prow of a boat cutting through water: "Ah! But her launchèd passion when she sings / Wins on the hearing like a shapen prow / Borne by the mastery of its urgent wings / Or, if she deign her wisdom she doth show / She hath intelligence of heavenly things / Unsullied by man's mortal overthrow" (ll. 9–10). The awkward mixed metaphor (a boat with wings?) hardly clangs since the romantic notion of a voice "taking flight" with passion or song seems so commonplace. The way the song "wins" the ear is significant, because Hopkins's first objection to this poem is the fact that Bridges's song does *not* win his ear, though it may trick his eye. Hopkins writes: the "barbarous rhyme of *prow* and *show*: I can't abide bad rhymes and when they are spelt alike I hate them more."[6]

Despite specific criticisms like those addressing the sonnet about which he seemed to obsess, Hopkins praised the twenty-four sonnets that would make up *The Growth of Love* much more generously than Bridges had responded to "The Wreck of the Deutschland." Hopkins writes: "[t]he sonnets are truly beautiful, breathing a grave and feeling genius, and make me proud of you." After a few more quibbles Hopkins moves to a discussion of Bridges's rhythm: "About the rhythm. You certainly have the gift and vein of it, but have not quite reached your perfection. Most of your Miltonic rhythms (which by the way are not so very marked as your letter led me to suppose they would be, and I think many modern poets employ them, don't they?) are fine" (34–38).

Hopkins continues with a discussion of Milton's prosody ("I have paid much attention to Milton's rhythm"), writing that he is thinking about writing something about the remarkable choruses of *Samson Agonistes*: "I think I have mastered them." Hopkins mentions the paper by J. A. Symonds, "The Blank Verse of Milton,"[7] as part of an ongoing interest in the prosody of Milton that he and Bridges shared. Both Hopkins and Bridges were working on rhythmic experiments ("you will see that my rhythms go further than yours do in the way of irregularity," writes Hopkins), experimenting with a new system that they wanted to master. Bridges writes to his friend Lionel Muirhead about his revisions to the first twenty-four sonnets as early as 1878: "They will be *better than anything I have done*, and 2 of them <u>are I hope successful in a new metrical system of which I hope great things</u>."[8] Mention of the new system leads to a discussion of Hopkins, but he returns to his new ideas for the revisions and expansions of *The Growth of Love,* closing the letter by saying that the new poems will provide an "[e]<u>ntirely new system of rhythm introduced into sonnett-writing.</u> [*sic*] See what excitements we have."[9] Bridges's enthusiasm for the "entirely new system of rhythm" mirrors Hopkins's description of sprung rhythm in his author's preface (which Hopkins wrote in 1883 "or not much later"),[10] in which he comments that "the rhythm in which the following poem is written is new,"[11] and, as he says in his 1878 letter to Dixon, "I had long had haunting my ear the echo of a new rhythm which now I realized on paper."[12] Critics have discussed how both poets were experimenting with sprung rhythm, though Bridges's experiments with rhythm were not limited to Hopkins's system; indeed, Bridges's concept of metrical mastery extended beyond the "new system" that he and Hopkins were inventing. Whereas Hopkins's focused on traditional meter and sprung rhythm, Bridges's investigations of

Milton produced both accentual and syllabic verse experiments. From the beginning of his poetic career, Bridges was able to investigate and attempted to master and stabilize multiple metrical systems, recognizing them as distinct and endeavoring to explain his understanding of these multiple systems to a wider audience.

Though Bridges had published at least two poems in sprung rhythm by 1880 ("On a Dead Child" and "London Snow") that became widely known, the poem, titled simply "Sonnet" in his 1879 collection *Poems*, is a direct conversation with Hopkins on the issue of metrical mastery.[13] Donald Stanford has noted that the four accentual poems Bridges published in this volume were distinguished by their small type, a practice Bridges continued in his 1880 edition of *Poems*.[14] Though these poems could be scanned according to an accentual-syllabic model, Bridges's practice of signaling his experiments with different types shows that he is also indicating the variety of verse forms possible in English—a pedagogical practice that he will continue throughout the course of his career.

MacKenzie speculates that Hopkins composed "The Windover" in 1877 and gave it to Bridges sometime in the middle of 1878, so it is possible that both Bridges's Sonnet 22 and Hopkins's "The Windhover" may be read productively in conjunction; Bridges was actively corresponding with Hopkins about "The Windhover" between 1878 and 1884.[15] Whereas "The Windhover" has become the most famous of Hopkins's entire oeuvre, and a favorite of critics, few have noticed the way that the poem is in dialogue with Bridges's sonnet.[16] In Hopkins's sonnet, the bird of the title, a windhover or a kestrel (falcon), is an allegory for Christ and for poetic inspiration. In the last two lines of the octave, Hopkins writes, "[m]y heart in hiding / Stírred for a bird, —the achieve of, the mástery of the thing" (l. 8).[17] Written only a year after he completed "The Wreck of the Deutschland," with its destabilizing opening salvo, "[t]hou mastering me, God," (in which we do not know which two syllables to emphasize according to Hopkins's own rules of the meter) the "mastery of the thing" here refers to Christ's mastery in creating the falcon, to the falcon's mastery of his flight (able to balance on its wings, stationary, as it rebuffs the "big wind," two words with diacritical marks for emphasis), but also to metrical mastery.

THE WINDHOVER

To Christ our Lord

I caught this morning morning's minion, king-
    dom of daylight's dauphin, dapple-drawn Falcon, in his riding
      Of the rolling level underneath him steady air, and striding
High there, how he rung upon the rein of a wimpling wing
In his ecstasy! then off, off forth on swing,   5

As a skate's heel sweeps smooth on a bow-bend: the hurl and gliding
   Rebuffed the big wind. My heart in hiding
Stirred for a bird, — the achieve of, the mastery of the thing!

Brute beauty and valour and act, oh, air, pride, plume, here
   Buckle! And the fire that breaks from thee then, a billion   10
Times told lovelier, more dangerous, O my chevalier!

   No wonder of it: shéer plód makes plough down sillion
Shine, and blue-bleak embers, ah my dear,
   Fall, gall themselves, and gash gold-vermilion.

If we read Hopkins's poems right, we will experience the "beauty and valour and act" that he witnessed, and the flash of beauty, the inscape of the poem, will be visible to us. Despite Hopkins's equivocation about his poetic vocation (whether he should be able to master the writing of poetry or whether that distracted him from his Jesuit calling, as well as how to reconcile those two important impulses), "The Windhover" is an *ars poetica* of how we might catch the beauty of Christ, ourselves, if we too are able to "master" the meter of this particular sonnet.

Hopkins revised "The Windhover" meter many times; as the manuscripts show, he crossed out "sprung" rhythm to write "falling / riding paeonic rhythm"; he changed the great colon between "big : wind" to two diacritical marks in line 7, and he added "the achieve of" in place of a dash: "stirred for a bird—for the mastery of the thing." Like "Buckle" and "chevalier," the "thing" has an exclamation point in all of the drafts. The chevalier is commonly read as Christ, and "Buckle" (the subject of many an exegesis) is the central crux of the poem, commonly read as the bird's dive downward after its suspension in air. But the "thing," I want to suggest, is not only the mastery, the achievement of Christ, of the bird, but also, as we witness the poet wrestling with the instability of his system (perhaps sprung, perhaps, significantly, falling, bird-like, despite a rhythm that seems to rise), he celebrates his own achievement, his own possible mastery. After all, he wrote to Bridges in 1879, "I shall shortly send you an amended copy of 'The Windhover:' the amendment only touches a single line, I think, but as that is the best thing I ever wrote I shd. like you to have it in its best form."[18] Hopkins wants admiration for his mastery in the poem as he admired Christ's mastery through the image of the bird; could a new rhythm stir a reader's heart "in hiding" toward seeing something beyond what is described in the poem?

In Bridges's "Sonnet—I Would Be a Bird," written concurrently with Hopkins's "The Windhover," Bridges turns the bird trope on its head, as if to signal the particular kind of formal awareness that both he and Hopkins bring to their poems.[19] Rather than the location of conventional song, the birds in "The Windhover" and Bridges's "Sonnet—I Would Be a Bird" are both symbols and considerations of metrical mastery. In Bridges's interpretation, he is not observing the mastered bird but has himself replaced the bird by mastering its form. Unlike Hopkins's observation, "I caught this morning's minion," in "The Windhover," here, the conditional "would be" of the first line also expresses an ambivalent desire, imagined in the octave as a bird metaphor that has no problem in a variety of climates:

> I would be a bird, and straight on wings I arise,
> And carry purpose up to the ends of air:
> In calm and storm my sails I feather, and where
> By freezing cliffs the unransom'd wreckage lies:
> Or, strutting on hot meridian banks, surprise   5
> The silence: over plains in the moonlight bare
> I chase my shadow, and perch where no bird dare
> In treetops torn by fiercest winds of the skies.

The most "sprung" moments of these first two lines are at the beginning, when Bridges sets up a series of what feel like trisyllabic substitutions, conventionally called anapests: I **would** be a **bird**, and **straight** on **wings** I a**rise**. The emphasis on "bird" and the lack of stress on both pronouns "I" folds the "I" into the action of "a**rise**," so that the subject is at once imagining the bird but also mimetically putting the bird's flight into the rising vowel sounds—Bridges is already experimenting with the phonetic effects that he explored in greater detail later in his career. Though not conventionally "sprung" in the sense of putting stressed syllables beside one another, the anapest in the middle of line 2 similarly hurries the bird's purpose, and the poem's, through the unstressed syllables after "up" to the end of the line:

> "And **car**ry **pur**pose **up** to the **ends** of **air**":

"[U]p" is suspended, midline, just before the line swerves into "to the ends of air." Of course "air" is already in "carry," so the meter itself is "carried" by the internal rhyming in the line. "In calm and storm my sails I feather, and where" seems a syntactic inversion for no other reason than to suspend the final two syllables "and where" as if on a cliff, and similarly, the setup of "surprise" in line 5 seems expressively perched as if to make us aware of the metrical movement, the shifty, slightly crooked flight, rife with internal assonance and consonance, of the bird-poet. The octave struts expressively that it can contain both slightly experimental lines and a number of regular lines. Whereas Bridges could flaunt the experiment more, he is tentative with the slightly accentual rhythm in the octave. Hopkins responded to these accentual experiments in February of 1879, writing, "the pieces in sprung rhythm—do not quite satisfy me. They do read tentative, experimental; I cannot well say where the thought is distorted by the measure, but that it is distorted I feel by turning from these to other pieces, where the mastery is so complete."[20] It is as if Bridges does not want to admit that he does not yet have mastery over this experimental new rhythmic form moving, instead, toward his own (more phonetic) exploration of the speeding and slowing effects of accent. But he writes his desire for mastery by imagining it in the sestet (ll. 9–14):

> Poor simple birds, foolish birds! then I cry,
> Ye pretty pictures of delight, unstir'd   10
> By the only joy of knowing that ye fly;
> Ye are nót what ye are, but rather, sum'd in a word,
> The alphabet of a god's idea, and I
> Who master it, I am the only bird.

Rather like a salvo, the sestet here turns the poet-as-bird into a writer who observes the desire to step back from the form with which he is working. Unlike the vision of "The Windhover," which stirs the poet's and reader's heart out of hiding, the sestet draws our attention to the simple conventions of the sonnet and the bird trope and steps outside of its own metaphoric realm.

Beginning with two stressed syllables in a row: "**Poor sim**ple birds!" followed by an extra unstressed syllable, there is a stumble at the end after the comma, with "**Fool**ish **birds, then** I **cry**." Emphasizing "cry" more forcefully because of the comma and the parallel rocking stressed-unstressed-stressed pattern preceding it (which we could just as easily read as another anapest), the rhythm continues to deemphasize the "I" to focus on what the bird, on what the bird's form, or the bird-as-form, cannot experience. Unlike the typical Shelleyan bird trope of the poetic voice taking flight to the heavens, here Bridges disdains how the birds, mere "pretty pictures of delight," remain "unstir'd," knowing only the joy of flight, but none of the accomplishment. Whereas Hopkins's heart "stirred for a bird, the achieve of—the mastery of the thing," here Bridges responds that the bird cannot achieve mastery without the poet's hand. Line 12 forces us to focus on the word "nót" by using a diacritical mark for stress. This poem's significance is heightened by both the visible idea of metrical scansion and the fact that this is the only diacritical mark (other than a French accent on the word mêlée) that Bridges leaves in the entire sixty-six sonnet sequence of *The Growth of Love*. Bridges is calling our attention to his metrical project and demanding that we read the poem on a deeper level. It is *not* the bird that is of interest here: "ye are nót what ye are, but rather, sum'd in a word / The alphabet of a god's idea." The poet, who employs his own alphabet of metrical order, is able to "sum" in a word; it is the poet, and not the bird, who is the master. Bridges employs a more clinical, mathematical "sum" of the metrical parts that make a "whole" of the line and of the poem, even getting rid of the "m" and "e" as if to show that he is adding up only what is necessary, including removing the personal pronoun in all its forms: "sum'd in a word." This metrical alphabet is neither poor, nor simple, nor foolish, and it is the mastery of it that Bridges wants to transmit to his readers. His metrical performance *is* mastery; there is no equivocation here as there is in Hopkins's poem, despite his reticence to fully embrace the experiment in the octave. Here is an early instance in which Bridges asserts his hopes for English meter, daring to display its possibilities in the guise of what will become a long sonnet sequence—"and I / Who master it, I am the only bird." This poem shows Bridges as a young poet "stirred" by the joy of his own achievement in mastering meter and working along the same lines as his colleague. Though Bridges, in Hopkins's mind, has not quite mastered his new form, Hopkins still praises the final tercet about mastery, writing that "[t]he Bird-sonnet shews the clearest distortion, though the thought of the last tercet is truly insighted" (71). The bird-as-poetic-expression is recast (or re-sum'd) by both Hopkins and Bridges in the mid-1880s as a metaphor for metrical mastery, but it was Bridges who would carry out his obsession with mastery to such an extreme that it would guarantee his obsolescence as a metrist, poet, and even a historical figure in the twentieth century.

Inventing the Britannic

Though Gerard Manley Hopkins and Coventry Patmore are better known for their metrical experiments, Robert Bridges was a crucial interlocutor for both. His book *Milton's Prosody* had a greater impact on the metrical landscape than Patmore's *English Metrical Law*. But in 1883, Bridges and Hopkins had not yet popularized their ideas about accentual meter. Bridges wrote to Patmore asking him to give an account of his experiments in accentual meter: "[I] hope that you would not be disinclined to give an account of what Hopkins and I call the new prosody." Patmore was about to revise *English Metrical Law* for reissue, and both Bridges and Hopkins wanted the revisions to reflect their own experiments. (Patmore's "new prosody" consisted not only of marking meter as a "series of isochronous intervals" but also moving metrical "law" into the metaphysical and mental realms.) Bridges told Patmore that *his* verses demonstrated the "new prosody" more popularly or practically than Hopkins's, though he was careful to note that Hopkins's verses demonstrated the new prosody more correctly. In the same letter, Bridges demurs, "I shall never write on prosody myself."[21] Of course, Bridges had by that time already written on prosody. In the preface to his 1879 edition of *Poems*, he stressed speech accent as the key to a reading of the poems in sprung rhythm. He also agreed to write an essay, "On the Elements of Milton's Blank Verse," for Henry Beeching's 1887 school edition of *Paradise Lost*, to be published by the Clarendon Press. In the advertisement at the front of the edition, Beeching writes, "The essay on Milton's scansion is contributed by a friend. It is hoped that it will succeed in making intelligible the really simple, but (to judge by the notes of commentators) frequently misunderstood rules of Milton's prosody in *Paradise Lost*. As a guide to the young student the poetical elisions are marked in the text by an apostrophe."[22] To mark how Bridges imagined Milton pronouncing his text aloud, he, like Hopkins, used an additional mark on the poem so that the student could perform the poem as Bridges imagined it. But it was not only an apostrophe that Bridges provided to aid with reading. In his first attempt at classifying Milton's system, Bridges gave a list of typical extrametrical syllables as well as four examples of the way that Milton's prosody fell under a rule that corrected and standardized the variety of elisions found in Shakespeare. He wrote, "[t]hese, which were common under Shakespeare, Milton in *P. L.* reduced, and *brought under law*"(3, emphasis mine). Bridges's first goal in this early version of the text is to assert that a metrical law can be extrapolated from an intense reading of Milton's prosody; as a pedagogic practice, therefore, Bridges is showing students that a poet's use of meter adheres to his or her own laws rather than a larger, inherent design in the language.

By writing that Milton was aware of and practiced his own law of elision in *Paradise Lost*, Bridges was engaging directly with John Addington Symonds, whose essay "The Blank Verse of Milton" had appeared in *The Fortnightly Review*[23] as well as in his collection *Sketches and Studies of Southern Europe* in 1880. Rather than defining blank verse, Symonds's argument resembles that of Saintsbury, asserting (without much investigation):

> [b]lank verse has been the metre of genius, that it is only used successfully by indubitable poets, and that it is no favorite in a mean, contracted, and unimaginative age. The freedom of the Renaissance created it in England. The freedom of our own century has reproduced it. Blank verse is a type and symbol of our national literary spirit—uncontrolled by precedent or rule, inclined to extravagance, yet reaching perfection at intervals by an inner force and *vivida vis* of native inspiration.[24]

Symonds reclaimed Milton from Samuel Johnson's accusation of "haste" and concluded that his erratic substitutions must be read "for the sense" and that it would take "the work of much study and prolonged labor."[25] Bridges's prolonged labor produced, in this first instance, four detailed laws of elision and two laws of contraction as well as a detailed summary of the stress patterns of Milton's verse and the possibilities of inverted feet, plus a list of all the possible positions of the caesura. Taken together, all of these details provide the rules under which the poem should be read,[26] each verse contracting in specific ways to the particular rules that, taken together, make the verses seem much more syllabic in nature than the free-substitution, foot-based model that Symonds proposes. Like Bridges's own poems, his evaluation of Milton shows that the genius of the poet proceeded according to a series of laws, of difficulties overcome, and it was *this* genius that symbolized the beauty of the national meter.

Rather than content himself with this prefatory material, Bridges wanted to circulate these prosodic rules beyond Beeching's edition; he published a separate edition of the essay in pamphlet form the same year. Bridges did not believe that he had produced the definitive account of Milton's prosody because the prosody was not the same poem by poem. Therefore, Bridges expanded his study by publishing *The Prosody of Paradise Regained and Samson Agonistes* as a supplement in 1889, the year of Hopkins's death. It is arguable that most of Bridges's ideas about the prosody of *Samson Agonistes* would not have been possible without his correspondence with Hopkins, whose own work with the speech rhythms of *Samson Agonistes*, in particular, was formative in the concept of "sprung rhythm." Though the supplement appears, at first, merely to give a sense of the further variations that Milton explored in his other poems, it quickly turns polemical, and could read as a defense of Hopkins's own experimental poems. After quoting a few lines with inverted first feet, he asserts: "Those who think such verses rugged and harsh are unfit to criticize Milton—as the most must always be, because the more elaborate the rhythm, the fewer can appreciate it; and Milton's rhythms require of the reader more than what commonly passes for a good ear."[27] He continues, vehemently: "Most 'lovers of poetry' merely love sing-song. Ritum, ritum, ritum, is rhythm to them, and anything which will not go ritum is harsh; or that and diddledy diddledy are all their notion of rhythm. But that the University of Oxford should print such a vulgar instruction of the youth of the country may well astonish" (8).

The sophisticated knowledge of metrical complexity would render a student more, not less civilized. Here, Bridges distinguishes between the regular "lover of poetry," conditioned in school to discard all but the most regular rhythms, and sets out to correct these miseducated readers by directing them to the text for which this is a supplement. In so doing, Bridges is redeeming Milton as well as English meter from a simple, conventional understanding of metrical form as associated with rhythmic regularity (a trend that is explored in further detail in the following chapter).

But Bridges was far from finished; in 1893 he published, in limited issue, a revised and expanded version of the text, titled *Milton's Prosody: An examination of the rules of the blank verse in Milton's later poems, with an Account of the Versification of Samson Agonistes*, and general notes, bringing the same book out in regular issue the following year. In this, he expanded his (rather syllabic) view of *Paradise Lost* and continued to make his case for the stress-prosody of *Samson Agonistes*. Finally, in 1901, Bridges published a more definitive volume, titled simply *Milton's Prosody*, alongside William Johnson Stone's *On the Use of Classical Metres in English Verse*. The fact of Bridges's constant revisions shows that as he was working through Milton's blank verse he was trying to think through his own ideas of English meter. Although he did not name it as such, the 1901 version of *Milton's Prosody* is actually a treatise about all meter in English based on his study of Milton. Or, as one reviewer heralds, "Mr. Bridges's ambition, however, goes further than the analysis of Miltonic prosody. He designs this essay, with its appendices, to be at least a basis for a scientific scheme of English prosody at large."[28] The 1901 edition of *Milton's Prosody* quickly sold out.

But what was Bridges's scheme? Originally expanding his study of Milton to include a consideration of Milton's blank verse in *Paradise Lost* and his very different, more various stress rhythm in *Samson Agonistes*, it was clear that Bridges felt that there was more than one way to read English meter. In both the 1901 and the 1921 revision, Bridges includes a chapter on the prosody of accentual verse, explaining the differences between syllabic and accentual verse and making a case that there was quite an explicit difference between the two (a distinction he outlines toward the end of his appendix on the "Accentual Hexameter").[29] By the 1921 "definitive edition," the title became *Milton's Prosody with a Chapter on Accentual Verse*.

Bridges's impulse is to provide rules by which to understand and reeducate readers about the whole of English verse in its bastardized and somewhat backwards evolution. Despite his strenuous detail, he is careful to assert that his "laws" are merely "the tabulation of what my ear finds in English stressed or accentual verse: but they appeal confidently to the reader's ear for confirmation."[30] He uses the words "heavy," "light," and "short" to denote the quantitative value of syllables and outlines six hypotheses toward the rules of stress prosody, but is careful to note in rule four that the ear may be tempted, or tricked, into hearing regular metrical units (that which we have been trained to call iambs and trochees, etc.) rather than the more important irregular speech units of the stress. This outdated method is not, in his mind, "true analysis":

> I am convinced that if any one who hankers after classical analogies will provisionally cast his fancy aside, and examine the real English construction of the verse, he will never, after understanding it, wish to superimpose upon it a foreign and needless explanation. For the stressed rhythm is a sufficient account of itself: its analysis is complete, and if it is not altogether more beautiful, it is more variously beautiful than any other. I would even say that the analogy with Greek or Latin verse is confusing and worse than useless.[31]

Though elsewhere he demonstrates how English verse can be read as analogous to Greek—that is, with similar primal importance of the verbal unit— here he moves toward a definition that repudiates comparisons with what could be seen as foreign, or non-English. This is not to say that Bridges did not believe that experimentation based on classical meter was not possible (indeed, he explored this possibility thoroughly); rather, Bridges is attempting to clarify that stressed rhythm in English makes more sense when we discard the measuring system of Greek and Latin and so, in this way, aligns his views a bit more closely with that of the Anglo-Saxonists Walter Skeat and, prior to him, Edwin Guest. Though Bridges lists disyllabics and trisyllabics that still correspond roughly to iambs, trochees, anapests, and dactyls, it is the patriotic fourth stress unit, the mid-stress trisyllabic, that demonstrates his commitment to inventing a truly English interpretation of stress. He proposes to rename this foot the "Britannic" (the name for the foot demonstrating its pronunciation—unlike any other metrical terminology). By naming the stress unit after the country it represents, Bridges is effectively wrenching the history of the particular system from the sign—a complicated history about which he just has taken great pains to educate us. Furthermore, he goes on to democratize the new meter—"a 'Britannic' is the commonest trisyllabic unit of stressedverse." Asserting that this newly named mid-stress, trisyllabic foot is the key to understanding the nature of the commonest poetry, he compromises, providing visual signs with which to scan verses that, according to his earlier assertions, should depend solely on the ear.

Granted, the "Britannic," as it is the most democratic of feet, allows the most freedom and so is not strictly bound to position on the line. He admits the dynamic structure of the verse toward the end of the essay, writing "[t]his is the account of these verses. A consistent prosody is, however, so insignificant a part in what makes good English poetry, that I find that I do not myself care very much whether some good poetry be consistent in its versification or not: indeed I think I have liked some verses better because they do not scan, and thus displease pedants" (99). Indeed, contemporary critic Donald Stanford finds Bridges's explanation of accentual verse unnecessarily complicated, since "in accentual verse the number of stresses to a line is constant and the stress must coincide with normal speech accent."[32] Bridges's propensity to justify his hypothesis based on speech is caught again between what he knows *his* ear is qualified to hear—the normal speech accent of English—and what he knows others, who would be beginners to a standard way of speaking and hearing English, would need to *see* in order to properly believe what they were expected to *hear*. Bridges's lofty ideal would be to banish diacritical marks altogether and trust the true phonetics of English (based on classical understanding and scientific knowledge of English's evolution), though he cannot begin to convey these revisions for the vocalized, modern form of the language without the appearance of diacritical marks—the visions of ancient signs marking the skin of the versification to measure our distance from the skeleton within.

Dynamic Reading

In a telling account of the history of the volume that appears at the end of the 1921 edition of *Milton's Prosody*, Bridges writes, explicitly, that his main goal in writing and revising his account was to correct the tendency to read Milton (and, implicitly, any poet's meter) improperly. This modest history of the volume rapidly expands into a technique for protecting the whole of English verse and language from sinking more deeply into ignorance, which he finds society reluctant or too frightened to remedy. He writes defensively, insisting that his original intention was to contribute "such an account of the versification as should knock out the prevalent usage of misreading the rhythm; for it was generally thought necessary and correct to mispronounce words so as to make them scan with regular alternate accent." He continues: "[T]hen, after the book was printed as a separate treatise, young poets started using Miltonic inversions so freely in their blank verse that champions of the prevailing orthodoxy raised an indignant protest in the newspapers, wherein the discussion grew so incredibly hot that a London evening journal advertised 'prosody' as an attractive item in its daily papers."[33] Though he gestures to the debates in which he participated, it is only in his private letters that he accuses metrists like Saintsbury, Skeat, and T. S. Omond of wrongly determining the direction of scholarship about English versification; in his public writing he makes every attempt to be conciliatory and unifying in the presentation of his scholarship. Ever since the public interest in prosody was fueled by the debates, Bridges laments, "this book has been on false footing." Here, in the 1921 edition, he attempts once again to "set the facts on their proper phonetic basis, but I am well aware that good intentions cannot make up for lack of early training in phonetics; it is a subject that needs a young ear, and my late adventures in the field can only modestly claim to be of use . . . " (113–14). The direction, then, of the 1921 edition, is toward criticizing England's failures to correct the issues he brought up in each edition in the thirty-three years that the book was in print, and to include his revised and mature thinking about the state of pronunciation and the general misuse of the language (a topic that became more and more important to him after the war). Bridges emerges in the early twentieth century as a crusader against "the tyranny of schoolmasters and grammarians,"[34] whose attempts to preserve the purity of English result in bemoaning the state of non-phonetic spelling and publishing versions of his poems in his own invented system of phonetic speech.

Most prosodic scholars, however, did not accept Bridges's prosodic mastery. Joseph Mayor, of Cambridge, attacked both Bridges and Skeat[35] in the 1901 (second) edition of *Chapters on English Metre*, taking issue in particular with Bridges's attempt to define the elision of extrametrical syllables in Milton's lines. Mayor's tone is high-handed: "I feel some doubt as to what would be Mr. Bridges's explanation of a line such as the following: "That cruel serpent. On me / Exercise most."[36] In an unpublished letter to Mayor as Bridges is revising the 1921 edition, Bridges asks Mayor how he himself would scan the line: "I remember that in controverting my contention that Milton in P.L. consciously excluded what I called 'extrametrical syllables' from any [---] of the verse but the final place you quoted against me [a line]: 'The infernal serpent on me exercise most.' I am writing to ask if you have any objection to telling me how *you* accented or shaped the word <u>exercise</u> in that line."[37] Mayor's reply does not acknowledge Bridges's question. His form letter response shows that he is entirely unwilling to engage Bridges on the level of pronunciation, which is what Bridges is getting at when he asks him to explain how he would have "accented or shaped" the word.[38] What is remarkable about this scholarly disagreement is less that they disagree than the choice of lines over which they argue. Both men are admirers of Milton, and both, as if to suit their own prosodic purposes, quote line 927 from book ten of *Paradise Lost* as: "That cruel serpent. On me exercise most," as if Milton's line is asking for the metrical scholar to exercise his prosodic methodologies on the text of the poem. However, Milton's line does *not* read "exercise most." The line, as if in defiance of all metrical attempts to standardize, reads: "That cruel serpent: on me exercise *not*" (emphasis mine). Bridges is rebelling against what he feels is an unfairly prescriptive approach to English language teaching; by standardizing phonetic spelling, the rules of English meter would emerge as harmonious with the past and would be truly English in character; the "exercises" of schoolmasters and grammarians, in Bridges's mind, are to blame for the inefficient state of English literary education. Mayor, on the other hand, represents the prescriptive ends of meter as a grammar—the cruel serpent of grammar exercises "most" in Mayor's concept of English literary education, whereas Bridges wants to reform it altogether.[39]

Perhaps fueled by the opposition of scholars like Mayor, in the 1921 edition Bridges does not hesitate to use *Milton's Prosody* as a platform for education reform: "I wish that the book may do something to conquer the prejudice which still opposes reform of this fundamental defect in our early education." He attacks the community to which he appealed repeatedly for validation, implicitly including, among others, his dear friend Henry Bradley, editor of the *New English Dictionary* (later the *OED*) and frequent correspondent:

> [T]here are very few of my contemporaries who will listen to common sense in this matter, or allow the clear light of scientific method to dispel the mystifications which prevent our children from understanding the elements of speech. And the further they proceed in the higher education the more hopelessly are they involved and confirmed in their ignorance: the barbarous distortion of Latin in our great schools is strenuously upheld as a reasonable propriety which it is almost a national offence to discredit.[40]

Bridges recognizes British society's attachment to the classical languages and all that they signify, but like other reformers eager to demystify the abstractions of linguistic signs, Bridges is attempting to be more nationalistic than the nationalists. By proposing a system that reverts to a conception of prosody that existed before the earliest pollution, he wants English ears to be able to hear again and hear clearly. We may read many of his proposed revisions as logical, democratic, and toward the promotion of the true greatness of English.

To do this, he has to devalue the sanctity of the mispronounced verbal sign, relying on formal *verbal* unity as opposed to formal literary structure—he abhors the "pedantry of scansion" and believes that true English speech, if pronounced properly, will naturally vocalize English verse as it should be heard. He asserts that the voice tone must translate words to the "plane of ideas and emotions" in Greek as in English. "In versification," he writes, "we know that the manner to which every one is accustomed, even though it be pedantry, has a far greater propriety to our ears than that which we should rightly prefer if we were not prejudiced by custom—the ridiculous distortion of sense and speech-rhythm in the chanting of the Psalms by the trained choirs of our Cathedrals is a good example" (13). And Bridges meticulously shows where the earliest corruption occurred: in the Latin language, when it wrongly discarded accent and instead attempted to imitate Greek verse form based on quantity. This mistranslation was then passed down through Chaucer to corrupt the English ears that Saintsbury will assert are perfect and privileged. Bridges is extremely careful, throughout *Milton's Prosody,* to show how he arrived at his conclusions by a systematic evaluation of Milton's verses; in order to prove the possible positions and numbers of accents and possible syllabic values, he cites particular lines throughout *Paradise Lost.* Despite this critical attention to prosodic detail, he asserts that the "rules" he is explaining are essentially "permissive, [Milton] indicates no rule for their use; their application is arbitrary. . . . Milton came to scan his verses in one way, and to read them in another" (34–35). Prosody, in this way, is proved to be an interpretive exercise for both poet and reader; rather than a guide as to how to vocally emphasize accents in a line, the "rhythm overrides the prosody that creates it. The prosody is only the means for the great rhythmical effects, and is not exposed but rather disguised in the reading" (36). By teaching the reader the system in which to scan the poem's prosody, the text encourages the reader to appreciate the poem's rhythmic effects at a higher level. Put most simply, by providing even provisional prosodic rules against which the rhythm rebels, Bridges wants the reader to begin to hear (rather than rely on wrenched pronunciation based on visible metrical signs) the variety within the verse—to Bridges's ear, the beauty of verse in its variety.

Mastery for the Masses

Though the few scholars who notice the historical divisions in the study of English prosody often cast the debate in terms of "accent" versus "quantity," or "stress" versus "time," the very definitions of "accent," "quantity," "stress," and "time" in English verse were dynamic, malleable, and shifted in specificity and abstraction depending on the intended audience, which I hope I have by now shown. Opposite of Bridges's willingness to explore multiple foundations and definitions of meter, Saintsbury devoted an enormous amount of energy to fixing the terms for poetic form. He felt strongly that the history of English poetry would clearly prove his opinions about English prosody, but he was also invested in a reading practice that he seemed to take for granted as that shared by all Englishmen. A teacher of Greek and Latin and even Hebrew at a young age, Saintsbury, like most young men of his generation, learned in just three or four years of school, "the first three books of the *Aeneid*, the Odes of Horace, some Homer, and most of the iambic part, with some of the choruses, of two or three Greek plays," which he described as "large patterns and examples of the most perfect literary form that the world has produced."[41] This is a typical assessment from a student educated at King's College School in London and Merton College in Oxford, where there was not yet regular instruction in English literature when Saintsbury finished his studies in 1868. Yet Saintsbury asserts that he formed his ideas about English prosody solely by reading English poetry.[42] And as this proclaimed prosodic autodidact's 1878 review of Coventry Patmore's *English Metrical Law*[43] reveals, even at the young age of thirty-three, Saintsbury (like Patmore, Bridges, and Hopkins) was not only fully aware of the complicated nineteenth-century prosodic debates, but he had already formed strong opinions about them. In this 1878 review, Saintsbury displays what would become his characteristic style of dismissing prosodic systems that did not satisfy his own nascent ideas of what an English foot should be and do:

> Mr. Patmore does not seem to have made quite as valuable a contribution to the literature of the subject as he might have made; the fatal old quarrel between accent and quantity has drawn him to take part in it with the usual result. The truth seems to be that English verse is to be scanned both by quantity and accent, and that no verse is really good which does not answer to this double test. Those who rely only upon accent give us slipshod doggerel; those who rely only upon quantity give us variations on the original "Tityus happily thou," and so on.[44]

He provides no information to back up his claim that the "truth seems to be" that English meter is scanned by both accent and quantity. His devotion to this singular understanding of meter is reinforced when, less than ten years later, he asserts his belief in an English foot measurable by both accent and quantity and based explicitly on classical meters, in his *History of Elizabethan Literature* (1887): "I must entirely differ with those persons who have sought to create an independent prosody for English verse under the head of 'beats' or 'accents' or something of that sort."[45] For Saintsbury, the question of English independence was a crucial issue; he felt that verse must not rely solely on accent without some form of quantity or else it loses its link to the classical languages. This assertion comes as a result of Skeat's reissue of Guest's imposing and "epoch-making" *History of English Rhythms* (1882) a mere five years earlier. Guest believed accent to be "the *sole* principle"[46] that regulates English rhythm and that English has no metrical quantity.[47] Guest's notion of an English prosody independent of the classics epitomized one of the schisms between prosodic perspectives at the time. The competing histories of prosody in the late nineteenth century were also competing histories of Englishness: were the nation's literary and national origins in the great Shakespeare and Milton, or were they in the Anglo-Saxon and Old-English tradition? One camp valued the continuous line of poetic thought from Shakespeare to Swinburne, and the other prioritized preserving the narrative of steady beating Anglo-Saxon rhythms against the foreignness of classical verse forms. The latter explained the English literary tradition as influenced by a native beat that rebelled against and repelled various foreign yokes (the Guest/Skeat model), whereas the former conceived of it as a stream that had various influences that were absorbed, colonized, and interpolated as part of an evolution (the Saintsbury model, though a bit less neatly). Saintsbury's mission was to guarantee that Guest's theories would not prove to be any more influential.[48] He would accomplish this not only by undermining Guest's *History* and arguing vehemently against the accentual system, but by replacing Guest's looming two-volume project with three volumes of his own.

In prosodic manuals, size does matter. In Saintsbury's next step toward foot domination, he published *A Short History of English Literature* (1898). Guest's *History* was 738 pages; Saintsbury's "short" history was 818 pages (the later, three-volume *History of English Versification* ran to a staggering 1,577 pages). In the *Short History*, Saintsbury makes clear his view that, in English prosody's history, just as in the history of the English language and people, there was a distinct break with Anglo-Saxon influences; therefore, there was also a break with Guest's solely accentual basis for English meter. In his introductory section, "The Making of English Literature," he claims that "the true and universal prosody of English instead of the cramped and parochial rhythm of Anglo-Saxon"[49] came about from the influence of Latin. He titles this section "the transition,"[50] and it is, in many ways, a blueprint for the section he titles "The Mothers" in his larger *History of English Prosody*. (The *Short History* was in its eighth edition by 1913.) Between 1898 and 1905, Saintsbury published revised editions of *A History of Nineteenth-Century Literature* (1900 and 1901) and *A History of English Criticism* (1900, 1901, 1902). Both of these divulged and elaborated on his intent to disseminate his faith in the English foot to the "general brain"; that is, how he could extend his conception of English meter to the masses.

Saintsbury's essay, titled simply "English Versification," is quite possibly the most succinct summary of his views on the matter. Yet it was not published as part of his three-volume *History,* nor did it appear as an English Association pamphlet. Rather, this essay was the introduction to a handbook for poets by Andrew Loring, titled *The Rhymer's Lexicon* (1905). "English Versification" was at once an advertisement for Saintsbury's forthcoming three volumes as well as a clear distillation of them. Saintsbury here defines the history of English Versification *not* as "a struggle between native and foreign rhythm, but of the native material of language adapting itself to the pressure of the foreign moulds, and modifying those moulds themselves by the spring and 'thrust' of its natural qualities."[51] The result, he writes, "is one of the most interesting things in literature. . . . By looking both ways—from earliest to latest and from latest to earliest—we can distinguish a new form of verse, characteristically English in its blended originality, which takes the general rhythmical form of Low Latin and French, but which adapts them to, or adapts to them, the primaeval English tendency to syllabic equivalence."[52]

The "blended originality" of English verse form is a point of pride in his longer *History*; by 1905, Saintsbury was becoming the representative for standard English meter based on a subtle blending of classical (foreign, quantitative) and Anglo-Saxon (native, accentual) meter. Though his own understanding of these meters seemed fluid, malleable and, indeed, unstable, the more destabilized and conceptual his opinion seemed the more ardent he became in his assertion of their fundamental Englishness. The result of this careful blending, he felt, was a dependable and timeless conception of English meter and a conception of Englishness as distinct from the classics: a culmination rather than a deviation. As a founding member of the English Association and a professor at the University of Edinburgh, Saintsbury balanced more than just Anglo-Saxon accents and classical quantities; he was defending a characteristic Englishness that could value the classical languages as a necessary part of English literature at a time when they were under siege. There had been a loud and angry reaction against the reinstatement of compulsory Latin after the 1902 Education Act,[53] and Saintsbury was performing the role of the English literary historian while at the same time trying to preserve the connection between English literature and its classical pasts. Skeat, on the one hand, was uninterested in classical verse terms altogether and was supplanting the classics in the academy with the rise of his own discipline, Anglo-Saxon, arguing that this should be the basis and history of English literature rather than the classical languages. Robert Bridges, on the other hand, saw both sides of this equation, wanting students to see the benefit of the Anglo-Saxon literary past while, at the same time, understanding the ways that classical verse forms could be useful as one way, among many, to expand the possibilities for English prosody. That is, for Bridges, the purity, diversity, and freedom of English meter meant understanding each distinct possibility (the accentual, the syllabic, etc.) as a separate system that required its own kind of training and its own possibility for mastery. His characterizations of each system contained within them some hope for a broad-reaching and inclusive future for English meter and the nation. Saintsbury, ambitious though he was, was defensive about the rise of Anglo-Saxon as part of English literary study and wanted desperately to preserve not only the classics as a discipline but his understanding of the classical English gentleman, with an education that set him apart from others. Though Saintsbury may not have wanted to acknowledge it, his work reveals that in order to understand English meter one had to be educated in a certain way.

The quick rise of English education—and the uncertainty, after the failures of the Boer War, whether the education system was doing its proper job in creating a strong, competitive, and patriotic class of potential soldiers[54]—accelerated the pace and passion of prosodic debate outside the classroom and increased the circulation of and demand for texts that would teach English poetry and meter along purely national lines. Pamphlets and tracts from the English Association, established in part by Henry Newbolt in 1906, and the Society for Pure English, established in part by Bridges in 1913, worried over the fate of English pronunciation, spelling, and reading practices—issues that they believed might help solve the prolific and zealous debates over defining English meter. Like the concurrent experiments of phoneticians Henry Sweet and Alexander Ellis, popularized by George Bernard Shaw in *Pygmalion*, pronunciation reforms to standardize English might erase some distinctions between the working- and upper classes.[55] Though this local application of education reform had broader social reform as its aim, Saintsbury's prosodic writing expressed an increasing anxiety that both pronunciation reform and social reform might too broadly democratize the field of English literary study. If English meter was truly accessible to all, then how might we measure the poets against the mere versifiers?

Increasingly, the foreign names for classical feet were called into question and students were taught to feel English poetry according to "natural" accents (traced to an Anglo-Saxon past) divorced from the valueless and hegemonic classical system of iambs and trochees. American prosodist C. E. Andrews called this conflict in 1918, "prosodic wars."[56] It enlisted, as I have described, those committed to moving the concept of English meter away from its classical origins, and even away from the popular concept of feet, into a more capacious metrical system. Sometimes this system was syllabic, sometimes accentual, and it could reflect varieties of dialects and even welcome other languages. These hopes for English meter were altogether not new but their nationalistic and defensive stance in the Edwardian era had been increasing steadily with each expansion of the education system; every new expansion seemed accompanied by new anxieties about what English literary education meant for national culture. Educators and poets alike had high expectations for Saintsbury's three-volume *A History of English Prosody from the Twelfth Century to the Present Day* (1906–10), in which the issue, for Saintsbury, was no longer explicitly the contest between Anglo-Saxon or classical measures but rather how the blend of these two metrical heritages could constitute a characteristic English meter and, more importantly, could most accurately measure the ideal English character. Saintsbury's dependence upon an essential Englishness, which could be deduced from masterful poetics and instilled in the masses through prosodic acuity, would only deepen his drive toward commandeering the culture's understanding of the "foot."

The English Ear

Saintsbury wanted it both ways. On the one hand, he wanted to popularize the foot-based system as natural for those with an English ear, and on the other hand wanted all Englishmen to possess an ear precisely like his own, despite his bitter awareness that they did not. In his introduction to Loring's 1905 *The Rhymer's Lexicon*, Saintsbury lays out his metrical principles:

> "lines" . . . possess a definite rhythm based on what is called double and triple time; that these integers (the lines) are made up of corresponding or proportionate fractions to which it has been usual to give the name of "feet," though some object; that they are as a rule tipped with rhyme, whether in simple sequences or pairs or in more complicated sets called stanzas. It is upon the nature and constitution of these fractions that the hottest and most irreconcilable difference prevails among prosodists. Some prefer to regard them merely from the point of view of the accented syllables which they contain, while others consider them as made up of "long" and "short" syllables precisely as classical feet are, though not combined on quite the same systems; and yet others hold different views.[57]

Saintsbury insists on the portability of the "foot" across time. And yet, for those without a classical education, these feet may still seem foreign. Saintsbury finds a way around this dilemma by promoting a kind of national metrical intuition over formal training: the English ear. He writes, "the ear recognizes for itself, or is made to recognize by the sleight-of-hand of the poet, one broad distinction of value between syllables—the distinction which is denoted, in classical prosody, by the terms 'long' and 'short.'" But Saintsbury demands that issues such as *time* in utterance, sharper or graver *tone*, lighter or heavier *weight*, louder or softer *sound*, and thinner and denser *substance* do not matter in terms of the distinction between English and classical prosody. Saintsbury instead simply suggests that "everybody (if he would only admit it) recognizes the fact of the broad difference" (xvi). We hear them, he says, but we might not admit that we do. Despite the metaphors of stepping-stones, fence posts, and walking to which the word "foot" lends itself, Saintsbury detracts attention from his obvious and innocent allusion to earlier usages of the term: "call them feet, spaces, isochronous intervals, or abracadabras, every English verse can be divided up . . . into so many groups of 'long' and 'short' syllables which have metrical correspondence with each other in the line and in other lines . . . call the name iamb or abracadabra, trochee or tomfool, the *thing* is there from the *Brut* to the *Barrack-Room Ballads*" (xix). From the earliest rhymed history of England to patriotic tales of soldiers, Saintsbury asserts that the history of meter and of England is unified, indivisibly, by these groups of syllables that preexist and predate even our ability to name them—name them whatever you like, but Saintsbury likes to call them *feet*. The English ear, as he construes it, is particularly adapted to detect and judge them.

But even if Saintsbury gives plenty of examples of the best poetry in English with his descriptions and praise, the book itself cannot provide the "ear train-ing" of the native Englishman who is classically trained, though Saintsbury does not say this directly. That is, implicit everywhere in the three volumes is the fact that the classical methods through which Saintsbury was trained pre-pared him for what he then translates into an innate sense of rhythmic sound that haunted his thinking about rhythm and meter. This "innate sense" also played extremely well on the way that the national education system was teaching English poetry. For Saintsbury, an "English ear" that could naturally hear metrical feet based loosely on a classical measure of scansion was the true English ear—the true, classically trained, public school educated, elite English ear. History, as far as metrical training was concerned, was transformed into nature, but only for those with access to a classical education. Saintsbury ar-gues, in a direct attack on Guest and Skeat, that although there is a natural English ability to both see and hear the beauty of English verses, some artificial training is beneficial:

I hope it is not impertinent or pedantic once more to recommend strongly this joint eye- and-ear reading. It does not at all interfere with the understanding of the sense or enjoyment of the poetry, and it puts the mind in a condition to understand the virtue and the meaning of the prosody as nothing else can. One of the innumerable privileges of those who have received the older classical education is that they have been taught (in at least some cases) to read scanningly.[58]

The eye and an ear are a "combined instrument," "properly tuned," that will reveal English meter to be "a real and living rhythmical organism" (184). But if it is between a theory of scansion, which is intended for the eye, and pronun-ciation, intended for the ear, the remaining two volumes lean toward the ear.

The eye, directed by signs that may be visible to all and therefore less interpretive, less dependent on an elite education, might be frighteningly democratic.

Saintsbury did not invent the concept of an "English ear" (it was already evident in schoolbooks and elocution manuals); nor did this concept resemble the "natural" pronunciation that Murray may have intended in the *Grammars* that I discussed in chapter 1. For Saintsbury, the "English ear" meant a certain kind of pronunciation coupled with refined hearing. Prins notices how Saintsbury's discussion of Tennyson's "Hollyhock Song" in volume three of his *History of English Prosody* is especially striking for the way it emphasizes a particularly English reader: "One reads it," Saintsbury writes, "wondering how any human ear could be 'tortured' by it, but wondering still more how any <u>English</u> ear could be in the least puzzled by its metre."[59] Above mere human understanding, the English ear is undeniably privileged. In this statement, Saintsbury claims that the true English *ear* is able to detect true *English* meter. He exclaims: "Our business is with English; and I repeat that, *in English*, there are practically no metrical fictions, and that metre follows, though it may sometimes slightly force, pronunciation." Though at times he focuses on the regular combination and alternation of metrical feet in various forms, the book also makes a case for iambic meter and, specifically, for ballad meter, as particularly English. The ballad meter is "very much ours"; "the ballad quatrain, or common measure . . . perhaps the most definitely English—blood and bone, flesh and marrow—of all English metres. It comes the most naturally of all to an English tongue and an English ear."[60] Joining the forms of English verse to the forms of English bodies, Saintsbury emphasizes the instinct, the internal feeling that English speakers and hearers should have for prosodic forms. Not only do these forms prove that you are an Englishman, they bind you to other Englishmen, with whom you also share "blood," "bone," "flesh," "marrow," "tongue," and "ear." This rhetoric sounds particularly Anglo-Saxon, and it is the same one called upon on the other side of the Atlantic by prosodists such as Sidney Lanier and Frances Gummere, but here the blood and bone of the collective Anglo-Saxon body is yoked, idealistically, to a classically educated, trained, and civilized English ear.

Not only must one's ear be tuned, like Saintsbury's own, to hear, for example, blended classical feet in English verse, but one must also (it is his hope) understand and absorb the characteristics that these blended, natural feet create. Saintsbury's narrative of the evolution of English feet is imbued with the same militaristic swagger as the patriotic poems that were being taught in state-funded schools: English feet evolved into their "orderly and soldierly fashion" over time, grouped into syllables and then into lines like so many regiments. Indeed, English metrical feet form "vast armies" that English citizens, future armies, are conditioned to hear "naturally." It is a matter of national pride that English readers should, can, and do cultivate their faculties in order to correctly appreciate poetry.

But if Saintsbury's idealized and "natural" English ear is, in fact, a classically trained organ, how does he promote the English foot soldier among the general reading public, the majority of whom did not have access to (much less sustained training in) classical languages and literatures? Rather than define explicitly what he means by "feet," Saintsbury again and again insists on an innate sense of rhythm. What he does give us, in 1906, is a justification, along militaristic lines, of the ascendancy of his favorite metrical foot, the iamb: "To get the vast armies, the innumerable multitudes of [iambic verse] that exist[s] in English, into trochaic form, or in most cases even into a suggestion of trochaic rhythm, you have to play the most gratuitous, unliterary, and unnatural tricks upon them, and you often produce positively ludicrous or nauseous results."[61]

Saintsbury, as one might expect, prefers iambic to trochaic rhythm, but values the trochee highly as the necessary variant for the iamb. However, his ability to diagnose English verse as iambic rather than trochaic is dependent only on his ability to hear meter; he states simply and vexingly, "my ear informs me." In this early appendix to the first volume he also makes his first declaration of the self-evident truths of English feet. The iamb is the "ruling constituent," the anapest "omnipresent." Of the dactyl he has "no doubt . . . at all," despite its tendency to "tip up" into an anapest; Why does it do this? He writes, "I do not know why; and though it would not cost me five minutes to turn the statement of the fact into a jargonish explanation thereof on principles very popular to-day, I decline to do anything of the kind. The English language is made so and I accept the fact" (402–3), and thus he urges us to accept the fact as well. Though part of Saintsbury's inherent charm is his confidence that we will take his word for it, his lack of technical guidance leaves us with the one thing he has been convincing us we have—our ear. Our understanding of English prosody is at once intensely individual, therefore, but also, necessarily collective. Rather than being taught what the iamb *is* (or was) and how to mark it and memorize it, as a student in a classical classroom would have been, Saintsbury infuses his concept of English meter with an Edwardian article of faith in the steadfast and sturdy nature of the language, of an England in which the iamb is and always has been the ruling constituent. Just like the schoolchild learning about English poetry through narratives of military glory, like the countless histories of England that justified and extolled imperial expansion, Saintsbury's English meter spoke to and fostered what he imagined was a specifically national character.

A Prosodic Entity

Though reviewers of *A History of English Prosody* did not take Saintsbury's word for it, we, as English speakers, largely have. After being accused of not defining the "the English foot," he added an appendix to the third volume, in

1910, titled coyly, "What Is a Foot?" Here he summarizes his position along military lines once again: "[F]rom almost the first 'syllable of recorded time,' when English became fully English, its verse arranges itself—haltingly at first, then in a more and more orderly and soldierly fashion—in certain equivalent groups of syllables themselves, which, in turn, are grouped further into lines."[62] This definition does not appear in the main text, however; Saintsbury hides it in an appendix, one of the many additions he includes in the 1910 volume three. Again, "it is the result *to the ear* which decides"[63] whether it hears something long, or short, or loud, or soft, or accented by degrees. But Saintsbury is just as reticent, four years after the start of his project, to provide an answer or definition. He admits, "sometimes you may be unable to go positively right, because there are two or more available interpretations of the riddle" (522). We might think, then, that feet, for Saintsbury, are abstract equivalent spaces, like Coventry Patmore's isochronous intervals, or T. S. Omond's "time-spaces."[64] But this is not the case. Despite the interpretive freedom he grants, for Saintsbury, English feet are no abstraction, even though they are sometimes equivalent and interchangeable. He writes, "I take them as something real." They have personalities; the foot "is a member of a line-body," "a prosodic entity":

> But . . . there abide these three—iamb, trochee, and anapaest—in the English aristocracy of poetry. The iamb is with us the staple of poetic life: it will do any work, take on any colour, prove itself at need the equal of the other two, which it often summons to reinforce it. The trochee is the passion of life; not easily adaptable by itself, except for special moments, comic or tragic, frivolous or plaintive, as it chooses, but seasoning and inspiriting the iamb constantly and yet strangely. And the anapaest is the glory of life, though its uses differ in glory.[65]

Here, Saintsbury uses patriotic and Biblical rhetoric and admits what he has been subtly insisting all along, or subtly hoping to convince us that we already knew: English meter is (just like Latin or Greek) something "aristocratic," and it also requires faith. (The allusion to St. Paul particularly aligns the iamb with "faith.")[66] Not only are these three feet singled out as equivalent to the glories of classical meter, but they are imbued with the nationalistic characteristics of a military regiment: they will do their duty, they will support one another, they will do any work. His particularly Edwardian emphasis on the English-ness of English meter—to the level of the dutiful iamb—plays into the expectations of poetry's nationally educated audience in the years leading up to the First World War. By refusing to engage with the complexity of English meter, we can read Saintsbury's *History* as an attempt at stabilization for the healthy, collective, patriotic view of English meter and, by extension, English poetry's role as a stabilizing, patriotic force in national culture. Saintsbury's equivocation and failure in the *History*, however, reveals deeper insecurity that all prosodic investigations and perhaps even all national identifications, no matter how ardently we assert that they are "natural," are matters of sheer and stubborn faith—unstable, historically contingent categories that may be artificial constructions both then and now.

So far we've seen how Bridges and Saintsbury can be used to represent two opposing camps in the "Prosody Wars." Saintsbury sought a purely "English" metrical scheme that depended upon a perpetuation of the class differences in education, whereas Bridges sought a naturalization of English meter through universal accessibility. Given the climate of the Victorian education system, it is not surprising that Saintsbury's behemoth crusade against a conception of meter flexible enough to incorporate the dynamics of time and the differences of class and nationality took precedence. The Victorian bias—that a mind un-trained in classics was somehow unprepared for the larger world—persisted long into the Edwardian and Georgian periods and particularly during the First World War.[67] Despite the growing popularity of English as an efficient means to educate the masses and even, toward the turn of the century, the creation of English departments in the major universities, the association be-tween the elite public schools and classical education remained secure, creat-ing a network of gentlemen whose academic knowledge was specific to the insulated world of their particular alma mater.

The characteristics of a classical education went beyond the mere acquisi-tion of Latin and Greek; it included a nostalgia for past glory directly tied to England's potential for greatness, a guarantee of postgraduate success and a mark of refined taste, rigorous study based on approved pedagogical methods meant to discipline the character of young men, a stubborn and determined ignorance of English literature (which was not yet a course of study at Oxford when Bridges and Saintsbury were students there),[68] and specialized academic knowledge down to the particular pronunciation of Latin at each school. And yet, during Bridges's and Saintsbury's lifetimes, the characteristics of classical learning would be adopted, altered, defended, and questioned by the progress of English literature and language as an alternative seat of humanist learning. Their ideas about English prosody and how it should be taught must be under-stood, in part, as a consequence of the ways that their generation was marked by the loss of, and anticipatory nostalgia for, the valuable English characteris-tics that were seen as a unique result of a classical education.

And yet, despite the ways Bridges was clearly marked by his classical educa-tion, he did not believe in classical pedagogy, nor did he think that Greek should be compulsory by any means. In 1919, Bridges summarized his posi-tion in a humorous poem: "For teachers know examination / To be the crown of education: / Since minds like plants cannot be trusted / To keep their root-lets well adjusted, / They who would rear them must examine'em / To gauge th'effect of what they cram in 'em."[69] Methods of classical education shifted away from the turn-of-the-eighteenth-century model: boys between the ages of five and eleven were drilled in Latin and Greek so that they could enter the public schools, commune with the greats, and become model citizens. Latin was taught first, then Greek through the Latin. Efficiency prevented any detailed understanding of the particulars of vocalized Greek and Latin (the teacher's "pronunciation" was often good enough for the pupils), and toward the late nineteenth century even the Greek and Latin grammars were composed in English rather than Latin, reflecting the premium placed on pedagogical efficiency. The pedagogical methods of classical education at the turn of the nineteenth century were admired and abhorred, but despite all external pressures, promoters and detractors alike could not escape the entrenched association between classical education and rules, measure, and order.

In this context, Bridges, who attended Eton in the late 1850s and early 1860s, was seen as "one of the finest products that the social and educational caste system of England could produce."[70] Bridges and Saintsbury shared a typical classical education (and a birthday).[71] The pedagogic model for teaching Latin and Greek—through memorization, translation, and composition—is one obvious cause of the brewing disdain for classical pedagogy at the end of the nineteenth and beginning of the twentieth century; outdated methodologies especially marginalized the teaching of Greek.[72] James Brinsley-Richards, a colleague of Bridges at Eton who seems only to be known for his popular memoir, *Seven Years at Eton* (1857–64) confessed, "in truth we learned very little, beyond maundering by rote Latin rules as many as were wanted for the day's lessons; and from day to day we forgot what we had committed to our tongues' tips the day before."[73] The students learned physically "by rote," yet did not commit the rules to memory; the vocalized discipline of language intending to shape the young pupil's mind through its rigid form, according to this memoir, does not even reach the student's mind. Indeed, the rules were so transient in Brinsley-Richards's mind that they came alive only on the "tongue-tips" of the students; the dead languages resuscitated only when spoken, not awakened by any nostalgic memory of comprehension or humanistic transformation. Classical pedagogy turned classical verse forms into abstractions that symbolized more than they actually meant.

Bridges became poet laureate in 1913 and the first poem that he published, "Flycatchers," was significant both because within it he states his disdain for the pedagogical methods of the classical education he received but also because in publishing the poem in Harold Monro's *Poetry and Drama* he aligns himself with a younger generation whose civilizing literature was English and who did not necessarily believe in the necessity of the classical traditions.[74] In "Flycatchers," Bridges recalls "a time sixty summers ago / When, a young chubby chap, I sat just so / With others on a school-form rank'd in a row, / Not less eager and hungry than you."[75] The pupils, "ranked" by their progress in class and ordered in a row, are figured as birds: "sweet pretty fledglings, perched on the rail arow / expectantly happy" (l. 1) and waiting for the professor to endow them with knowledge. But the professor is no mystical scholar, he is here an "authoritative old wise-acre" who "stood over us and from a desk fed us with flies" (l. 10):

> Dead flies — such as litter the library south-window,
> That buzzed at the panes until they fell stiff-baked on the sill,
> Or are roll'd up asleep i'the blinds at sunrise,
> Or wafer'd flat in a shrunken folio.
> A dry biped he was, nurtured likewise   15
> On skins and skeletons, stale from top to toe
> With all manner of rubbish and all manner of lies.

Both a critique of "dry as dust pedantry" and an "experimental poem" in what he calls "free rhythm,"[76] the poem exploits the pervading early twentieth-century anticlassical sentiment in subject matter, turning Greek and Latin words into corpses exhumed for each young generation of hopeful birds. The useless continuity of the system, in which the professors teach what they were taught to keep the system alive, is condemned as "rubbish and lies," the dead letters literally "litter," and the classical "fly leaves" are transformed into dead flies. The professor is reduced to his scientific and metrical classification of "a dry biped," (as in "two feet") inhumanly droning grammatical shapes, skins, and skeletons into the pupils.

Though the meter of the poem is, in 1913, still undeveloped, it previews Bridges's later experiments in neo-Miltonic syllabics, the lines not adhering to a strict syllabic count as we understand it today, but instead observing the system of English quantity that Bridges had carefully worked out in his study of Milton's prosody. The formal tension in this poem is not necessarily between tradition and experiment; both accentual and syllabic patterns are irregular, which brings the all too regular rhyme to the forefront (an effect that falls out of Bridges's later verses entirely). As if to mimic the droning repetition of a typical lesson, Bridges ends the majority of his lines with rhymes on the word "row," a mockery of the kind of order expected in the classroom: arow, below, ago, so, row, trow, aglow, window, folio, toe. The archaic "trow" appears as a rhythmic jolt, to call attention to the artificiality of the scheme and the poet casting for a word to fit into his composition. The repeated "oh" sounds add a sickening echo of the possibility of punishment, as in line 13, "buzzed at the panes until they fell stiff-baked on the sill" (read as "pains") echoes both physical consequence and a futile longing for escape. The only other repeated rhyme in the poem is "flies," appearing always with the image of being fed, in lines 4, 11, and 18. We hear "lies" in "flies," of course, lies that have been repeated from generation to generation. No other sound is heard, here, other than the buzzing to escape; the poem confirms the assertions that the imposition of classical grammatical forms was something forced in by the mouth. Even the "eye" sound of "lies/flies" is stifled, "blind[s] at sunrise," in the dark turn at the end. The stiff figure of the professor is ironically "nurtured likewise"—withered, unwise, dry with the old lies.

Though Bridges had a deep and abiding interest in the classics, classical meters, and foreign verse forms in general, he saw in Milton's prosody a way that English verse might break free from its artificial reliance on classical scansion. Along with Hopkins, Bridges was avidly engaged in thinking through the problems that a purely "English" system of scansion presented. Why do we scan based on the classical model, a model that must be inaccurate, since we have no conception of how a dead language sounds? *Milton's Prosody* became a salvo for English poetry's misunderstanding of classical meter and an attempt to put forth new ideas for English prosody on a broad scale. Saintsbury, on the other hand, preferred to replace the abstraction of classical meter with the abstraction of English meter, taking for granted that enough of England would be properly trained to hear with the kind of classical ear he imagined. Bridges's proposals, in a series of appendices added to and revised for each edition of the book, attempt to clarify and purify what he saw as the gross miseducation of the English ear in accepting the inaccurate and abstract system based on the classical model and promoted by Saintsbury. In sum, Bridges believed that a better understanding of meter might mediate between the classical languages and English. In his introduction to the 1901 edition, he writes, "[i]f we consider how familiar classical poetry is to English poets and how much it influences their practice, this definition of the English syllables [along the lines Stone proposes] is a necessary study for those who, through habits of English pronunciation, consciously or unconsciously misread classical verse."[77] The publication and subsequent popularity of these pamphlets should be read as an anticipatory protest against the 1902 Education Act, in which compulsory Latin and Greek, modeled on what Stone and Bridges both agreed was a false understanding of classical prosody, was again enforced by the state. Bridges complained to Henry Bradley, editor of the *OED*, in 1904: "I was disappointed in the result of voting on the compulsory Greek. We shall have our way in all these matters in a few years, if we stick to it. It vexes me that they are bothering my boy with Greek, he has only just got over his Latin troubles. . . . His time is being wasted—and most boys are in the same condition."[78] In this 1904 letter, we see that Bridges still has some faith that reform is possible, though he has little faith that schoolmasters will be able to give his son an accurate understanding of Latin and Greek. But reform was not likely; between 1904 and the First World War, schools promoted an increasingly abstract model for English meter and the modernist avant-garde arose to protest the metronome of similar-sounding metrical poetry that they wrongly associated with Victorian poetics. The potential for dynamism, for reformed phonetic spelling and standardized pronunciation, and for a truly technical and linguistic understanding of the various possibilities for English prosody, lost out to the pedagogic and patriotic necessities of the Edwardian period. Bridges's interests became the purview of the scientific study of prosody that evolved away from English departments and into linguistics departments in the 1920s. Saintsbury's model of an abstract, interpretive, and essentially nationalistic model is that which we have inherited as our traditional prosody in English departments to this day.

And yet Saintsbury's particularly Edwardian emphasis on the Englishness of English meter—to the level of the dutiful iamb—plays into the expectations of poetry's nationally educated audience in the years leading up to the First World War. By refusing to engage with the complexity of English meter, we can read Saintsbury's *History* as stabilizing for the healthy, collective, patriotic view of English meter and poetry's role in national culture. Saintsbury popularized the theory that meter is interpretive, subjective. The laws of verse, variously argued and defended in the Victorian period as universal, began to emerge in the Edwardian period as a manifestation of the individuality so valued by the culture of the twentieth century. Despite the complexities and oversimplifications of the prosody wars, the phenomenon of actual war artificially consolidated the pedagogical model for meter; the need for order and discipline in education outweighed that of defining a metrical category as complex as the evolving Edwardian culture it represented. Rather than agree with his reviewers that he could have done more to settle the matter, we might read Saintsbury's reticence to provide a technical answer to the problem of prosody as a symptom of a deeper anxiety at the beginning of the twentieth century—that all prosodic investigations, and perhaps even all national identifications, were matters of sheer and stubborn faith.

❧ 4 ❧

The Discipline of Meter

Young men, whose knowledge of grammar, of the minutest details of geographical and historical facts, and above all of mathematics, is surprising, often cannot paraphrase a plain passage of prose or poetry without totally misapprehending it, or write half a page of composition on any subject without falling into gross blunders of taste and expression. I cannot but think that, with a body of young men so highly instructed, too little attention has hitherto been paid to this side of the education; the side through which it chiefly forms the character. . . . I am sure that the study of portions of the best English authors and composition, might with advantage be made a part of their regular course of instruction to a much greater degree than it is at present. Such a training would elevate and humanise a number of young men, who, at present . . . are wholly uncultivated; and it would have the great social advantage of tending to bring them into intellectual sympathy with the educated of the upper classes.
—Matthew Arnold, *General Report for 1852*

Certainly the appetite for ballads and the power of getting sustenance from them in very early life, and a love for other kinds of poetry, does not necessarily follow in later years.
—Henry Newbolt, "British Ballads," *English Review*

Woe be to him who makes a hell of this earthly paradise, who plants the fair meadows of poesy with the thorn of grammar, the briar of etymology, and the prickly, unappetizing thistle of historical notation, who mars the face of Beauty herself with the mask of learned triviality, so that the children come to think of her, their elder sister, as a hideous witch, a harsh taskmistress.
—J. Dover Wilson, "Poetry and the Child," *The English Association Pamphlet*

Patriotic Pedagogy

The "prosody wars" I describe in chapter 3 run parallel to a split among educational theorists and practitioners about the uses of English poetry in the state-funded classroom. Whereas some still believed in the character building and disciplinary aspects of teaching classical languages through the rote learning of verse forms well into the twentieth century, around the turn of the century many educational theorists began to see an opportunity in the teaching of English poetry to promote a kind of "ordered liberty," especially among younger students. English poetry in and outside of the classroom, once freed from the comparison to classical poetry, sustained its own division between "verses" (used mainly for memorization, discipline or drill, and the history lesson) and "poetry," which represented the best of English literature but that might prove too difficult for the younger student whose mind had not been conditioned by convention. English meter was the center point of this growing distinction; seen as at once naturally felt and artificially imposed, the curriculum of versification, still largely based on the classical model of scansion in English grammar books, diminished in the English literature classroom and was replaced by a concept of meter that imagined poetic rhythm as that which could be felt naturally without having to understand the potentially off-putting terms used to name those rhythms.[1]

Traditional accounts of the late nineteenth- and early twentieth-century "rise of English"[2] have exposed the ideologies behind English literary study on a broad scale. From the beginning of institutionalized English literary education—ostensibly with Lord Macaulay's great "Minute on Education" in 1835 through Matthew Arnold's *Culture and Anarchy* in 1869—great works of literature, and especially poetry, were believed to have the power to civilize and shape the otherwise disordered minds of the masses and thus safeguard English society from "savages" (or the philistine working class), a sentiment with roots in the writing of Samuel Johnson, William Wordsworth, and John Stuart Mill, among others. Chris Baldick, in *The Social Mission of English Studies 1848–1932*, outlines how schools that promoted English studies were seen as part of the "protection of society," a "guarantor of social stability," and reveals how Macaulay believed that teachers should be trained and paid by the state on the same principle as soldiers.[3] Both Baldick and Terry Eagleton note that English was first taught at working men's colleges, and that the ideologies of "protecting" society not only meant civilizing the working classes but also teaching them to defend the empire. John Churtin Collins, himself at one time an extension lecturer for working men's colleges, wrote in his 1891 manifesto, *The Study of English Literature* (a plea to establish a school for English at Oxford): "[The people] need political culture, instruction, that is to say, in what pertains to their relation to the State, to their duties as citizens; and they need also to be impressed sentimentally by having the presentation in legend and history of heroic and patriotic example brought vividly and attractively before them."[4]

Though there is a vast field of literature about the complicated history of English education, the rise of English as a discipline in the elite public schools, the battle for English in the universities, and literacy and learning among the working classes, scholars have tended to generalize about the ascendancy and importance of poetry as a civilizing power in the Arnoldian sense, on the one hand, and the "heroic and patriotic" ideologies of Englishness in the state-funded classrooms of the lower and middle classes, on the other.[5] Looking only at the examinations based on the Revised Code (the series of reforms in the 1860s called "payment by results," which rewarded schools for passing their students through tests in "reading, writing, and arithmetic"), we miss the more nuanced, metrical ways that English poetry performed patriotic ideologies in the state-funded classroom. Arnold, like many prosodists I described in the previous chapter, valorized the formative disciplinary aspects of the poetry recitation lesson *not* because of the subject matter of the poems but because of an idealized concept of rhythm. The poetry in the English language classroom, despite its questionable metrical quality, contained lessons meant to imprint good English morals (the progress of the child into citizen) or historical narratives that joined England's military past to the sturdy rhythms of school poems (the progress of the nation). In this period, I argue, we can trace a public conception of English verse form that has little to do with the controversies about iambs and trochees that raged throughout the nineteenth and early twentieth centuries, and everything to do with a concept of national history, rhythmically marching through time to a naturally, instinctively felt "beat." This "beat" had been argued by Edwin Guest and his followers (practitioners of "Guestianity," as Saintsbury derisively calls them) to be "native" to England as opposed to the foreign imposition of classical verse forms and, an obsession with the "beat" as a native instinct mapped easily onto the philological fascination with Anglo-Saxon origins though it had existed as "emphasis" and "accent" in prosodic discourse prior to the nineteenth century. Recall that Guest's *A History of English Rhythms* was published in 1838; in 1882, Walter William Skeat, a prominent Cambridge professor of Anglo-Saxon (and editor of the *Etymological English Dictionary* from 1879–82, and 1910), reprinted it.[6] Saxon-centric accounts of England's history in the nineteenth century (above all, as Asa Briggs has noted, in radical writing)[7] trickled into the late nineteenth-century classroom, where textbooks in history that were used primarily in the state-funded schools promoted racial Anglo-Saxonism as English national identity.[8]

Outside the classroom, the controversy about how to define or measure the beat, or accent, concerned prosodists, physiologists, and educators well into the twentieth century. But concurrently, for the average schoolchild, this beat was simply, naturally "English." The public conception of English rhythm obfuscated the more complicated distinctions between accent and quantity, fetishizing the metrical "ictus" (defined by Patmore in 1857 as the "beat" and abstracted to mean "accent," as in a beat that is "marked by accent," according to Patmore)[9] as the primary "pulse" of English poetry and national culture through the ages. The circulation of poetry with a distinctive stress-based rhythm—begun in classroom verses, thematized in poetry by Henry Newbolt, and later, poets as diverse as Edward Thomas, Thomas Hardy, and Jessie Pope, and satirized in newspapers tired of the overwhelming outpouring of patriotic poetry from the front—became associated with English patriotism and, more generally, with English meter, though it is altogether distinct from the pedantic practice of scanning poetry along classical lines.

Newbolt—poet, prosodist, legislator, and propagandist—emerges as a central and complicated figure whose work in all of these domains weaves a complicated tapestry for the subsequent future of English meter in the national imagination. Unlike Bridges (who compromised his metrical beliefs when he published poems for the propaganda office), Newbolt both promoted and capitalized on his role as a public poet marching to a particularly English drum. The audience for poetry, at first attracted to but then powerfully repelled by the patriotic impulse of his verse and the thousands of others like it, developed a distaste for public "verse" in general and the amateur "versifiers" who produced it. If simple, often ballad-like English patriotic verses were for the masses, then the elite classes (and the "modernists") began to imagine that "Poetry" required a redemption that could only be achieved by the avoidance of regular rhythm and patriotic themes. Pound's line, "to break the pentameter, that was the first heave,"[10] has been largely read as a salvo against outdated Victorian metrical regularity; but the line itself is in pentameter: "to BREAK the penTAMeter, THAT was the FIRST HEAVE," and shows that neither Pound's reading of the nineteenth century, nor our reading of the modernist reaction "against" meter, is as sharply defined as it seems. Rather than reading the modernist "heave" as a break, this chapter complicates and enriches our understanding of a period in which the generic understanding of English poetry was redefined, and shows the important ways that English meter was central to that redefinition. One of the stakes of English meter in this period is something quite different than our histories of poetics have imagined—not a progress toward liberated modernist and postmodern form, nor a rejection of Victorian form, but rather a fierce attention to a part of poetic form that has been hidden in plain sight: the beat.

Matthew Arnold's Metrical Intimacy

The 1861 Newcastle Commission "on the state of popular education in England" recommended that student teachers study English "just as the Greek and Latin Classics are read in superior private schools."[11] In 1867, English Literature was introduced as an optional special subject in schools, but according to the Schools Enquiry Commission Report (otherwise known as the Taunton Report) published in 1868, neither Latin nor Greek were taught in nearly half of the endowed grammar schools.[12] In 1870, Forster's Education Act encouraged the expansion of elementary education and the following year, English literature was recognized as a class subject in the upper three grades (standards four through six) of the now-compulsory elementary schools (47–48). Because of pressure from the "payment by results" scheme of the 1862 Revised

Code, the legislation of which was administered by "her majesty's inspectors" (HMIs), more traditional prescriptive grammar books were gradually replaced in the late nineteenth century by "readers" geared toward helping the students pass their exams in "the three Rs." In his 1867 General Inspector's Report, Matthew Arnold disparages the type of popular poetry that children in the fifth form read aloud for examination: "[p]erhaps it may be permitted to an ex-professor of poetry to remark that in general the choice of poetry in these books is especially bad. . . . When one thinks how noble and admirable a thing genuine popular poetry is, it is provoking to think that such rubbish as this should be palmed off on a poor child for it with any apparent sanction from the Education Department and its grants."[13]

This report was reprinted in the magazine, *The Museum*, as "Teachers and the Education Bill," one of many articles that represented a general concern about the administration and curriculum of the state-funded school system, about the place of English in the public schools and universities, and about the position of both the subject of English and the newly educated English middle-class subject in the empire. Though poetry recitation was not mandated as part of specific examinations until 1875 (and English literature added to the list of "specific subjects" in 1876), Arnold's Inspectors' Reports, again and again, single out poetry as a civilizing and cultivating force in the state-funded classroom. Arnold, like Bridges, Saintsbury, and Newbolt, imagined English poetry through their classical training; that is, they felt, as did many others of their generation, that English literature was best understood and appreciated after substantial training in the classics. But Arnold's classical ideals were compromised by the realities of working-class education, and in place of the rigors of memorizing classical verse forms Arnold imagined that memorizing English poetry could provide some measure of the mental discipline that the classics had provided the upper classes.

According to the *Classified Catalogue of School, College, Classical, Technical, and General Education Works*, English grammars slowly began to replace classical grammars toward the end of the nineteenth century, and English recitation readers and anthologies of poetry became equally as important as books that only covered English grammar.[14] English poetry was taught as a recitation subject, not as a means to understanding the language, as it would have been for the study of classics. Ian Michael and Manfred Görlach have begun to collect information about English grammar books published in the nineteenth century (they estimate that almost 2,000 texts existed).[15] A study of English grammar books in the United States before 1850 shows that "prosody," as the fourth part of the traditional textbook, only occupied 7 percent of the book when it was included at all. The "rubbish" that Arnold derided, therefore, did not accompany any lesson in English prosody or pronunciation; rather, the poetry in the "standard readers" of state-funded schools was not part of a lesson in poetry at all.

Though Arnold does not name the poem or the book, he does say that the "specimen of popular poetry" he disparages, titled "My Native Land," comes from a "Fifth Standard book of a series much in vogue."[16] One such series "much in vogue" was *Chambers's Narrative Series of Standard Reading Books, specially adapted to the Requirements of the Revised Code including those in Writing, Arithmetic, and Dictation* (1863).[17] The editors of *Chambers* anticipate Arnold's dismay at the class of poetry found in the readers. In the introductions to the *Standard Reading Books* for Standard III, the preface orients the teacher, stating "a few of the simpler trisyllables were used in Standard II. In Standard III they are more freely used. . . .The verses are religious, moral, and humorous, and will be found free from errors of taste at least, though scarcely meriting the name of Poetry. In Standard IV poetry, in the proper sense of the word, for the first time appears" (iii). The preface to Standard IV states: "[p]oetry suitable for children now takes the place of what in the earlier books cannot be dignified by a higher name than verses" (iii). Verses do not "merit" the distinction of being named "Poetry"; they are meant to teach both religion and morality, as well as help students learn to say more complex trisyllabic words. In the table of contents for Standards IV through VI, poetry and verse appear together, intermingled but distinguished by a parenthetical, as in "Lucy Gray" (poetry) or "Little White Lily" (verse). Most of the verses are anonymous, and some of the anonymous verses are attributed to a certain tradition, as in: "Old Ballad" or "Old Song," (as opposed to the occasional attribution "From the French"). A host of generic assumptions go into the building of this particular reader pertaining to songs, ballads, and poetry with a capital "P," but it is clear that many songs and verses are intended to teach the proper "received" pronunciation that was gaining ground in the latter half of the nineteenth century, along with religious, moral, and, significantly and increasingly, patriotic values. "My Native Land," not attributed to an author, is incorrectly named "A Song" by the editors, as if to emphasize that it is not to be mistaken for a "poem." Arnold prints the entire poem in his report, as if to mock it:

MY NATIVE LAND

She is a rich and rare land
Oh! She is a fresh and fair land,
She is a dear and rare land,
This native land of mine.
No men than hers are braver,   5
The women's hearts ne'er waver;
I'd freely die to save her,
And think my lot divine.
She's not a dull or cold land,
No, she's a warm and bold land;   10

Oh! She's a true and old land,
This native land of mine.
Oh! She's a fresh and fair land,
Oh! She's a true and rare land,
Yes, she's a rare and fair land   15
This native land of mine.

The "song" "My Land" is by Irish nationalist poet Thomas Davis,[18] and so the addition of "Native" to the title shows the textbook editors are either unaware that Davis's land is Ireland, not England, or they are intentionally erasing the Irish national aim, and by erasing Davis's name they appropriate the poem (and the country) into a three-beat English patriotism.

Davis had been praised over ten years earlier in an *Irish Quarterly Review* (1855) article as one "gifted with the power to awaken a nation to a sense of its own position, or to fill the mind of a people with proud consciousness of the glory which belongs to them."[19] The reviewer writes that Davis's poems possess "everything which ballad poetry ought to possess; a certain happy elasticity of rythm [*sic*], irrepressible animation, energetic and appropriate phraseology, and a racy tone which is truly the literary counterpart of the conversational character of the Irish peasantry" (700). Finally, "unworthy of his country must he be who can read the inspiring lyrics of Davis without feeling his heart beat high with patriotic emotion, and without experiencing animative impulsive sympathy with many of the heroic sentiments which they breathe." The *Irish Quarterly* reviewer singles out Davis's "ballad" as one that could animate the impulses—the pulses, even—of the Irish peasantry, infusing their veins with nationalist blood and bringing the country to life and glory. Erasing the "nation" of Ireland from "My Land" and adding "Native" to the title (lifted gently from the poem's refrain) specifically affected the impressionable English school children of 1867. Similarly, readers of Arnold's 1868 article in *The Museum* (in which the poem is reprinted in full) were invited to view the poem as a particularly unworthy example of what Arnold found "genuine" and "noble" in poetry. As opposed to Arnold's view of "poetry," Davis's "verse," even more of a "ballad" when given an anonymous author by the *Chambers* editor, inspires the collective readership in the classroom to feel something, well, collective. Though Lionel Trilling has argued that Arnold "embraced the whole of the racial assumption and was at pains to show how the English are an amalgam of several "bloods"—German, Norman, Celtic," in his discussion of poetry it is the subtlety of more subdued accents and more versatile versification that Arnold values in his poetry, even if the poem's form might display traces of these various elements.[20] Though Arnold finds Davis's verses unworthy of the lower and middle classes in the late 1860s, by the turn of the century patriotic and heroic verses would infuse the textbooks of the state-funded English classrooms, and even Arnold would begin to come around to the *Irish Quarterly* reviewer's opinion that verses could help the collective feel a sort of "animative, impulsive sympathy" with the nation.

We can see Arnold's increasing frustration with the unmet pedagogic potential of English literature and especially poetry in his reports into the 1880s—frustration in no small part generated because of his public position as the poet-critic who would replace the nation's religion with its "unconscious poetry." In his now famous statement from the introduction to another school text, Thomas Ward's 1881 multivolume *The English Poets,* Arnold writes, "the future of poetry is immense, because in poetry, where it is worthy of its high destinies, our race, as time goes on, will find an ever surer and surer stay."[21] In his 1878 General Report, three years earlier, Arnold makes a case for the formative power of memorizing poetry and argues against those who find it out-of-date:

> Learning by heart is often called, disparagingly, learning by *rote* and is treated as an old fashioned, unintelligent exercise, and a waste of time. It is an exercise to which I attach great value, and it tends, I am glad to say, to become general in the schools of my district, partly because the teachers know that I am in strong favor of it. Poetry is almost always taken for this exercise, not prose; and when so little is done in the way of learning by heart, poetry should certainly have the preference.... [I]n almost all inspected schools, in my district at any rate, the whole upper part of the school would each year learn by heart from one to three hundred lines of good poetry.... The advantages of this to me seem indisputable. If we consider it, the bulk of the secular instruction given in our elementary schools has nothing of that formative character which in education is demanded.... But good poetry is formative; it has, too, the precious power of acting by itself and in a way managed by nature, not through the instrumentality of that somewhat terrible character, the scientific educator. I believe that even the rhythm and diction of good poetry are capable of exercising some formal effect, even though the sense be imperfectly understood.... [A]n effort should be made for this one exercise, to fix the standard high. Gray's *Elegy* and extracts from Shakespeare should be chosen in preference to the poetry of Scott and Mrs. Hemans, and very much of the poetry in our present school reading books should be entirely rejected.[22]

Just as Davis's Irish ballad was held up for derision, the works of popular Scottish poet Walter Scott and popular "poetess" Felicia Hemans, though they proliferated in "Standard" readers[23] do not measure up to Arnold's high standard for the kind of poetry that "exercise[s] some formal effect" through "rhythm and diction." Shakespeare and Gray might be too difficult, but the rhythm will act on its own "even though the sense be imperfectly understood."

Rhythm, itself perhaps only understood by Arnold as more subtly manipulated rhythm, made into good English meters by the best English authors, will have a "natural" effect that will shape the student without them even knowing that it is happening; this is similar to the belief that through the disciplinary rigors of mastering classical versification, the English pupil need not understand the Latin poetry he or she is learning, as long as it exercises the correct disciplinary effect. This "natural" effect is related to the uses of metrical mnemonics discussed in chapter 1: "a rhyme may glide into the mind / like wedge into the oak, / Op'ning a broad, marked path for prose." This verse, from Jane Bourne's *Granny's History of Rhyme*, carries within it multiple discourses that were circulating in the nineteenth century: that form's effect could be insidious (gliding) and act upon you without your knowledge; that, as in the case of Hopkins's poetics, it could be violent and striking (a wedge into an oak); and that it was in some way linked to the native body of the English reader.[24] Arnold, along with hundreds of scholars after him, does not pause to consider the ways that the easily apprehended rhythmic narratives of Hemans and Scott secure their popularity with the non–classically trained masses. Two years later, Arnold aligns this specialized "formal effect" with discipline directly. Rhythm and diction—in good poetry—might discipline the student to become the right kind of English citizen:

> The acquisition of good poetry is a discipline which works deeper than any other discipline in the range of work in our schools; more than any other, too, it works of itself, is independent of the school teacher, and cannot be spoiled by pedantry and injudiciousness on his part. . . . Good poetry does undoubtedly tend to form the soul and character; it tends to beget a love of beauty and of truth in alliance together, it suggests, however indirectly, high and noble principles of action, and it inspires the emotion so helpful in making principles operative. Hence its extreme importance to all of us; but in our elementary schools its importance seems to be at present quite extraordinary.[25]

Arnold insists on "good poetry" to open "the soul and imagination" (1878, 192) yet either fails to notice or chooses not to see how the tropes of form and discipline in English poetry are enacted through themes of discipline and duty in the poems the students actually read, as well as in their physical classroom activities. Unlike the awareness and understanding of metrical form on which Bridges insists for metrical "mastery," for Arnold the meters of good poetry, its "rhythm and diction," will form a superior character naturally, subtly, as if the meter will be intimately folded into the student's consciousness. Though he does not name "meter" directly, it is the meter that clearly disciplines the student in a differently classical sense or, rather, without the requirement of the student sensing that he is being disciplined or formed at all. The power of this metrical intimacy to civilize is a crucial benefit, for Arnold, of good English poetry.[26]

The poetry Arnold derides contains what becomes rhythmic ideologies that are present in the songs and chants that accompanied military—sometimes called metrical—drills in the late nineteenth and early twentieth centuries. Military drills had been introduced in schools as early as 1871 and were hugely popular in the Edwardian era. The popularity of discipline and drill in state-funded elementary schools, private grammar schools, and "public schools," has been the subject of many studies by J. A. Mangan, who argues that game culture is part of the general rise of an English culture of masculinity based on school sport.[27] This masculine centrism and the insertion of tactical prowess into education presages the increased militarism of pedagogical methods. Mangan often uses Newbolt's poetry as an example of military athletic culture, particularly his famous poem, "Vitae Lampada," which equates war to a public school cricket match. John M. Mackenzie, Pamela Horn, and Stephen Heathorn have looked at drill culture as inculcation into a national identity tied crucially to the empire.[28] The Earl of Meath, who founded the "Lad's Drill Association" in 1895, also founded the "Empire Day" movement that Horn and Tricia Lootens[29] note, flourished in the Edwardian era as a result of the pervasive insecurity about the physical degeneracy of English soldiers after the failures of the Boer War. Though military drill in schools promoted a very different kind of discipline than that which Arnold imagines for recitation, I am interested in the moments when physical discipline (drill marching) and mental discipline (recitation) join together. The "National Service League" movement of the Edwardian era began around the passage of the 1902 Education Act, which reintroduced the study of classics as a subject in the national language classroom. General Earl Roberts pleaded in protest that compulsory classical subjects be replaced with compulsory military drill in schools[30]; Saintsbury and Roberts exchanged quite a few letters and Rudyard Kipling published a tribute to him in 1914, titled "Lord Roberts," which included the lines "Never again the war-wise face, / The weighed and urgent word / That pleased in the market-place — / Pleaded and was not heard!"[31] Its militaristic aspects, as well as the way poetry could be used in the direct service of the nation, were highly relevant in the period from the Boer War until the First World War and were, indeed, a disciplinary aspect of the imperial project.

Even before the turn of the century, rhythmic movement and imperialist sentiment were joined in slim volumes containing physical exercises intended for school use. Veronica Vassey's *Tiny Verses for Tiny Workers* (1898), is one such handbook. The books usually included a "gun drill" for boys, to be practiced with wooden rifles, and "fan" or "scarf" drills for girls. Boys' drills also included wooden exercise dumbbells, and both boys and girls marched, were taught to stand at "attention," and to pace according to different musical time. Below are two examples from Vassey's book:

GUN DRILL (for boys)
We shall be soldiers   Enter boys with guns.
With our guns,
We'll show you how we fight,   Then follows a gun-drill, accompanied
And guard our Queen   by some bright air on piano
And country dear,
For England's good is might.   March off to music.

SCARF DRILL (for girls)
Oh, see our pretty   Enter girls with coloured scarves
Coloured scarves,
We hold them at each end;
We'll dance, and sing,   Scarf drill follows
And show you all
How easily we bend.   March off to music.

We see here a progression from recitation to exercise class in the curriculum of the day, from the theme of Davis's "she is a rich and rare land" to the marching accompaniment of "we shall be soldiers with our guns." Military drills were often accompanied by patriotic songs like "God Save the Queen." Students marched to create the form of a flag, particularly for Empire Day (with the girls in one color and the boys in another) or to create other patriotic formations—an anchor to represent England's nautical prowess, for example.

What has gone unremarked about the drill movement and the subsequent popularity of Empire Day was the prominence of poetic recitation. In *The Victorian and Edwardian Schoolchild*, Pamela Horn outlines how patriotic poetry and imperial nostalgia were joined with the celebration of Empire Day.[32] A typically Edwardian phenomenon, Empire Day ceremonies spread to over half of the state-funded schools by 1907. The celebrations included hoisting and saluting the Union flag and singing the national anthem and other patriotic songs. Addresses were given to the children by visiting speakers on the duties of British citizenship and upon some aspect of the empire. Recitation of a poem illustrative of "heroic duty and self-sacrifice on behalf of the nation" followed. Proceedings concluded with a rendering of Rudyard Kipling's "Recessional," which, as Lootens points out, had entered not only the *Oxford Book of English Verse* but also the hymn book of the Church of England by 1901.[33] Kipling composed "Recessional" for Queen Victoria's diamond jubilee in 1897, and it was recited along with the national anthem:

God of our fathers, known of old,
Lord of our far-flung battle-line,
Beneath whose awful Hand we hold
Dominion over palm and pine
Lord God of Hosts, be with us yet,   5
Lest we forget lest we forget!

The tumult and the shouting dies;
The Captains and the Kings depart:
Still stands Thine ancient sacrifice,
A humble and a contrite heart.   10
Lord God of Hosts, be with us yet,
Lest we forget lest we forget!

Far-called, our navies melt away;
On dune and headland sinks the fire:
Lo, all our pomp of yesterday   15
Is one with Nineveh and Tyre!
Judge of the Nations, spare us yet,
Lest we forget lest we forget!

If, drunk with sight of power, we loose
Wild tongues that have not Thee in awe,   20
Such boastings as the Gentiles use,
Or lesser breeds without the Law
Lord God of Hosts, be with us yet,
Lest we forget lest we forget!

For heathen heart that puts her trust   25
In reeking tube and iron shard,
All valiant dust that builds on dust,
And guarding, calls not Thee to guard,
For frantic boast and foolish word
Thy mercy on Thy People, Lord![34]   30

Kipling was known for his patriotic verses such as "The English Flag," "McAndrews Hymn," and "The Song of the English" and was only later praised (albeit ambivalently) for his metrical virtuosity (T. S. Eliot equated him to Swinburne).[35] At the time "Recessional" was published, critics were uncomfortable praising both his poetic mastery and his subject matter; often the two were confused, as in an 1899 study by Richard Le Gallienne, which praises him as a poet of the people at the same time that he derides the artistry of his poems:

Mr. Kipling is a master of captivating sing-song, a magician of the catches and refrains of melodies that trip and dance, and gaily, or mournfully, or romantically, come and go, there has perhaps been no such master before him in English; and he is this largely because he has had the wisdom to follow Burns, and with many of his ballads to popular or traditional airs, which must be allowed their share of the success. He is, so to say, the Burns, not of steam, but of the music hall song.[36]

Le Gallienne's criticism inspired a number of articles in Kipling's defense, emphasizing the way that "since 'the Recessional' . . . and other poems of that character, he has really become a great national influence."[37] But despite the fighting spirit with which Kipling is often associated, he was critical of empire in the poem that was widely memorized and recited in praise of it. The responsibility—what Kipling elsewhere called the burden—of the British Empire is imagined linguistically, religiously, and even prosodically in "Recessional." Linguistic forgetting, in which tongues are wildly, frantically boasting, equates the uneducated Englishman with the "lesser breed" who is "without the Law"—both the Law of the Lord and the law of the Empire, though, for schoolchildren there was no guarantee that this law included the law of verse.[38] That is, in line 21, his reference is to Romans 1:18 in which the gentiles are instructed not to boast "against the branches. But if thou boast, thou bearest not the root, but the root thee." If the English boast supremacy over the colonies, they forget that it is the colonies that support the Empire. Likewise, if the entire imperial project forgets a higher order, then it will fail. John Le Vay writes that in "Recessional," Kipling is "clearly (though distantly) envisaging the decline and fall of the British empire"[39] and yet the poem serves to revive the Edwardian schoolchild's allegiance to "country and King" by inscribing Kipling's meters in the minds of the impressionable young citizen. Kipling highlights the alliterative four-beat lines throughout the beginning of the poem: "Lord of our far-flung battle-line," (2); "Hand we hold," (3); "palm and pine," (4); "tumult . . . shouting," (7); "Captains and the Kings," (8); "Still stands . . . sacrifice," (9); "humble . . . heart" (10). In the third stanza, as the "far-called" navies melt away, so too does the confident formal alliteration. The warning of stanza 4, beseeching the Lord to "be with us yet" lest the Law is replaced with "wild tongues," stabilizes again by stanza 5 with the "heathen heart" (25) now disciplined into industry, repeating "dust," "dust," "guarding," "guard" and "frantic," "foolish." The pathos of this repetition is also evocative of the forgetting that the poem prescribes; the memorable lines "lest we forget" will not be forgotten, but the poem's warning serves a dual purpose, then: offering an apologia for the "untrained" and volatile tongues that British imperialism has loosed upon the world, and a promise, through repetition, to train English subjects "within the Law" in order to differentiate them from the "heathen heart." Both linguistic and national, Kipling's reiterated verse serves as a reminder that the Edwardian period was fraught with repetitions of linguistic insecurity left over from the late Victorian era. Here, the Arnoldian ideal is realized by the hundreds of schoolchildren who are unable to explain the verses, but who have been subtly and metrically disciplined to believe that they know them naturally.

Following Arnold's hopes for English poetry, though perhaps unknowingly, legislators and reformers toward the end of the century recoiled from any study of English poetry that would repel the young student. P. A. Barnett, an invested inspector of training colleges for schoolmasters and a former English professor, was one of many authorities who wrote educational books and pamphlets around the turn of the century. His *Teaching and Organisation,* (first published in 1897 and reprinted four times before 1910) is subtitled a "Manual of Practice" for teachers. In it, Barnett discards the "mere mental gymnastic" of Latin and Greek and cautions teachers to choose poetic examples in English that "need not offer irresistible philological temptation" but rather appeal to the "general interest." He emphasizes "poetry of the least degree of difficulty" that is "simplest and most familiar in form."[40] Barnett writes,

> We expect the study of literature to put our pupils into intimate relations with high ideals and examples of conduct, to give them a taste for the most refined and purest intellectual pleasures, and to send them away with some knowledge of the form and matter of the highest achievements of thought. . . . [The type of] literary subject fit for the young pupil is the epic or heroic poem, a sweeping pageant of wise kings and brave heroes. (141–42)

The study of English poetry could not only promote the national character but also impart a sense of loyalty, duty, sympathy, and sentiment in the mind of the English schoolchild. Though this subtle inculcation took place through the poetic techniques of meter, rhythm, and rhyme, students were encouraged to avoid anything that would repel them from loving English literature and to see themselves as part of a long line of military heroes, following the rhythms of English verse without question.[41] These educational trends paved the way for the establishment and quick proliferation of the patriotic recitations of Empire Day, and they also secured the almost overnight success of poet Henry Newbolt.

Henry Newbolt's Cultural Metrics

In Newbolt's autobiography, *My World as in My Time* (1932), he recalls walking with his nurse and hearing "a drum and fife at a little distance and saw a small detachment of troops in scarlet, marching away over a wooden bridge."[42]

When he asks his sister why she doesn't look at them, she replies: "I don't like to see them—they're dressed like that to go to their death." The small section of the chapter is titled "The Sound of Death," and he concludes it by meditating: "I had no sense of grief or fear—only a sudden intimation that there was something mysterious happening or about to happen, something which made these soldiers grander and more beautiful, but at the same time took them away for always, beyond our sight and hearing" (9). Newbolt never served in the military; he quit practicing law to write poetry when he achieved near-overnight fame for his 1897 book, *Admirals All*. His poems and stories focused on tales of soldiers and patriotic glory, which meshed perfectly with the expectations of "English literature" for children brought up with the recitation readers and drill culture of the state-funded English education system. Despite this mass-cultural popularity, however, Newbolt was associated more immediately with public school culture, a certain elite class of readers. By uniting both audiences in a metrical community, Newbolt bridged a divide between English literary and classical education. This bridge allowed for the institutionalization of English literary study in ways that Arnold had hoped for—that is, with the study of English literature forming the basis of a sound humanistic education—and in many ways that he had not. Newbolt's poetry was hugely popular and, in its popularity, accessibility, and themes, associated his own brand of swinging English meter to blind English patriotism. Newbolt worked toward institutionalizing English studies, greatly impacting the study of prosody: in 1906 he was instrumental in the creation and activities of the English Association (the organization that ensured English literature would find its role as a school subject); he wrote poetry and novels for the government propaganda office during the First World War; in 1921 he was the primary author of *The Teaching of English in England*; and in the 1920s he edited his own series of schoolbooks for Nelson's. But for Newbolt, as seen in his reaction to the drum-and-fife passage of his autobiography quoted above, Patmore's metrical "ictus" was a drum-beat linked to English military action. The lasting impact of Newbolt on the study of English prosody was not his work to institutionalize English studies, but specifically the way his poetry unified a collective readership for rhythmic, patriotic poetry that embodied Arnold's metrical intimacy so widely and broadly that it became artificial once again, seen and heard as a jingoistic anomaly that clanged falsely in the differently tuned ears of post–First World War readers.

Newbolt's role in popularizing a certain concept of literary Englishness has been viewed as the last gasp of an idealized Victorian imperial stance, from its promotion of the public school values of athleticism and sacrifice to its perceived jingoism.[43] It is commonplace among scholars of experimental Modernism to show how Newbolt's particular brand of blind patriotism and poetic propaganda provided the backdrop against which the international movements of experimental Modernism rebelled.[44] But Newbolt's poems were

merely the most famous example, from the writer with the pedigree of a classical education, of a wide variety of imperial verses circulating in school textbooks and in the public press—a circulation that increased and even exploded
during the First World War. Newbolt's verses trope the drumbeat of steady,
easily perceived rhythm and therefore imagine an English audience that responds to his verses physically, as a patriotic call. Though not all ballads, Newbolt's poems evoke and envision a national collective unified behind "the nation's cause."[45] Yet this unification, while upholding Arnold's aims, ultimately
reverses them.

Though Newbolt experimented in classical meter and syllabic verse, most
reviews of his first book, *Admirals All* (1897), focused on the poem's effect
on the reader: "When he is well set in a swinging metre, Mr. Newbolt's verve
and virility are tremendous," a review in *Literature* states. "Here are all the
qualities of ballad poetry—simplicity, directness, a vivid impression, and the
quick sympathy which leaps from word to eye, and makes every reader yearn
to be up and doing."[46] Newbolt's ballads, like those of Thomas Davis, appealed
directly to the reader's keen sense of duty. Newbolt's "swinging metres" were
successful precisely because they played into Edwardian era patriotic sympathies—simple, crafted narratives that nonetheless satisfied the nation's goals
for poetry. A *Globe* reviewer (quoted in the promotional pages of *Admirals
All*) wrote, "[w]e should like to see these stirring verses in the hands of every
high-spirited youth in the Empire." The poems are "stirring" because of the
way their narratives seem to comment on, at the same time as they are propelled by, Newbolt's distinctively English rhythm. The *Scotsman* reviewer explicitly stated that Newbolt's choice of form was inherently appropriate to the
national spirit it promoted: "All the pieces [in *Admirals All*] are instinct with
the national English spirit. They are written in a sturdy rhythmical speech,
worthy of their high themes."[47] The reviewer's use of the word "instinct" is key
here—the national spirit is imbued in the sturdy rhythms, to use the formal
definition of "instinct," but this saturation of spirit in rhythm is also conceived
as an "instinct"—a pattern that is perceived to be innate or natural rather than
learned.

Newbolt's poetry nationalizes anew Arnold's argument about the beat;
joining rhythm to national duty and sacrifice, Arnold's intimate collectivity is
put on broad and ostentatious display. In the title poem "Admirals All," Newbolt lists admirals who share names with England's poets ("Here's to the bold
and free! / Benbow, Collingwood, Byron, Blake, / Hail to the Kings of the
Sea!"), emphasizing that writing poetry and defending the country are joined.
Newbolt's two most famous poems, "Vitae Lampada" and "Drake's Drum,"
both appear for the first time in *Admirals All* and thematize the power of
rhythm to inspire patriotic, military action. Although both poems have been
and should be read in the context of the Boer War,[48] each circulated widely in
anthologies and were reprinted in Newbolt's books *The Island Race* (1898),

and *Poems, New and Old* (1913-17), and in countless newspapers and war anthologies. "Drake's Drum" resembles one of Kipling's "Barrack-Room Ballads," many of which also contain references to soldiers responding to drums.[49] Unlike Kipling's verses, however, Newbolt's have none of the "deep ambivalence about what Victoria's soldiers were actually fighting for."[50] In the first stanza of "Drake's Drum," Drake is "in a hammock and a thousand mile away" as he dreams "arl the time o' Plymouth Hoe." The poem is easy to read, and before the drum is even introduced, Newbolt varies the first paonic ballad meter with a line that demonstrates thematically how all activities on the ship take place in a steady, rhythmic drum time: "An' the **shore-lights flash**in', an' the **night-tide dash**in.'" All activities (dancing, lights flashing, the tide) take place in rhythmic time with the drum and with the sturdy, alternating four- and three-beat verses, but this line, with its internal rhyme and mirrored three beats, evokes its own ordered echo within the poem.

In the second stanza, when Newbolt shifts the meter from first paeons to tighter trochees before the mirrored three beats, it is in Drake's voice: "Take my drum to England, hang et by the shore, / Strike it when your powder's runnin' low" (ll. 13–14). He then increases the beats again in line 15, as if to imitate the more somber cadence that the drum might produce were he actually needed: "If the **Dons sight Dev**on, I'll **quit** the **port** o'**Heav**en / An **drum** them **up** the **Chan**nel as we **drummed** them long **ago**" (ll. 15–16). Here, to "drum" is to punish and to "drum" the Spanish invaders up the channel is to "beat" them in battle. The first stanza, then, metrically performs the orderly dancing to Drake's drum before his death, and the second metrically performs the drum and the enemy's defeat. In the final stanza, he is "listenin' for the drum" and we are instructed to "call" for Drake in times of national need: "Call him on the deep sea, call him up the Sound, / Call him when ye sail to meet the foe; / Where the old trade's plyin' an' the old flag flyin' / They shall find him ware an' wakin, as they found him long ago!" Any Englishman can "call" on this legend and he will respond "up the Sound." The legend of Drake's drum, written here, evokes the continuity of English loyalty through the ages but also, importantly, likens that legend of English military glory to the ability to hear and repeat a sound.

The poems in *Admirals All* and *This Island Race* were learned by heart, chanted, and sung across England, the Empire, and beyond, with American and English periodicals publishing most of his poetic work during the next year.[51] *Admirals All* first appeared in Elkin Matthews's series, *The Shilling Garland,* in 1897 and ran through four editions in two weeks and twenty-one editions before *The Island Race* was published in 1898. Even before the books were published, individual poems circulated in the *Gentleman's Magazine,* the *Spectator,* and the *Pall Mall Gazette.* Newbolt records in his memoirs *My World as in My Time* how the publication of the poem "Drake's Drum" itself acted as a drum, responding and helping the nation in a time of crisis[52]; he noticed that the placards for the *St. James's Gazette* in which the poem was published bore "two words only, in enormous capitals: as if it were the beat of the Drum made visible" (186). Capitalizing the word "Drum" here aligns the legend of the drumbeat with the legend of the general himself, enmeshing national duty with national rhythm.

Many critics have argued that Newbolt's popularity and the popularity of patriotic poetry in general was due to the rise of militarism at the turn of the century,[53] and the "verbal symbols of ideological commitment" to the great public schools.[54] Newbolt's poetry further attuned that audience, troping the drum and a natural ability to hear and follow rhythm as essential aspects of English military history, glory, and sacrifice; thus, reading and "feeling" English poetry through its rhythm (perhaps even a hazy understanding of its meter) was conceived of, by Newbolt and others, as an essential aspect of English citizenship. Though Drake's legend was taken up many times by other poets in the Edwardian period,[55] it was Newbolt who turned the old wives' tale into a legend that emblematized, through a rewriting of English history, how a rhythm could inspire military heroism and sacrifice. Newbolt himself was impressed by the popularity of the poem, recording in his autobiography the many times that readers contacted him to tell him that they *heard* the actual drum, both at the close of the Boer war and the close of the First World War.[56] The drum, then, in its Edwardian and Georgian uses, is not only the historical legend of Drake's unifying rhythm but, in the poem itself, an example of the unifying rhythms imagined in all English poetry that calls citizens to collective action.

In Newbolt's poems leading up to and during the First World War, the drumbeat shifts from one of national duty to a more specific march toward death, the ultimate sacrifice. In "The Song of the Guns at Sea," dated 1909, and published in the 1916 *Poems, New and Old,*[57] Newbolt subdues the regular ballad meters of his earlier nautical poems:

O Hear! O hear!
Across the sullen tide,
Across the echoing dome horizon-wide,
What pulse of fear
Beats with tremendous boom?   5
What call of instant doom
What thunderstroke of terror and of pride
With urgency that may not be denied
Reverberates upon the heart's own drum?
Come! . . . Come! . . . for thou must come!   10

Here, without the actual drum of rhythm, Newbolt tries to achieve a kind of echoing repetition. When that fails, he evokes the echo of a drum sound in the use of exclamation points and ellipses. "Rejoice to obey," we are told, "the beat that bids thee draw heroic breath, deep-throbbing till thy mortal heart be dumb." The beat of the drum has become guns and the heart's pulse, and it seems poised to beat the mortal heart to death.

In Newbolt's 1918 book, *St. George's Day and Other Poems*, the inspiring drum of his earlier poems transforms into a funeral march, and he fetishizes the drumbeat to near absurdity in a poem about a collection of soldiers who are too tired to march. In "The Toy Band," subtitled "A Song of the Great Retreat," Newbolt tells the story of General Tom Bridges (Robert Bridges's nephew), who creatively inspired his regiment to march by playing "Tipperary" and "The British Grenadier" on instruments found in a toy shop. He returns to this scene many times in his memoirs and letters; indeed, he recycles it from an episode in one of the books he writes for the British Propaganda Office, *Tales of the Great War* (1916):

> When the reason is out of action, you must call to something deeper, more instinctive. Everyone who has ever marched to a band knows how music adds to your marching power without your thinking of it . . . he paraded in the square, playing 'the British Grenadiers,' not probably with a very rich tone but in exact and spirited time. The beat of it got into the dead men's pulses and made them soldiers again. They staggered up and followed the toy band out of the town, and down the long dark road toward Nyon.[58]

Indeed, in the accompanying illustration, the caption reads, "the beat of it got into the dead man's pulses," to emphasize that the soldiers act without thinking once they hear the beat.

The poem teaches us about the poet's ability to use simple, childlike materials to suit a national need; to return to the "ritum, ritum" that the poet believes the public expects. The eerie nursery rhyme sing-song and nonsense words do nothing to brighten a scene in which "half a thousand dead men" are marching. The soldiers are an unthinking, automaton audience, reanimated only by the "penny drum" and urged to fight despite their physical limitations.

The Toy Band

A Song of the Great Retreat

Dreary lay the long road, dreary lay the town,
Lights out and never a glint o'moon:
Weary lay the stragglers, half a thousand down,
Sad sight the weary big Dragoon.
"Oh! If I'd a drum here to make them take the road again,   5

Oh! If I'd a fife to wheedle, come boys come!
You that mean to fight it out, wake and take your load again,
Fall in! Fall in! Follow the fife and drum!

"Hey, but here's a toy shop, here's a drum for me,
Penny whistles too to play the tune!   10
Half a thousand dead men soon shall hear and see
We're a band!" Said the weary big Dragoon.
"Rubadub! Rubadub! Wake and take the road again,
Wheedle-deedle-deedle-dee, Come, boys, come!
You that mean to fight it out, wake and take your load again,
Fall in! Fall in! Follow the fife and drum!"   15

Cheerly goes the dark road, cheerly goes the night,
Cheerly goes the blood to keep the beat;
Half a thousand dead men marching on to fight
With a little penny drum to lift their feet.
Rubadub! Rubadub! Wake, and take the road again,   20
Wheedle-deedle-deedle-dee, Come, boys, come!
You that mean to fight it out, wake and take your load again,
Fall in! Fall in! Follow the fife and drum!

As long as there's an Englishman to ask a tale of me,
As long as I can tell the tale aright,   25
We'll not forget the penny whistle's wheedle-deedle-dee
And the big Dragoon a-beating down the night,
Rubadub, Rubadub! Wake and take the road again,
Wheedle-deedle-deedle-dee, Come, boys, come!
You that mean to fight it out, wake and take your load again,   30
Fall in! Fall in! Follow the fife, and drum![59]

Here, Newbolt demonstrates what seems to be a near desperate belief in the power of this martial, English rhythm, and in his own power as someone able to employ that rhythm, to bring people together and inspire self-sacrifice and love of country. As in his early poem, "Admirals All," Newbolt joins the military general to the poet, both with the power to move their audience toward action. But the difference between the prose text and the poem is significant: in the prose version, as "the beat of it got into the dead man's pulses," the men were roused, revived and saved from death—or, rather, from court martial— by the sound of the "beat." In the poem, the "Englishmen" are boys: "Rubadub, Rubadub" and "Wheedle-deedle-deedle-dee" making a school game out of battle and almost bragging that the "half a thousand dead men / soon shall hear and see / that we're a band." Although clearly attempting to be onomato-

'The beat of it got into the dead men's pulses.'

Figure 2. "The beat of it got into the dead men's pulses." In Henry Newbolt, *Tales of the Great War.* Originally published by Longmans, Green, and Co. in 1916 (with 7 color plates and 32 illustrations in black and white, by Norman Wilkinson and Christopher Clark), p. 185.

poetic with the "wheedle" of the whistle and the "rubadub" of the toy drum, Newbolt's infantilizing war scene in the service of idealizing and glamorizing the power of music and poetry (indeed, his own power as a poet of wartime) seems violently out of place; a cartoonish, audaciously false presentation of the happy soldier, "cheerly" singing along.

"The Fourth of August: A Masque," a poem full of "love of country" and "freedom that lives by service," and which closes the volume, reverses this move in a stage note: "A funeral march is heard: the Boy beats his drum to it and turns to go . . . the funeral march changes to a high triumphant movement." The "natural," self-sacrificing drumbeat pulse and impulse has finally been exposed by 1918 as a false rhythm, unnatural and horrifying, and even more offensive than the popular poetry of the thousands of patriotic poets whose work flooded the public press at the beginning of the war.[60] In his "masque," Newbolt wrenches the funeral march into triumph, again eerily yoking the drumbeat of the nation to a death march. The only poem in which Newbolt imagines himself on the actual front, "A Letter from the Front" is also the only one in "free verse," as if the scene of an English officer with a domestic cat on the front was somehow inappropriate for meter. English rhythm, in Newbolt's hands, is pure propaganda; without duty and imperial sacrifice, there is no need to shape rhythm into lines at all. Unlike for Bridges, who felt that free verse and other experiments could fit into a shifting and dynamic English national identity, able to accommodate multiple forms, for Newbolt, meter without patriotism would not fit into his project of a collective metrical and national identity.

Private Meters, Public Rhythms

Newbolt realized Arnold's dream of a cultural metrical identity by way of institutionalizing a military-metrical complex. Yet this was not the whole story. Newbolt defined and troped a national rhythm in his poetry, naturally felt, one to which Englishmen instinctively responded. However, Newbolt, like Robert Bridges and George Saintsbury before him, was also a classically educated Englishman, and so despite the rhythmical rigor of his widely published poetry, he was still perplexed, like many writers in the period, about the problem of maintaining a distinction between the "natural" rhythms that he promoted in his poetry and the pedagogy that would line up those rhythms into an order that could be called an "English meter." Rather than promote the monolithic military-metrical complex in which his poems participated, his writing on prosody reveals a compromise between the way that poetry should be read, written, and understood by mass culture and the way that poetry, at a higher, more technical level, should be classified and discussed by the more educated classes and then disseminated to the culture at large. His 1904 essay, "The Future of English Verse," shows that he, too, wants to protect the less educated from the complications of versification, though he longs to provide an explanation that will allow the layperson some measure of understanding:

"[T]o any but a very intelligent and cultivated audience I should not . . . suggest that blank verse is not the simplest thing in the world. As Mr. Bridges has said, 'Most "lovers of poetry" merely love sing-song: *ritum, ritum, ritum* is rhythm to them, and anything which will not go *ritum, ritum* is harsh."[61] Newbolt agrees with Bridges that an education in English meter is not necessary in order to love poetry. His meditation on variety in blank verse gives way to a history of English versification beginning with Latin verse ("the Founder of the Family"). In his critical attempt at simplicity, Newbolt faults both newspaper critics and random authorities (specifically "Evans on Versification")[62] for making arbitrary rules for poets to follow, especially rules that do not acknowledge natural "stress" in English. "To everyone but a few makers of authoritative books," he contends, "the stresses in English are more important than the syllables" (376). He continues, "look at the simplicity of it. You set out to write a poem, say in short couplets; you put the words of your story in their natural order, with their natural pronunciation and stresses; you do not need to trouble yourself about iambs and trochees; anapaests or dactyls are no more to you than anacondas or pterodactyls; when you have got four beats or stresses you have got a line, and you go on to the next" (379).

Stressed verse will thrive in England because it has grown up in its "native soil" (380). Newbolt is an advocate for simplicity, avoiding the kind of conservatism and pedantry that he sees in critics and false prosodic authorities. Like Saintsbury's promotion of the foot as natural to an "English ear," for Newbolt, the Anglo-Saxon beat is simple and natural, with beats and stresses. This movement toward Anglo-Saxon versification that Newbolt describes is similar to the fantasy of classical meters in English that Arnold imagined, transposed onto the new and more militaristic national metrical history of English. For Arnold, that is, English meter would awaken a culture you did not know was inside you and civilize you out of the masses and into a kind of distinction. For Newbolt, the beat recognizes you and pulls you toward it, so that you became not just part of a culture but of a nation, in the twentieth-century sense of the word.

Despite Newbolt's reputation for simplified meters and his attempt to explain English meter in the simplest terms, he was involved in the complicated national debates concerning English education and meter's complex role in that curriculum. One way in which he sought to solidify meter's role was by urging his contemporaries to explore and solidify related or constituent terms to meter, such as "rhythm." As editor of *The Monthly Review*, Newbolt pestered Bridges for ten years to write an article about rhythm that he could publish in the magazine. In 1900, Bridges wrote excitedly to Newbolt about his preparations for the second edition of *Milton's Prosody*. Looking at the manner in which Bridges summarized his arguments to Newbolt, it is clear that their correspondence, though perhaps not as technical as Bridges's correspondence with Joseph Mayor or Henry Bradley, contained discussions of English meter.[63] On December 17th, 1902, Bridges responded to a letter from Newbolt: "I will try and put together my ideas on rhythm for you this Xmas. I really think I can make the matter very simple, readable, and convincing" (422). In January, Bridges writes: "I was quite forgetting about the Rhythm. It is developing — Will be in 3 parts as I see it now" (424).[64] And yet, in an April 3, 1903 letter, Bridges's response to an inquiry by Newbolt shows how anxious Newbolt was for some treatment of rhythm in English by Bridges, whereas

Bridges's concerns had turned almost entirely to the promotion of phonetic spelling:

> What seems to have happened is this: I asked if you would like a *phonetic* article. You replied. Yes of course I am expecting your article on *rhythm*. I replied. I meant *phonetics*—to this *no response*. I therefore thought no more of it. . . . Rhythm. This subject has a way of developing in all directions. Better wait till you come down here. I am getting on *very* well with it, but there is no hurry. I have written nothing.[65]

Bridges felt that he had clarified Milton's rhythms for the masses and had moved on, at this point, to his more pressing concern with the salvation of English through reformed spelling and signs for pronunciation. His comment that "this subject has a way of developing in all directions" was a clarification for Newbolt. Bridges had spent his career parsing out the complications of defining English prosody, and offered Newbolt some comments on Newbolt's own prosodic essay in 1908 (despite never finishing the essay on "rhythm" that Newbolt had requested). Bridges writes: "your distinction between prosodies of blank verse and lyric seems misleading. Whatever prosody lyric poetry may adopt in England, yet the best lyric in the world (that is the best of Shelley and Keats) will preserve its prosody alive . . ." Bridges goes on to explain the evolution of prosody to Newbolt in a boxed diagram, showing a progression from quantitative, syllabic, and stress prosodies into quantitative verse becoming syllabic and syllabic verse giving way to stress. "I think that what happened may be exhibited in a diagram" (552; see figure 3):

> Again there was this similarity in methods 1 and 2, viz., that as in the best syllabic verse the practice was sometimes unjustifiable on its own theory, so in the best quantitative verse of the Greeks there is a freedom which allows *many* false quantities. What is sought is a beautiful rhythm, and the value of the prosody is difficult to explain. But it would seem absolutely necessary to have some recognized scheme as a basis; and such a scheme, owing to the nature of language, must be in some respects artificial, and this artificiality is a direction determined by the scheme. (552–53)

Their correspondence primarily shows both parties' involvements in the dialectic regarding prosody in the context of national identity. But a secondary revelation can be found here, as well: if Arnold's intimate meter was distorted into Newbolt's national meter, then Bridges's project of metrical multiplicity represents a very different kind of nation than the one that Newbolt's theories propose, even if Bridges explains the evolution of stress verse as a natural pro-

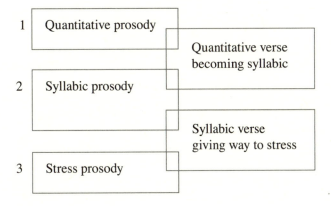

Figure 3.

gression in the continuum. While Newbolt seems to embrace his version of English national meter as the culmination of this evolution, Bridges wants to keep each strain of the tradition alive, always evolving, and part of a variety of choices available to English poets.

There are no more technical prosodic discussions in their correspondence until 1912, when Bridges asks, "did you ever ask anyone to test the ordinary scholar's theory of classical prosody by reading hexameters in true longs and shorts with the initials of the feet accented? It is a truly effective demonstration" (617). It is in this same letter that Bridges offers to return Newbolt's copy of Mayor's *English Prosody* to him.[66] In an undated letter that is most likely from 1912 (because of a reference to Saintsbury's book on English prose rhythm), Bridges educates Newbolt about the fallacies of Saintsbury's system ("I really think that the average ass would understand this form of demonstration" [921]). Their correspondence shows that both Bridges and Newbolt, who were involved in poetics, politics, and pedagogy in complex ways, were keenly aware of the struggles over what prosody in English *meant,* not only for their own practice but for that of generations of schoolchildren whom they meant to keep on proper footing. Whereas Bridges was against Saintsbury's hegemony of the foot, preferring to diversify and destabilize any notion of traditional meter with multiple metrical systems, Newbolt merged his classicism with patriotism and chose to promote the national meter (read: rhythm) that would appeal to a public already accustomed to the practice of learning patriotic verses by heart.

Newbolt's influential report on national education, *The Teaching of English in England*, shows that he espoused the same values for English education that he did for English poetry. Yet, despite his personal interest in the specifics of English prosody, Newbolt shies away from suggesting the adoption of any one prosodic system in the classroom. He is pleased to find that children "can recite a surprising number of separate poems, selected by themselves from their anthology, and have read and appreciated many others; [children] who compile and transcribe anthologies of their own, and delight in composing of poems."[67] Children, in 1921, are not the issue. They have "a natural love for beauty of sound, for the picturesque, the concrete, the imaginative, that is to say, for poetry." It is the teachers who need to be reined in. Teachers are warned against "undue insistence on perfect memorizing, destructive explanations, and ill-concealed indifference, or even distaste." They must be especially talented to instruct their pupils in verse-writing, because "the danger is great that principles of prosody, only half understood, or perhaps entirely erroneous, may be enforced in such a manner as to reduce the lesson to a mere mechanical drill" (110). Here is an echo of Arnold's denigration of "mere verses" and a strain of the intimate cultural discipline possible through those "great principles of prosody." In the report, the pupil's freedom is paramount—to choose passages for memorization, to feel empowered to appreciate English literature. English is the eye opener, the study that can refresh the pupil to the appreciation of all literature—even the classics. Newbolt's report is a culmination of trends that were solidifying over the course of the first twenty years of the 1900s. His postwar sentiment toward the English language, and English poetry, must be read in light of the way that English language, rhythm, and meter had become severed from scientific or linguistic study in the Edwardian classroom and transformed into an almost privileged birthright.[68] He writes, in the introduction to his report, that the various influences, or tributaries, that formed English literature, have been conquered by an idea of Englishness that is understood to be native to England:

> To every child in this country, there is one language with which he must necessarily be familiar and by that, and by that alone, he has the power of drawing directly from one of the great literatures of the world. Moreover, if we explore the course of English literature, if we consider from what sources its stream has sprung, what tributaries it has been fed, and with how rich and full a current it has come down to us, we shall see that it has other advantages not to be found elsewhere. They are mingled in it, as only in the greatest rivers they could be mingled, the fertilizing influences flowing down from many countries and from many ages of history. Yet all these have been subdued to form a stream native to our own soil. The flood of diverse human experience which it brings down to our own life and time is in no sense a degree foreign to us, but has become the native experience of men in our own race and culture. (13)

Newbolt's legacy, then, is not only the patriotic verses for which he is known, but also the way in which those verses exemplify the rhetoric that was being played out in the classroom. Newbolt, in effect, subdued his own interests in classical meters in favor of presenting a unifying rhythm to English patriotic culture. The echoes of and in Newbolt's poems remind us only of one aspect of this particularly Edwardian figure; Newbolt's report, consolidating an idea of English literature in the postwar period, guaranteed that the dichotomy between "native" rhythms and "foreign" meters would continue throughout the twentieth century.

Newbolt's own assertion of accent as the true and native basis for English verse mirrors common distinctions between simple or lowly "verses" and more metrically complex, and therefore artificial, "poetry." The *NED* defined poetry in 1907 as "a composition in verse or metrical language, or in some equivalent patterned arrangement of language; usually also with choice of elevated words and figurative uses, and option of a syntactical order, differing more or less from those in ordinary writing. In this sense, poetry in its simplest sense or lowest form has been identified with versification or verse."[69] Newbolt's patriotic rhythm was part of a broader movement in education that abstracted "meter," misunderstood as accent, stress, or particularly "beat," as an invisible unifying cultural force. Likewise, "verses" by amateur poets inspired by the war, by the marching rhythms of military action, were folded into a pedagogic and critical assessment of the state of poetry in general in the Georgian period. C.F.E. Spurgeon, in her 1917 English Association pamphlet, *Poetry in the Light of War,* links the outpouring of poetry to the national education system with some satisfaction:

> This war, which has taught and is teaching us so many things has, it seems to me, brought into relief and emphasized certain qualities in poetry, and the prominence of these qualities has in its turn raised some questions in my mind with regard to the teaching of literature . . . there has been a quickening of interest in poetry, both among those who are fighting and those who stay at home, that people who read it little before have been led to read it more, while those who cared for it before the war have found that caring increased and intensified. Some people have expressed great surprise at this. We have all of us perhaps felt a slight thrill of surprise mingled with satisfaction. But the fact that there has been any surprise felt is a proof that the matter of poetry is either imperfectly understood or imperfectly remembered. For if it is remembered, it is clear that it is no more surprising that a soldier before battle or those in anguish of spirit at home should turn to poetry and find in it refreshment and sustenance, than that a hungry and physically exhausted man should find pleasure in a meal of bread and wine.[70]

According to Spurgeon, the aims of national education in regard to poetry, then, have been satisfied in that "the matter of poetry" is remembered in times of "anguish of spirit," even if it is not understood. This sentiment is a complication of Arnold's hope of intimate metrical civilization; here, poetry has become an external cultural bond, a place to find patriotic sustenance, community, and collective identity.

As organizations like the English Association (established in 1906) and the Society for Pure English increasingly worried over the use of poetry and the way it was taught, versification manuals rushed to provide structure to the newly inspired poetry-writing masses. Joseph Berg Esenwein and Mary Eleanor Roberts's *The Art of Versification,* published in 1913 and again in 1916, was one of a surge of such manuals. They warned: "If you wish to turn your philosophy, or your patriotism, or your religion, into poetry, well and good, but the fact that your philosophy is deep, or your patriotism lofty, or your religion lovely, will not of necessity make your poetry so—the spirit must be clothed upon with body, and the body must be of form suitable for the appareling of so deep, lofty, and lovely a spirit."[71]

Notice how patriotism is interchangeable with religion here (a sentiment also found in the 1914 introduction to *Songs and Sonnets for England in War Time*: "God, His poetry, and His music are the Holy Trinity of war"[72]). Meter, Esenswein and Roberts's book explains, means measure, and "the syllable marked by the stress of the voice necessarily corresponds to the beat of the foot in marking time." English rhythm and meter are "born of music," and "the rhyming games of children are a survival of the primitive instinct to associate foot-movements with chant or song."[73] Going one step further than Saintsbury, here, Esenwein and Roberts renaturalize the idea of the "foot" as a human foot, attached to a dancing (marching) body. Rhythm is a primal instinct, as Newbolt argues, and so is our ability to mark, or measure that rhythm, by literally moving our feet in time with the beat. This continuation of the nineteenth-century naturalization of "the foot" takes away all foreign notions of Greek terminology; indeed, even "the foot" is now linked to the nation's concerns.

The poems with less "delicacy of workmanship" are directed toward stirring an audience to action. Along with countless war poetry anthologies, popular *Punch* poetess Jessie Pope's *War Poems* and *More War Poems* were published in 1915, followed in 1916 by *Simple Rhymes for Stirring Times*. Her poem "The Call" at once evokes and mocks Newbolt's patriotic verses: "When that procession comes, / Banners and rolling drums — / Who'll stand and bite his thumbs — / Will you, my laddie?" (ll. 21–24). Her poem, "Who's for the Game," is a direct response to Newbolt's "Vitae Lampada." Pope's poem begins:

Football's a sport, and a rare sport too,
Don't make it a source of shame,
Today there are worthier things to do,

Englishmen, play the game!
A truce to the League, a truce to the Cup   5
Get to work with a *gun*.
When our country's at war we must all buck up —
It's the only thing to be done!⁷⁴

The variation between iambs and anapests seems to follow Saintsbury's characterization—the iambs are mobilized, ready for action, ready for glory. Pope's
two most prominent anapests here, "with a *gun*" and "to be done," make explicit, along the lines of Newbolt's later war poems, the morbid ways that glory
is acted out in wartime.

The excitement of poetry used to motivate the country excited Thomas
Hardy, whose poems were reprinted and recirculated even more than Jessie
Pope's. Hardy's poem, "Song of the Soldiers," was published first in the *Times*⁷⁵
in response to Newbolt's call for patriotic verse. Newbolt was the liaison to the
government propaganda office and Hardy was a participant in the group (indeed, he wrote a draft of the poem on his way home from its first meeting).
The poem was reprinted in a pamphlet by itself a week later; it was popularly
known as "Men Who March Away" and was reprinted in many wartime anthologies, including George Herbert Clarke's popular 1917 *A Treasury of War
Poetry*.⁷⁶ The original title, with its dactyl and trochee, gestures to the falling
march the entire poem emblematizes, but the three-beat rhythms make a
mockery of marching; the poem stumbles, reluctantly participating in the national metrical project of easy "English" rhythms and asserting, rather aggres-
sively, that Hardy's understanding of meter did not necessarily speak to the
same metrical communities as Newbolt's or Pope's.

What of the faith and fire within us
Men who march away
Ere the barn-cocks say
Night is growing gray,
To hazards whence no tears can win us;   5
What of the faith and fire within us
Men who march away?

Is it a purblind prank, O think you,
Friend with the musing eye
Who watch us stepping by,   10
With doubt and dolorous sigh?
Can much pondering so hoodwink you!
Is it a purblind prank. O think you,
Friend with the musing eye?

Nay. We see well what we are doing,   15
Though some may not see —
Dalliers as they be! —
England's need are we;
Her distress would set us rueing:
Nay, We see well what we are doing,   20
Though some may not see!

In our heart of hearts believing
Victory crowns the just,
And that braggarts must
Surely bite the dust,   25
March we to the field ungrieving,
In our heart of hearts believing
Victory crowns the just.

Hence the faith and fire within us
Men who march away   30
Ere the barn-cocks say
Night is growing gray,
To hazards whence no tears can win us:
Hence the faith and fire within us
Men who march away.   35

This poem echoes popular sentiment in the lines, "England's need are we" and "March we to the field ungrieving, / In our heart of hearts believing / Victory crowns the just," yet these are the only lines in the poem that participate fully in the regularized rhythms of wartime verses. The rest of the poem might be described as metrically reticent. Perhaps, from Hardy's vantage point, we might read his slow, irregular meters as a sign of his own hesitation in participating in Newboltian poetic propaganda, as well as concern over the way that militaristic meters had become the expected norm. Indeed, the poem is about unevenness; with its seven-line stanzas and lurching near-ballad measure. In the first stanza the march is halting, as if the soldier starts to march along to the beat and then pauses three times at the end of each three-beat line. The first stanza is the most rhythmically regular and the third is the most awkward: "Nay. We see well what we are doing, / Though some may not see — / Dalliers as they be! — / England's need are we." Whatever meter Hardy is employing here, we are forced to believe that he knows what he is doing, because the line "Nay. We see well what we are doing" seems to sprawl out to carry far more than the four accents he set as his pattern earlier. As if to mask the four beats, he adds a pause for punctuation after "Nay," so that the line, to me at least, seems to read "**Nay. We** see **well what** we are **do**ing." However, if you hurry through the pause after "Nay," the line reads in trochees, only forcing one dactyl at the end: "**Nay** we **see** well **what** we [are] **do**ing." Hardy is far too sophisticated a metrist for me to doubt that he had some idea about what this uneven, uncomfortable marching song might mean to readers.[77] He refuses to embrace the dominance of the artificially upbeat iamb, here, and only employs it when calling attention to the dangers of marching too blindly: "To hazards," in line 5, and the "musing eye" "who watch us stepping by / with doubt and dolorous sigh." This musing, doubting eye watches the downward steps of the men who march away with the same kind of reticence that the poet demonstrates in his downbeat meters. This is not to say that Hardy couldn't have composed a more rousing poem, but he equivocates between his sophisticated and mass readers here. As his thinly veiled autobiography explains:

> That the author loved the art of concealing was undiscerned. For instance, as to rhythm. Years earlier he had decided that too regular a beat was bad art. He had fortified himself in his opinion by thinking of the analogy of architecture, between which art and that of poetry he had discovered, to use his own words, that there existed a curious and close parallel, both arts, unlike some others, having to carry a rational content inside their artistic form.[78]

And yet, also in *Wessex Poems* Hardy had reprinted "The Sergeant's Song" (originally published in *The Trumpet Major* [1880]) with its refrain "rollicum-rorum, tol-lol-lorum, / Rollicum-rorum, tol-lol-lay!" and its highly regular beat. For Hardy then, the equivocation about how to appeal to the masses but maintain a kind of metrical integrity is readable in his wartime poems. Even when we read the rousing rhythms of Newbolt's poems as simply emphatic without reading them in the context of the military metrical complex in which these poets were participating, we miss the way they were also interested in prosody and might have figured their ability to participate in more than one metrical community. We have not known, until now, what to make of these poems, nor what to make of the thousands that were pouring in from the front during the First World War. Rather than reading these poems as a way to participate in a collective national identity, scholars both then and how have read them as an affront to the high offices of "Poetry," a confusion of seemingly regular meter, militaristic themes, and a wartime notion of Englishness.

The Sound of the Drum

The division in nineteenth-century readers between poetry and verse continued and deepened in the twentieth century. Though Arnold hoped that memorized poetry would discipline the newly enfranchised masses, the poetry that circulated in schools was less remarkable for its metrical achievement and more memorable for its blatant patriotism. The poetry of Newbolt thematized this "native rhythm" as something that would unify a collective to action, pushing his drum trope far past propriety and toward a surreal, disconnected sense of actual battle (or actual meter). Meanwhile, the prosody wars remained unresolved, and poets like Bridges, Hardy, and Newbolt participated in a public "metrical" project of publishing simple, patriotic poems for the masses while at the same time continuing to write metrically innovative poems and discuss the possibilities of English prosody among themselves.

For Bridges and Hardy, especially, the difference between the poems written for the propaganda office and their usual output is especially remarkable, and critical opinion has tended to ignore the war poems. Poet, critic, and soldier Edward Thomas admired "Men who March Away," calling the poem "the only good one concerned with the war"[79] and describing it as "an impersonal song which seems to me the best of the time, as it is the least particular and occasional." This commendation shows how, generally, Thomas was reticent to embrace the poetry of wartime, but it also brings to light the continued discontinuity between the contemporary attitudes of poets and prosodists and the historical narrative that defines them to later generations; Thomas, too, has been characterized as a war poet. As early as 1914 in an article titled "War Poetry,"[80] Thomas criticized the speed with which poets wrote poems about the war, noting that only

> a small number of poems destined to endure are directly or entirely concerned with the public triumphs, calamities, or trepidations that helped to beget them. The public, crammed with mighty facts and ideas it will never digest, must look coldly on poetry where already those mighty things have sunk away far into "The still sad music of humanity." ... They want something raw and solid, or vague and lofty and sentimental. (342)

Thomas feels that the editors who publish these poems and the public who consumes them are just as much to blame for the surge in bad war poetry as the poets who write them—if, that is, they can be considered poets, and if these are even poems. Thomas makes a clear distinction between "War Poetry" and the "verses" or "hymns" that were flooding the public press. "A patriotic poem pure and simple hardly exists," he writes, adding that "[v]ery seldom are poems written for occasions, great or small, more seldom for great than for small. But verses are, and they may be excellent. Virtually all hymns are occasional verses" (343). Thomas distinguishes between "poetry" and "verse" along the lines of both content (verse takes on "occasions") and quality (he intimates that if a poem is patriotic, its quality suffers). Yet, Thomas does not condemn or exalt either form outright; he merely distinguishes between them. He wants to praise the better specimens of verse only if they are understood as such and not if they are held to the standards he reserves for poetry. This reservation can be attributed to his belief that verses "are written for a certain people or a certain class. The writer of hymns or patriotic verses appears to be a man who feels himself always or at the time at one with the class, perhaps the whole nation" (343). These verses, which are not "great poetry" nor are they "what is wanted," are written by a writer "who picks up popular views or phrases, or coins them, and has the power to turn them into downright stanzas" (344). To this reviewer, verses that are meant for something other than mere diversion are dangerous—rather than convince you to follow along to the beat of a country's drum, they are artificially, dishonestly asking you to follow along to your death. The simple verse form comes to signify artificial patriotic sentiment as well as dishonest forms in general.

Like Hardy, Bridges, and Newbolt, Thomas participated in the patriotic poetics of the First World War but still reserved judgment for the "verses" that he felt were beneath him. Thomas felt that Kipling and Newbolt "belong to a professional class apart" and hoped that others, like Hardy, would write "even better yet," expecting "the work of other real poets to improve as the war advances, perhaps after it is over, as they understand it and themselves more completely" (344). Part of the reason that Kipling and Newbolt were considered poets distinct from those pouring out military verse is because they had already distinguished themselves, as discussed above, as poets whose main theme was, in some way or another, English national identity.

In *To The Lighthouse* (1927), a novel that famously relegates death and war to parentheses, Virginia Woolf brackets the observation that "the war, people said, had revived their interest in poetry."[81] However, the martial rhythms of patriotic pedagogy had laid the groundwork for what many editors called a "poetry boom." In 1917, Harold Monro, editor of *Poetry and Drama* and owner of "The Poetry Bookshop,"[82] complained, "we find ourselves at this moment almost unprovided with verse that we should care to publish." Rather than understanding the overwhelming public output of poetry as a result of the rhythmic-imperial education provided in the Edwardian period or the outpouring of metrical handbooks participating in the prosody wars, Monro blames the proliferation of simplified metrical verses, which he refuses to call poetry, on sheer ardent patriotism: "We get the impression of verse-writers excitedly gathering to *do something* for their flag, and as soon as they begin to rack their brains how that something may be done in verse, a hundred old phrases for patriotic moments float in their minds, which they reel into verse or fit into sonnets—and the press is delighted to publish them."[83]

In the same vein, *The Egoist* published a poem under the pseudonym "Herbert Blenheim," titled, "Song: In War-time," mocking the proliferation of wartime metrical verses in the public press:

At the sound of the drum,
Out of their dens they come, they come,
The little poets we hoped were dumb,
The little poets we thought were dead,
The poets who certainly haven't been read   5
Since heaven knows when, they come, they come,
At the sound of the drum, of the drum, drum, drum.

At the sound of the drum,
O Tommy, they've *all* begun to strum,
With a horrible tumty, tumty, tum;   10
And it's all about you, and the songs they sing
Are worse than the bullets' villainous "ping,"
And they give you a pain in your tumty-tum,
At the sound of the drum, of the drum, drum, drum.

At the sound of the drum,   15
O Tommy, you know, if we haven't all come
To stand by your side in the hideous hum,
It isn't the horrors of war we fear,
The horrors of war we've got 'em here,
When the poets come on like waves, and *come*
At the sound of the drum, of the drum, drum, drum.[84]

This parody is both a play on "Drake's Drum" and a commentary on the way that military activity has provoked monotonous, militaristic meters. The "horrors of war" are not on the battlefield, but in the poetry that attempts to describe the battlefield, the poetry written for "Tommy" by poets who haven't been "read." That the "little poets" have not been "read" refers both to the fact that these so-called poets are not well read and also that they are only being "read" or published because of the occasion of war. These poets, who "come on like waves," are so powerful that they dissuade the writer from standing by Tommy's side—it is not the "horrors of war" that the writer fears—indeed, "hideous hum" and the chaotic collection of the bullets with their "villainous ping," are preferable to the endless, maddening repetition of the "drum, drum, drum." The actual battlefield is preferable to the battles over who has access to writing English poetry, especially when poetry is reduced to a repetitive, jingoistic incantation in praise of the nation.

Thomas lamented that the "poetry boom" had been caused by men, "turned into poets by the war, printing verse now for the first time," who "pick up popular views or phrases . . . and turn them into downright stanzas." He explained, in the same 1914 review referenced above, that "These poems are not to be attacked any more than hymns. Like hymns, they play with common ideas, with words and names which most people have in their heads at the time . . . they go straight to the heart of the great public which does not read poetry."[85]

Perhaps we could venture that they do not read poetry, but they have been conditioned to read verse. This discourse was influenced, of course, by the advent of literary Modernism, but it was also significantly influenced by the institutions of the state that educated these certain people, this certain class, to believe that English poetry was certainly accessible to them; by marching in time with those simple rhythms, there was something both redemptive and social in sending the poem home to be published. Victorian greats like Hardy were writing this kind of poetry—even the poet laureate reeled off a few verses—and there was something clearly hopeful and redemptive about writing verse rather than poetry, or writing verse thinking that it was poetry. Though these soldiers had been taught that English rhythms were their legacy, their inability to manipulate more complex and subtle meters—their alienation from English versification—prevented them, on the formal level, from engaging in what the critics insisted was an exclusive definition of poetry.

Edmund Gosse's 1917 review, "Some Soldier Poets," catalogues some early war poetry as if to place it prematurely in the context of English literary history.[86] "The earliest expressions of lyric military feeling came from veteran voices," he writes, referring to Hardy and Bridges. He reports, "already, before the close of autumn 1914, four or five anthologies of war-poems were in the press, and the desire of the general public to be fed with patriotic and emotional verse was manifested in unmistakable ways" (298). Indeed, it was the audience for the poetry boom that amazed so many critics during the war. Gosse continues,

> The immediate success of the anthologies . . . proved that the war had aroused in a new public an ear for contemporary verse, an attention anxious to be stirred or soothed by the assiduous company of poets who had been ripening their talents in a little clan. These had now an eager world ready to listen to them. . . . There has never before, in the world's history, been an epoch which has tolerated and even welcomed such a flood of verse as has been poured forth over Great Britain during the last three years. These years have seen the publication, as I am credibly informed, of more than five hundred volumes of new and original poetry. (298)

Gosse and Woolf both recognize how the war facilitated the acceptance of poetry—be it well crafted or "monotonous," as Gosse calls it. The "delicacies of workmanship" had, in many cases, been overshadowed by the need to stir "the pulses of their auditors." Just like Newbolt's rhetoric at the beginning of the century, poetry of the First World War is asked to both "stir" and to "subdue," and yet the distinction between poetry and verse is sharpened in this moment by the thematic and formal evaluations of poets and critics like Thomas, Murry, Gosse and, later, Pound, Eliot, and Yeats. Such poets and critics were suspicious and tired of the outpouring of poems that spoke to a kind of collective Englishness, at the same time that they participated in the myth that true poetry was what the nation needed in wartime. What began in the late nineteenth century with Matthew Arnold as a cultural dream of a nation intimately civilized by poetic form transformed through the education system and the poetry of Newbolt into a trope of drumbeats and militarism that was often accompanied by simple poetic meters, which was then, in turn, supported by established poets like Hardy and Bridges choosing to write verses that participated in this military metrical complex. In addition, the thousands of soldier poets who had been conditioned in schools to "read verse," were therefore taught to imitate the patriotic rhythmic ideology—an embodiment of the failure, really, of Arnold's pedagogic project. The stigma of meter becomes, at the end of the First World War, a stigma about militarism and its strong association with verse for England's sake, with "meter" losing its variety and complexity and marching to a very distinctive, yet still very English "beat."

❧ 5 ❧

The Trauma of Meter

A thousand suppliants stand around thy throne,
Stricken with love for thee, O Poesy.
I stand among them, and with them I groan,
And stretch my arms for help. Oh, pity me!
—Wilfred Owen, "To Poesy" (1909)

Above all I am not concerned with Poetry. My subject is War
and the pity of War. The Poetry is in the pity.
—Wilfred Owen, unpublished "Preface" (probably May 1918)

Wartime, Poetics

The above epigraphs, written nine years apart, demonstrate a transition between Edwardian and Georgian poetics. Wilfred Owen, son of a stationmas-
ter and early "supplicant" to poetry, did not attend any of England's great public schools. He is, rather, a success story of the military metrical complex of
England's state-funded school's national curriculum. In Owen's 1906 copy of
Palgrave's Golden Treasury, he scribbled a circle around the word "Paeon" in
dark ink, writing out the definition in an adolescent scrawl: "A song in honor
of Appollo [*sic*] — a song of triumph." English poetry had triumphed over the
classics as representative of the nation's greatness for Owen and many other
poets of his generation. Classical meters were English meters and English poetry was the highest form of the country's literature—a triumph, mostly, of
Edwardian education.

The story of the "Georgian Revolt" runs parallel to the story of the rise of
experimental Modernism in poetry. Robert Ross asserts that Georgian poetry
was part of the "larger twentieth-century revolt against Humanism; . . . the
poetic phase of a widespread revolt against Academism among all the arts;
and, specifically in the field of poetry, a reaction against the dead hand of the
Romantic-Victorian tradition."[1] Critics who work on the coteries of the period (the poets publishing in Edward Marsh's wildly popular *Georgian Poetry*
series, the Imagists, the Futurists, and the Vorticists) tend to use "meter" as a
stand-in for convention and tradition in verse. But as we have seen, both mass

and elite cultures were invested in a concept of English meter that stood for an idealized "Englishness." Pitting "Romantic-Victorian tradition" against "free verse" skims over the ways that the Edwardian era specifically contributed to both of those discourses. Owen, Robert Graves, and Siegfried Sassoon are poets and soldiers whose work benefits from reevaluation in the dynamic context of metrical culture in England before and during the First World War. In the first section of this chapter, I discuss how Owen and Graves were "supplicants" to the Edwardian concept of English poetry in the early stages of the war. Their transition to being "less concerned with poetry" has everything to do with the way that English meter shaped how these soldiers approached their service and how their ideas were changed by the pressures of modern warfare. More specifically, their ideas about the communities of English meter were both affirmed and complicated by the chaos of battle and neurasthenic trauma. In this chapter, I read the trauma of soldiers' experiences as a synecdoche for the dissolution of broader concepts about English national culture during and after the First World War. The disciplining and ordering intention that English meter accrues before the war becomes at once horrifying and comforting during and after the war. The trauma of meter, for both soldier-poets and early twentieth-century readers, was the realization that meter as a stable category was illusory. To recover from trauma, through a method of therapy provided by the very idea of "meter" that had betrayed them, was to acknowledge the collective agreement—sometimes manifest as an individual desperate need—to believe in meter's stability anyway.[2]

The phenomenon of wartime neuroses during the First World War forced psychologists to fashion theories that grasped the centrality of practice to psychic healing. In instances of neurasthenic trauma, often psychologists were charged with the task of realigning linguistic ruptures, manifested by expressive stammers or even complete aphasia. Owen was hospitalized for shell shock and Graves was also prevented from returning to the front because of his mental state. In the second section of this chapter, I juxtapose the interdisciplinary techniques employed by Owen's doctor, Captain Arthur J. Brock, a classicist and sociologist on staff at Craiglockhart War Hospital, with the methods of Dr. W.H.R. Rivers, an anthropologist fascinated by the theories of Freud. For Brock's patients, ordered activities provided a lifeline to the unique social world of the hospital and surrounding town, forming a method of healing through which shell-shocked officers were efficiently "cured" so that they could return to the front. The success of these "ordered activities" was particularly remarkable for linguistic disorders. Rhythmically controlled time became an empowering practice for patients adept at composing metrical verses; composing in meter, for many patients trained in poetic craft, was a new kind of therapeutic activity that coupled the expressive aspects of Freudian psychotherapy practiced by Dr. Rivers (narrating traumatic experiences in order to "move through" them) with sociological ergo-therapy, or, "cure by functioning" promoted by Captain Brock. Brock's method also promoted a different kind of metrical culture—which we could call "metrical" insofar as temporal and spatial ordering become more important than narrative and/or expressive models.

Ordering time and prosodic ordering at Craiglockhart illustrate, in microcosm, many wartime and postwar anxieties about poetic form. Soldiers at the hospital were reeducated to embrace forms and orders that had become meaningless to them while at the same time they were encouraged to express their mistrust of all forms and orders. That is, while soldiers participated in ordered activities designed to help them reintegrate into the social world, they were also encouraged to express their emotions and feelings freely through Freudian talk-therapy. Sassoon and Owen, who were patients of Dr. Rivers and Captain Brock, respectively, both composed poems at the hospital that deserve rethinking within these new psychotherapeutic models of poetic production: specifically, through the continuous supplementary aspect of Freudian narration, on the one hand, and the active metrical exercise of fitting fragments of experience into a predetermined order, on the other. This metrical writing under the auspices of rehabilitation promised to reintroduce the writer to the social world through the history of form.

As I have discussed in the preceding chapters, poetic meter was increasingly seen as a symbol of English national culture in this period. However, until recently, poetic meter has seldom been considered a historically significant connection to the social world. Indeed, meter is rarely discussed in detail in the many classic texts about First World War poetry. Paul Fussell, author of the two monumental texts *Poetic Meter and Poetic Form* (1965) and *The Great War and Modern Memory* (1975), was close to connecting soldier-poetry to English national meter, but read tropes and myth making in soldier-poetry as preconditions of the ironic modern age. In a discussion of Cowper's "The Castaway" in relation to Edmund Blunden's "Rural Economy," Fussell acknowledges "an English reader would find it hard to experience that stanza form without recalling at least bits of Cowper's poem."[3] What Fussell means is "an English reader" who had read a good deal of Cowper and knew his particular poetic form. Fussell is mainly interested in intertextual images, symbols, and pastoral allusions, but he acknowledges that Blunden may be aware of the "artistic shape in which he has lodged" his "concern," tracing the "semblance" between himself, Cowper, and the men who appear in his poem. It is surprising that Fussell uses the verb "lodged" for Blunden's choice of form, as if Blunden had Cowper's poetic form in mind and either moved his sentiment inside the intact meter or stuck it there by force. The semblance at which Fussell hints, however, is precisely the substance of intertextual meter; it ties Blunden to his distinctively English past, and writes him into the history of "immortalizing" the dead who may or may not be redeemed. Cowper's "Castaway" would have been a useful reference for Fussell: "tears by bards or heroes shed / Alike immortalize the dead" (219). Fussell's dismissal of Cowper's meter misses the way that Blunden's meter references the social world and comments on how the soldier's relationship to those communities beyond the war (the prewar schoolroom, hearth, and home) will be irrevocably altered. "What husbandry could outdo this? / With flesh and blood he fed / The planted iron that nought amiss / Grew thick and swift and red, / And in a night though ne'er so cold / Those acres bristled a hundredfold" (205). An expansion of hymn meter, the final two lines of the sestet stanza are a repeated third rhyme (ababcc); Blunden's poem subverts the pastoral into a harvested graveyard, and Cowper's heroic poem becomes a plot, too, out of which Blunden can dredge poetic tradition in order to make it morbidly his own.

Fussell, Samuel Hynes, and Jay Winter have shown how the "literariness" of the First World War promoted the use of typical romantic images in soldier poetry, with each critic careful to point out the privileged class education available to the officer-poets who produced the now famous poetic images of the Great War. In the classic *The Great War and Modern Memory*, Fussell argues that pastoral tropes and intertextual references to the great works of English literature "signal a constant reaching out towards traditional significance . . . an attempt to make some sense of the war in relation to inherited tradition" (57). He cites specific symbols to make his point: "Intact and generative are the traditional values associated with traditional symbols—white blossoms, stars, the moon, the nightingale, the heroes of the *Iliad*, pastoral flowers" (61). Indeed, Fussell's influential assertion that soldiers were not "merely literate" but were "vigorously literary" (157), is reinforced by Samuel Hynes's *A War Imagined*. Hynes writes that, "it was clear by the end of 1914 that this war would be different—it would be the most literary and the most poetical war in English history."[4] Fussell and Hynes agree that English literature gave soldiers a sense of pride, purpose, and value; the heroic themes of their literary traditions provided a justification for their activities. Jay Winter, in *Sites of Memory, Sites of Mourning*, is dismissive of any poetic function of war poetry save the tropological: "[s]ome poems were experimental; others were written in conventional forms. Much of it arose out of the perceived need not to reject out of hand traditional languages about the dead, but rather to reformulate and reinvigorate older tropes about loss of life in wartime."[5] Both Winter and Fussell briefly acknowledge the consolatory function of hymns, but their main points relate to remembered Biblical imagery that the hymns conjure, evoking familiarity and comfort. These scholars show us how English and classical literary education influenced officers and provided comfort for them; I hope to build on their work and complicate it by showing how actively soldier-poets recognized their relationship to poetry and poetic form as equivocal, volatile, and distressing.

Though critical discourses about First World War poetry showed how popular anthologies like *Palgrave's Golden Treasury* and the *Oxford Anthology of*

English Poetry provided comfort for soldiers on the front, they neglected to discuss how soldier-poets had been trained, prewar, in the particularities of English poetic craft. Soldier-poets were conditioned by the martial meters of patriotic verses in schoolbooks and the public press before and during the war to see themselves as part of a collective English culture, bound to defend the language of Shakespeare. Heroic patriotism had been portrayed through a particular kind of English metrical poetry that was often directly allied to military service. Military and metrical drill, as I explored in the previous chapter, relied on similar ideologies of discipline and protecting the "mother country." Though these poetic practices provided comfort for soldiers on the front, there is also evidence that many soldier-poets were already questioning the rhetoric of formal Englishness that prewar poetry promoted. In *No More Parades* (1925), Ford Madox Ford presents a fictionalized account of how English poetic forms were used to counter the effects of mental crises. The protagonist, Tietjens, attempts to write his way out of a nervous breakdown by speedily composing a sonnet: "He said to himself that by God he must take himself in hand. He grabbed with his heavy hands at a piece of buff paper and wrote on it in a column of fat, wet letters:

a
b
b
a
a
b
b
a, and so on."[6]

Tietjens writes the sonnet in "two minutes and eleven seconds" on "buff" paper with "fat," "wet" letters, the upright letters taking on the traits of a healthy body. Immediately after, the broken-down bodies of soldiers enter the room, returning from battle: "[t]heir feet shuffled desultorily; they . . . held in unliterary hands small open books that they dropped from time to time." Tietjens's empowered "literary" hands act of their own volition, writing the sonnet as he barks orders simultaneously to men around him, careful "never to think on the subject of a shock at the moment of a shock."[7] Captain Tietjens's hands, in their practiced exercise of writing in English meter, order his mind so that he can continue to give orders to the men around him—"unliterary" men whose own "feet" shuffle aimlessly. Predicated by the national curriculum and by the resulting inundation of popular war poems in the public press, military feet and metrical feet are joined here—not to inspire a patriotic collective, but rather to allow for the automatic composition of a *line* meant to discipline and protect an individual officer and then his company.

Ford's fictional account renders all the more illuminating the fact that in addition to poetry anthologies, Wilfred Owen owned the 1908 reprint of R. F. Brewer's popular manual, *Orthometry, or, The Art of Versification and the Technicalities of Poetry.*[8] This handbook encourages poets to understand metrical laws so as to "at least accustom the beginner to the proper use of his *feet* before trusting him to untried *wings*," and praises how English poetic forms have become successfully imprinted in the minds of all Englishmen. Brewer's manual declared that

> [t]he study of our poets has now happily attained a footing in the curriculum of nearly all our public schools and colleges; while the millions who attend our elementary schools have suitable poetic passages indelibly impressed upon their memory in youth. All but pessimists anticipate good results of this early training upon the tastes and re-creative pleasures of young England of the twentieth century. (ix–x)

Ford, Owen, Graves, and Sassoon were all products of an education system that "impressed upon their memory in youth" memorable passages from English poetry. In a wartime context, memorized poetic forms took on new meaning. It is not only the "re-creative" pleasure of writing poetry (read both as "recreation" and that which can be created again and again), but also the importance of training that emerges when these prosodic discourses are considered in light of actual military operations. The idea of using writing as a form of mental ordering relied on the assumption that education had done its work before the war; traditional poetic forms had to have been successfully inscribed into an officer's memory for them to be used as aids in his rehabilitation. Even to the nonofficer class, marching songs and other forms of patriotic narratives had been passed down by the school system wherein military drill and metrical drill had been established as counterparts in the late nineteenth century.[9] How did the war refashion the disciplinary and therapeutic aspects of metrical writing?

Sad Death for a Poet!

In 1913, Owen wrote to his mother that he was leaving the Vicarage at Dunsden, escaping the "hotbed of religion" and murdering his "false creed," that is, leaving the Church of England. He imagines how poetry will now become his religion:

> It has just struck me that one of the occult Powers that Be may have overheard the ancient desire of my heart to be like the immortals, the immortals of earthly Fame, I mean, and is now on a fair way to granting it. . . . Only where in me is the mighty power of Verse that covered the

multitude of their sins. . . . I still find great comfort in scribbling; but lately I am deadening to all poetic impulses, save those due to the pressure of Problems pushing me to seek relief in unstopping my mouth.[10]

The ability to express himself freely in poetry gives Owen "relief" despite a lack of "poetic impulse." Though this is hardly a depiction of metrical order, Owen admits that the expressive aspect of writing is a comfort to him. In the same letter, he includes an early draft of the poem, "On My Songs" (inspired by James Russell Lowell's sonnet, "To the Spirit of Keats"),[11] which shows his assumption of and equivocation over the poetic legacy he hopes to continue:

> Though unseen poets, many and many a time,
> Have answered me as if they knew my woe,
> And it might seem have fashioned so their rime
> To be my own soul's cry; easing the flow
> Of my dumb tears with language sweet as sobs,   5
> Yet are there days when all these hoards of thought
> Hold nothing for me. Not one verse that throbs
> Throbs with my heart, or as my brain is fraught.
>
> 'Tis then I voice mine own weird reveries:
> Low croonings of a motherless child, in gloom   10
> Singing his frightened self to sleep, are these.
> One night, if thou shouldst live in this Sick Room,
> Dreading the Dark thou darest not illume,
> Listen; my voice may haply lend thee ease.[12]

When the poetry of other "unknown" or "distant" poets ceases to comfort Owen, he turns to writing his own verses. Here, Owen imagines writing verses as a way of healing himself and then, potentially, lending a healing verse to others. Verses metrically "throbbing" that do not "throb" with his heart are artificial, external, and are not guaranteed to provide comfort. The line: "Yet are there days when all these hoards of thought / Hold nothing for me. Not one verse that throbs / Throbs with my heart, or as my brain is fraught" shows that the perceived physiological comfort of a meter "throbbing" in time with a heart cannot "hold" a thought that will soothe the poet's fraught "brain." Though "throbs" / "throbs" does seem to evoke a steady beat, its placement at the end of line 7 and the beginning of line 8 creates a palpitation, as it were, set up by the caesura of "me. Not" in the middle of line 7. That is, the phenomenological aspects of meter, so willingly believed by many generations of poets so as to become part of the tradition, fail Owen when he needs it most, when he himself is ill. It is not physical, but mental comfort that he requires from this tradition, which he recognizes is something of a fantasy of youth, akin to a "low crooning," a meaningless comfort. His poem is made of "weird reveries" and the metrical "throb" of his own composition might translate his "sob" into a "song" that he will call "his," and the poem, though it hopes to "lend ease" to a future reader, enacts its own potential inability to comfort an audience.[13] Though Owen subtly considers the difference between reading and writing poetry here, he finds diversion, at least, in composing a poem in a traditional metrical form. After writing a roundel about Hercules in 1914, he explains to his cousin Leslie Gunston that "I find it exceedingly easy to write one without having either emotion or ideas."[14] We can trace how Owen clearly values poetry as a means of uncensored expression at the same time as he finds it delightful that he can compose easily in a fixed form—a dual awareness that predates his enlistment.

Two months after the declaration of war, Owen was in France working his way toward rationalizing a reason to enlist. Though he wouldn't join the Artists' Rifles until November 1915, he was indecisive about his "duty" to defend England and its language versus his "duty" toward writing poetry. On November 6, 1914 he wrote to his mother: "Now I <u>may</u> be led into enlisting when I get home: so familiarize yourself with the idea! It is a sad sign if <u>I do</u>: for it means that I shall consider the continuation of my life of no use to England. And if once my fears are roused for the perpetuity and supremacy of my mother-tongue, in the world — I would not hesitate, as I hesitate now — to enlist" (295).

Owen considers his sacrifice particularly great in the context of language and poetry, since it is possible that the "continuation" of his life might lead to important poetic contributions to the mother tongue. The idea of a "mother" country and "mother tongue" surfaces in a letter to his own mother—who was far away when he was living in France and working as a tutor in Bordeaux— and carries multiple ties to the communities of home: national, literary, and familial. Nearly a month later, he honed his argument, seeing himself as Keats's direct disciple, one in a long line of important poets:

> The *Daily Mail* speaks very movingly about the 'duties shirked' by English young men. I suffer a good deal of shame. But while those ten thousand lusty louts go on playing football I shall go on playing with my little axiom: — that my life is worth more than my death to Englishmen.
>
> Do you know what would hold me together on a battlefield? The sense that I was perpetuating the language in which Keats and the rest of them wrote! I do not know in what else England is greatly superior, or dearer to me, than another land and people. (300)

Owen's idea of what could "hold him together" in combat is shaped by his relation to the community of "English poets," of which he sees himself a part.[15] By 1915, he was reading *Servitude et Grandeur Militaires* by Alfred de Vigny

and quoting this line to his mother: "<u>If any man despairs of becoming a Poet,
let him carry his pack and march in the ranks</u>." He continued, "I don't despair
of <u>becoming</u> a Poet.... Will you set about finding the address of the 'Artists'
Rifles' as this is the Corps which offers commissions to 'gentlemen returning
from abroad'"(342). Artists' Rifles interested Owen because Lord Leighton
(1830–96, president of the Royal Academy 1878–96), Millais (1829–96, Pre-
Raphaelite cofounder), and Forbes Robertson (1853–1937, actor and theater
manager), were all members, as he exclaimed to his mother in a letter two
weeks later. Once Owen enlisted and had begun his military training, however, he complained to his brother Harold that his poetic training was woe-
fully inept in the face of his new duties: "What does Keats have to teach me of
rifle and machine-gun drill, how will my pass in Botany teach me to lunge a
bayonet, how will Shelley show me how to hate or any poet teach me the trajectory of the bullet?"[16] Owen may not have realized, at this stage, how much
poetry would help to keep him together on the battlefield, in the Casualty
Clearing Station, and at the War Hospital.

Apparently free of such hesitations, Robert Graves enlisted almost immediately after the outbreak of war. His first book of poems, *Over the Brazier*, however, also contains poems in which he imagines his work's reception and questions his relationship to the poetry he was taught to value. The book is divided
into three parts. The first part, "Charterhouse," is the name of Graves's public
school, where he encountered poetry for the first time; in his memoir, he records: "I found a book that had the ballads of 'Chevy Chase' and 'Sir Andrew
Barton' in it; these were the first two real poems I remember reading. I saw
how good they were."[17] The poems in "Charterhouse" show an admiration for
"anthems, stately, thunderous" ("Ghost Music") but also show Graves's playful
and irreverent attitude toward the constraints of English meter. His long
poem titled "Free Verse" (reprinted as the final poem in his 1917 *Fairies and
Fusiliers*), begins:

I now delight
In spite
Of the might
And the right
Of classic tradition   5
In writing
And reciting
Straight ahead
Without let or omission
Just any little rhyme   10
In any little time
That runs in my head:
Because, I've said,

My rhymes no longer stand arrayed
Like Prussian soldiers on parade　　　　　　　　　　　　　15
That march,
Stiff as starch,
Foot to foot,
Boot to boot,
Blade to blade,　　　　　　　　　　　　　　　　　　　20
Button to button,
Cheeks and chops and chins like mutton.[18]

Graves's poem is regulated by "any little rhyme" without any regular time, performing its own delusion with traditional verse forms,[19] and seeing what happens when he puts them into "uniform." The lines, "My rhymes no longer stand arrayed / Like Prussian soldiers on parade" are the most metrically regular lines of the poem, and directly link metrical form to military form. "Foot to foot" becomes "boot to boot," and then, dangerously, "blade to blade." Military discipline is preceded by the disciplines of "classical tradition." Graves accuses poets, who attempt to artificially arrange their poems into "meaningless conceits," of being "petty." The action of "disciplining" language into poetic form is allegorized as violent, and the verbs Graves uses to describe the desecration of language allude to both violence during wartime and that of English ideas of propriety:

How petty
To take
A merry little rhyme
In a jolly little time　　　　　　　　　　　　　　　　35
And poke it
And choke it
Change it, arrange it
Straight-lace it, deface it,
Pleat it with pleats,　　　　　　　　　　　　　　　　40
Sheet it with sheets,
Of empty meaningless conceits,
And chop and chew
And hack and hew
And weld it into a uniform stanza,　　　　　　　　　　　45
And evolve a neat
Complacent, complete,
Academic extravaganza![20]

The "rhymes," like Saintsbury's armies of soldierly feet, are welded "into a uniform stanza," "button to button," "neat" and "complacent," "complete." And yet Graves, himself a captain, participates in this "academic extravaganza" in his loosely formed "free verse," which is, with its odd "straight-laced" rhyme, anything but "free." Like Owen's lament that the "throb" of metrical beats does not align with his heartbeat, Graves makes the act of aligning metrical feet menacingly corporeal. The verses are chopped, chewed, hacked, and hewed like mutton. The "might and right" of classical and military tradition are made ironic; Owen's later allusion to Horace's "sweet and meet," becomes, for Graves, "sweet" and "meat": the coming butchery of the soldierly bodies can be read as powerfully foreshadowed by the complacency with which soldierly feet are hacked into Graves's Skeltonic lines.

Despite the chilling collision of military and metrical form in "Free Verse," (later titled, provocatively, "In Spite," in 1927), the second section of *Over the Brazier* titled "La Bassée" (referring to the Battle of La Bassée in the fall of 1914) considers the familiar themes of military and poetic glory. "The Shadow of Death" laments (like Owen's prewar letter) that dying young for Graves would also mean the end of his poetic gift. "Here's an end to my art! / I must die and I know it, / With battle murder at my heart — / Sad death for a poet! // Oh my songs never sung, / And my plays to darkness blown! / I am still so young, so young, / And my life was my own." Graves's unwritten poems are mourned like dead soldiers or his dead children: "song, / I may father no longer" (19). In the sonnet, "The Morning Before Battle," Graves contrasts how he "carelessly sang, pinned roses on my breast" in the octave, to the stark final three lines of the sestet that anticipate the now famous image from T. S. Eliot's *The Waste Land*: "the pale rose / Smelt sickly, till it seemed through a swift tear-flood / That dead men blossomed in the garden close" (21). Though war and poetry seem incommensurate in these two poems, Graves comments on how the war inspires less macabre transformations. "A Renascence" describes the "white flabbiness" of arms turning into "brown and lean . . . brass bars," men who have "steeled a tender, girlish heart, / Tempered it with a man's pride, / Learning to play the butcher's part / Though the woman screams inside" (13). The inherent chauvinism of these lines is amplified by the fact that metrical poetry must be made into a manly art. The men are taught to "leap the parapet" and "stab the stark bayonet" but the rebirth is not their transformation from effeminate bystanders into hardened heroes, rather it is the transformation of this military world—and the misery it brings with it—into poetry. Graves performs the transformation of brute action into the potentially more redemptive act of writing poems, thus enacting the rebirth of the title: "of their travailings and groans / Poetry is born again."[21]

Graves refused to reprint many of these early war poems in later volumes, though he continued to elaborate on the problems of military and musical form in his memoir *Goodbye to All That* (1929). "La Bassée" is where Graves questions the innocence of marching songs and demonstrates how these take on a maddening repetition and murderous connotations:

"[t]hat night we marched back again. . . . The men were singing. Being mostly from the Midlands, they sang comic songs. . . : *Slippery Sam, When we've Wound up the Watch on the Rhine,* and *I do like a S'nice S'mince Pie,* to a concertina accompaniment. The tune of *S'nice S'mince Pie* ran in my head all next day, and for the week following I couldn't get rid of it."[22]

In the ten pages after his first introduction of this song, Graves describes in vivid detail a brutal disaster of communication, resulting in thousands of casualties: "the barbed-wire entanglements protecting [the old front line] had not been removed, so that the Highlanders got caught and machine-gunned between their own assault and support lines" (129); "We went up to the corpse-strewn front line" (132); "I was surprised at some of the attitudes in which the dead stiffened—bandaging friends' wounds, crawling, cutting wire" (134). The survivors eat meat pie and deaden their nerves with whiskey before they line up to wait for the next stage of attack, and the menacing song about meat pie returns:

> We waited on the fire-step from four to nine o'clock, with fixed bayonets, for the order to go over. My mind was a blank, except for the recurrence of *S'nice S'mince S'pie, S'nice S'mince S'pie . . . I don't like ham, lamb or jam, and I don't like roley-poley . . .*
> The men laughed at my singing. The acting C.S.M. said: "It's murder, sir."
> "Of course it's murder, you bloody fool," I agreed, "But there's nothing else for it, is there?" It was still raining. *But when I sees a s'nice s'mince s'pie, I asks for a helping twice. . .* (137)

Amid descriptions of corpses souring on the front—"I vomited more than once while superintending the carrying. . . . The colour of the dead faces changed from white to yellow-grey, to red, to purple, to green, to black, to slimy" (137)—the song manically repeating in the officer's head takes on the connotation of murder, the soldiers' decomposing bodies in direct contrast to the whiskey and meat pie that the survivors eat. The joking expression, "it's murder, sir," expresses what they have just carried out, and are about to repeat. The expression also proves that the song, on endless repetition in their minds, is agitating rather than calming or ordering. Graves's character dismisses the complaint by continuing to sing, and as such, anticipates that this song and this war will continue by the refrain, "I ask for a helping twice." The irony of this passage is that the officer has assimilated the view of the troops; even the simplest forms of comfort have lost meaning here and have come to symbolize the brutal and empty goals of battle. The endless repetition, both of the tune's recurrence in his mind and his performance of it, signifies form's inability to console or even distract the soldier from his circumstances. Repetition appears again in the wake of inconsolability through the popular First World War marching song, "We're Here Because We're Here." The song is an example of the foot-beat rhythm growing almost maddeningly repetitive, to the tune of "Auld Lang Syne"—a song about past joyous times that ironically refers to those times being brought back into the present again and again, as well as the tune to which popular histories of England were sung (as I discussed in chapter 1). Here, "let auld acquaintance be forgot," becomes a more apt subtext for the song's proliferation of nonmovement. There is no mention of "there," the home where old acquaintances await, and sung on the march, the song erases each new place the soldier lays his feet; he is at once 'here' and 'here' and 'here,' a veritable nowhere. The song: "We're here / Because / We're here / Because / We're here / Because we're here" enacts the trap of progression within no progression as well as the feeling of being "nowhere" at all on the larger scale of the theater of war. The war is "here" and "everywhere," just as the soldier's tune demands no beginning or past, and no end or future.[23]

Though both Owen and Graves considered their poetry to be a patriotic contribution to the national language, Graves's early poem comments on meter and militaristic discipline and violence, and his prose about war comments on the way sing-song verse meant to comfort can quickly turn sinister. Owen's letters foreshadow his breakdown when he imagines that an idea of Keats could "hold him together" on the battlefield and his subtle awareness in the poem "On my Songs" that the "throb" of poetry, at times, "holds nothing" for him is evidence of a latent disillusionment that would become manifest in the Craiglockhart War Hospital. There is much in both Owen's letters and poems and Graves's poems and memoir about the intermingling of military forms and musical and metrical forms. On a typewritten copy of Graves's poem "Free Verse," Owen copied out another poem from *Over the Brazier*: "Sorley's Weather":

When outside the icy rain
Comes leaping helter-skelter,
Shall I tie my restive brain
Snugly under shelter?

Shall I make a gentle song,   5
Here in my firelit study?
When outside the winds blow strong
And the lanes are muddy?

With old wine and drowsy meats
Am I to fill my belly?   10
Shall I glutton here with Keats?
Shall I drink with Shelley?

Tobacco's pleasant, firelight's good
Poetry makes both better.
Clay is wet and so is mud,   15
Winter rains are wetter.

Yet rest there Shelley, on the sill,
For though the winds come frorely,
I'm away to the rain-blown hill
And the ghost of Sorley.[24]

Both poems were ostensibly from Graves's manuscript pages; war poet Charles Sorley was killed in action in October 1915 and his collection *Marlborough and Other Poems* was published posthumously in 1916. Here, Owen and Graves agree that Shelley and Keats are not useful in the current storm, but Owen is still thinking about how poetry might make things better. In a poem Owen wrote at Craiglockhart, called "The Poet in Pain," he criticizes those who would write of the horrors of war without experiencing it: "Some men sing songs of Pain and scarcely guess / Their import, for they never knew her stress."[25] It is his task, still imagining the representation of the nation's greatness in its poetry, "to write of health with shaking hands, bone-pale, / Of pleasure, having hell in every vein" (ll. 11–12). We could read "to write of health with shaking hands" as "to write *to* health"—no longer the health of the larger nation, but the health of the smaller community of officers who found themselves cut off from the poetic and national ideals that led them to enlist in the first place. Like Tietjens imagining the healthy bodies of his fat, wet letters, the responsibility to preserve and protect English poetry, and the figure of the English poet, shifted so that the writing of English poetry became part of the process of healing the psyches of wounded soldier poets.

Therapeutic Measures

W.H.R. Rivers was among the many medical officers interested in new treatments for neurasthenia or, as Rivers preferred to call it, anxiety and substitution neurosis. Anxiety neurosis interested Rivers because it required that the patient attempt to "lift" the repression in his mind through a process of confronting, narrating, and therefore "metabolizing" the memory that, by his methods, had been "thrust out of [the patient's] consciousness."[26] This ability to renarrate an event in order to recontextualize it was the unique ability of officers; Rivers expressed boredom with the men of the ranks he had treated at Maghull War Hospital, recording that "the characteristic of the uneducated person is that the mental outlook of adult life does not differ appreciably from that of childhood."[27] Rivers believed that officers possessed a higher faculty for expression in general due to their education, but also understood that their upbringing formed part of a culture of repression in British society that required men to "move on" from difficult memories without confronting or expressing them, especially officers who were expected to repress fear in order to lead a regiment confidently into battle. This culture of repression, for Rivers, was the root cause of many nervous disorders—repression that had "germinated in the nursery and [been] perfected in the English public school."[28] Though Rivers criticizes this tendency in English society, it is this very ability to express traumatic memories in well-crafted English narratives that attracted him to the highly educated officer-patients at Craiglockhart.

Before transferring to Craiglockhart, Rivers worked closely with Dr. William Brown at Maghull, where both doctors developed their therapeutic methods. Brown's idea, *autognosis*, largely adapted from Freud, was based on the new belief that anxiety neuroses were based in pathogenic associations between past and recent events and the resulting confusions over meaning. In "W.H. R. Rivers and the War Neuroses," Allan Young explains that the job of therapy was to expose these links and clarify these misunderstandings (369). Brown emphasized "long talks between the physician and the patient." The physician's task, among others, was to help the patient sort out any temporal dislocation between past and current events through redirecting the patient's attention toward "a neglected aspect of his experience,"[29] in an attempt to transform traumatic memories into tolerable, and even pleasant, images. Rivers gives the example of a patient who witnessed the violent death of his friend; a shell had blown apart the man's body. The doctor points out that quick death of his patient's friend, though gruesome, was painless, and that this friend is now free from harm, thus allowing the patient to "dwell upon his painful memories" by casting them in a new (albeit grimly positive) light. Dr. Rivers's patient, Sassoon, published four poems in the hospital literary magazine *The Hydra* in 1917.[30] "Repression of War Experience" (the title of a 1917 lecture and 1918 *Lancet* article by Rivers) was not among the poems Sassoon published at Craiglockhart, perhaps to protect Dr. Rivers from thinking his nerves were out of order. The poem illustrates what Sassoon thought of Rivers's methods and of the process of therapy in general:

> it's bad to think of war,
> when thoughts you've gagged all day come back to scare you;
> and it's been proved that soldiers don't go mad
> Unless they lose control of ugly thoughts
> That drive them out to jabber among the trees.   5
> Now light your pipe; look, what a steady hand.
> Draw a deep breath; stop thinking, count fifteen,
> And you're as right as rain . . .[31]

This ironic narration shows the harm caused by repression, despite the belief that "it's bad to think of war." The poem ends with the subject running mad among the trees.

Sassoon describes the order of daytime treatment and "wholesome activities" at the hospital as "elaborately cheerful. Brisk amusements were encouraged, entertainments were got up, and serious cases were seldom seen downstairs" (23), but he later contrasts these organized amusements with the chaotic and uncontrollable aspects of the war neuroses. Day and night are contrasted as interludes controlled by either the medical staff or by the anxiety neuroses, but never by the patient's own repaired will.

> [B]y night [the doctors] lost control and the hospital became sepulchral and oppressive with saturations of war experience. . . . One became conscious that the place was full of men whose slumbers were morbid and terrifying — men muttering uneasily or suddenly crying out in their sleep. . . . In the day-time, sitting in a sunny room, a man could discuss his psycho-neurotic symptoms with his doctor, who could diagnose phobias and conflicts and formulate them in scientific terminology. Significant dreams could be noted down, and Rivers could try to remove repressions. (87–88)

"Muttering" or "suddenly crying out" is calmly transcribed into "scientific terminology" that the doctor "notes down," diagnosing and renarrating the symptoms into a cheerful reinscription of the experience in the patient's mind. In Sassoon's description, daytime is unsettling and unsatisfying, as if we could already anticipate the contrast with incommunicable and sudden terror, shouted to the reluctant audience of other sleepless soldiers in the inevitable night. The descent into chaotic memories is described in bracing detail as that which is truly present in the patient's mind—a place to which the doctor, despite his nodding encouragement, will never have complete access. "[B]y night each man was back in his doomed sector of a horror-stricken front line where the panic and stampede of some ghastly experience was re-enacted among the livid faces of the dead. No doctor could save him then. . . . Not then was their evil hour, but now; now, in the sweating suffocation of nightmare, in paralysis of limbs, in the stammering of dislocated speech" (87).

Here, Sassoon narrates what will be familiar to us as the definition of trauma: that the moment when the memory occurred is less powerful than its haunting and endless return, mocking the deliberate military march of any disciplined order and seizing the patient's mind with an unordered "stampede" of nightmare. Sassoon's dramatization of the doctor's attempts to "remove repressions" feels ironically inefficient when compared to the patient's disorienting collapse of past into present and the resulting dislocation of expression manifested bodily by the stammer. Rather than "reenacting" an experience for the listening doctor, experiences are involuntarily "reenacted" for the now livid audience of the dead and are, through their haunting recurrence, performed nightly on the stage of the patient's neurasthenic psyche.

Time's collapse was manifest, for many patients, in the inability to control or adequately manipulate speech—what Sassoon calls "the stammering of dislocated speech"; though speech is always located "elsewhere," the metrical grid provided both spatial and temporal orientation. The metrical aspect of recovery is evident in Sassoon's 1918 letter to Graves, in which words cram together nonsensically until the appearance of Dr. Rivers soothes the patient into almost mocking, yet ordered, double dactyls: "Sleeplessexasperuicide, O Jesu make it stop! / But yesterday afternoon my reasoning Rivers ran solemnly in, / With peace in the pools of his spectacled eyes and a wisely omnipotent grin." Not only does Rivers's appearance coincide with dactylic regularity in this line, but Sassoon, as a patient, transforms his self-loathing into self-appreciation (albeit ironic) through Rivers's guidance into the patient's "grey" unconscious: "And I fished in that steady grey stream and decided that I / After all am no longer the Worm that refuses to die. / But a gallant and glorious lyrical soldjer." A "lyrical soldjer," however, who resents how his mind is "crammed with village verses about Daffodils and Geese" and begs his doctor to free him of his misery: "O Rivers please take me. And make me / Go back to the war till it break me."[32] This passage is a case study for Captain Brock's assessment of speech-disruption among sufferers of neurasthenic trauma: "The various affections of speech tend to run into one another; moreover, along with the stammer of the tongue we not infrequently observe a distinct 'mental stammer.'"[33] Here, we see how Sassoon's writing runs together the unhealthy letters, cramming the dactylic "sleeplessness," "exasperate," and "suicide" into a stammering and traumatic metrical and material effect on the page. At once ironic and expressive, the passage consciously or unconsciously plays out the psychic condition Brock describes.

Brock elaborates on the officer's unique relationship to disrupted time and speech in his 1923 book, *Health and Conduct*:

> The shell-shock patient is out of Time altogether. If a "chronological," he is at least not a historical being. Except in so far as future or past may contain some memory or prospect definitely gratifying, or morbidly holding him, he dismisses both. He lives for the moment, on the surface of things. His memory is weak (amnesia), his will is weak (aboulia), he is improvident and devoid of foresight. He is out of Space, too; he shrinks from his immediate surroundings (geophobia), or at most he faces only certain aspects of it; he is a specialist à Outrance.[34]

Brock's analysis shows how the patient is both immovably moored in time and space—unable to move forward through language, so repeating sounds in a loop—and how the patient somehow unconsciously chooses his extreme detachment from both time and space. His thoughts cannot move forward, nor can his speech. The patient must be reeducated to see himself in time as part of a continuum, and he must reintegrate into the social world and his surroundings to face all aspects of experience. Brock advises treating the whole patient, not merely the symptoms: "[T]he far-seeing doctor will not allow the urgency of the local expression to blind him to the much more important general condition (otherwise — if he confines himself to dealing with symptoms — it will probably be as with the heads of the Hydra — '*uno avulso, non deficit alter.*'"[35] Brock's treatment methods were also Hydra-like in their efficiency— highly coordinated and diverse activities at the hospital were Brock's solution for treating patient "inco-ordination" (146). The patients' responsibility to manage their own time—through an endless array of physical and social activities—would, in Brock's reckoning, force them to actively and metrically order their mental chaos by virtue of thinking through new contexts of time (the five-beat line of a poem, a first-person narrative or short-story, a play) and space (a diagram of the city, a lecture on botany, a description of local museums).

Brock encouraged patients to write metrical poetry but warned against the dangers of "art for art's sake," where art became a kind of drug that separated the patient from the social world; art for art's sake could be seen as an extreme form of *outrance*. To counter this artistic tendency, artists and writers in the hospital were encouraged, indeed, required, to "produce beautiful objects of immediate and practical utility," with the hopes that Brock could eventually "orchestrat[e] the work of all our artists towards cooperative programmes of regional or civil scope."[36] Objects of art, then, were subject to discipline just like any other "activity," though as an exercise, writing was specifically a form of communication with a larger collective—of other patients, possible patrons (hospital magazines raised money for the hospital, and patients were charged for copies), and an imagined community of literary connoisseurs and other publishing poets.

Meter's role as part of this connective tissue, hearkening back to prewar poetic forms, was perhaps the most important aspect of Brock's therapy for Owen and other literary-minded patients. The ability to manipulate poetic language into English poetic form linked these soldier-poets to the larger field of English writing and of the country in general. In the hospital, even the poetic self was part of the collective history of the region and country; not isolated, but participating in his heritage, in the preservation of his own past and future, and in his own rehabilitation. Learning these tools relied on discipline and labor; what Brock called "ergo-therapy" reconnected the soldier to the social and physical world—to the structure and communities of language and country—from which he had become severed through the unnatural mechanizations of modern warfare.

On March 22, 1917 Owen quoted from memory a long passage from Elizabeth Barrett Browning's *Aurora Leigh*, condemning "many tender hearts" for stringing "their losses on a rhyming thread." Owen confessed to his sister that he, too, had perhaps "sow[ed] [his] wild oats in tame verse"; he added, "this passage winded me, yea wounded me."[37] In a long letter to his brother one month later, we see Owen's reliance on rhythmical form despite a reluctance to unconditionally endorse the traditional English poetic form haunting his letters. Owen laments the lack of a drumbeat as he describes to his brother the sensation of "going over the top":

I kept up a kind of chanting sing-song: Keep the line straight!
Not so fast on the left!
Steady on the Left!
Not so fast! (458)

Owen begins "Keep the line straight!" on the same line as the letter, then indents the next three lines into a stanza for a little marching poem. The four lines, read together, each have three strong beats, but each also wavers with extra syllables as if to show how difficult it is to keep this line, or any line, "straight." He seems to identify corporeally with the rhythmic form, as if by making the drumbeat himself, in his mind and voice, he will encourage his feet and those of his men to move forward. Reading the meter of these four, three-beat lines shows how Owen, himself, broke them as if to indicate how the "chanting sing-song" was, in his mind, charged with the responsibility of keeping him moving forward. It is clear, however, that the only lines that allow the quatrain's movement are those crammed with syllables around the beat; that is, the iamb and anapest of "**Not** so **fast** on the **left**" lifts the line up and hurries it through the unaccented syllables of the words "on the" so as to keep time with the line, just as "**Steady on** the **Left**" slows through "**Steady**," shaking the pronunciation of the word so that it becomes unsteady. The three monosyllables that are also, perhaps, three stressed syllables, exclaim "Not so fast!" and show the poet and the soldier's inhibitions about moving forward, seeming to pull the small poem back into itself—a retreat from metrical feet altogether. Absolving the line from any unstressed syllables, any "sing-song" is a direct confrontation of that standard metrical culture; a retreat from regularity as the soldier-poet approaches that other three-syllable space of "no man's land." This small quatrain indicates the simultaneous forward and backward instincts of cresting the top of the trench into no man's land. But the poet's employment and manipulation of, as well as his deviation from, metrical forms also shows the poet-soldier's wavering line; Owen cannot keep the line straight, nor can the (poetic) line keep him (mentally) straight. He composed this particular letter from the casualty clearing station in straight lines following standard issue ruled paper, after suffering the shell blast that would manifest itself as neurasthenia.[38]

Owen arrived at Craiglockhart on June 23, 1917 and met Dr. Brock in his office for the first time four days later. Brock recognized that Owen was a "devotee" of writing; in the hospital, his poems took up issues of feet, rhythm, music, and sound as primary and secondary themes, especially in the war poems. Three instances show how assignments by Dr. Brock directly influenced Owen to associate survival with his ability to manipulate poetic form, (metrically, as he had been taught). First, Owen was assigned a report on Outlook Tower in Edinburgh—a tall medieval house adapted as a center for sociological studies. On July 14, 1917, Owen read the following notes to his doctor: "I perceived that this Tower was a symbol: an Allegory, not a historic structure but a poetic form. I had supposed it to be a museum, and found it [a] philosophical poem: when I had stood within its walls an hour I became aware of a soul, and the continuity of its idea from room to room, and from storey to storey was an epic."[39] Owen fuses the spatial allegory of poetic form to the temporal allegory of narrative structure—an order for wholeness. He acts out Brock's desire that the patients participate in the larger community, but through his reconsideration of poetic form he sees himself as part of a specifically literary community; indeed, through Owen's poems we are able to perceive poetic form as a kind of historic structure.

Brock saw the mechanizations of modern war as inherently unnatural and sought to reunite his patients to their social as well as natural environments. The land, of course, was Britain, and geographic knowledge—an ability to map out one's surroundings, to navigate—was an important part of "reconnecting to one's environment" as well. Brock composed an article about the Anteaus myth for *The Hydra*, noting how "His story is the justification of our activities. When we come here the first thing we do is to get on our legs again. . . . Thus we come "back to the land" in the most literal, as well as the more metaphorical sense."[40] Like Owen's assignment to write about Outlook Tower, Brock saw Owen's concern with poetic form as one way that the neurasthenic soldier could reorder his understanding of himself in time and in the larger context of English writers. Owen simultaneously worked on a presentation for the newly created "Field Club" at the hospital and on his second literary assignment for Dr. Brock, the composition of a poem about the Anteaus myth.[41]

Owen approached the composition of his Anteaus poem as a spatial problem. He wrote to his mother, "On the Hercules-Anteaus Subject — there are only 3 or 4 lines in the Dictionary. So I shall just do a Sonnet."[42] By the time he wrote to his cousin Leslie Gunston a few days later, the poetic form progressed from the two stanzas or two rooms of a sonnet to a larger blank verse epic, or what Owen calls "a strong bit of Blank." This lengthening of form from finite to continuous in both the Outlook Tower essay and the Anteaus fragment

demonstrates Owen's consideration of a possible literary, or heroic, future—a perpetuation of life like the perpetuation of the English poetic tradition he imagined for himself as a younger poet. In addition, by sharing
the poem with his cousin Leslie, Owen reached out to his prewar poetic
community.

> . . . How earth herself empowered him with her touch
> Gave him the grip and stringency of Winter,
> And all the ardour of th'invincible Spring;
> How all the blood of June glutted his heart,
> And all the glow of huge autumnal storms
> Stirred on his face, and flickered from his eyes. (477)

The sound patterns of this early version of the poem foreshadow Owen's later
mastery of interwoven sound structures. Each season seems to have its own
sound sown within the line; the "er" sound of line 1; the soft "i" and "n" of line
2; the "ah" and "er" of line 3.[43] These alliterative effects are signaled by metrical
stresses as well, alternating within Owen's stringent blank verse. The "blood of
June" that "glutted the heart" of Anteaus can be read as a memory of the blood
of June in the battlefield Owen has escaped. These powers, drawn from the
seasons of the earth, are only available to Anteaus when his feet are firmly
planted on the earth, to the roots of words and to their geographies of phonemes and inner structures, not just the metrical forms imposed on language
from without. The "stringency" and discipline of winter must come before the
"ardour" and "invincible" spring of the young and hopeful soldier until finally
the blood of June battles triumphs. In a letter written the same day to his
mother, he quotes a longer excerpt from the beginning of the poem, describing
how Hercules was "baffled" by the strength of his opponent, and fixed his feet
firmly to the earth. The line, "And yet more firmly fixed his graspèd feet,"
shows how the strength of the ten-syllable line is bolstered by the diacritical
mark promoting an artificial second syllable in "graspèd" (in a later version,
Owen revised this word to "grasping" to keep the two syllables and remove the
diacritical mark). The figures in the poem struggle through their feet—Hercules's feet are "firmly fixed" though the poem's metrical feet are not, jostling
between iambs and trochees. The poem's feet are more like Anteaus, pulled
away from the firm ground of English poetic form: "How, too, Poseidon
blessed him fatherly / With wafts of vigor from the keen sea waves, / And with
the subtle coil of currents — / Strange underflows" (477). The word "coil" is
also promoted to two syllables here, expanding a word that means contraction
to arbitrarily lengthen the line to ten syllables. The poet is wrestling with unruly feet themselves, the beginning of a metaphor for time and measure that
appears in many of his later war poems and, most significantly, in his substantial writing for *The Hydra*.

The most notable activity Brock prescribed for Owen was the editorship of *The Hydra*. Most hospitals that treated shell shock had small papers or gazettes that published hospital activities, though none were quite as literary as *The Hydra*.[44] Not only did *The Hydra* provide the kind of comradeship between officers that Brock recommended, it specifically demonstrated the indelible forms of education that each officer carried. Through its frequent allusion to literature, classics, and the arts, the magazine allowed the officers to associate with both their social class and with past communities of school and home. The journal was entirely patient-run—evidence of Brock's influence. Already relying on the forms of classical knowledge shared by most officers, the first editorial states: "The name of the journal will indicate what we wish its character to be: many headed—many sided" (April 28, 1917). The name *Hydra* was not only a reference to Hercules's labors, but also referred to the fact that the hospital was a former hydropathic sanitorium, dubbed "the hydro" by its wards. Through the articles published in *The Hydra* (especially during the four months when Owen was editor), we come to understand how writing at Craiglockhart was a part of the therapeutic process of organizing neurasthenic time.

For instance, the September 15, 1917 issue, under Owen's editorship, includes an eerie cartoon of Captain Rivers, drawn by "one who has not seen him." Rivers is dressed as an Oxford tutor and stands on a pedestal of books while four officers sit in the background passively waiting for the wand-bearing wizard to cure them. (From the Casualty Clearing Station, Owen wrote to his sister Mary on May 8, 1917: "The Nerve Specialist is a kind of wizard, who mesmerizes when he likes: a famous man."[45] The soldiers in the drawing show no sign of functioning or taking control of their own activities; they sit slumped in chairs as if in a trance. A scroll in Latin swirls above Rivers's head: "Styx Acheron Phlegethon Lethe Cytis Avernus," but upon closer examination we see that the doctor is reciting, the scroll leading ominously back to his mouth. The pun on "rivers" is clear in the translation from the Latin; these are the names of "rivers" Virgil and Dante encounter in *The Inferno*. Rivers stands on the stage of literature with a book ignited in flame in his left hand, asking his charges to confront their own personal hell of traumatic memories, as if to show how despite all the discipline and authority in their education and military training, there will always be a chaos threatening to ignite at any moment. There is, in the postures of the slumped men, the sense of complete passivity; despite the mesmerism of the "wizard" doctor, there seems a distinct possibility that these men are broken beyond repair. In this way, the cartoon offers another subtle questioning of the military and therapeutic orders the men are expected to follow in the hospital. The cartoon, then, shows how education and psychotherapy are perhaps inadequate forms of discipline and self-preservation in the face of neurasthenic "hell." This scene replicates and mocks the forms of classical education to which the officers were privileged, while at

Figure 4. Cartoon of Captain Rivers, anonymous, published in *The Hydra* on September 15, 1917. Copyright Jon Stallworthy, Wilfred Owen Estate. Courtesy of the Bodleian Library, OEF Wilfred Owen Collection, Box 37.

the same time showing how they are dependent on these same forms in the hospital.

The Hydra received enough financial support by September 1917 that the editorial committee pleaded for more submissions and a different cover for what was to be the "new series" in November 1917 (the month of Owen's discharge). "We make a last appeal for an attractive cover design—a promising futurist thing, if you will; anything but a future promise" (September 29, 1917). We may read a grim humor in his phrase, "future promise." In the fantastic new cover (see figure 5), the rigid military forms of the original cover picture (with its austere-looking officer standing in front of the square hospital building) are blasted away by the fluid drawing of a soldier propelled backwards by a shell blast shaped like the multi-headed hydra, both a classical reference and a gesture to the former use of the hospital. The hospital is barely visible, perched up on a hill in the far right corner, and the scorched earth below resembles the pocked moonscape of Owen's 1917 poem, "The Show": "a sad land, weak with sweats of dirth, / Grey, cratered like the moon with hollow woe" (155). The soldier has lost hold of a book; in both this drawing and the cartoon about Rivers, literature's ability to heal is dramatized and, ultimately, questioned. It is as if, in some small way, these artists demonstrate that literary form cannot possibly contain the horrific and fantastical visions of a world blown apart and scorched by war.

Owen attempted to steer the magazine toward his own literary aspirations by begging for more verse submissions in every editorial. Though Owen printed two of his own poems in the magazine (anonymously), his editorials provide indirect mediation on coming to terms with the different requirements of therapy at Craiglockhart, and show how his own poetic writing might be read for "marks" of neurasthenic disconnection from time's proper marching. In many places in the magazine we see the contrast between Brock's methods, geared toward work and activity, and Rivers's, geared toward expression of repressed experiences. Unlike Sassoon's characterization of Rivers's methods, in which the doctor asserts control over a passive patient's chaotic psyche, Brock's patients are hyperaware of their own active attempts at control. Brock writes:

> In the act of normal individual functioning . . . all the elements of time are involved. [The subject's] present action bears relation not only to his actual circumstances but is based on his past experience . . . and reaches forward into his future. The action of a neurasthenic does not show this equilibrium, this evenly-balanced flow . . . the attention of the neurasthenic may become temporarily arrested upon some element of his past or future experience, and he develops a worry or definite *phobia*.[46]

Figure 5. New Series. Cover design by Mr. Adrian Berrington, published in *The Hydra*, November 1917. Mr. Adrian Berrington is credited by A. J. Brock in the May 1918 editorial of *The Hydra*. Copyright Jon Stallworthy, Wilfred Owen Estate. Courtesy of the Bodleian Library, OEF Wilfred Owen Collection, Box 38.

Brock called the fear of properly functioning in linear time, "ergophobia." The magazine takes on "ergophobia" as a leitmotif, spoofing one officer who cannot think of a useful hobby and begins to have nightmares about his inability to occupy himself, and scolding patients who do not submit writing to the magazine as sufferers of "hydra-phobia."

In homage to and mockery of Dr. Brock's goals of adherence to linear time, Owen's August 18, 1917 editorial recounts the misadventures of "Private Time," condemned by "Colonel Eternity" to Eternal Field Punishment for "refusing to stand still on parade."[47] The soldier is ordered to "Mark Time." Though "Marking Time" is a military command requiring that the soldier lift each foot six inches off the ground without moving forward, here it stands in evocatively for shell shock—the patients are unable to move forward in time and are thus mentally marching in place. For officers like Owen, trained in classical and English verse writing, "marking time" would also be familiar as a method for scanning classical quantitative verse (dividing it into "feet"). Like Owen working out his metrical feet in lines of verse while recovering from trauma in the hospital, the character of Private Time is compelled to "mark time" strapped to the earth on eternal march. He eventually grows weary, but a policeman, aptly named "Private Watch," is hired to make sure "Private Time" does not "stand still." Of course, the officer's body is never moving forward because it is the earth that moves beneath his feet; "marking time" is merely "putting down the feet" without making progress, as arbitrary as any order. Metrical exercises are made arbitrary, just like precise military footwork that, in this instance, prevents the soldier from moving forward. Both Private Time and the policeman grow weary after so much work: "It was, and is, called 'the Small Hours,' and is open from 1:30am to 4:30am." Private Watch steals into these hours and "*Time, in his absence, stands still, and has a rest. And hence arise many of our troubles*" (emphasis Owen's). Owen's piece ends:

> But a way has been found. Knights of the Bedchamber, your vigils are at an end! Not long ago a magazine called *The Hydra* came into being. Its main idea was to contain things written while the policeman was in "The Small Hours." Then others started to read what had been written, and immediately fell asleep. Forgotten were the maladies, even to the very worst, which, in our opinion, is *Hydra*-phobia. When men lay out a golf-course, buy a pipe, or engage a cook, they do so with a purpose. When men start a magazine they do so because — because — we offer a "ticket" for the answer. (7)

The stammer of "because — because" could show the writer's doubt as to what the true purpose of *The Hydra* is, but, referring to the paper on which the magazine is printed, the "ticket" of writing and reading is seen as a way out of malady. In the magazine, writing is considered part of the cure—both because the writing is so poor it causes one to fall sleep, but also because the fact of writing might help the process of expressing the repressed memories that cause the nightmares. The impossible ticket, the dream of every soldier, was the "ticket" that meant official discharge from the army, especially for medical reasons, before the full period of service was up. To "work one's ticket" was to attempt, through scheming, bribing, or malingering, to get out of the army, and came to be known as a genial and facetious suggestion that a man was mentally defective. Despite the jovial tone, we see Owen's interpretation of the intolerability of waiting until dawn, of the dreams that double-back to memories, of the trap of trauma. In this article, we see the physical staggering of the tired soldier forced to march transformed into a soldier whose symptoms prevent him from moving forward in time. The arbitrariness of the military exercise is also a sly reference to the arbitrariness of writing under the auspices of rehabilitation.

Bent-Double

At Craiglockhart, officers who were unable to imagine themselves outside the traumatic "stopped time" of neurasthenic trauma were sometimes able to piece together a functional relation to time's movement through writing poetry, though their recovery meant an inevitable return to battle. As Brock's successful Anteaus, Owen learned to manipulate the complex relationships between his feet and his head, action and expression, and returned willingly to the front where he continued to write with an increased self-awareness. Re-reading Owen within the larger contexts of English national meters and the metricality of therapeutic healing, we can see how his poems try to reconcile the empty patriotic promises of prewar poetry and militarism. Indeed, with this in mind, Owen's habit of scanning below a poem seems particularly evocative, as if the marks do not need the letters beneath them to provide some form of comfort. His poems often contain metrical marks, and revisions show him trying to think through the complexities of metrical form.[48] However, in the poems he writes at Craiglockhart and after, Owen critiques the dangers of following rote militaristic feet and struggles with the question of how poetic form's future possibilities for meaning might be always determined by its inability to preserve, comfort, or even endure.

Owen composed a fragment in his last months at Craiglockhart (dated August–September 1917) titled, "All Sounds Have Been as Music." The 18-line poem begins: "All sounds have been as music to my listening: / Pacific lamentation of slow bells, / The crunch of boots on blue snow rosy-glistening, / Shuffle of autumn leaves; and all farewells." The poem continues on to name country bells clamoring and a host of other traditionally pastoral images, but the fourth stanza includes "startled clarions" and "drums, rumbling and rolling thunderous." Here, the crunch of boots is swept up in the idealized country life, and he leaves the last stanza unfinished, taking up these images and sounds as part of the betrayal he explores in his most famous war poems, "Anthem for Doomed Youth" and "Dulce et Decorum Est." In "The Calls," written in May 1918, some six months after his return to service, he begins each stanza envisioning a world measured by regular sounds, "a dismal fog-hoarse," "quick treble bells," "stern bells," "gongs hum and buzz," each occurring at a specific hour (much like his descriptions of military time in his letters). The fourth stanza dramatizes the "clumsiness" of soldiers trying to follow along in some sort of forced regularity: "A blatant bugle tears my afternoons. / Out clump the clumsy Tommies by platoons, / Trying to keep in step with rag-time tunes, / But I sit still; I've done my drill."[49] The manuscript copy shows that Owen deleted the lines "I've had my fill" and "Here I've no rime that's proper." Regularized external sounds, then, are allegorized in Owen's poems as disciplines or forms aware of and suspicious of their own value while, at the same time, the internal sounds of the poem, contracting and expanding in his metrical manipulation, simultaneously support and reject this allegory. "The Calls" admits that the sounds and forms of military and literary discipline are necessary, even if he has no "proper" way to express this unfortunate necessity. Other more blatantly antiwar poems violently question the necessity of military and metrical discipline.

There are many examples that demonstrate Owen's formal reckoning but few are as effective as his now canonized "Dulce et Decorum Est," which he began writing at Craiglockhart in October of 1917.

> Bent double, like old beggars under sacks,
> Knock-kneed, coughing like hags, we cursed through sludge,
> Till on the haunting flares we turned our backs
> And towards our distant rest began to trudge.
> Men marched asleep. Many had lost their boots   5
> But limped on, blood-shod. All went lame; all blind;
> Drunk with fatigue; deaf even to the hoots
> Of gas shells dropping softly behind.
>
> Gas! GAS! Quick, boys! — An ecstasy of fumbling,
> fitting the clumsy helmets just in time;   10
> But someone still was yelling out and stumbling,
> And flound'ring like a man in fire or lime . . .
> Dim, through the misty panes and thick green light,
> As under a green sea, I saw him drowning.
>
> In all of my dreams, before my helpless sight,   15
> He plunges at me, guttering, choking, drowning.

If in some smothering dreams you too could pace
Behind the wagon that we flung him in,
And watch the white eyes writhing in his face,
His hanging face, like a devil's sick of sin;   20
If you could hear, at every jolt, the blood
Come gargling from the froth-corrupted lungs,
Obscene as cancer, bitter as the cud
Of vile, incurable sores on innocent tongues, —
My friend, you would not tell with such high zest   25
To children ardent for some desperate glory,
The old Lie: Dulce et decorum est
Pro patria mori.

The form of Owen's poem is itself "bent double," like the soldiers it describes. Many critics have noted the poem's similarity to the Shakespearean sonnet form as well as its implicit reference to Wordsworth's "Leech-Gatherer": "Such seemed this Man, not all alive nor dead, / Nor all asleep — in his extreme old age: / His body was bent double, feet and head / Coming together in life's pilgrimage."[50] The poem is, in fact, two sonnets, bent and doubled in the middle at lines 13 and 14, where the lines that would normally form the final couplet in a Shakespearean sonnet simply begin a new rhyme: "light" and "drowning." Despite the formal buckling or juxtaposition with the second sonnet, the formless figure of the dying man provides a perfect thematic coda to the first octave, in which the men's marching is subdued in a sort of sleep. Indeed, in the sestet, the man's figure is obscured and shapeless as if underwater, his image seen through dim, thick, green light. The verbs and adjectives in the first sonnet—trudge, lame, blind, drunk, deaf—subdue the imagined activity into an embalmed slumber (these verbs reminiscent of what one would witness in the halls of Craiglockhart) Even the flares become part of a hazy backdrop, and the menacing shells drop "softly," like petals.[51] Likewise, the soldier's movements are calm and imperceptibly shuffling to a failed attempt at iambic pentameter, as if the spondaic opening of "Bént dóuble" and "Knóck knéed" of lines 1 and 2 show the extra step each man must take. When the lines settle into five stresses, in lines 3, 4, 5, 7, and 8, the iambs are consistently irregular, alliterations causing frequent trochaic and spondaic substitutions. The iambic pentameter seems perceptible enough, but the fact that these steps are complicated suggests that Owen, here, is lulling us into an expressive reading of regular accentual-syllabic meter. We might imagine that we think we know what kinds of steps the soldiers should be able to take, but are unable. Only line 4, of these beginning lines, adheres to the perfect five-beat iambic pentameter line: "And towárds our dístant rést begán to trudge." The meter marches asleep here, stumbling through a rhythm that is ruled by sound patterns rather than any traditional military or literary discipline. Line 6, the longest line of the first octave, is heavy with extra stresses and halts with three pauses—"But límped ón, // blóod-shód. // Áll went láme; // áll blínd"—as if this ten-syllable line could be divided into four, two-beat lines (complete with the pararhyme of "blood" and "blind"). The men's feet and the metrical feet limp on, shod in no protective form for the rhythmic beats.

Lines 9 through 12 express metrically the gasping repetition of "Gas! GAS! Quick, boys!" Quickly, the soldiers move—fumbling, stumbling, and fitting—as the form performs, back into the traditional ten syllables "just in time." The stumbling and fumbling of the poem is juxtaposed against the rigidity of lines 11 and 12, which are, like line 4, in exact pentameter, as if tradition somehow regularizes this chaotic moment; that is, Owen flaunts a moment of extreme metrical regularity at the chaotic center of the poem. We hear the iambs again from the middle of line 10—"the clúmsy hélmets júst in tíme; / But sómeone stíll was yélling oút and stúmbling, / And floúnd'ring líke a mán in fíre or líme"—with Owen careful to elide the "e" in floundering to keep the realigned meter regular. The man, "still" in the middle of the chaos, is caught up in the trudging slumber of the traditional iambs. Instead of a calm, sleep-ridden march, the meter of this first sonnet is thrown into suspicion. When called upon, the soldiers who could recover from their stumbling to move "just in time" were saved from the defeat of the trapped soldier, the "someone still" of the sestet. But not only is the iambic pentameter of a traditional sonnet bent and doubled in this poem; the sound structure in the first sonnet also performs a sort of bent doubling. If the meter of the first sonnet stumbles, the sound structure stammers—both the metrical and alliterative effects in the poem manifesting symptoms of trauma in their formal performances. In each line in the first octave, the sounds double on either side of a real or imaginary caesura (bent/beggars, coughed/cursed, til/turned, toward/trudge, men/many, blood/blind, drunk/deaf). Some of these sounds gesture toward Owen's experiments in pararhyme, taking out the vowel center of a word and leaving the skeletal structure of the beginning and end consonants, but these stammering sounds also show how subtle repetition, like the stumble of metrical feet, coaxes the poem forward to the sound that occurs in the middle of the line while also demanding that it double back to the sound at the beginning. These effects fade in the would-be sestet: "still" morphs into the sounds of "stumbling" in line 11, and "sea" into "saw" in line 14, neither a true stammer but more a "see-saw" of imbalance to signify the defining feature of the first sonnet's movement.

The second sonnet's movement performs an "about—turn," presenting its three quatrains in reverse, beginning with the couplet of "sight" and "drowning," heralding the theme of the second part of the poem, the sight of endless drowning from which the now marching soldier cannot look away. The stumble of broken iambic pentameter in the middle of the poem stands out against the measure of meter surrounding it. Rather than stammer through the explanation of the aftereffects of the event (the stammer and stumble are, themselves, aftereffects), the second sonnet foregrounds the difficulty of expressing the shocking central action—a man dying in the poisoned air—not only to an audience that has now become blind and deaf to the realities of war because of the "Old Lies" of tradition with which they themselves have been poisoned, but also through the very forum of poetic form. Lines 15 and 16 isolate the first person—his recurring nightmares, the "helpless sight" of traumatic memories lurching back toward him. Daniel Hipp notes that Owen shifts the verb tenses from past in the octave through progressive verbal forms in the sestet into present tense in these lines and, reading lines 15 and 16 as the completion of a quatrain, asserts that "the repetition of "drowning" at the expense of conventional rhyme emphasizes the persistence of the visual image within the poet's unconscious mind, which like the unfinished "sonnet" has remained unresolved."[52] According to Hipp, these two lines signal the mirror image of the second sonnet, pitting "I saw him drowning" against "before my helpless sight" as twin feelings, meant to emphasize both the transition of a past memory into a present nightmare but also to show a dissatisfaction with forms that save only some.

Meter and movement transform here, after the chaos of gas, from an automatic march back from the front into a different kind of awareness for the soldiers; the soldiers are marching with the same feet, but their paces occur with a forced and artificial regularity, symptomatic of the uneven, uncontrolled figure who disrupts the regularity in the middle of the poem, and whose figure now threatens to disrupt it again. The return to a fervent iambic pentameter in line 17 answers and, in some ways, remedies the chaotic image jolting in front of the soldiers in the wagon. Lines 17 through 28 are one long, rambling, accusatory sentence with relatively straightforward syntax. As readers, we are jolted by frequent spondaic substitutions in this second sonnet: "you too;" "white eyes writhe;" "high zest;" "old Lie." The only perfectly iambic line of the second sonnet, line 21—"If you could hear, at every jolt, the blood"—calls our attention to these jolts, this blood, and our own ear's ability to hear them in the second sonnet. "Dulce et Decorum Est" does not perform an upright, decorous form, and it illustrates in its breaking of the Latin meter in the final line how neither English nor classical meter can withstand the threats of modern forms of war. The Latin tag from Horace, "'Tis sweet and mete to die for one's country," allows us to rethink the word "mete"; both "just punishment" to die for one's country that we are urged "not to tell," and the measure of this sacrifice, which, through meter, is "told" in the poem's stumbling prosodic performance. The poem's formal status, bent-double and attempting to recover from the trauma at its center, gives the reader an awareness of forms as both possible and impossible emblems of recovery and survival. But finally, the poem's own verbs are evidence for the true war poet's task:

cough, curse, turn, trudge, limp on, fit, choke, smother, pace, gargle, *not* tell—though the poem's form recovers from its own chaotic center to show the *necessity* of telling, and the bittersweet triumph of steady, controlled pacing as the only possible method for that telling. The second sonnet's accusation is also its central opposition: "If you too could pace . . . you would not tell." That is, substituting "pacing" for "hearing," we can read the lurking hysteria in the middle of the poem both literally and allegorically—as an anxiety about the way that pacing and time significantly prevent the poem from "telling" its own formal absurdities, and as an anxiety from the figure of the writer as choking soldier, witnessing his own inability to tell, pace, measure, or order experience.

Owen died before he could fashion his own poetic monument, and his critical legacy has been shaped and reshaped by critics who see his progression as either Georgian (a Romantic pastoral legacy) or temporally modern. Within the context of Craiglockhart, we can read Owen's later poems as partial products of therapy that reeducated its patients to recognize and confront their hysteria, reordering its reception in the mind through a reconnection to the physical and social world. Meter's place in that particular microcosm was at times allegorical, at times literal, but almost always empowering. This counterpoint—in which deliberate and measured language is at once an exercise in recovery from modernity's chaos as well as a constant reminder of the tyrannies of historical order that led to formal rupture in the first place—serves as an important double movement for famous war writers such as Owen, as well as for the thousands of soldier-poets whose names did not find their way into the canon.

The Kindred Points of Heaven and Home

Outside a few scattered reviews, Owen was not considered a great poet by the general reading public until the publication of the 1931 *Selected Poems*, edited by Edmund Blunden. Even after this reprinted edition, Owen was still classified as a "war poet." Blunden's edition was reprinted nine times before C. Day Lewis's expanded edition was published in 1963. In contrast, the first edition of Owen's poems, edited by Siegfried Sassoon (with the help of Edith Sitwell, who had published Owen's poems in her anti-Georgian journal, *Wheels*), sold only 730 copies in the eleven years following its publication. Despite the relative success of the 1931 edition, however, W. B. Yeats famously refused to include Owen in his *Oxford Book of Modern Verse, 1892–1935*:

> I have a distaste for certain poems written in the midst of the great war; they are in all anthologies. . . . The writers of these poems were invariably officers of exceptional courage and capacity, one a man constantly selected for dangerous work, all, I think, had the Military Cross; their

letters are vivid and humorous, they were not without joy—for all skill is joyful—but felt bound, in the words of the best known, to plead the suffering of their men. In poems that had for a time considerable fame, written in the first person, they made that suffering their own. I have rejected these poems for the same reason that made Arnold withdraw his "Empedocles on Etna" from circulation; passive suffering is not a theme for poetry. In all the great tragedies, tragedy is a joy to the man who dies; in Greece the tragic chorus danced.[53]

Yeats's protest against Owen shows how much form and content had become separate issues in the 1930s, and allows us to consider retrospectively how the reviews in 1920 still held poetry to a kind of formal national standard that lingered in the culture despite the unresolved issue of how to teach prosody in the classroom.

Yeats's introduction makes no mention of the potential formal qualities of Owen or any other war poet. Reviews in the 1920s, however, were nearly obsessed with Owen's formal experiments, perhaps desensitized to the subject matter of the war due to those many anthologies to which Yeats refers. Owen's use of consonant and assonant rhyme, which he harmlessly called a "vowel-rime stunt" in a letter to Sassoon, was often blamed (in reviews) for disfiguring his verses, "preventing them from ever achieving greatness." Owen had been warned; as early as 1917, Robert Graves wrote, "Owen . . . you are a poet but you're a very careless one at present. One has to follow the rules of metre one adopts. Make new metres by all means, but one must observe the rules where they are laid down by the custom of centuries."[54] Even in Graves's chastisement, "new metres" are expected to observe and respect the old ones. Owen believed, like Bridges and Hopkins, that the boundaries of English prosody needed to be expanded. His own preface, however, directed some reviewers to pay attention to the content of his poems ("the pity") over the potential expansion he was proposing in the poetry's form.

Critics sentimentalized his early death, as in *The Sunday Times* in 1920: "in him was lost to English literature a man who might have done much."[55] And acknowledging the instructive, journalistic quality of the verses, a reviewer for *The Daily Herald* wrote, "[these poems] should be read by everybody who has any sentimental illusions about the war."[56] It was noble, but also dismissible, that Owen and his editor Sassoon were both soldier-poets "attempting in English verse to express the inexpressible 'real thing.'"[57] *The Daily News* and most other papers concluded that the 'real thing' was pitifully inexpressible. However, an editorial choice by Sassoon leaves out the manuscript page, entitled: "points to note about my Sounds," in which Owen asserts that his sounds are "1: 'correct,' as regards feet and rhyme, but the system of rhymes is not necessarily classical; 2: they conform to the essential unity of idea and a solemn dignity of the treatment."[58] This small page indicates Owen's awareness of and struggle with his craft. His early reception was influenced by the soldier-poetry fatigue of many poetry readers and the assumption that poetry about the war participated in the military metrical complex. Sassoon's reception avoided this fate because of his journalistic, ironic swagger and his blatant critique of the war. Owen's latent critique was metrical, experimental, and reeducated readers, just as he had been reeducated, to be suspicious of the forms and orders that profess to protect.

Early reviews gingerly avoid mentioning the immeasurable distance from front line to newsroom and focus squarely on the formal distance created by pararhyme, which Owen only used in a handful of poems. *The Daily News* reports "the thing confessed ha[s] not quite been fused with the music of the confession. Owen was <u>experimenting</u> with words and with <u>strange</u> consonantal rhymes: when he died, he had not yet arrived at mastery."[59] Critics were dismayed by his "curious" and "slightly irregular system of consonantal identity in place of rhyme." Though some reviewers called his rhymes "highly original experiments," most were *not* impressed, calling them mere "onomatopoeic trick[s]." Though Owen's poems stood out as unique and sensitive among the deluge of generally unoriginal soldier poetry, his experimental technique seemed inappropriately alienating. A *Times Literary Supplement* reviewer summarizes:

> The intention is to chastise our sensibility . . . to shake us and wake us, as has been done not infrequently through certain alliterative devices, regularly, indeed, in the old Saxon metres. But our ear now being tuned to vowel-rhyme, the poet avails himself of our disappointment to increase the biting severity of his strokes; and so, profiting not only by what he gives but by what he withholds, he gets an effect of total desolation.[60]

Like the reviews of Sassoon, many of the reviews of Owen's poetry found the lack of perfect rhyme in to be alienating rather than comforting; they did not meet the expectations of the war poem, nor did they participate openly in the expected metrical project. Only John Middleton Murry acknowledged, in 1921: "those assonant endings are indeed the discovery of genius." Murry can't quite bring himself to name Owen's line endings "rhyme," but he also does not call them dissonant—Murry thus exchanges the potential disapproval for dissonant rhymes with approval for "assonance"—a positive term for Owen's genius invention. In his discussion of "Strange Meeting," Murry writes: "The reader who comes fresh to this great poem does not immediately observe the assonant endings. At first he feels only that the blank verse has a mournful, impressive, even oppressive, quality of its own; that the poem has a forged unity. . . . The emotion with which it is charged cannot be escaped; the meaning of the words and the beat of the sounds have the same indivisible message."[61]

For the average reader, Murry intuits, there is something not quite right about the unity of the poem, yet for Murry the strangeness is part of the poetry's point: the poem's form *is* forged artificially and aware of its artificiality, but for the average reader who has been conditioned to expect a different kind of poetic form, this artificiality was a jarring flaw. A *Manchester Guardian* reviewer eagerly attacks Owen's experiments for "a calculated deflection from the kindred points of heaven and home, which are rhymes."[62] By avoiding this "tonal completeness," the reviews agree that Owen's form distances the reader from these perfected and accepted forms of English verse. His rhyming is "removed," and the poems, like an irresponsible officer leading us astray, "lose command of the ear."

That Owen would be expected to have command of an "ear," and that his divergence from this responsibility brings him away from spiritual and national success (heaven and home), are concerns that we have seen predicated in the Edwardian classroom. It is this attempt to align poetic form with heaven and home that is so distasteful to 1930s-era reviewers, who read war poetry because it is "important" but not necessarily because it is good poetry. Yeats, again, summarizes this tendency with his defensive misreading of Owen's poetry:

> My anthology continues to sell & the critics get more & more angry. When I excluded Wilfred Owen, whom I consider unworthy of the poets' corner of a country newspaper, I did not know I was excluding a revered sandwich-board Man of the revolution & that some body has put his worst & most famous poem in a glass-case in the British Museum—however if I had known it I would have excluded him just the same. He is all blood, dirt & sucked sugar stick (look at the selection in Faber's Anthology—he calls poets 'bards,' a girl a 'maid,' & talks about 'Titanic wars'). There is every excuse for him but none for those who like him. . . ."[63]

Yeats's focus on Owen's early, less experimental poems, unfairly places him among those poets who had not yet discovered the possibilities of stretching English meter's limit. In Yeats's letter, Owen's poetry stands in for the products of Edwardian education, anthology culture, and easy-to-swallow "Georgian" poetry. What Owen's poetry—indeed, what a reevaluation of poetry from this period—teaches us is that in order to rehistoricize the complicated role meter played in Edwardian education and in the prosody wars, we must resist the temptation to be dismissive when the products of prosodic experiment are perhaps not as experimental as they could be: like Pound's disappointment with Bridges (which we will examine in the concluding chapter) and Yeats's resistance to Owen—rather, we must see Owen's poetry as the outcome of the dynamic and changing contexts of national culture in which English meter's instability played a crucial role.

In his 1934, *A Hope for Poetry*, C. Day Lewis writes: "Gerard Manley Hopkins died young in the year 1889. His poems were not published until 1918, the year Wilfred Owen was killed. Hopkins would have been a poet under any circumstances: Owen, I am inclined to think, was made a poet by the war."[64] Though Owen certainly identified himself as a poet before the war, the fact that Lewis puts Hopkins and Owen together is important. As many scholars have noted, the experiments of Hopkins when read in the context of the modernist avant-garde in 1918 seemed less revolutionary than they had in 1889. Likewise, Owen's poems seemed less revolutionary than they indeed were when read in the context of the thousands of soldier poems and the output of rhythmic, accentual verses of the early twentieth century. But Lewis's assessment, in 1934, is apt: "Owen commends himself to post-war poets largely because they feel themselves to be quite in the same predicament; they feel the same lack of a stable background against which the dance of words may stand out plainly, the same distrust and horror of the unnatural forms into which life for the majority of people is being forced" (14). Hopkins knew already, and agonized over, the lack of a stable background; in his way he and Bridges attempted to invent new metrical possibilities. Owen was taught that the background was stable though it had never been; that was the trauma of meter for him and many other soldier poets, and that is why their poetry deserves reevaluation in light of the competing metrical histories and shifting concepts of national identity I am describing here.

❧ 6 ❧

The Before- and Afterlife of Meter

If life is not always poetical, it is at least metrical. Periodicity rules over the mental experience of man, according to the path of the orbit of his thoughts. Distances are not gauged, ellipses not measured, velocities not ascertained, times not known. Nevertheless, the recurrence is sure.
—Alice Meynell, *The Rhythm of Life*

See, they return; ah, see the tentative
Movements, and the slow feet,
The trouble in the pace and the uncertain
Wavering!
—Ezra Pound, "The Return"

Metrical Modernism

Few writers benefitted more from the boom in soldier poetry and the explosion of popular verses during the First World War than the poets associated with what we now call "modernism." But modernist writers, especially, deserve reconsideration and recontextualization within the shifting cultural and educational contexts of the Edwardian and Georgian eras. In "Prolegomena," published in Harold Monro's *Poetry and Drama* in 1912,[1] Ezra Pound writes, "I believe in an 'absolute rhythm,' a rhythm, that is, in poetry which corresponds exactly to the emotion or shade of emotion to be expressed. A man's rhythm must be interpretive, it will be, therefore, in the end, his own, uncounterfeiting, uncounterfeitable." If the poetry of Newbolt was arguing for a collective "metrical" national identity (that Newbolt and Bridges nonetheless understood as highly individualized), then Pound replied with an even more individualized idea of rhythm—something that begins and ends with each poem. In "A Few Don'ts," published in *Poetry* magazine in 1913, Pound continues to imagine rhythm as individual and authentic as opposed to the collective counterfeit of metric patterns—a divide, I argue, between an at-once individual and universal "rhythm" and an elite, external, and artificial "meter" that he narrates as if it is distinct from his own metrical investigations, the expired product of another age. It is important to recall, too, that the artificial "meter" of patriotic poetry was already an abstracted, misrepresentative description for rhythm. To Pound, the collective military-metrical project I described in chapter 4 is read as derivative; they merely "shovel" in words to "fill a metric pattern or to complete the noise of a rhyme-sound."[2] Pound not only misunderstands the upsurge in a rousing Edwardian English accentual rhythms as "metric" (and forgivably so), he is also suspicious of the simultaneous obsession with defining English meter for the discipline of English literary study and linguistic science. Pound advocates a simultaneous awareness of and need for historical forms as well as a complete disregard for them at the moment of writing. He writes "[p]ay no attention to the criticism of men who have never themselves written a notable work. Consider the discrepancies between the actual writing of the Greek poets and dramatists, and the theories of the Graeco-Roman grammarians, concocted to explain their meters." Rather than reading metrical explanations, he suggests, "let the candidate fill his mind with the finest cadences he can discover, preferably in a foreign language" (4, 5). If grammar fixes and stabilizes, so, too, by extension, does meter. Pound's desire for a rhythmic fluidity rests on a descriptive rather than prescriptive approach to poetic form; and yet "to describe" would be also to fix. By assuming that "cadences" can be absorbed phenomenologically, somehow at the level of "instinct," Pound both troubles and supports the assumption of inherent abstract national rhythms so promoted by the grammarians of the eighteenth century through Henry Newbolt. And yet, rather than a universal "Englishness," the cadences and rhythms Pound supposes for poetry are somehow universally "poetic"—beyond the realm of grammar or meter, and require the "shock and stroke" of each individual.[3]

Pound's belief in an at once "universal" and "individual" rhythm was, in many ways, as class-determined as Saintsbury's or Bridges's. By shoveling words into preexistent molds, poets employing a metric pattern without making it their own were guaranteeing their obsolescence and displaying their vulgarity, their lack of an elite understanding of ancient forms. (Indeed, the class implication of Pound's day-laborer word choice shows that he is much more aligned with the educated elite than the common man that he implies he would be freeing from the shackles of meter.) He admits that he has devoted himself to "the ancients" ("pawed over") in order "to find out what has been done, once and for all, better than it can ever be done again" and yet he concludes, "I doubt if we can take over, for English, the rules of quantity laid down for Greek and Latin, mostly by Latin grammarians." Pound reveals his familiarity with Bridges's experiments here, but puts himself in Bridges's role: the only mention of Bridges, however, is to admit that "Robert Bridges" is "seriously concerned with overhauling the metric, in testing the language and its adaptability to certain modes."[4] Yet his vitriol against "the metric" is everywhere evident; Pound continues to elaborate on the violence of traditional metrics: "don't chop your stuff into separate *iambs*. Don't make each poem

stop dead at the end, and then begin every next line with a heave. Let the beginning of the next line catch the rise of the rhythm wave, unless you want a
definite longish pause."[5] Pound's language supports the narrative of a violent
break with the past as well as the violence that meter can do to a poem. He
narrates "rhythm" as an ideal hybrid form that mediates between the individual and the community, and yet his assumption that any and all metrical systems are hegemonic and rigid belies his ignorance of nineteenth- and early
twentieth-century poetics. Indeed, the modernist revival of the term "cadence"
rather than "meter" or "rhythm" marks a return to Lindley Murray's original
1795 definition of versification, back to elocution and performance imagined
through the image of the printed page. Everything should be fluid; even the
"pause," a primary element of versification, is abstracted into "definite longish."
Though bad poetry will begin the next line "with a heave," Pound will redraw
the lines of poetic tradition by declaring in his *Pisan Cantos* more than forty
years later the famous statement I quoted earlier: "To break the pentameter,
that was the first heave" (Canto 81). The first "heave" was really Pound's misreading of nineteenth-century meter, or rather, collapsing a variety of metrical
experiments into one collective project of predictable verses. Pound did not
"break" the pentameter, as his five-beat line roughly demonstrates, but he
dares us to dwell on his "that" after the "break" of the midline caesura, as if to
cast his line precariously into four beats. But I have shown the artificiality of
"that" break, or Pound's imagined divide, and argued why and how the pentameter and the four-beat line would have been something that so many poets
invested with meaning, and how one or the other could be read as variously
"natural" or "artificial." Pound knew that to retroactively impose a structure on
the past would allow him to bury it, exhume it differently, and make it part of
his own invention. However, this same retroactive imposition of stability is
strikingly similar to what was happening in English meter with the burial and
exhumation of classical meters from the end of the nineteenth to the early
twentieth centuries. The perceived stability of English metrical forms was
based on a variety of factors, but it was the supposed stability of classical meters on which English meter was ostensibly, partially, and perhaps erroneously
based in the late nineteenth century. In fact, fewer and fewer poet-critics believed in this particular classical metrical genealogy. Pound's infamous "break"
with the pentameter and his restrictions against using "strict iambs" obfuscates
the rich heritage of experiment, debate, and contested metrical discourses that
circulated throughout the nineteenth century and into the twentieth. Later
on in "A Retrospect," Pound muses, "I think progress lies rather in an attempt
to approximate classical quantitative metres (NOT to copy them) than in a
carelessness regarding such things."[6] He adds the note, "let me date this statement to 20 August 1917," significantly indicating that, in 1917, there were
various kinds of experiments at work in the field of English meter and that *vers
libre* was just *one* of a multitude of possibilities in the early twentieth century.

Pound neglects to mention, perhaps because he would rather not acknowledge it, that meter in the Victorian era was similarly experimental, contested, and varied—a proliferation of concepts rather than a unified field.

As I have by now made quite clear, Bridges's exacting prosodic experiments—themselves evidence of the proliferation of concepts about verse form—have been overshadowed by the more popular free verse experiments of Pound, Eliot, Williams, and other artists associated with the anti-Georgian literary movements of the 1910s and 1920s, embedded though those experiments were with various metrical forms not at all "free." The divide between poet-prosodists like Bridges and Pound parallels the divide between the formal investigations of linguistics departments and those of English departments, in which the constant search for a "right" answer and the abstraction of metrical form secures that the very freedom it allows will be just flexible enough to survive as the kind of law about which professors like to argue. Pound and Bridges, however, were more alike than either acknowledged. In 1936 Pound refused to write a short memoir of Bridges, joking to Eliot,

> I take it all I gotter do is to talk about Britches, not necessarily read the ole petrifaction? . . . Rabbit Britches indeed!!! . . . proposed title of article: 'Testicles versus Testament.' An embalsamation of the Late Robert's Britches. All the pseudo-rabbits: Rabbit Brooke, Rabbit Britches . . . I spose I can cite what I once said of Britches? I managed to dig about 10 lines of Worse Libre out of one of his leetle bookies. Onct. And then there iz the side line of Hopkins. . . . In fact, the pooplishers ought to donate a Hopkins and the Hopkins letters so az to treat Britches properly. Background for an article that wdn't be as dull, oh bloodily, as merely trying to yatter about wot he wrote.[7]

The association of Robert Bridges with Rupert Brooke (Rabbit Brooke) here is significant. Both "rabbits" are infantilized, indeed animalized through Pound's dialect. Though ostensibly phonetic, Pound's playful dialects also efface the serious phonetic experiments of Shaw, Bridges, and other phoneticians in the early twentieth century—the very discourse that has continued to trouble over the problem of pronunciation and versification in linguistics to this day. But more importantly, by placing Bridges alongside the war hero Rupert Brooke, Pound essentially devalues Bridges's experiments, experiments that Pound himself had valued at the start of his career—although he does know that Bridges should be treated "properly," "wot he wrote" is somehow instantly forgettable, as forgettable as any war poet.

In a letter dated the next day, Pound decides to not even attempt an article about Bridges, saying it would be a "falsification of values" and that Bridges is already "a corpse of the null" (280, 281). His mention, in the prior letter, to *The Testament of Beauty* is also a show of how frustrating it must have been for

Pound that the poet whose legacy he was trying to desperately to unseat had, with *The Testament of Beauty*, outsold and outshone the kind of poetry Pound wanted to promote. Though Pound only stated his condemnation of Bridges privately, it shows how much Pound revised his views toward poetic mastery in the years after the war. The younger, less famous Pound felt little but envy for the poet laureate in October 1915, when he reviewed Bridges's *Poems Written in 1913* in *Poetry Magazine*: "beyond dispute, his command of the sheer mechanics of quantitative verse can be looked on with nothing but envy. I have a grave respect for any man who is restless and persistent in the study and honor of his craft."[8] Pound singles out two poems from the volume, "Fly-catchers," which I discussed in chapter 3, and "a brief epigram, bitter as Palladas, full of emotional violence held in by rigid, delicate barriers "[title in Greek]":

> Who goes there? God knows. I'm nobody. How shall I answer?
> Can't jump over a gate nor run across the meadow.
>
> I'm but an old whitebeard of inane identity. Pass on.
> What's left of me today will very soon be nothing. (43)

Though Bridges's verses, as Pound predicted, have been forgotten in contemporary discussions of literary modernism, exhuming Bridges's works might "embalm" him (and provide "summation") differently than the "enbasalmation" Pound eventually imagined. But earlier in the same review, Pound outlines how little poets know of accentual and quantitative verse today, writing a brief history of all verse forms as essentially free (including "vowel-chants" from Egypt and "polyrhythmical sequairies and litanies" from the middle ages) and then continuing to blame the metrical rigidity on mid-Victorian culture:

> And after all these things came the English exposition of 1851 and the Philadelphia Centennial, introducing cast-iron house decorations and machine-made wood fret-work, and there followed a generation of men with minds like the cast-iron ornament, and they set their fretful desire upon machine-like regularity. . . . [T]he indigenous Anglo-Saxon rhythms were neglected because society did not read Anglo-Saxon. And the most imitative generation of Americans ever born on our continent set themselves to exaggerating the follies of England. (41)

Though Pound is aware that Bridges's name "is almost a synonym for classic and scholarly poetry," he resents that Bridges's knowledge of verse form could lead him to name one of the poems in his new volume an "experiment in free verse," calling it a "smack in the eye" to the provincials who merely imitate machine-like verses. But Pound's retelling of literary history shows how little he knew of the Anglo-Saxonist movements in England and America, though his own interest in Anglo-Saxon was certainly a product of these. Likewise, by dating "machine-like regularity" of "cast-iron" verses at mid-century, he simplifies the projects of poets whom he knows are more metrically complex than this history allows. But even if Bridges, architecturally, might be compared to "a pseudo-renaissance classic façade," Pound relents that there are poems in his volume "comparable with the best in the language." The review reveals both Pound's wish to be recognized as an authority (amid multiple competing authorities: Saintsbury, Skeat, Mayor, Brewer, etc.) on matters metrical and historical as well as his nearly resentful admiration for Bridges, whom he must admit is already recognized—and should have broader recognition—as a master of multiple metrical forms.

Two years before Pound's review, Bridges published "A Letter to a Musician on English Prosody" in the same issue of *Poetry and Drama* (1913),[9] in which Edward Thomas published his views of war poetry and where Pound published a number of poems. If Pound's insistence, in "A Retrospect," that poets should "compose in the sequence of the musical phrase, not in sequence of a metronome," is abstract and collapses metrical regularity in all its forms to a ticktocking time-keeper, Bridges's explanation so intricately describes the complexity and difficulty in the history and future of English metrical study that his "letter," in its very expertise, unseats Pound's authoritative statements. Even "a musical phrase" is troubled in Bridges's account. Less a "letter" and more a mini-metrical treatise along the lines of the views Bridges expressed in *Milton's Prosody*, the coexistence of these texts in the same periodical shows how, despite Pound's own narratives of rhythmic invention, he was aware of —though pretended a willing ignorance of—the ways that other poets were explaining and attempting to understand English verse rhythm. Lines from *Hugh Sewlyn Mauberly*, in particular, gesture to his need for inclusion in this rehistoricization of prosodic form. Participating in the same discourses as Owen, Pound writes, "Died some, pro patria, / Non "dulce" non "et décor" . . . / walked eye-deep in hell / believing old men's lies, then unbelieving" (12). Why would Pound, or any poet in the 1920s, buy into the broken promise of poetic form in English? Pound engages with this metrical discourse at the same time that he attempts to reject it so that he can position himself as the arbiter and authority. Like Saintsbury and Patmore rejecting the metrists who came before them, Pound performs the characteristic move of negatively characterizing his predecessors. Though Pound was not a product of the English education system, he was sufficiently educated to understand the ideologies of English poetic form that he refused, yet at the same time could not help but inhabit. Eliot's poetry and prose are similarly inflected with traces of the rise and fall of meter, and deserve reexamination along historical and prosodic lines, as does the complex prosodic discourse and recasting of tradition evident in the poems of Robert Frost, Mina Loy, H.D., William Carlos Williams, and even, perhaps especially, Yeats.

Eliot defines Pound's metric according to an "adaptability of metre to mood, an adaptability due to an intensive study of metre, that constitutes an important element in Pound's technique. Few readers were prepared to accept or follow the amount of erudition [in *Personae and Exultations*] ... or to devote the care to reading them which they demand."[10] Eliot then summarizes Pound's substantial "erudition" but concludes that the poems require "a trained ear, or at least a willingness to be trained" (167). Eliot, writing in 1917, seems to contextualize Pound's metric in terms of an "English ear." And yet this definition and formation of a reading practice according to an "ear" was conceived as a new critical model in the 1920s. "How to read meter" became a question severed from English historicity and politics, cut from any lingering association with metaphysics, and was transformed into a secular and ahistorical reading practice. Pound, Eliot, and other poets of this formative Victorian-Edwardian-Georgian moment, deserve reconsideration within the shifting contexts of English philology and education that I present here, figured literally and allegorically in changing conceptions of metrical form in English.

Make It Old: Robert Bridges and Obsolescence

"As for the nineteenth century," Pound writes in "A Retrospect," "with all respect for its achievements, I think we shall look back upon it as a rather blurry, messy sort of period, a rather sentimentalistic, mannerish sort of period." Until Swinburne, Pound attempts to persuade us, "poetry had been merely the vehicle ... the ox-cart and post-chaise for transmitting thoughts poetic or otherwise."[11] Pound is emphasizing the newly mechanistic nature of modernist rhythm, as opposed to the rural, agricultural, provincial meters of old that, without a trace of acknowledgment as to why or how these rural, agricultural, or provincial meters were otherwise conscripted into the service of a national Anglo-Saxon past (working class, nativist, persistent, and steadfast).[12] We have seen what Pound made of Robert Bridges, and his recasting of Bridges as a "corpse of the null" has done its work to keep Bridges's life and work hidden. But what did Bridges make of Pound and the new generations of poets who would prefer that the laureate fade away, back into the Victorian era where he belonged? It is true that Bridges had always been associated with a kind of "older" style; he looked backward toward Milton and to classical verse forms. He published multilingual *The Spirit of Man* wartime anthology when he was eighty-four years old. But however slow his poetic output might have been in later years, he continued to experiment and to perfect what he felt was a more delicate form of free verse, all the while aware of and attempting to educate his audiences about the histories and possibilities for accentual, syllabic, and quantitative verse traditions in English. In his late-career poem, "Poor Poll," Bridges reveals his disappointment that his life-long pursuit to reveal the multiplicity of metrical forms, their historicity and possibility, is either too technical for the mass public or rather, too belated. That is, his understanding (just as Pound's) of English poetics relies on an education that is no longer possible in the national school system, without an intimate knowledge of classical verse forms.

Bridges published "Poor Poll" in 1923. Ostensibly a reference to John Skelton's 1521 poem, "Speke, Parrot," which was also written at a time when the ideologies of classical education were under debate, Bridges both commented on the resurgent interest in Skelton and alternative verse forms as well as used the platform of metrical experiment to address the deterioration of Western civilization.[13] When it was first privately circulated, on a quarto sheet, he included a preface as well as "metrical elucidations" to flaunt his accomplishment and perhaps obfuscate the latent critique in the poem (this preface and the metrical elucidations were not reprinted with the poem in Bridges's lifetime or in any subsequent edition of his poems). After Milton, he decided to use a twelve-syllable verse line; not only could all speech fit within that structure, but speech and metrical forms from most Western languages:

> I saw . . . that all the old forms of 12 syllable verse, the Greek iambic, the scazon, the French Alexandrine, etc., would be admitted on equal terms. It was partly my wish for liberty to use various tongues that made me address my first experiment to the parrot, but partly also my wish to discover how a low setting of scene and diction would stand; because one of the main limitations of English verse is that its accentual (dot and go one) bumping is apt to make ordinary words ridiculous; and since, on theory at least, there would be no decided enforced accent in any place in this new metre, it seemed that it might possibly afford escape from the limitations spoken of. And thus I wrote "Poor Poll"[14]

Readers of his collected verse would find the poem under the heading, "Neo-Miltonic Syllabics," (all in the twelve-syllable line) along with a few other poems in the same style, but unless one were a prosodist who had followed Bridges's development through the appendices of *Milton's Prosody*, or happened to be a colleague in the Society for Pure English, the common reader would encounter a poem that referenced various meters but did not clearly settle into a recognizable accentual-syllabic pattern. The poem is at once welcoming and repelling; the "low setting of scene" is appropriate for a wide audience, but the multilingual references speak to a select few. Bridges's poem weighed in on the state of English and classical education; written in the same year that Newbolt's *The Teaching of English in England* was published (1921), it expresses both joy and regret over the report's conclusion that literature "must never be treated as a field of mental exercise remote from ordinary life"; it certainly shows agreement that "if a child is not learning good English he is learning bad English, and probably bad habits of thought."[15] But the report and poem diverge; the report states the classics "will always remain, among the best of our inherited possessions, and for all truly civilized people they will always be not only a possession but a vital and enduring influence . . . ," yet the status of "civilization," postwar, is less redeemable in Bridges's eyes than Newbolt's. It would seem, through his Neo-Miltonic syllabic meter, that Bridges had discovered and wanted to promote a modern poetic form to replace the classical model, a more capacious, yet still historically respectful English verse form in the post–First World War moment. And yet, like Eliot's *The Waste Land*, Bridges's "Poor Poll" expresses grave doubts that any form can hold in the wake of such tragedy.

Whether Eliot could have spoken to the poet laureate about his metrical experiment is speculative. "Poor Poll" was published in June of 1923, a month before Virginia Woolf finished setting the type on *The Waste Land* (and after years of Ezra Pound "tightening [its] meter"), so there is little hope for the critical discovery that Bridges's poem is a kind of shadow poem for Eliot's. The two poems side by side show Bridges, the elder statesman of English meter, and Eliot, the up-and-comer, engaging with the waning power of the classical concept of "meter" in English. Both poems are macaronic: Eliot's *The Waste Land* includes lines in German, French, and Italian as well as references to Swinburne and Tennyson. Bridges's "Poor Poll" includes lines in German, French, Italian, Latin and Greek (all solidly resting in the twelve-syllable lines) and references Pindar, Dante, and Goethe; Bridges's Sibyl at Cumae is a parrot in a Miltonic cage. The 97-line poem, at first glance, seems an idle, Browningesque narrative about a man discussing the nature of knowledge with his house parrot, but the poem twists and turns into a metametrical allegory and anticipatory elegy for the loss of a particular understanding of English meter and national culture.

> I saw it all, Polly, how when you had call'd for sop
> and your good friend the cook came & fill'd up your pan
> you yerked it out deftly by beakfuls scattering it
> away as far as you might upon the sunny lawn
> then summon'd with loud cry the little garden birds   5
> to take their feast. Quickly came they flustering around
> Ruddock & Merle & Finch squabbling among themselves
> nor gave you thanks nor heed while you sat silently
> watching, and I beside you in perplexity
> lost in the maze of all mystery and all knowledge   10
> felt how deep lieth the fount of man's benevolence
> if a bird can share it & take pleasure in it.[16]

The well-trained bird is able to communicate that he is hungry and that he wants to share with the free garden birds, though given proper names (Ruddock and Merle and Finch) can only "squabble" and "give . . . no thanks nor heed" of Poll's kindness; the caged bird has the freedom to communicate and to enact benevolence, whereas the wild birds, though in possession of proper names, cannot properly use speech nor manners. Without proper education, without the proper cage of civilizing meter, the bird-subjects are savage. The captive parrot silently watches as the poet wonders beside her and the other birds eat below her, not giving any explanation for her actions; her ability to communicate is linked only to personal need and to a perceived benevolence, not to any sort of inquiry or understanding—a sharp distinction between beast and poet, and an unsubtle reference to the humanist rhetoric of English education more generally.

Bridges imagines, however, that a certain primitivism could teach the English moralists a thing or two. From lines 13–21 the poet muses as to what the bird's philosophy would be if she indeed could have one, pitting his own ability to reason ("I thought" [l. 13], "thus reason'd I"[l. 19])—as well as the way that this reasoning power makes him a unified "I"—against "the darkness" in which Poll must live. The "feeble candle-power"(l. 17) of her mind, and her "pall," is both her insipid nature and now gloomy casket-like cage and, of course, her name. The metrical metaphor of the cage becomes a metaphor for cognition more generally:

> If you, my bird, I thought, had a philosophy
> it might be a sounder scheme than what our moralists
> propound: because thou, Poll, livest ín the darkness   15
> which human Reason searching from outside would pierce,
> but, being of so feeble a candle-power, can only
> show up to view the cloud that it illuminates.
> Thus reason'd I: then marvell'd how you can adapt
> your wild bird-mood to endure your tame environment   20
> the domesticities of English household life
> and your small brass-wire cabin, who shdst live on wing
> harrying the tropical branch-flowering wilderness:

The bird, here, is a symbol of ignorant doom and of domesticated freedom and wildness; the poem imagines her in "the tropical branch-flowering wilderness"(l. 23) with some regret, as if, like this new meter, the parrot is some tamed poetic impulse that cannot recognize the freedom that the cage of form provides. Indeed, Bridges is already the master of both this form and the bird; notice the possessive "my bird," and the fact that the diacritical mark on the word "ín" oddly forces us to emphasize that Poll lives in darkness, in the cage, in the poet's mind (just as, recall, Bridges showed us that *he* was "the only bird" in his Sonnet 21); her inability to recognize either the metrical or mental "cage" in which she finds herself separates her from man. For a meter that is supposed to avoid wrenched pronunciation, this diacritical mark reminds us, too, that we are "in" a form of the poet's making, that Bridges is mastering *us* in a meter that we might not understand.

Bridges then describes how man, like the parrot, has been trained to "follow along" or "mimic" without understanding—a model for metrical mimicry that belies deeper ignorance. Whereas this mimicry in both man and bird is commonly praised as "civilized," the passage quickly turns to a violent indictment of what the false civilization masks.

> Yet Nature gave you a gift of easy mimicry
> whereby you have come to win uncanny sympathies   25
> and morsell'd utterance of our Germanic talk
> as schoolmasters in Greek will flaunt their hackney'd tags
> θωναντα συνετοισιν and κτημα ες αει,
> η γλῶσσ ομωμοχ, η δε θρην ανωμοτος
> tho' you with a better ear copy ús more perfectly   30
> nor without connotation as when you call'd for sop
> in irrepressible blind groping for escape

There is much to sift through here; lines 27–29 directly criticized the pedantic classical schoolmasters, who can have no ear for a dead language and yet flaunt their skills nonetheless. It is also a critique of the pedantry Bridges finds in the teaching of English verse—based on no unified theory of meter, English pedagogues model English verses on the classical system without understanding its inadequacy (derived from the misunderstanding of Latin meter). The ictus on the word "ús" in line 30 is the second diacritical mark that the poet employs in the English text of the poem, guiding the reader's eye to the word, the reader's voice to emphasize it, good pupils of (inaccurate, worse than useless) scansion that we are.

In the following line (31), this perfect "copy" of our speech is "not without connotation," tempting us to dig more deeply in the two lines of Greek. Both Greek lines reiterate through intertext Poll's ability to mimic and inability to truly reason or understand, and thus also refer to the schoolboys—grown up into Bridges's reading public—who have ironically repeated the forms of grammar without the wisdom to which line 28's first Greek tag alludes, from a Pindaric Ode (01.22.04) "speaking to the wise." To the non-classically trained reader (a growing majority in the 1920s), these tags are mere repetitions to the ignorant, and Bridges keeps it that way. In his gloss he only writes "a Greek iambic line"—showing that the meter *is* the substance; there are three lines here from three different writers—the second from Thucydides (1.22.4), "a possession for all time." Thucydides was referring to the afterlife of his own work, but here Bridges may mean that these memorized tags are, for better or worse, 'for all time' and that, despite the lack of set quantities in English, the "time" of his syllabic meter allows Thucydides a properly "timed" memorial here. The third and most significant translated intertext is in line 29, from Euripides' *Hippolytus* (l.612)—a play all about the broken promises of speech—"my tongue swore but my mind is unsworn." Though the tag seems to refer back to the parrot, who can talk as if she is tame but possesses a "wild-bird mood," I find it more useful to think of those parroting schoolboys, formed but not transformed by what their tongues have been trained to repeat—the disappointment of a classical education, as in Bridges's poem "Flycatchers." Though the lines in Greek demonstrate Bridges's ability to absorb it in his English meter, his choice of lines is a subtle critique of the misuse and misunderstanding of classical languages and classical education at the end of the nineteenth century and beginning of the twentieth.

As if to reinforce the disembodiment of the repeating, insipid and unknowing tongue, line 32 strips away all admiration associated with the domestication of the bird's tongue by showing how barbarous and uncontrollable it really is.

> all with that stumpy wooden tongue & vicious beak
> that dry whistling shrieking tearing cutting pincer
> now eagerly subservient to your cautious claws
> exploring all varieties of attitude   35

The "stumpy wooden tongue and vicious beak," make the bird's spirit itself seem dangerous and threatening, a wooden tongue that has 'sworn' not to produce any wisdom. Indeed, civilized life contains its own potential barbarism. The parrot's "irrepressible blind groping for escape" and "dry whistling shrieking tearing cutting pincer" are perverse references to the supposed domesticities of English household life. Domesticity and education both contain deeper threats; easy mimicry, under the guise of "cultivation," forcibly masks a kind of primal urge and robs us of some important natural instinct—quite a comment on English values embedded here. The poem's pileup of adjectives begins to gain momentum, the phrases "stumpy wooden tongue" and "vicious beak" mimic the threat, with violent dentals and plosives hammering down. Here is no imitation of man's benevolence; the uncanny ability to imitate human speech is now reduced to an inhuman "dry whistling," heard in the nasal, guttural trochaic downbeat of "shrieking, tearing, cutting, pincer." The bird has been driven mad with mimicry into an entirely physical, violent being, its speech ability alienated from the spiritual; it can only explore "all varieties of attitude / in irrepressible blind groping for escape." Speech, relegated to the insipid, imitating tongue, is itself dissected from any spiritual meaning, just as the bird figure is reduced to a physical object blindly groping for escape from its artificial environment.

Poll's savage need to escape is personified as "the very figure & image of man's soul on earth / the almighty cosmic Will fidgeting in a trap" (ll. 37–38),[17] but the poet pities the bird, understanding how the rigidities of parroting Greek tags might inspire a kind of "quenchless unknown desire for the unknown life."

> —a very figure & image of man's soul on earth
> the almighty cosmic Will fidgeting in a trap —
> in your quenchless unknown desire for the unknown life
> of which some homely British sailor robb'd you, alas!   40
> 'Tis all that doth your silly thoughts so busy keep
> the while you sit moping like Patience on a perch
> ———Wie viele Tag' und Nächte bist du geblieben!
> *La possa delle gambe posta in tregue* —
> the impeccable spruceness of your grey-feather'd poll   45
> a model in hairdressing for the dandiest old Duke
> enough to qualify you for the House of Lords
> or the Athenaeum Club, to poke among the nobs
> great intellectual nobs and literary nobs
> scientific nobs and Bishops *ex officio*:   50

A British sailor has stolen the bird from its origin and the poem faults him (l. 40) for making the bird "endure" English country life. English and British, as concepts, are called to question here: both have become unbearably tame (the sailor is "simple") and have forgotten some ancient, wilder, and nobler origin. Bridges gestures to the ancient and noble founder of his meter in line 41: "'Tis all but doth your silly thoughts so busy keep," from Milton's hymn, 12 syllables—a simplified alexandrine line without the traditional caesura. Now, the bird's thoughts are also simplified, or "silly," as she sits "moping like Patience on a perch." We are reminded that mastery is the only true "bird," not this poor simple model. But Bridges's eagerness to demonstrate his own mastery causes the poem to flounder a bit, and the next lines, in German and Italian, seem to perform only the fact that they fit into his metrical experiment.

If one is fluent in German, one might recognize this line from Goethe's "Bericht: Januar": "Wie viele Tag' und Nächte bist du geblieben!" ("for how many days and nights have you stayed"). From the notes, we learn that this line earned inclusion because of another metrical variation—the second to last foot is a dactyl in a line of trochees. Goethe's poem is an address to Cupid, and demands whether he has become "the only master in the house"—another subtle reference to domesticity and domination. The line from Italian,

La possa delle gambe posta in tregue ("The position of your legs after a moment of repose") is from Dante (also a favorite of Eliot's) and shows the same metrical variation—that is, a trisyllabic foot in place of a two-syllable foot. Bridges absorbs these foreign lines into his English meter, but he has chosen the lines because they demonstrate the three-syllable foot that he believes the "commonest" foot in the English language. These foreign lines, pardon the pun, had their foot in the door, with Bridges's invented foot for the new century— the Britannic—marching back into a poem based on the meter of the English master Milton. He seems to flaunt his ability to showcase these lines in the narrative that follows, about Poll's own ability to imitate a "Duke," a member of the "House of Lords," or the "great intellectual nobs and literary nobs." The properly mastered meter will allow imitation in a number of languages and classes, both high and low. Just as Eliot and Pound imitate lower-class dialects, Bridges shows here how Dante's vernacular form can be called upon to represent elite learning—vernaculars and elite languages change depending on how those great intellectual and literary "nobs" choose to portray and read them.

The performance of the poet's virtuosity turns elegiac just after its midpoint, around lines 50 to 60. Here, Bridges stops mocking the bird and starts to sound like a man, in very old age, thinking about what he has or has not accomplished:

> nor lack you simulation of profoundest wisdom
> such as men's features oft acquire in very old age
> by mere cooling of passion & decay of muscle
> by faint renunciation even of untold regrets;
> who seeing themselves a picture of that wh: man should-be   55
> learn almost what it were to be what they are-not.
> But you can never have cherish'd a determined hope
> consciously to renounce or lose it, you will live
> your threescore years & ten idle and puzzle-headed
> as any mumping monk in his unfurnish'd cell   60
> in peace that, poor Polly, passeth Understanding —
> merely because you lack what we men understand
> by Understanding. Well! well! That's the difference
> *C'est la seule différence, mais c'est important.*

Indeed, the poem begins to personify its maker; Bridges has spent his life attempting to educate himself and other poets about the true potential of English verse, only to arrive surrounded by those who are only interested in parroting, imitating, and abstracting meter without truly understanding the history that lies behind it. The "wh: man should be" casually hints at Bridges's lost hope for pronunciation reform; his own private shorthand, which "should be" recognized but was never adopted. Likewise, he effaces the hope from earlier in the poem that the bird might have some desire for understanding and now accuses it of the sort of "puzzlement" he experienced at the beginning. He gives up, essentially, in lines 57 and 58: "you can never have cherish'd a determined hope / consciously to renounce or lose it," as the poet has, and, postwar, as the nation has. The bird is "idle and puzzle-headed" and lacks "what we men understand / by Understanding." Despite this conclusion, the poet still asks the bird, still asks his poem and his hope for poetic meter: "would you change?" He answers his own rhetorical question in the next twenty lines by showing that ignorance is preferable to eventual dismemberment—both physical and metrical.

Lines 63 ("Well, well") and 64 ("*mais*") are the only lines with definite caesuras and both seem to indicate a reckoning; the pause creating a transition between the renounced hopes of the poet for his caged-bird-free-verse and an attempt at justifying his activities in the face of these lost hopes. He begins his address again, "Well! well! that's the difference / *C'est la seule différence, mais c'est important.*" The poem immediately imagines the dangers of all of the acts from which reason has been detached:

Ah! your pale sedentary life! but would you change?   65
exchange it for one crowded hour of glorious life,
one blind furious tussle with a madden'd monkey
who would throttle you and throw your crude fragments away
shreds unintelligible of an unmeaning act
dans la profonde horreur de l'éternelle nuit?   70
Why ask? You cannot know. 'Twas by no choice of yours
that you mischanged for monkeys' man's society,
'twas that British sailor drove you from Paradise —
Ειϑ ωφελ ' Αργους μη διαπταασϑαι σκαφος!
I'd hold embargoes on such a ghastly traffic.   75

Why ask?, he seems to ask himself, concluding again, "you cannot know." But then the freedom to have "one crowded hour of glorious life" freed from the civilized cage, even if that hour risks destruction and dismemberment, is called "Paradise." The Greek line he quotes in line 74 is telling—it's the first line of Euripides's *Medea*, in which the nurse wishes that the ship had never set sail from Argos to arrive in Colchis[18] (where Medea commits the darkest of her tragic acts). Medea, the foreigner who is accused of speaking a "barbarous" language to go along with her "barbarous" acts, has also, in effect, been "stolen away" across the water. Bridges, in his ironic stance against all unregulated foreignness in the English language, writes, "I'd hold embargoes on such ghastly traffic," and though he seems to assert that he would protect us from ruin, we know that his attitude toward English meter has been, by the 1920s, irreparably poisoned.

The sustained address to the parrot throughout the poem can be read as a subjective slide into the poet's consideration of his own dissatisfaction with his self and his craft. The "I" in the poem moves through states of perception: "I saw"; "I beside you in perplexity / lost in a the maze of all mystery and all knowledge, felt how deeply"; "Thus reason'd I"; "I'd hold embargoes"; and finally, the movement that begins on line 76, "I am writing verses to you." Bridges flaunts the poem's antivocality. The diacritical marks must be seen; the dead languages cannot possibly be heard. Though the poet is writing to a bird, his grief is for English poetry, and an audience for that poetry who may be *"absolument incapable de les comprendre, / Tu Polle, nescis ista nec potes scrire"* —both the French and Latin again telling, in a foreign tongue, how all reason is foreign to a simple creature who can only imitate—she does not know these things and is not able to know them.

> I am writing verses to you & grieve that you shd be
> *absolument incapable de les comprendre,*
> *Tu, Polle, nescis ista nec potes scrire: --*
> Alas! Iambic, scazon and alexandrine,
> spondee or choriamb, all is alike to you —   80
> my well-continued fanciful experiment
> wherein so many strange verses amalgamate
> on the secure bedrock of Milton's prosody:
> not but that when I speak you will incline an ear
> in critical attention lest by chánce I míght   85
> póssibly say sómething that was worth repeating:
> I am adding (do you think?) pages to literature
> that gouty excrement of human intellect
> accumulating slowly & everlastingly
> depositing, like guano on the Peruvian shore,   90
> to be perhaps exhumed in some remotest age
> (*piis secunda, vate me, detur fuga*)
> to fertilize the scanty dwarf'd intelligence
> of a new race of beings the unhallow'd offspring
> of them who shall have quite dismember'd & destroy'd   95
> our temple of Christian faith & fair Hellenic art
> just as that monkey would, poor Polly, have done for you.

These meters, in particular, demonstrate our inability to realize the terms of meter in the early twentieth century—our guide, the scazon from Martial, in which Bridges changes the name to "Polle," should lead us to understand that line 79 is a quantitative scazon in English; lines 80 and 82 are also English quantitative lines, but though he is littering his lines with clues about the foundations and future of his English meter, their meaning is lost on us.

The poem elegizes what the bird-as-form, bird-as-English-tongue, cannot know. "Alas! Iambic, scazon and alexandrine, / spondee or choriamb, all is alike to you / — my well-continued fanciful experiment / wherein so many strange verses amalgamate / on the secure bedrock of Milton's prosody" (ll. 79–83). The metrical forms are named, here, like the proper names given to the squabbling birds at the beginning of the poem. The geologic amalgamation of these different forms on the bedrock of Milton should be triumphant, and yet the poem throws its metrical names out as if to challenge the reader to appreciate this gift, the parrot/poet here bored like the bird who shares with the wild birds who disregard his generosity—take it: "all is alike to you."

Who could go through the poem and truly distinguish one strange verse form from another, the poem seems to ask. Who would even recognize the bedrock of Milton? This lack of critical understanding is signified in the most sustained use of diacritical marks to indicate accent in the entire poem. As if to show that England will not and cannot believe what it cannot see, Bridges writes: "not that but when I speak you will incline an ear / in critical attention lest by chánce I míght / póssibly say sómething that was worth repeating" (ll. 84–86). The poem finally shifts the poet-parrot to the poet-reader, that is, the listening reading public that can only hear experiments, not detect them visually. It is only "when I speak" that we "incline an ear" with critical attention, not when we read. By slipping into iambic pentameter and then reversing the foot in line 86, the poem mocks what is easily repeated out loud and demonstrates that perhaps the preservation of these forms will never be correctly repeated because of the level of training required to read them correctly, and the level of inquiry required to even detect that they exist.

After the "worth repeating:" we might expect to find a list of repeatable forms, a final gesture of what we might still be expected to learn. His parenthetic statement asks us to reflect, finally, after an entire poem of proving that our intellect is not capable of adequate reflection (do you think? [l. 59]). This question at the end of the poem seems an ironic question to the answer his other question set out: "Why ask? You cannot know," you cannot think, you do not think. Literature becomes mere "pages"— "that gouty excrement of human intellect / accumulating slowly & everlastingly / depositing, like guano on the Peruvian shore, / to be perhaps exhumed in some remotest age" (ll. 87–89). The reference to guano here is particularly telling because of the influence of Huck Gibb's money on the progress of the Oxford English Dictionary. Gibb's family fortune, made by the export of Peruvian guano, loaned Gilbert Murray enough funds to publish part one of the dictionary in 1884. Despite this reference to the enormous success in preservation for English language and literature, one dependent on accumulation and standardization, the intellect-as-excrement image is both humorous and damning. Bridges seems to think that his intellectual experiment has already been buried in his lifetime.

Though, once spoken, the poem might be "worth repeating," it laments its own eventual future: both disremembered (never repeated) and its complex metrics, its carefully composed skeletal structures of prosody, essentially "dismembered"[19]—torn limb from limb. The fate of classical prosody, the "temple of Christian faith & fair Hellenic art," is told in the last Latin tag, now sequestered to the parenthesis *piis secunda, vate me, detur fuga*. This line, from Horace's sixteenth epode "to the Roman people" (Ad Populum Romanium), tempts a reading of England's future like the fate of Rome Horace describes: "this land shall again be possessed by wild beasts. . . . The victorious barbarian shall trample upon the ashes of the city . . . there can be no better destination than this; namely, to go wherever our feet will carry us. . . ."[20] But where would England's metrical feet carry her? The dismembered feet of England's meters were already scattered throughout the poetry of the 1920s, destined to survive the rest of the twentieth century only in metrical fragments, ghosts of a civilization that was never quite successful. Bridges, talking to his brass-wire-entrapped parrot, changes the Latin form in his quotation from "datur" to "detur," a subtle move to the modal to show how escape from ignorance is not just one possibility, but the only possibility; one he exemplified by a lifetime of metrical experimentation and one that we are only at the beginning stages of recovering. If one studies the history of meter today, one will see that it involves reassessing the myriad assumptions about meter, the confusions and complications that he tried—as any metrists today tries in his or her own way—to elucidate.

Alice Meynell's "English Metres"

The story I have begun to tell here is a narrative of masculinity, of a male-centric, Anglo-Saxon identification that suppresses and ignores the ways that women poets writing concurrently were participating in and troubling concepts of English national meter and English national identity. I have not investigated, nor have I given ample space to investigating the implications of the homosociality in the communities imagined by Gerard Manley Hopkins and Wilfred Owen. Nor does space permit me to theorize about the implications of homosexual identification in each of these poet's oeuvres; both of them were hostile toward women at different points in their careers and believed women to be lesser poets: poetasters and poetesses, mere versifiers (attributed with lesser intellect, in Hopkins, and home-front ignorance, in Sassoon, though Owen was a great admirer of Elizabeth Barrett Browning). There is much work to be done in the ways that assumptions about gender and education impact and play out in the metrical discourses of the period. From Anna Letitia Barbauld's support of the schoolroom-as-nation to the countless schoolmistresses who wrote metrical histories, grammar books, songbooks, and drills (from Jane Bourne to Veronica Vassey), to the slant-rhymes of Elizabeth Barrett Browning to the experiments of the hundreds of "poetesses" (male or female) in the nineteenth century and the subsequent modernist reception, rejection, and repression of these experiments (like Christina Rossetti's "goblin metrics," so expertly theorized by Anne Jamison in *Poetics en Passant*), the gendering of meter—both English and classical, deserves sustained study. Henry Newbolt learned a great deal about meter from Mary Coleridge, and Coventry Patmore learned from Alice Meynell. The absence of women as main characters in this study by no means indicates that women were not participating in, creating, critiquing, and influencing metrical discourses in the nineteenth and early twentieth centuries. Yopie Prins's work in *Victorian Sappho* (Princeton, 1999) is foundational; *Ladies' Greek* (2013) will be as well. Work by Jason Rudy, Linda K. Hughes, Linda Peterson, Emma Major, Ben Glaser, Carrie Preston, and Emily Harrington has begun to correct these male-centric metrical narratives. Because few female poets, beyond Alice Meynell and Adelaide Crapsey, published prosodic treatises or manuals, I have left them out of this initial study, just as I have left out a good many male poets who also wrote about meter (it was such a common practice that nearly every poet wrote something about his or her metrical practice in a private letter at some point). I hope that this book serves as a first step toward expanding our understanding of metrical discourse to include all of the narratives of metrical and national identity that have been suppressed by literary history. As a gesture toward the work that needs to be done, and that will be done, in this area, I want to close this book with another 1923 poem by a poet who participated in the abstraction of meter as corporeally, natively English in complicated and lasting ways. In the same year that Eliot published *The Waste Land* and Bridges published "Poor Poll," Alice Meynell published "The English Metres" in her collected *Poems*. Wilfred Owen's *Poems*, edited by Sassoon, had been published in 1920 and reprinted in 1921, and Hopkins's *Poems,* edited by Bridges, had been receiving the rare baffled review since its appearance in 1918. Like all of the poets I discuss in this project, Meynell meditates on metrical form in the broader contexts of English national culture in her poems, "The Laws of Verse" and "The English Metres." These poems provide a suitable postscript to a project in which many poets were concerned that the fate of the "English metres" in the twentieth century would mean their erasure from the script of literary history altogether.

Like Robert Bridges in Sonnet 21, and like Hopkins in "The Windhover," in Alice Meynell's "The Laws of Verse," she makes verse itself the bird, not a poetic inspiration that will fill a form:

The Laws of Verse

Dear Laws, come to my breast!
Take all my frame, and make your close arms meet
Around me; and so ruled, so warm, so pressed,
I breathe, aware; I feel my wild heart beat.

Dear Laws, be wings to me!
The feather merely floats. Oh, be it heard
Through weight of life—the skylark's gravity—
That I am not a feather, but a bird.

Here, Meynell addresses Shelley, Bridges, and the laws of verse themselves. The laws of verse seem to be the laws of Christ, of devotion, but she is also the master of these laws.

Addressing meter as "English" in "The English Metres" staunchly positions Meynell among those who believe that classical feet are not only acceptable but perhaps also laudable as representatives of the measure of English poetry. Meynell does not bother to justify her terminology—she writes as if the Greek words for metrical feet are not only appropriate but as if they have become a crucial part of an English landscape. Despite her adoption and naturalization of these laws, this is another subtle elegy for an understanding of meter that will disappear along with classical education. Like Saintsbury, Meynell asserts that "English meters" exist and have characteristics that align them with the nation, and yet there is a metametrical narrative at work in this poem as well, in which the poet mourns the poem's inability to be understood as a metrical allegory.

The English Metres

The rooted liberty of flowers in the breeze
Is theirs, by national luck impulsive, terse,
Tethered, uncaptured, rules obeyed 'at ease'
Time-strengthened laws of verse.

Or they are like our seasons that admit   5
Inflexion, not infraction: Autumn hoar,
Winter more tender than our thoughts of it,
But a year's steadfast four.

Redundant syllables of Summer rain,
And displaced accents of authentic Spring;   10
Spondaic clouds above a gusty plain
With dactyls on the wing.

Not Common Law, but Equity, is theirs —
Our metres; play and agile foot askance,
And distance, beckoning, blithely rhyming pairs,   15
Unknown to classic France;

Unknown to Italy. Ay, count, collate,
Latins! With eye foreseeing on the time
And numbered fingers, and approaching fate
On the appropriate rhyme.   20

Nay, nobly our grave measures are decreed:
Heroic, Alexandrine with the stay,
Deliberate; or else like him whose speed
Did outrun Peter, urgent in the break of day. (ll. 1–24)

Though these poems were published in 1923, we see that they are rooted in Edwardian concepts of metrical freedom and wartime conceptions of poetic form. For instance, the first stanza calls English meter "by national luck impulsive, terse, / Tethered, uncaptured, / rules obeyed 'at ease' / Time-strengthened laws of verse." Meter itself is like a soldier 'at ease,' still serving the country, but not bound to perform any duty. English laws of verse are "rooted" in history, but this history has taught them to strive toward freedom. Her own diction is "terse" and "tethered" here, as it describes the "impulsive" and "uncaptured" laws of verse, demonstrating that her own practice shows that she admits to adhering to some sort of law, though she also admits that this law has not been "captured" by any adequate description. The English laws of verse are always rooted in England, but they are still "at liberty," though "by national luck" (and the cultural contexts I outline in the six chapters of this project), they have been strengthened and codified somewhat by the passage of time.

Meynell measures time by metrical seasons ("a year's steadfast four") and, like meter, the four seasons "admit inflexion, not infraction." Just like meter, the seasons might be different than our expectations of them: "winter more tender than our thoughts of it." Her own four-beat lines, here, are as inevitable as the seasons but nonetheless subtler than any description. In the third stanza, nature is allegorized into meter "redundant syllables of Summer rain, / And displaced accents of authentic Spring." The metrical feet, rather than taking on the characteristics of actual feet, sprout wings and fly: spondees are clouds, dactyls are "on the wing." Rather than reference the standard iamb and trochee here, Meynell inserts the most controversial metrical feet (the spondee and dactyl) as if to show how natural these have become—an inevitable part of the English landscape. The "bird" as inspiration, as metrical mastery, as repeating and trapped parrot, has become the metrical foot itself: not the poet or the poem, but that term with which we describe the poem is "on the wing."

Nor does Meynell adhere to a strict iambic meter, though she could be alluding to "heroic" and "urgent" iambs in Saintsbury's terms in stanza 5. The poem welcomes dactyls and spondees, and it is not, though it seems like it almost should be, a lesson in expressive reading. Unlike Coleridge's "Lesson for a Boy," Meynell does not employ dactylic feet in the line "with dactyls on the wing," nor are there spondees in the line "spondaic clouds above a gusty plain." Authentic spring, in Meynell's metrical allegory is not configured in the line through displaced accents, and even the amphibrach and dactyl of "redundant syllables" seem altogether necessary. There is no stanza in which the form, actual or allegorical, imposes itself; the three lines of pentameter followed by one of trimeter never succumb to a strict iambic except in the playful line in stanza 4: "Our metres; play and agile foot askance." In Meynell's poem, agile feet of English meter can play without fear of reproach.

And yet, the fourth stanza alludes to Common Law versus Equity, thus referring to a legal, rather than natural, origin of "our metres." English meters have "Equity" instead of "Common Law," where metrical form would be decided solely on precedent and custom (despite how they are rooted in history). By using this legal terminology, Meynell alludes to the British and American system of ethical modification to the rule of law. Modification based on fairness is the rule to which Meynell refers here, and this flexible interpretation of the laws of verse is "unknown to classic France," and "unknown to Italy" (in stanza 5). Though the English meters are natural, their modification—indeed, codification—might be seen as unnatural or external. The English meters are defined in opposition to their continental counterparts. Even the Latins are seen as too strict, "with eye foreseeing on the time / And numbered fingers, and approaching fate, / On the appropriate rhyme," their verses leading inevitably and predictably to a conclusion we can count on.

"Nay nobly our grave measures are decreed:" she refers to the history of English verse in this final stanza—the heroic couplet, (those "distant, beckoning, blithely rhyming pairs") and the Alexandrine, but again, "decreed" and "stay" have a slightly legal tone to them. English meters have all the freedom they need in 1923, and yet unless they are "decreed" noble, deliberate, they might take on too much speed. John (20:1–9) outruns Peter "urgent in the break of day," to see the resurrected Christ. Here, the poem favors the nobility, the heroism, and the deliberation of the national meters, fearing that without a lawful decree, without the "rooted liberty," verse might be too young, too eager, too quick to discard the careful wisdom of the past. Because both John and Peter are disciples to a "higher law" (Meynell is Catholic), their reticence to let go of the laws of English meter and the freedom they entail, coupled with the eagerness to rush into a new poetic era, are written into this final stanza.

This reticence, born of a Victorian education that respected the misunderstood laws of verse; this freedom, from Edwardian education and the changing conceptions of poetic form (and Englishness in general); and this eagerness to change the law entirely, especially in the 1920s, are all products of cultural change that affected the status of poetry in England. Like Bridges's elegiac turn in "Poor Poll," Meynell's "English Metres" is an ode to English metrical freedom at the same time that it is an elegy for those who will not understand English meters in the way that Meynell has been deliberately, nobly, luckily educated to understand them. As twenty-first-century critics, we might prefer this eagerness; but we must understand that our critical inability to read meter historically is a culturally produced phenomenon, one that this book takes slow, deliberate steps to retrace.

Toward a Critical Prosody

In addition to recovering and recontextualizing poets whose projects seem to fall outside of the received narrative of English literature's formal evolution—most importantly, reading metrical projects as part of a larger metrical discourse, not discarding formal poetics as merely "formal," and understanding that "form" meant different things to different poets at different moments—historical prosody reveals how the history of our profession is intertwined with the history of form. Our traditional approach to meter has been to assume that it imposes "order" onto emotions and onto experience. But what if, as I have shown, the allegory for "order" is destabilized to begin with? Maybe the emotional and experiential elements of the poem are not bound to an agreed-upon stability. The instability generated by multiple and competing metrical discourses correlated with an unstable national culture in the nineteenth century, in particular. Poets may identify with certain forms at certain moments and use and manipulate formal conventions, but a ballad written by Wordsworth comments on those conventions differently, say, than a ballad written as an imitation of a popular music hall song at the end of the nineteenth and beginning of the twentieth centuries or, indeed, differently than the lyrics to a popular song on the radio today. Metrical forms circulate, change, and accrue different meanings at different moments, and this is as readable and important in our understanding of the formation of "poetry" as a concept as the poems themselves.

If we accept that many of our contemporary associations with the word "meter" became fixed in the nineteenth century, what other ways were educational and institutional discourses influencing the reception of poetry in the twentieth century? What other assumptions might we call to question? This book has started to bring to light many competing nineteenth-century prosodic theories and, more importantly, to show what was at stake for the poets and prosodists who attempted, and often failed, to institute these new and

various English meters. I realize, as I hope you do as well, that I cannot account
for all varieties of metrical discourse in the nineteenth century. Rather, I am
learning to ask, when poets were inventing or experimenting with prosodic
systems, with what else, in addition to the measure of the line, were they wrestling? Why was the question of English meter even a question? How did meter
permeate discussions of religion, education, psychology, and disciplinary formation in general? What does "meter" mean if we refuse to take for granted
that our traditional understanding of iambs and trochees is an artificial, cultural construct? The "rise and fall" of meter I narrate here certainly shows the
broad sweep of excitement about defining English meter in a time of disciplinary formation and change (the decline of classics, the rise of "English"), but as
these disciplines were also calling up metrical narratives in new ways at different moments, what meter "means" changes from one community to the next
at each moment. "Meter" and metrical discourse is constantly rising and falling; that is, its status can be "on the rise" in one community just as it is falling
out of favor in another, depending on what associations these communities are
making, and what battles are being played out and for what reasons. But just
because forms or conventions might be best understood as unstable, it does
not mean that we should not honor them anyway; realizing and gesturing to
an inherent instability at the heart of "formal" discourse does not close the
aesthetic possibilities of a poem, shuttling it into cultural studies and considerations of material culture. Rather, considering the political and aesthetic dimensions of poetry's instability might allow us to look closely at the places
where forms seem "fixed," asking why that is the case. Paying attention to the
historical contingencies of poetic form at the same time that we attend to the
poem both broadens and deepens our engagement with poems in/and history
and also gives us the opportunity to question the assumptions that we make as
readers when we encounter texts.

All of this is to say, my historical approach to prosody is to provide a more
nuanced picture of the formal contingencies of the poem at a specific moment,
while also remaining aware of why we are invested in this particular practice.
The narrative of competing metrical forms has multiple strands that apply to a
variety of cultural domains: our associations between certain metrical forms
and certain social classes, between metrical tropes and gender, and between
perceived metrical stability and perceived institutional or ideologically complex hierarchies of power (the church, the domestic sphere). Providing concurrent formal histories—incomplete though they may be—to these generative allegorical readings of prosodic form, are important parts of the practice
of historical prosody. Historical prosody is by no means limited to meter;
meter is just one part of it, and much work needs to be done on pronunciation,
rhyme, rhythm, alliteration,[21] and so on. Likewise, work beyond the prosody
of the poem toward the history of formal circulation can, should, and has recently begun to extend beyond England and into the colonial world, as well as

more deeply into the interiors of domestic spaces and concepts of gendered poetics.[22] This book focuses on meter because meter is where we have stabilized these concepts—twentieth-century poetic criticism has, largely, relied on concepts of genre and form in order to narrate the nineteenth century as a foil to the twentieth. The abstraction of meter, its lack of historical specificity in mid-twentieth-century criticism, I argue, is due to these disorganized, multiple, and competing narratives. It is this failure to achieve a definitive reading—despite the desire to achieve it—that I find heartening about the project of historical prosody. That is, even in a text as didactic as the prosody handbook or an author's notes on how to read a poem, I find the struggle to instruct the reader, and the inherent acknowledgment that the metrical structure of the poem will not successfully transfer across readers and across time, expressive of the many ways English national identity—and stable "identity" in general—was and is fundamentally in flux.[23]

Rather than collapse the metrical history into a simple opposition of Anglo-Saxon or classical ideologies, I have read these myths of origin as two of many that come into play when poets approach metrical form. Beyond the history of the language, the development of industrial culture, mechanization, changes in musical culture, different approaches to the body, to performance, to all kinds of systems and orders, played some role in a poet's thinking about poetic form. All of these influences—transatlantic and cross-channel poetics, translations and foreign travel—might be important and generative considerations for poets experimenting with English poetic form. That many poets were attracted to a stable metrical system is clear, and their attempts to achieve and define these systems and what those attempts teach us is the subject of this study. But the very unfixed nature of many metrical conventions, on the one hand, and the too-fixed nature of their abstract definitions that then inspired a model for endless critical discourse, on the other hand—created anxiety for poetry readers of every class and educational background. And this anxiety about form still pervades the discipline of English literary studies, where "poetic form" appears as that last bastion of elite training, the one place where we have a right to a "right" answer, the place where a poem's meaning might be explained, once and for all, with the help of a teacher trained in the system that will demystify it. And yet, as I have been arguing, the very poets with whom we have charged the responsibility of fixing these conventions and metrical systems doubted the sustainability of conventional forms, doubted their security for the future of the English language and English culture. They knew, or were beginning to realize, that many systems were possible for English verse but the contingencies of pedagogy meant that these various possibilities—those that would, perhaps, reveal the hybrid nature of the English language—might create insecurity in the young student/subject, and so that is not how we have been teaching English meter. And even this realization—that one model would prevail and be called quintessentially "English" at the expense of other possible ways of reading both "poetry" and "verse," of identifying "Englishness" within literary studies—was figured metrically, formally, in the early twentieth century by the poets who Modernism has buried. It is up to us to exhume these multitudinous metrical narratives so that we might further understand our own unstable relationship to poetic form and culture and to generate new ways of thinking about poetic form's historical contingencies as well as the contingencies of our own contemporary reading practices.

❧

Introduction: The Failure of Meter

1. The records to which I refer here were destroyed in the Second World War and not the First World War.

2. *Versification*, according to its bibliographic record, was "a monthly magazine of measure and metre." Only two issues are now listed in the online catalog and both are missing. In *The Western Antiquary: Or, Devon and Cornwall notebook,* vol. 11, the editor records, "We have received several numbers of a little serial called 'Versification,' edited by Alfred Nutting. Its chief feature is the publication of original poems by amateur authors, to which the editor appends critical notes as to the style and quality of compositions." ("Current Literature," *The Western Antiquary*, 30).

3. Bradbury and McFarlane, "The Name and Nature of Modernism," 21.

4. Nadel, *Cambridge Introduction to Ezra Pound*, 26.

5. Cavitch, "Stephen Crane's Refrain," 33.

6. Beasley, *Theorists of Modernist Poetry*, 1.

7. Lewis, *Cambridge Introduction to Modernism*, 4, 3.

8. Herbert Read, in 1933, writes: "it is not so much a revolution, which implies a turning over, even a turning back, but rather a break-up, a devolution, some would say a dissolution. Its character is catastrophic" (*Art Now*, 58–59); C. S. Lewis, in 1954, writes: "I do not see how anyone can doubt that modern poetry is not only a greater novelty than any other 'new poetry' but new in a new way, almost a new dimension." (*De Descriptione Temporum: An Inaugural Lecture*, 13).

9. Bradbury and McFarlane, *Modernism*, 21.

10. Cavitch writes: "the perpetuation of such liberation narratives is powerfully motivated, and deeply inscribed in our scholarship, our course syllabi, and our anthologies and editions" ("Stephen Crane's Refrain," 33).

11. This literary historical narrative, I am arguing, is largely based on reactions to the poetry of the movements associated with the modernist avant-garde as well as reviews of these poems by the scholars now known as the "New Critics." For "difficulty" in modern poetry, see Steiner, "On Difficulty," 263–76; Christie, "A Recent History of Poetic Difficulty," 539–64.

12. Pound, *The Pisan Cantos*.

13. Prins, "Nineteenth-Century Homers and the Hexameter Mania," 229–56.

14. For recent exciting work in Victorian prosody, see Hughes et al., in the "Victorian Prosody" special issue of *Victorian Poetry*, edited by Meredith Martin and Yisrael Levin.

15. This patriotic narrative of curricular reform in the English education system was often figured as an issue that pertained only to the men who would grow up to become soldiers and, indeed, the masculine aspects of English rhythm's march through time was certainly a trope that appeared again and again. But I want to signal that this nar-

rative was promoted and disseminated by schoolmistresses in the classroom and by the female authors who wrote the majority of English grammar books in the nineteenth century. Poets like Alice Meynell, Mary Coleridge, and Jessie Pope also participated in a discourse that promoted the concept of English meter's preexistence in the heartbeats and footsteps of particularly English bodies, a discourse, I argue, that escalates and is articulated in a particularly nationalistic way at the turn of the twentieth century.

16. Doyle, *English and Englishness*, 19.

17. Beer, *Open Fields*; Dowling, *Language and Decadence in the Victorian Fin de Siècle*; Mugglestone, *Lost for Words*.

18. Hugh Blair, *Lectures on Belles Lettres and Rhetoric*, 227.

19. Fussell, *Theory of Prosody in Eighteenth-Century England*, 3.

20. Ibid.

21. Ibid.

22. Abbott, ed., *The Letters of Gerard Manley Hopkins to Robert Bridges*, 231.

23. See Armstrong, *Victorian Poetry*; Prins, "Victorian Meters," 89–113; Cavitch, "Stephen Crane's Refrain," 33–54; Hughes *The Cambridge Introduction to Victorian Poetry*; and especially Jamison, *Poetics en Passant*.

24. Levine, "Formal Pasts and Formal Possibilities in English Studies," 1241–56.

25. In *Hardy's Metres and Victorian Prosody*, Taylor begins to reveal the complexity of Victorian metrical criticism. Though focused primarily on Hardy's verse forms, the early chapters argue for the "abstraction" of meter into a system or "law" against which the "freedom" of spoken language, with its various unmeasured quantities, was in tension. Markley's *Stateliest Measures* reveals Tennyson's classical metrical experiments in English were meant to evoke a kind of national Hellenism.

Chapter 1: The History of Meter

1. Enfield, *The Speaker*.

2. Guillory, "Mute Inglorious Miltons," 100.

3. Ibid., 101.

4. Nonconforming Protestants, but also Quakers, Catholics, and Jews.

5. Rule V, Enfield, *The Speaker*, 7.

6. Walker, *Elements of Elocution*, 263.

7. "Prosodic regularity forces the ordering of the perceiver's mind so that it may be in a condition to receive the ordered moral matter of the poem, just as, in ethics and religion, a conscious regularizing of principles and even of daily habits is the necessary condition for the growth of piety" (Fussell, *Theory of Prosody in Eighteenth-Century England*, 43).

8. Burt, *A Metrical Epitome of the History of England Prior to the Reign of George the First*, vii.

9. It is distinct, too from the "metrical romances" of earlier centuries, romances that were being translated and circulated in the nineteenth century. For more on the popularity of the metrical romance in the early nineteenth century, see St. Clair, *The Reading Nation in the Romantic Period*.

10. *Cf.* Prins, "Metrical Translation: Nineteenth-Century Homers and the Hexameter Mania."

11. Eighteen thousand copies sold in ten years; 100,000 by 1875 (from Cunningham, *The Victorians: An Anthology of Poetry and Poetics*, 72).

12. Published in 1587 and reprinted in 1815 (this is the edition I am quoting), the *Mirror for Magistrates*, edited by Joseph Haselwood was included in the eighteenth century in Elizabeth Cooper's *The Muses Library* (1737) and Edward Capell's *Prolusions* (1760) before Thomas Warton's *A History of English Poetry* (1781) popularized it once more. John Haselwood edited an edition in 1815 for Longman and based his on the 1587 edition. *The Mirror* was also reprinted in the series *Cassell's Library of English Literature* in the volume *Shorter English Poems*, selected, edited and arranged by Henry Morley (1883).

13. De Sackville, surely the most famous author of *The Mirror*, writes how he was inspired much like Caedmon: awakened from sleep, or in a sleepy dream, he is visited by spirits who force him to write: "one after one, they came in strange attire / but some with wounds and blood were so disguised / you scarcely could by reason's aid aspire / to know what war such sundry death's devised" (*Cassell's Library,* 183).

14. A three-part series in English, Roman, and Hellenic history was written "after the method of Dr. Grey" at midcentury: Grey, *Wilcongsau, or, Mnemonic hexameters: after the method of the Memoria Technica of Dr. Grey: English History*; *First Thebaloi, or, Mnemonic Hexameters, after the method of the Memoria Technica of Dr. Grey: Hellenic History*; and *Regdol or Mnemonic Hexameters after the method of the Memoria Technica of Dr. Grey: Roman History*.

15. Grey, *Memoria Technica*, vii–viii.

16. He admits that he lifted the ancient history from "Mr. Hooke, the Roman Historian" and took parts of *A Poetical Chronology of the Kings of England* from *The Gentleman's Magazine*. Valpy, *A Poetical Chronology of the Kings of England*, 4.

17. "Poetical Chronology of the Kings of England," T. M. Esq. in "Poetical Essays," *Gentleman's Magazine* printed in serial, monthly between September 1773–January 1774, 454–55, 511, 571, 613, 655.

18. Ibid., 5, 6.

19. Metrical histories of *Charles the Great* and the *War of the Roses,* for example, focused on specific events in English history.

20. There were easily three times as many metrical histories, epitomes, and chronicles published in the nineteenth century as in the eighteenth century.

21.   Poor Edward the Fifth was young killed in his bed

        By his uncle, Richard, who was knocked on the head

        By Henry the Seventh, who in fame grew big

        And Henry the Eighth, who was fat as a pig! (Collins, *Chapter of Kings*)

22. See Strabone, "Samuel Johnson Standardizer of English, Preserver of Gaelic"; Strabone, *Grammarians and Barbarians: How the vernacular revival transformed British literature and identity in the eighteenth and nineteenth centuries*, 69; and Elfenbein, *Romanticism and the Rise of English*.

23. Dibdin. *A Metrical History of England; or, Recollections in Rhyme of some of the most prominent Features in our National Chronology, from the Landing of Julius Caesar to the Commencement of the Regency in 1812 in two volumes*. Although a review in *The Monthly Catalogue* faults the compilation as being "an amplification of the well-known 'Chapter of Kings,'" it admits that it is "something more" (Francis Hodgson, Review of Dibdin, 437).

24. A clever idea in theory, but in practice his narrative vacillates between heroic couplets and ballad meter. Herbert F. Tucker, in *Epic: Britain's Heroic Muse 1790–1910* writes, "one hardly knows what to call" Dibdin's history (150) and concludes that the poem displays "a nationalism secure enough to make fun of itself" (151).

25. Hall, "At Home With History: Macaulay and *The History of England*," *At Home with Empire*, 32–52, as well as Hall, McClelland, and Rendall, *Defining the Victorian Nation*.

26. London University's matriculation examination made history compulsory from the start (1838), and it was included in examination requirements of the Civil Service (1854–55, 1870) and the Army (1870). The Schools Inquiry Commission and publishing house data shows that the four most popular books were Mangnall's *Historical and Miscellaneous Questions for the use of young people,* reprinted many times between 1804 and 1891; Gleig's *School History of England;*, W. F. Collier's *History of the British Empire*; and Ince's *An Outline of English History*. From Howat, "The Nineteenth-Century History Textbook," 147–58.

27. "In committing the fibre of a material so raw to the metrical loom, a coarse tissue must necessarily be worked out—coarse but genuine—a greater regard having been paid to its durability than its appearance" (Raymond, *Chronicles of England*, xvii).

28. Rossendale, *History of the Kings and Queens of England from King Egbert to Queen Victoria*, preface, no page number.

29. Montefiore, *The History of England in Verse* (London: Ward, Lock, and Tyler, 1876), 2.

30. Robson, "Standing on the Burning Deck: Poetry, Performance, History," 148–62.

31. Other books with mnemonic ciphers include Feinaigle, *The New Art of Memory Founded on the Principles Taught by Gregor von Feinaigle*; Fauvel-Gouraud and Miles *Phreno-mnemotechny*; and Fuller, *The Art of Memory*: In Byron's *Don Juan*, he jokes about Donna Inez's perfect memory, which did not need the aid of Feinaigle the hack:

> —memory was a mine; she knew by heart
> All Calderon and the greater part of Lopé
> So that if any actor missed his part
> She could have served him for the prompter's copy;
> For her Feinaigle's were an useless art,
> And he himself obliged to shut up shop, — he
> Could never make a memory so fine as
> That which adorned the brain of Donna Inez.
> (*Don Juan*, I, xi, 1818)

Lewis Carroll's *Memoria Technica* (s.n.), which was a numerical cipher but certainly influenced by the new memorization techniques, wasn't published widely until 1888 (though there was a small 1877 edition).

32. Bourne, *Granny's History of England in Rhyme*, 1.

33. Mann, *School Recreations and Amusements, Being a Companion Volume to King's School Interests and Duties, Prepared Especially for Teachers' Reading Circles*, 175–76.

34. Stray and Sutherland, "Mass Markets: Education," 359–81, 359, 360.

35. I am moving quickly through the period leading up to the 1860 education reforms; Richardson's *Literature, Education, and Romanticism: Reading as Social Practice 1780–1832* provides an excellent survey of broad educational movements in the period.

36. See Mugglestone, *Lost for Words*; Dowling, *Language and Decadence in the Victorian Fin de Siècle*; Vincent, *Literacy and Popular Culture in Britain 1750–1914*; and Strabone, *Grammarians and Barbarians*. Also, Tony Crowley *Standard English and the Politics of Language*; St. Clair, *The Reading Nation in the Romantic Period*; Cohen, "Whittier, Ballad Reading, and the Culture of Nineteenth–Century Poetry."

37. *Cf.* Cureton, "A Disciplinary Map for Verse Study."

38. I have benefited from the work of English language historians Manfred Görlach and Ian Michael, especially, as guides to the development of grammar teaching in nineteenth-century England. See Görlach, *English in Nineteenth-Century England: An Introduction* and Michael, *The Teaching of English from the Sixteenth Century to 1870*.

39. See Spoel, "Rereading the Elocutionists: The Rhetoric of Thomas Sheridan's 'A Course of Lectures on Elocution' and John Walker's 'Elements of Elocution.'"

40. See Woods, "The Cultural Tradition of Nineteenth-Century 'Traditional' Grammar Teaching"; Fries, "The Rules of Common School Grammars."

41. Though Elfenbein's recent *Romanticism and the Rise of English* takes into account grammatical debates about usage in the late eighteenth and nineteenth centuries, prosody has received little attention.

42. Strabone, "Samuel Johnson: Standardizer of English, Preserver of Gaelic."

43. Johnson, *Dictionary*; Fussell, *Theory of Prosody in Eighteenth Century England*, 25–26. Fussell speculates that "an acquaintance with John Rice's *Introductions to the Art of Reading with Energy and Propriety*" (London, 1765) may have caused Johnson to add the new sentence to his revision of *The Dictionary*" (26, n.116).

44. Percy, *Reliques of Ancient English Poetry: Consisting of Old Heroic Ballads, Songs, and other Pieces of our earlier Poets, (Chiefly of the Lyric kind.) Together with some few of later Date*.

45. Strabone, *Barbarians and Grammarians*, 283.

46. Percy, *Reliques*, 261.

47. Review of *King Alfred's Anglo-Saxon Version of the Metres of Boethius, with an English translation and notes*, in *A Gentleman's Magazine*, vol. 158: 49.

48. Turner, *History of England*, 264–65.

49. Some important early nineteenth-century publications in Anglo-Saxon studies were Thomas Whitaker's 1813 version of *Piers Plowman*; John J. Conybeare's 1814 "English Paraphrase" of *Beowulf* contained in *Observations on the metre of the Anglo-Saxon poetry; further observations on the poetry of our Anglo-Saxon ancestors* (London: Archaeologia, 1814); Conybeare, *Illustrations of Anglo-Saxon Poetry*; Joseph Bosworth's *Elements of Anglo-Saxon Grammar*; and Kemble, *A Translation of the Anglo-Saxon poem Beowulf*. Versions of *Beowulf* appeared in nearly every decade of the nineteenth century thereafter (A. D. Wackerbarth, 1849; Benhamin Thorpe, 1865; Thomas Arnold, 1876; James M. Garnett, 1882; H. W. Lumsden, 1883; John Gibb, 1884; G. Cox, E. H. Jones, 1886; John Earl, 1892; Leslie Hall, 1892; William Morris and A. J. Wyatt, 1898).

50. Murray, *Grammar*, 207.

51. Sheridan, *A Course of Lectures on Elocution Together with Two Dissertations on Language* and *A General Dictionary of the English Language . . . to which is prefixed A Rhetorical Grammar* (London: J. Dodsley, Pall-Mall, C. Dilly, and J. Wilkie, 1780).

52. Coote, *Elements of English Grammar*, 278–83.

53. Woods, "The Cultural Tradition of Nineteenth-Century 'Traditional' Grammar Teaching," 8.

54. On Murray, see Read, "The Motivation of Lindley Murray's Grammatical Work."

55. Murray, *English Grammar*, 146.

56. Ibid., 1839, 71.

57. Ibid., 1867, 224.

58. This wholesale lifting of Sheridan's text only appears in the 4th edition of Murray's *English Grammar*, in 1798, and is not in the first three editions (1795, 1796, 1797).

59. Ibid., 1798, 203.

60. This allegory of walking, predating the Wordsworthian walking composition, will be taken up in Coventry Patmore's theory of isochronous intervals, though Patmore's pace does not come from footsteps themselves but from the regular appearance of an accompanying fence-post—the mind, for Patmore, must perceive the metrical grid for the body to follow.

61. Murray, *English Grammar Adapted to the Different Classes of Learners*, 203. This text is identical in all editions following; it appears on p. 252 of the sixth American edition, *English Grammar Comprehending the Principles and Rules of the Language* (New York: Collins & Co., 1829), and the fifty-eighth edition, (London: Longman, Hurst, 1867), 203.

62. Sheridan, *The Art of Reading*, 27.

63. Murray, *Grammar*, 190.

64. Ibid., 203.

65. Murray and Flint, *Abridged Grammar*, 78.

66. Saintsbury gives only passing notice to Murray in his *History of English Prosody*, stopping to reprimand him for relying too much on accent and not enough on quantity, but admits that his doctrine that "we have all that the ancients had, and *something they had not*" is "uncommonly near the truth, though I dare say he did not know how true it was. For the fact of the matter is that we have the full quantitative scansion by feet, which is the franchise and privilege of classical verse, without the limitations of quantitative syllabisation with which that verse was hampered. We have their Order and our own Freedom besides" (156).

67. Guest, *A History of English Rhythms*, 111.

68. There is no record in the history of linguistics for the study of prosody, nor is there a survey like Fussell's extremely useful *Theory of Prosody in Eighteenth Century England*. For useful histories of language study in nineteenth-century England, see Anna Morpurgo Davies, *History of Linguistics* and Aarsleff, *The Study of Language in England 1780–1860*.

69. Potter, *The Muse in Chains*.

70. Prins, "Victorian Meters," 93.

71. Hollander, *Vision and Resonance: Two Senses of Poetic Form*, 19.

72. Prins, "Victorian Meters," 90–91.

73. Goold Brown, *The Grammar of English Grammars*, 827, 828.

74. As evidence of the necessity for simplifying and abstracting metrical rules for pedagogical purposes, the section on "versification" that appears in Goold Brown's often reprinted *First Lines of Grammar* reads: "Versification is the art of arranging words into lines of correspondent length, so as to produce harmony by the regular alternation of syllables differing in quantity" (Brown, *The First Lines of Grammar*, 145).

75. Patmore's article, "English Metrical Critics," appeared in issue XXVII, 127–61, 1857 of the *North British Review* in 1857 as "an article ostensibly reviewing George Vandenhoff's *The Art of Elocution*, Edwin Guest's *A History of English Rhythms,* and William O'Brien's *The Ancient Rhythmical Art Recovered.*" Sister Mary Augustine Roth's reproduction of Patmore's *Essay on English Metrical Law* includes an introduction in which she expertly traces the influences of Patmore's predecessors Joshua Steele, Hegel ("whose *Aesthetics* provided the philosophical basis for an "organic" theory of prosody unifying 'life' and 'law,' meanings and versification," ix), Daniel, Foster, Mitford, and Dallas. Patmore revised the essay and printed it as a "Prefatory Study on English Metrical Law" in the 1878 edition of *Amelia, Tamerton Church Tower, Etc.*, which was again reprinted in the 1879 four-volume edition of Patmore's collected *Poems* (in volume 2).

76. Patmore, "Essay on English Metrical Law," *Poems Volume 2*, 217. I am using the fourth edition of the second volume of *Poems*, which was printed (and reprinted) in 1886, 1887, and 1890, attesting to its popularity as well as the potential readership of the essay, which appeared in the appendix. Despite the importance that Dennis Taylor has given to this essay (as the harbinger of the "New Prosody"), few of Patmore's obituaries mention the essay, and a long *Atheneaum* piece (1896: Dec. 5, 797) only states: "a thoughtful essay, marked by fresh study, and displaying the genius of the poet in a very distinct and startling light." Saintsbury discards Patmore's metrical interventions in a June 15, 1878 *Athenaeum* review (757) [see chapter 3]. A long review in *The Examiner* (June 29, 1878) summarizes:

> it is ingenious and scrupulously exact in expression, and is conceived in a dignified spirit, but errs in recording as legitimate canons of rythmic (sic) art irregularities that are only to be pardoned in genius, not recommended to immaturity. For instance, it is dangerous to attempt, by any public recognition of time, to regulate the varied pauses that enliven and illuminate the best English verse. If once we drop the jog-trot measurement of lines by feet, on the ground that, what we call an iambus has, in fact, by an irregularity, become a trochee, we open the door to every sort of extravagance. By all means, let young people continue to be taught to scan in the old mechanical way. If they are poets, they will learn intuitively to arrange their time. . . . The whole of this study on metre, in short, is highly interesting, whether the reader agrees with it in detail or not. It is singular to find a poet defending with such dignity the theory of an art that he seems, in practice, so often to defy. (821–22)

Patmore himself asserts "I have seen with pleasure that, since then [1856], its main principles have been quietly adopted by most writers on the subject in periodicals and elsewhere" ("Essay on English Metrical Law," 215).

77. Vandenhoff and Poe, *A Plain System of Elocution*; Vandenhoff, *The Art of Elocution as an Essential Part of Rhetoric: with instructions in gesture and an appendix of oratorical, poetical, and dramatic extracts*.

78. *Milton's Prosody* was first published in 1887 as part of Henry Beeching's school edition of *Paradise Lost* as "On the Elements of Blank Verse," and it was reprinted in 1894 as a pamphlet all its own (Oxford: Clarendon Press, 1894), reprinted again in 1901 alongside Stone's treatise, and printed in final revised form in 1921.

79. Stone had published *On the Use of Classical Metres in English* in 1899 and it was reprinted alongside Bridges's *Milton's Prosody* in 1901.

80. Schipper, *Englische Metrik*. Translated into English in 1910 as *A History of English Versification*, trans. Jakob Schipper, the book was reviewed alongside Saintsbury's three volumes.

81. Omond, *English Metrists* and *A Study of Metre* were revised and reprinted. Omond was a frequent interlocutor with Mayor, Bridges, and Saintsbury.

82. I note the various editions of Patmore's text to point to the way that scholars were constantly revising and reprinting their work on meter, adding appendixes, rejoinders, responses, and clarifications based on the proliferation of discourse on the matter. On the proliferation of writing about meter in the nineteenth century, see the next section of this chapter, then Taylor, *Hardy's Metres and Victorian Prosody* and Prins, "Victorian Meters." On the rise of mass literacy, see St. Clair, *The Reading Nation in the Romantic Period* and Vincent, *Literacy and Popular Culture in Britain 1750–1914* and *The Rise of Mass Literacy: Reading and Writing in Modern Europe*.

83. See Taylor and Prins, also, more recently, Hall, "Popular Prosody: Spectacle and the Politics of Victorian Versification," or Pinch, "Love Thinking."

84. Trench, *On the Study of Words*, 64.

Chapter 2: The Stigma of Meter

1. Thomas Sheridan's third edition of *A General Dictionary of the English Language* revises "rhetorical grammar" to "prosodial grammar" and emphasizes that the grammar he wishes to provide therein refers only to oratory (lxxx).

2. Norman MacKenzie, "Introduction to the Fourth Edition," *The Poems of Gerard Manley Hopkins*, xiii.

3. Abbott, *Letters of Gerard Manley Hopkins to Robert Bridges* (*LI* in-text citation), 231; Abbott, *Further Letters of Gerard Manley Hopkins* (*LII* in-text citation); Abbott, *The Correspondence of Gerard Manley Hopkins and Richard Watson Dixon* (*LIII* in-text citation); House, *The Journals and Papers of Gerard Manley Hopkins* (*JP* in-text citation); Devlin, *Sermons: The Sermons and Devotional Writings of Gerard Manley Hopkins*; Hopkins, Author's Note on "The Wreck of the Deutschland" (*AN* in-text citation).

4. Miles, "Gerard Hopkins," 164.

5. "From the consequent miseries, the insensate and interminable slaughter, the hate and filth, we can turn to seek comfort only in the quiet confidence of our souls; and we look instinctively to the seers and poets of mankind, whose sayings are the oracles and prophecies of loveliness and lovingkindness." From Bridges, "Preface," *The Spirit of Man*. Hopkins's poems in *The Spirit of Man* include "Spring and Fall" (9), reprinted from Miles, ed., *Poets and Poetry of the Century*, vol. viii; the first stanza of

"The Wreck of the Deutschland" (53); "The Candle Indoors" (269); "In the Valley of the Elwy" (including Hopkins's note about the poem, 358); "The Handsome Heart" (along with the note that "the author was a Jesuit priest, and *Father* in line 2 is the spiritual title," 369); "The Habit of Perfection" (the first two stanzas; written when an undergraduate at Oxford, 385).

6. Most of Hopkins's poems prior to *The Spirit of Man* appeared in small publications, and though the notice they attracted came mostly from his Catholic audience, early twentieth-century readers were intrigued by his innovations. George Saintsbury reported of Hopkins's poems in 1910 that "it is quite clear they were all experiments," and that the lines, "of the anti-foot and pro-stress division" seemed to have syllables "thrust in out of pure mischief" (Saintsbury, *A History of English Prosody from the Twelfth Century to the Present Day*, 3:391).

7. Maynard, "The Artist as Hero," 259–60.

8. Clutton-Brock, unsigned review, 19.

9. Richards, "Gerard Hopkins," 195.

10. Hopkins also felt distress when faced with the physical form of the metrical mark.

11. Norman MacKenzie traces Hopkins's addition of the accent marks on lines 9 and 14 on Bridges's transcription from Manuscript A to Manuscript B. Variants in the manuscripts include "will" in italics from Manuscript A to "will." MacKenzie notes that this is "probably GMH's stress." In Mackenzie's *Poetical Works of Gerard Manley Hopkins*, he keeps the marks on the rest of the poem but chooses to italicize *will* (Richards, *Practical Criticism*).

12. Richards, *Practical Criticism*, 83.

13. William Empson takes issue with Richards's removal of the mark in *Seven Types of Ambiguity*, 148:

> Mr. Richards, from whom I copy this, considers that the ambiguity of *will* is removed by the accent which Hopkins placed upon it; it seems to me rather that it is intensified. Certainly, with the accent on *weep* and *and, will* can only be an auxiliary verb, and with the accent on *will* its main meaning is "insist upon." But the future meaning also can be imposed upon this latter way of reading the line if it is the tense which is being stressed, if it insists on the contrast between the two sorts of weeping, or, including *know* with *weep*, between the two sorts of knowledge. Now it is useful that the tense should be stressed at this crucial point, because it is these two contrasts and their unity which make the point of the poem.

Despite Empson's acceptance of the ambiguity on "will," he continues that "[i]t seems difficult to enjoy the accent on *are*, which the poet has inserted; I take it to mean: 'Sorrow's springs, always the same, independent of our attitude to them, exist,' permanently and as it were absolutely'" (149). In both instances, whether it is the two contrasts and their unity or the permanence of spring, Empson resolves Hopkins's use of metrical marks into an absolute intention that tends toward a reading that erases the possibility that the meter could mean something other than an indication of stability.

14. In a discussion of "Easter Communion," Griffiths writes, "two claims are made on the voice, claims which it can with difficulty meet simultaneously; it must hark back from 'shakes' to 'brakes' so that the rhyme may sound out and it must press on

from 'shakes' to 'them' so that the syntax may flow" (*The Printed Voice of Victorian Poetry*, 273).

15. *Cf.* Richards, *Basic English and Its Uses*; *So Much Nearer: Essays Towards a World English*. A few canonical "sound" focused studies of Hopkins's meter include J. Hillis Miller, "The Univocal Chiming," 89–116; Susan Stewart, "Letter on Sound," 29–52; James I. Wimsatt, *Hopkins's Poetics of Speech Sound: Sprung Rhythm, Lettering, Inscape*.

16. Earle, *The Philology of the English Tongue*, 585–620.

17. Abbott, *LII*, 218–19.

18. *Cf.* Plotkin, *The Tenth Muse*; Dowling, *Language and Decadence in the Victorian Fin de Siècle*.

19. Plotkin, *The Tenth Muse*, 37–38.

20. Müller, *Lectures on the Science of Language*, 384.

21. Trench, *On the Study of Words* (1851) and *English Past and Present* (1855), 117. Further references are given parenthetically in the text.

22. House, *JP*, 269.

23. Ibid., 127; Higgins, *The Collected Works of Gerard Manley Hopkins, Volume IV: Oxford Essays and Notes*, 306–7.

24. For an intricate reading of Hopkins's "Word" and "The Wreck of the Deutschland," see Daniel Brown, *Hopkins' Idealism*, 278–326.

25. Both White's *Hopkins: A Literary Biography* and Phillips's *Gerard Manley Hopkins and the Victorian Visual World* note the influence of Ruskin on Hopkins's philosophy of inscape in the visual world. It is no accident that "blood is red" so closely resembles Ruskin's meditation on perception in *Modern Painters,* especially the chapter, "Of the Pathetic Fallacy": "be it observed that the word *blue* does *not* mean the *sensation* caused by a gentian on the human eye; but it means the *power* of producing that sensation" (157).

26. House, *JP*, 129; Higgins, *Oxford Essays and Notes,* 312.

27. Bloom, *Gerard Manley Hopkins: Modern Critical Views*, 3, 2.

28. House, *JP*, 139.

29. Hopkins had used a grave accent as early as 1864 in his draft of "Floris in Italy." That mark occurs in a line that instructs us about how to use meter as a visual guide: "Beauty it may be is the meet of lines / Or careful-spacèd sequences of sound." In the "mete" or measure of lines, sound—an imprecise science—must be sequenced and spaced onto the page. The grave mark, promoting the normally unpronounced "ed," as is typical in poetic practice, spaces the line out to give it ten syllables.

30. Abbott, *LI*, 24.

31. Norman MacKenzie, *Poetical Works*, 56.

32. House, *JP,* 136. "Beating the bounds" of the Parish is an Ascension Day tradition. The priest would walk the grounds to show its boundary, saying a blessing at certain points. Boys with white birch rods would then rhythmically beat the spot until the priest moved on to the next boundary. Though parish maps have supplanted this tradition from some churchyards, Hopkins's observation of this event gives another meaning to his use of "white birch" in his poems. "This ancient method of impressing the parish's boundaries on the children's memory on Ascension day is still preserved by three Oxford parishes: St. Michael's at the North Gate, All Saints, and Saint Mary the

Virgin's. The bounds of St. Michael's pass through the old St. Peter's Rectory in New Inn Hall Street, where GMH then lodged" (n.1, 136, 348).

33. Norman MacKenzie, *Poetical Works*, ll. 3–5, 58.

34. Devlin, *Sermons*, 129.

35. House, *JP*, 195.

36. July 8, 1871: "I noticed two kinds of flash but I am not sure that sometimes there were not the two together from different points of the same cloud or starting from the same point different ways—one a straight stroke, broad like a stroke with chalk and liquid, as if the blade of an oar just stripped open a ribbon scar in smooth water and it caught the light; the other narrow and wire-like, like the splitting of a rock and danced down-along in a thousand jags" (House, *JP*, 212).

37. Hopkins, AN.

38. Abbott, *LIII*, 14–15.

39. Hopkins gladly erased the marks in order to try to assure the poem's publication, but *The Month* rejected it even without marks.

40. Abbott, *LI,* 51–52.

41. See MacKenzie, *The Poetical Works of Gerard Manley Hopkins*, 319–20. An interesting phenomenological reading of "The Wreck" is offered by William A. Cohen in *Embodied: Victorian Literature and the Senses*, 125–27.

42. The numbers in the left column record the distance from the left edge of the page for each line. The distance is equivalent for each line, so that in line 1, the eye has to wander past 4 spaces (tabs, when we type) before the supposed two beats of the line. The right column records the number of stresses in the line according to the "Author's Note." I have reproduced this spacing—as all editors perhaps should—because *the absence of words is part of the metrical pattern*. The stanza itself leans to the right, like a stroke for stress when viewed from far away:

(4)	Thou mastering me	(2)
(3)	God! giver of breath and bread;	(3)
(2)	Wórld's stránd, swáy of the séa;	(4)
(3)	Lord of living and dead;	(3)
(1)	Thou has bóund bónes and véins in me, fástened me flésh,	(5)
(1)	And áfter it álmost únmade, what with dréad,	(5)
(2)	Thy doing: and dost thou touch me afresh?	(4)
	Óver agáin I féel thy fínger and fínd thée.	(6)

43. *Arsis* means the act a raising or lifting the foot and *thesis* to the stamping down of the foot, corresponding in Greek quantitative meter to the short and long part of the metrical foot. In Latin accentual verse, the meaning was reversed: arsis came to mean the long part of the foot and thesis the shorter. This misinterpretation held when English accentual verse translated short and long feet into unaccented and accented syllables. Hopkins explains this to Patmore in an 1883:

Perhaps you do not know that the Latin writers exchanged and misapplied the Greek words *arsis* and *thesis*. *Arsis* is properly the rise of the foot in dancing or of the conductor's arm in beating time, *thesis* the fall of the same. *Arsis* therefore is the light part of the foot, I call it the 'slack'; *thesis* is the heavy or strong, the stress. For this reason some writers now refuse to say *arsis* and *thesis* and use *ictus* only. It is clear the Latin writers thought of *arsis* as effort, *thesis* as the fall to rest after effort. (Abbott, *LII*, 185)

44. Saville, *A Queer Chivalry*, 83.

45. In Dublin in 1885, a series of three meditation points—titled "Lance and Nails," "The Transfiguration," and "The Five Wounds"—elaborates this early metaphor of the stigmata to attaching your will completely to God's will: "Seeing Christ's body nailed consider the attachment of his will to God's will. Wish to be as bound to God's will in all things, in the attachment of your mind and attention to prayer and the duty in hand; the attachment of your affections to Christ our Lord and his wounds instead of any earthly object" (Devlin, *Sermons*, 255).

46. *Cf.* MacKenzie, "Spelt from Sybil's Leaves," *Poetical Works*.

47. MacKenzie notices the pattern of 5s: 5x2 stanzas in part one and 5x5 stanzas in part two. He also refers to Hopkins's early notebooks, "On the Origin of Beauty," in which a character asks the professor: "Out of five dots arranged in a particular way you make a cross, may you not?" (House, *JP*, 103; Higgins, *The Collected Works of Gerard Manley Hopkins*, 155).

48. An earlier version of this line reads, "O rose but thy crimson, the gashes in thee / They came at thy nailing against the cross-tree" (ll. 33–24).

49. "Rosa Mystica" was first published in *The Irish Monthly,* 26. 299 (May 1898): 234–35 and it was reprinted in Shipley's *Carmina Mariana*.

50. Hopkins, considering Christ's passion in early 1870, describes the wellspring of his emotion as a pressure like that of a knife:

> But neither the weight nor the stress of sorrow, by themselves move us or bring the tears as a sharp knife does not cut for being pressed as long as it is pressed without any shaking of the hand but there is always one touch, something strik-ing sideways and unlooked for, which in both cases undoes resistance and pierces, and this may be so delicate that the pathos seems to have gone directly to the body and cleared the understanding of its passage. On the other hand the pathetic touch by itself, as in dramatic pathos, will only draw slight tears if its matter is not important or not of import to us, the strong emotion coming from a force which was gathered before it was discharged: in this way a knife may pierce the flesh which it had happened only to graze and the grazing will go no deeper. (House, *JP*, 195)

51. Ibid., 11.

52. From Devlin, *The Sermons*: "the touch which only god can apply" (158).

53. Hartman, *The Unmediated Vision*, 49–67.

54. Miller, *The Linguistic Moment*, 260.

55. Hopkins's journal entry from August 29, 1867 recounts a meeting with a Miss Warren (whose nephew was a Fellow at St. John's Oxford); they took a walk (this epi-sode is recounted in MacKenzie, *Poetical Works*, 149). Hopkins records:

> Miss Warren told me that she had heard the following vision of an old woman. She saw, she said, white doves flying about her room and drops of blood falling from their "nibs" — that is their beaks. The story comes in Henderson's book of Folklore. The woman was a good old woman. . . . The room was full of bright light, the "nibs" bathed in blood, and the drops fell on her. Then the light be-

came dazzling and painful, the doves were gone, and our Lord appeared display-ing His five wounds. (House, *JP*, 153–54)

The ability of the beak to "mark" as a pen nib would mark on a page would not have been lost on Hopkins, here. MacKenzie notes that Hopkins used the word "nibs" four days later in his description of the Dartmoor furze.

56. As Hopkins prepared to revise "The Wreck of the Deutschland" to send to Pat-more in 1883, he found out that he had been appointed as a Fellow in Classics of the Royal University of Ireland (Abbott, *LI*, 263), a post that took him off English soil and away from the salvation of English souls altogether. This is, perhaps, another rea-son for his increasing interest in English *soil*, and the actual border of English and England. From his isolated vantage point in Dublin, his late poetry configures and reconfigures the multiple possibilities of connecting to God and to England.

57. Hopkins is writing about his rejection in *The Month* to his mother (*LII*, 138).

58. Abbott, *LI*, 46. Bridges famously despised "The Wreck of the Deutschland." As he was preparing the first edition of Hopkins's poems, in 1918, he wrote to Kate Hop-kins: "That terrible 'Deutschland' looks and reads much better in type — you will be glad to hear. But I wish those nuns had stayed at home" (Stanford, *Selected Letters of Robert Bridges*, 726).

59. Abbott, *LI*, 46. By January 1879, Hopkins was explicit about his wish to con-vert Bridges. He writes: "You understand of course that I desire to see you a Catholic or, if not that, a Christian or, if not that, at least a believer in the true God (for you told me something of your views about the deity, which were not as they should be)" (60).

60. Hopkins's family called him "the Crow of Maenefa" because of the similarity between black-gowned priests and crowish birds, and because of the crow's nests, seats atop trees near St. Bueno's College, where Hopkins studied in Wales (White, "Hop-kins as the Crow of Maenefa," 113–20).

61. Abbott, *LIII*, 27.

62. Patmore's article "English Metrical Critics" appeared in issue 27, 127–61 of the *North British Review* as "an article ostensibly reviewing George Vandenhoff's *The Art of Elocution*, Edwin Guest's *A History of English Rhythms,* and William O'Brien's *The Ancient Rhythmical Art Recovered.*" Sister Mary Augustine Roth's reproduction of Pat-more's *Essay on English Metrical Law* includes an introduction in which she expertly traces the influences of Patmore's predecessors Joshua Steele, Hegel ("whose *Aesthetics* provided the philosophical basis for an 'organic' theory of prosody unifying 'life' and 'law,' meanings and versification," ix), Daniel, Foster, Mitford, and Dallas. Patmore revised the essay and printed it as a "Prefatory Study on English Metrical Law" in the 1878 edition of *Amelia, Tamerton Church Tower, Etc.*, and it was again reprinted in the 1879 four-volume edition of Patmore's collected *Poems*. It is the correspondence between Hopkins and Patmore following this 1878 edition that is of interest to me here.

63. Abbott, *LI*, 119.

64. Though we cannot read the letter to which Hopkins is responding (Bridges de-stroyed his half of the correspondence), we can read that there was competition be-tween Bridges and Patmore; Hopkins ends his discussion of Patmore's theories in the January 1881 letter with "[b]ut about Patmore you are in the gall of bitterness." Recall that, two years later, Bridges approached Patmore about the possibility of mentioning in print the "new prosody" that Bridges and Hopkins had devised (it was also Bridges

who let slip that Hopkins was not only an astute reader of poems but a poet in his own right—and Hopkins's employment of his own theories may have been cause for Patmore to misunderstand and resist Hopkins's poems). Thus, amid the praise and niceties the two poets-critics exchanged, we sense a larger tension between Patmore, whose perceived expertise in matters of versification had only grown with the reissue of his treatise, and Hopkins, who speaks with an authority as assured as his poetic criticism. In the 1886 edition, the small "note" from the author states: "This Essay was first printed, almost as it now stands, in the year 1856. I have seen with pleasure that, since then, its main principles have been quietly adopted by most writers on the subject in periodicals and elsewhere." It was precisely "in periodicals" where Bridges's debates about classical meters were playing out concurrently, and where, as Patmore states in his essay, "a vast mass of nondescript matter has been brought up from the recesses visited, but no one has succeeded in rendering any sufficient amount of this secret of the intellectual deep," concluding "upon few other subjects has so much been written with so little tangible result" (*Coventry Patmore's "Essay on English Metrical Law,"* 3–4). Patmore never adopted any of Hopkins's suggested revisions, though he assured Hopkins that he would give his suggestions "my best consideration . . . before I reprint that Essay, which I propose to do . . . meantime I will only say that much of the substance of your very valuable notes will come rather as a development than as a correction of the ideas which I have endeavoured—with too much levity perhaps—to express" (Abbott, *LII*, 186).

65. Ibid., 152–58, 177.

66. Ibid., 166–71. Abbott MS. 185a Durham University Library. This is also the case for Hopkins's comments on *The Unknown Eros* Dec. 6, 1993, Abbott MS. 193a.

67. Ibid., 178–81, Abbott MS 190a 2–3.

68. Patmore, "Prefatory Study on English Metrical Law," 15.

69. Abbott, *LII*, 179.

70. Hopkins continues: "Also what we emphasize we say clearer, more distinctly, and in fact to this is due the slurring, in English, of unaccented syllables; which is the beauty of the language, so that only misguided people say Dev-*il*, six-*pence* distinctly" (Abbott, *LII*, 179).

71. Ibid., 183.

72. Hopkins went over Bridges's fair copy of his manuscript (MS B) over Christmas of 1883 as he was preparing to move to Dublin as a Fellow in Classics of the Royal University in Ireland (Abbott, *LI*, 263). Hopkins reached Dublin on February 18, 1884 and did not send his manuscript to Patmore until early March.

73. Though the "Author's Note" shows a confidence about the poet trusting the reader's performance, guided by the always subjective ear, Hopkins's correspondence with Bridges proves that Hopkins had not resolved the issue of using marks for accent in his own poems, and continued, in fact, to trust the eye over the ear. Because Bridges made fair copies of all of Hopkins's poems, Bridges could choose whether to leave the accent marks on or off. In this way, Hopkins could see his poems in a different handwriting with the original metrical marks erased and then, "make a few corrections," which often meant reluctantly returning his accent marks to his poems.

74. Devlin, *Sermons*, 127.

75. Rask, *Grammar*, 114.

76. Of course this, too, was at issue: Anglo-Saxonism created the myth of that national border. Anglo-Saxon has just as often been claimed as the ancestral heritage of Denmark.

77. Abbot, *LI*, 87.

78. William Quinn, "Hopkins's Anglo-Saxon," 25–32.

79. The history of philology reveals a great deal about the disappearance of the "mark" for accent on English writing. When Old English texts were translated into modern English, the modernized editions "changed the accentuation" of the Old English texts or deleted the accent marks altogether. Edwin Guest, in his 1838 *History of English Rhythms*, writes "they change the accents, which in certain cases are used to distinguish the long vowels; they compound and resolve words; and they alter the stops and pauses — or in other words the punctuation and versification — at their pleasure" (9). Guest brings up OE accent again on page 16: "there can be little doubt that modern accentuation in our language is mainly built on that of its earliest dialect; and that we must investigate the latter before we can arrive at any satisfactory arrangement of the former." And again, on page 277: "of all meters known to our poetry, that which has best succeed in reconciling the poet's freedom with the demands of science, is the alliterative system of our Anglo-Saxon ancestors." In a review of an Anglo-Saxon dictionary, Henry Sweet proclaimed: "A serious fault of these two editors is that they both deliberately suppress the accents of the MSS in their texts" (Sweet, *Transactions*, 119).

80. A typical (and relatively easy) line from a poem by Barnes: "An 'zoo they toddled hwome to rest, / Lik' doves a-vlee-en to their nest, / in leafy boughs a-swäyen" (Barnes, *Poems of Rural Life in the Dorset Dialect*, 51.

81. Abbott, *LI,* 162.

82. Abbott, *LII,* 222.

83. Barnes, *An Outline of English Speech-Craft,* iii.

84. Abbott, *LI,* 163.

85. Ibid., 246.

86. Ibid., 231.

Chapter 3: The Institution of Meter

1. Perkins, *History of Modern Poetry*, 41.

2. "A Poet of Content," rev. of *Shorter Poems* by Robert Bridges (454–55).

3. Green, "Robert Bridges: Studies in His Work and Thought to 1904," 93.

4. Bridges published this poem multiple times, as *XXIV Sonnets,* Ed. Bumpus, 1876; *LXXIX Sonnets,* Daniel Press, 1889; *LXIX Sonnets,* Smith, Elder & Co. Vol 1., 1898, and in *The Poetical Works of Robert Bridges*, 187.

5. Norman MacKenzie, commentary, *The Poetical Works of Gerard Manley Hopkins*, 470–71. MacKenzie notes that Hopkins suggests revisions to l. 3, "'Tis the joy the foldings of her dress to view" in Abbott, *LI* 35, 89, 141, and 243. Hopkins took such issue with the line that he omitted it from his translation.

6. Abbott, *LI,* April 3, 1877, 35. He goes on to say that Bridges has not reached "finality in point of execution, words may be chosen with more point and propriety, images might be more brilliant etc."

7. Symonds, "The Blank Verse of Milton," 767–81, reprinted in *Blank Verse*, 73–113; Symonds, appendix, *Sketches and Studies of Italy*, 411–28; and Symonds, appendix, *Sketches and Studies of the Southern Europe*, 325–84.

8. Stanford, *Selected Letters of Robert Bridges*, vol. 1, 127.

9. Ibid., 128.

10. The preface was included with the poem before Hopkins sent the poem to Coventry Patmore in 1884. Norman MacKenzie, *Complete Poems and Manuscripts,* 314.

11. Ibid., 118

12. Abbott, *LIII*, 14.

13. The sonnet became, initially, the twenty-third sonnet in his 1889 version of *The Growth of Love* and the twenty-second sonnet in all other editions. *Cf.* Holmes, "The Growth of *The Growth of Love*," 583–97; 55, 221.

14. Stanford, *In The Classic Mode*, 86. He lists "A Passer-by," "The Downs," and "Early Autumn Sonnet — So hot the noon" as the three additional poems in accentual meter.

15. See MacKenzie, *Poetical Works*, 376–77, for a detailed discussion of the manuscripts, and 144–46 for a copy of the earliest surviving autograph copy of the poem.

16. For a summary of readings of "The Windhover," by far the most discussed of Hopkins's poems, see ibid., 378.

17. "Mastery" has a sforzando sign above it, indicating slightly stronger stress and greater emphasis (ibid., 144).

18. Abbott, *LI*, 85.

19. *Cf.* Harrison, "The Birds of Gerard Manley Hopkins," 448–63; also, August, "The Growth of 'The Windhover,'" 465–68.

20. Abbott, *LI*, 71.

21. September 28, 1883, in Derek Patmore, "Three Poets Discuss New Verse Forms: The Correspondence of Gerard Manley Hopkins, Robert Bridges, and Coventry Patmore," 69–78.

22. Bridges, *Milton, Paradise Lost, Book I*, 5. Henry Beeching was one of Gerard Manley Hopkins's first editors (posthumous), including some of his poems in his turn of the century anthology *Lyra Sacra*. He also married Robert Bridges's niece.

23. Symonds, "The Blank Verse of Milton," 767–81, mentioned by Hopkins to Bridges in letter XXX, April 3, 1877 (Abbott, *LI*, 32–40).

24. Symonds, *Sketches and Studies in Southern Europe*, 361–62.

25. Ibid., 352. *Blank Verse,* which became a more famous volume, was published in 1895 and included the essays first published in the former book.

26. The rules he presented in 1887 included the rule of open vowels (all open vowels may be elided); the second rule of pure R (unstressed vowels separated by "r" may be elided). This rule has an interesting exception in Milton's use of the word spirit: "Milton uses the word spirit (and thus its derivatives) to fill indifferently one or two places of the ten in his verse). . . . The word is an exception" (22); the third rule of pure L (unstressed vowels before pure L may be elided, and here the exception is on the word "evil") and finally the fourth rule of the elision of unstressed vowels before N.

27. Bridges, *On the Prosody of Paradise Regained and Samson Agonistes.*

28. Unsigned review, "Mr. Bridges and Metre," review of *Milton's Prosody*, by Robert Bridges, 85. The review begins, "Mr. Robert Bridges' essay on Milton's prosody has long been recognized by metrical students as a work of standing value."

29. His appendices to the 1901 version included: Appendix A, The Extrametrical Syllable; Appendix B, On Elision; Appendix C, Adjectives in *able*; Appendix D, On Recession of Accent; Appendix E, Pronunciation in Milton; Appendix F, On Metrical Equivalence; Appendix G, On the Use of Greek Terminology in English Prosody; Appendix H, Specimens of Ten-Syllable Verse; (Appendix I is somewhat cleverly elided so we go straight to) Appendix J, Rules of Stress-Rhythms, which includes a second part on Accentual Hexameter.

30. Bridges, Robert Seymour and William Johnson Stone, *Milton's Prosody*, 1901, 88.

31. Bridges, *Milton's Prosody*, 1921, 94.

32. Stanford, *In the Classic Mode*, 90.

33. Bridges, *Milton's Prosody*, 1921, 113.

34. From the introduction to the *Society for the Purification of English*, which was founded in 1913 but suspended its proceedings due to the "national distraction" and resumed them again in 1918:

> Literary education in England would seem in one grave respect to lack efficiency, for it does not inspire writers with a due sense of responsibility towards their native speech. . . . The ideal of [this] proposed association is both conservative and democratic. It would aim at preserving all the richness of differentiation in our vocabulary, its nice grammatical usages, its traditional idioms, and the music of its inherited pronunciation: it would oppose whatever is slipshod or careless, and all blurring of hard-won distinctions, but it would no less oppose the *tyranny of schoolmasters and grammarians, both in their pedantic conservatism,* and in their *ignorant enforcing of newfangled 'rules,' based not on principle, but merely on what has come to be considered 'correct' usage.* The ideal of the Society is that our language and its future development should be controlled by the forces and processes which have formed it in the past; that it should keep its *English character,* and that the new elements added to it should be in harmony with the old; for by this means our growing knowledge would be more widely spread, and *the whole nation brought into closer touch with the national medium of expression.* (*SPE Tracts,* [London: Clarendon Press, October 1919]), italics mine.

35. Bridges had his own reservations about Skeat's crusades; in a 1909 letter to Henry Bradley, Bridges writes: "I think Skeat is an ass" and "Skeat is worthless."

36. Mayor, *Chapters on English Metre*, 98.

37. (Emphasis mine). This letter and its response are both unpublished. Dep. Bridges 36, folios 16–31, Modern Papers. Bodleian Library, Oxford. Bridges's letter is dated November 26, 1915 and Mayor's reply is dated November 19, 1915. Bridges's letter begins "Dear Sir," and Mayor's begins "My Dear Sir," showing that their relationship was strictly professional and perhaps antagonistic.

38. Ibid., November 29, 1915 response (unpublished):

> My Dear Sir, My reason for writing my book on "Modern English Meter" was to see how far the rules laid down by metrists, such as Dr. Guest and, in a lesser degree, by Dr. Abbott, are borne out by facts. For Ch. II and again, in Ch. X, variations from rules are to be found in our best poets from the time of Shakespeare onward, and are felt by the lovers of poetry to enhance its beauty. I have

ventured to clarify these under the heads as Feminine Rhythm, Enjambment, Position of Pauses, Interchange of Feet, Special Quality of Vowels and Consonants, Alliteration, Onomatopoea, etc., Believe me. Yours very truly, J. B. Mayor.

39. A 1902 review of both *Chapters on English Metre* by Joseph Mayor and *Milton's Prosody* by Robert Bridges was titled "The Battle of the Scansionists." "Simple as the matter might seem," the reviewer summarizes, "the eternal crux of a metrical systemist is to find some scheme by which he can label words as being in such and such a metre" (465).

40. Bridges, *Milton's Prosody*, 1921, 114.

41. Saintsbury, *Last Vintage*, 116; *Last Scrap Book*, 88–91. Both quoted in Dorothy Richardson Jones, *King of Critics: George Saintsbury*, 8.

42. Saintsbury, *History of Prosody from the Twelfth Century to the Present Day*, 3, 575.

43. Patmore published "English Metrical Critics" in *the North British Review* in 1857, expanding it and revising it as part of his volume of poems, *Amelia, & Tamerton Church Tower* in 1878.

44. Saintsbury, *Atheneaüm* 2642 (June 1878), 757. The last line refers to translating Horace's Odes into English.

45. Saintsbury, *A History of Elizabethan Literature*, 14. He continues, emphatically, *"[e]very English metre since Chaucer at least can be scanned, within the proper limits, according to the strictest rules of classical prosody: and while all good English metre comes out scatheless from the application of those rules nothing exhibits the badness of bad English metre so well as that application."* Saintsbury's *A History of Elizabethan Literature* was part of a four-part series that proved extremely popular in the 1890s, with twenty-two reprints in all, and two editions.

46. Guest, *A History of English Rhythms,* 108.

47. An archeologist and philologist, Guest established the Philological Society in 1842 that eventually began working on the *New English Dictionary.* An anonymous reviewer notes that "compilers of histories of English language and literature have quarried in Dr. Guest and appropriated his results," and that Guest refused to reprint the edition in his lifetime (323).

48. Despite Skeat's efforts, Guest's *A History of English Rhythms* was not that influential; it served more as a foil than anything else. The revival in the study of Anglo-Saxon literature, as a whole, was more directly responsible for a revived interest in Anglo-Saxon meter, as well as the influence of philological and metrical accounts of the evolution of English poetry and meter from Germany. A small note in *Notes and Queries* vol. 101 (January 20, 1900) responds to "Egeria"'s query regarding "Instruction on the Rules of Poetry": "There is, as far as we know, no such work as you seek. Dr. Guest on 'English Rhythm' is erudite, but scarcely popular," 60.

49. Saintsbury, *A Short History of English Literature*, 44.

50. Ibid., 39–47.

51. Loring, *The Rhymer's Lexicon*, iv.

52. Ibid., viii.

53. Eric Eaglesham writes that the authors of the Act—Robert Laurie Morant, James Wycliffe Headlam, and John William Mackail (classicists all)—believed that true mental discipline could only be learned through mastery of Latin grammar; English education had grown too quickly and without standards and, after the failures of

the Boer War, Latin could help the country get back on track. Eric Eaglesham, "Implementing the Education Act of 1902," 153–75. Christopher Stray makes a similar assertion: "Underlying the attachment to Latin grammar was a powerful emotional conviction that it was the exemplar of 'real' knowledge. . . . The stress on the power of discipline needs to be seen in this context, as a reassertion of permanence and stability" (Stray, *Classics Transformed*, 258).

54. *Cf.* Matthew Hendley, "'Help us to Secure a Strong, Healthy, Prosperous and Peaceful Britain,'" 261–88. See also J. O. Springhall, "Lord Meath, Youth, and Empire," 97–111, and R.J.Q. Adams, "The National Service League and Mandatory Service in Edwardian Britain," 53–74.

55. "Of the later generations of phoneticians I know little. Among them towers the Poet Laureate, to whom perhaps Higgins may owe his Miltonic sympathies, though here again I must disclaim all portraiture." George Bernard Shaw, "Preface: A Professor of Phonetics," 102.

56. Andrews, *The Reading and Writing of Verse*, ix.

57. Loring, *The Rhymer's Lexicon*, x.

58. Saintsbury, *A History of English Prosody*, vol. 1, 182.

59. Ibid., vol. 3, 188. *Cf.* Prins, "Victorian Meters," *The Cambridge Companion to Victorian Poetry,* 89–113.

60. Saintsbury, *A History of English Prosody*, vol. 3, 247.

61. Ibid., vol. 1, 529.

62. Ibid., vol. 3, 522. See Jason Rudy's excellent discussion of Carlyle's rhythms in *Electric Meters: Victorian Physiological Poetics*, 76–77.

63. Saintsbury, *A History of English Prosody*, vol. 3, 521.

64. Omond, *A Study of Metre*, xii.

65. Saintsbury, *A History of English Prosody,* vol. 3.

66. "And now abideth faith, hope, charity, these three; but the greatest of these is charity" (1 Cor 13:13). I am grateful to Liam Corley and Carolyn Williams for this reference.

67. Christopher Stray notes how, well into the twentieth century, "when ciphers were being used in wartime, the classical knowledge which excluded the lower ranks from such communications on one side simultaneously linked the officers and gentlemen on opposing sides" (Stray, *Classics Transformed,* 127).

68. George Saintsbury studied at Merton College until 1868; Bridges was at Corpus Christi; and Hopkins was at Balliol until 1867.

69. From "Verses Written for Mrs. Daniel," an unpublished poem written in 1919 publicly printed in facsimile at Oxford in 1932 and printed again in *Collected Poems*. Notice Bridges's subtle play on the word "rootlets," wherein "roots" is the root of the word. Botanical metaphors for metrical and grammatical education abounded in this period, with many calls to rely on proper educational "roots" so that the language student could "blossom" into the right kind of English citizen, quite unlike the earlier insidious grass of metrical form in the metrical histories I discussed in chapter 1.

70. Green, *Robert Bridges*, 37.

71. Phillips describes Bridges's education:

Once the basics of Latin and Greek were sufficiently grasped, the boys moved gradually through Horace, Ovid, Livy, Cicero, Catullus, Propertius, Caesar, Greek lyric and elegiac writers, Virgil, Homer, some Thucydides, Herodotus,

Demosthenes, Pindar, Plato's *Republic*, and a selection of Greek tragedies and comedies. The examinations which Robert took in at Eton in 1863 show clearly the emphasis on parsing, on translation, on being able to write in Greek and Latin.

Phillips also notes how in 1859 Eton became the first of the schools to be caught up in the Rifle Volunteer Movement, which soon spread to the universities and throughout the country. She writes, "by the summer of 1860 nearly half of the upper school boys at Eton (some 300) were enrolled in the Corps, among them Robert and his friend Lionel Muirhead" (Phillips, *Robert Bridges: A Biography*, 16, 22).

72. Palmer, in *The Rise of English Studies*, describes the evolving association with the Greek language as "purely literary" rather than "practical" or, as in the case of Latin and English, a method of studying "words as things." The "thinginess" of Latin and English grammar, and of words as signs (of meaning) in general, is certainly tied to the growing need to define grammar and philology as "scientific" as opposed to literary, a trend which caused divisions in English language departments between the literary and philological camps (Palmer, *The Rise of English Studies*, 13).

73. James Brinsley Richards, *Seven Years at Eton*, 17.

74. Harold Monro's stated aim with the publication he edited in 1912, *The Poetry Review*, was to make the review "the representative organ chiefly of the younger generation of poets" (10). Monro's *Poetry and Drama* was seen as the successor to *The Poetry Review* after he had a falling out with the society (*The Poetry Society*) that backed the original review.

75. Bridges, "Flycatchers," l. 7–8.

76. Bridges scrawled "Free rhythm" next to this poem in the holograph copy of his book manuscript.

77. Bridges, *Milton's Prosody*, 1901, v.

78. Bridges, *Correspondence of Robert Bridges and Henry Bradley,* 59.

Chapter 4: The Discipline of Meter

1. This is a later moment in the history John Guillory describes in his chapter, "Mute Inglorious Miltons," 85–133: "Coleridge understood very well that the life of this dialect was sustained by the schools, just as it was originally produced by the institutional lag between Latin and vernacular literacy." This "vernacular poetics" is, in some way, what I am attempting to argue for, here, but with an abstracted concept of "meter" that really means regular rhythm and has little to do with "meter" at all.

2. *Cf.* Eagleton, "The Rise of English," 15–46; Graff, *Professing Literature: An Institutional History.*

3. Baldick, *The Social Mission of English Studies 1848–1932,* 63.

4. John Churton Collins, *The Study of English Literature,* 148.

5. On education and English studies, see Eagleton, "The Rise of English," 15–46; Palmer, *The Rise of English Studies*; Court, *Institutionalizing English Literature*; Mathieson, *The Preachers of Culture*; Soffer, *Discipline and Power: The University, History, & the Making of an English Elite, 1870–1930*; Shayer, *The Teaching of English in Schools*. On education in England, see Neuberg, *Popular Education in Eighteenth Century England*, 93–138; Lawson and Silver, *A Social History of Education in England*. On the classical ideal of education, see McPherson, *Theory of Higher Education in*

Nineteenth-Century England; Vincent, *Literacy and Popular Culture*; Heathorn, *For Home, Country, and Race*; John M. Mackenzie, "Imperialism and the School Text-book." On Matthew Arnold and educational theory, see Wallcott *The Origins of Culture and Anarchy: Matthew Arnold and Popular Education in England*; J. Dover Wilson, introduction, *Culture and Anarchy*; Connell, *The Educational Thought and Influence of Matthew Arnold.*

6. Jakob Schipper published a similar account of English rhythm in 1882, *Englische Metrik* but it was not translated into English until 1910 as *A History of English Versification*, where, rather than comparison with Skeat's 1882 reprint of Guest (which it resembled) it was compared with George Saintsbury's three volume *History of English Prosody*, which derided any theory based solely on accent. The tension between "Teutonic" or "Saxon" theories of accent-based English rhythm and Anglo-Norman or hybrid theories markedly increased in the years leading up to the First World War.

7. *Cf.* Briggs, "Saxons, Normans, and Victorians," 215–35, and Parker, *England's Darling: The Victorian Cult of Alfred the Great.* What Hugh A. MacDougall calls the "racial myth" of origins in English literature (*Racial Myth in English History: Trojans, Teutons, and Anglo-Saxons*) is traced by Clare Simmons to the educational discourse of both Thomas Arnold and John Petherton. Arnold asserted that despite repeated invasions, English history began "with the coming over of the Saxons. We this great English nation, whose race and language are now overrunning the earth from one end of it to the other, — we were born when the white horse of the Saxons had established his dominion from the Tweed to the Tamar. . . . So far our national identity extends, so far history is modern, for it treats of a life which was then, and is not yet extinguished" (Arnold, *Modern History*, 30; Simmons, 72); and in an overview of Anglo-Saxon studies published in 1840, John Petheram expressed a hope that "the Anglo-Saxon tongue will, within a few years, form an essential part of a liberal education" (Petheram, *Anglo-Saxon Literature*, 180; in Simmons, 71). Even Charles Dickens, in his popular *A Child's History of England*, evokes the "law, and industry, and safety for life and property, and all great results of steady perseverance" of "the Saxon Blood" (*III, Tanchevitz*, 1853, 148–49); quoted in Philip Collins, *Dickens and Education*, 60. Both Thomas Arnold and James Kay-Shuttleworth believed that the lower classes were more likely to understand Saxon vocabulary. Arnold wrote that the distinction between rich and poor was marked in the use of French and Saxon words: "the language of the rich, which is of course that of books also, being so full of French words derived from their Norman ancestors, while that of the poor still retains the pure Saxon character inherited from their Saxon forefathers" ("The Social Condition of the Operative Classes," [1832], *Miscellaneous Works of Thomas Arnold*, 407), quoted in Simmons, 71; Kay-Shuttleworth wrote "those who have had close intercourse with the labouring classes well know with what difficulty thy comprehend words not of a Saxon origin, and how frequently addresses to them are unintelligible from the continual use of terms of a Latin or Greek derivation; yet the daily language of the middle and upper classes abounds with such words" (115). *Sir James Kay-Shuttleworth on Popular Education*; from "First Report on the Training School at Battersea," 1841.

8. Heathorn, *For Home, Country, and Race*, 402.

9. *Cf.* Patmore, "English Metrical Critics," chapter 3, part 5.

10. Pound, *Pisan Cantos* (written in military detention).

11. *Report of the Commission on the State of Popular Education*, 1861, Vol. 1, 120.

12. Baldick, *The Social Mission of English Studies 1848–1932*, 43.

13. Matthew Arnold, *Reports on Elementary Schools General Report 1852–1882*, 130.

14. For instance, comparing the 1876 *Classified Catalogue of School, College, Classical, Technical, and General Educational Works* (Sampson Low, Marston, Searle, and Rivington) with the 1887 *Catalogue* is already a daunting task. As stated in the preface to the 1876 edition, the 1871 catalogue was "simply a classified list of eight or nine thousand Educational books now in use in this country, issued by nearly one hundred and fifty publishers." But by 1876, the number of titles presented to the reader is nearer 15,000. Of these, the 1876 edition contained over 600 titles listed on classical subjects, including individual authors in the original or translation (i.e., Aeschylus, Plato), 212 titles under the heading Greek, and 255 under Latin (including testament studies) for a total of roughly 1,070 classical entries. For English subjects in 1876, authors are listed together under "English 'classics'" and total only 113, with nearly 1,000 titles listed under English in total (Anglo-Saxon 15; Elocution 36; Grammar and Composition 315; Literature 84; Poetry 54; Primers 89; Pronunciation 7; Readers 190; Spelling and Dictation 93; Rhyming Dictionary 2). Compare these numbers with the 1887 edition, which gives "nearer twenty-five thousand" titles, where there are over 2,445 entries for classical languages (600 in Latin and 345 in Greek) and over 1,700 entries for English (Anglo-Saxon 17; Elocution 48; Grammar, Composition and Dictation [formerly with spelling] 565—a huge increase; Literature 67; Parsing [new category] 21; Poetry 100 [nearly double the number from 1876]; Primers 123; Pronunciation 8; Readers 233; Spelling 109; English "Classics" 300 [more than double the number from 1876], and an additional single author category, Shakespeare 110).

15. Michael, *The Teaching of English from the Sixteenth Century to 1870*; Görlach, *An Annotated Bibliography of Nineteenth-Century Grammars of English*. As I discussed in chapter 1, there is much work to be done in evaluating how often these books were used, and by what classes.

16. Arnold, 120.

17. The *Chambers's* series was reprinted in 1870, 1871, 1873, 1880, and 1887, supplementing this selection, in 1879 and 1894, with a series of *National Reading Books*. *Chambers* also published a *Poetical Reader* in 1865.

18. The poem is titled "My Land." In an 1855 *Irish Quarterly Review* article by "N.J.G.," titled "A Quartette of Irish Poets," that reviewed *The Poems of Thomas Davis, Now First Collected. With Notes and Historical Illustrations* (Dublin: James Duffy, 1853), the cultivating powers of poetry are directed particularly toward Irish writers:

> If, by proper training or natural inclination, Irishmen would direct their intellectual powers to the cultivation of literature . . . it is not difficult to conceive how much brilliant success must attend their efforts. . . . There is nothing that would tend more surely to improve the national mind than a general cultivation of poetry: the more we would see our old traditions enlarged and decked out in poetic dress, the more, naturally, we should value them, and the more strongly attached we should be to the localities which gave them birth. . . . It is needless to say what a beneficial effect this movement would have on the national character: a morally independent feeling would of necessity be inculcated, and everything which we are taught to consider as arising from virtuous principles and

elevated views, all the blessings of freedom, in a word, would spring up and bless our people (698–99).

Davis's poem circulated in many Irish, British, and American anthologies in the late nineteenth and early twentieth centuries: from Davis, *The Spirit of The Nation, Ballads and Songs by the Writers of "the Nation,"* 219; Kennedy, *The Universal Irish Song Book,* 163; Cooke, *The Dublin Book of Irish Verse 1728–1909,* 251; Welsh, *Golden Treasury of Irish Songs and Lyrics; American Ideals: Selected Patriotic Readings for Seventh and Eighth Grades and Junior High Schools,* etc.

19. N.J.G., "A Quartette of Irish Writers," 697–731.

20. Trilling, *Matthew Arnold,* 212. Trilling is referring to Arnold's lectures, *On the Study of Celtic Literature.* In both *Celtic Literature* and *On Translating Homer,* Arnold thinks through various possible origins for English poetry in order to project into the future a stable national culture. Gross, who calls Arnold a snob, explains that "Arnold was deeply committed to the values of his own class, that of the university-educated gentleman — a social stratum lying somewhere between the Barbarians and the Philistines" (Gross, *The Rise and Fall of the Man of Letters,* 59; Arnold, *On the Study of Celtic Literature and On Translating Homer*).

21. Ward, *The English Poets,* 1.

22. Arnold, *Reports on Elementary Schools,* 186.

23. *Cf.* Robson, "Standing on the Burning Deck: Poetry, Performance, History," 148–62.

24. *Cf.* Rudy, *Electric Meters: Victorian Physiological Poetics;* and Blair, *Victorian Poetry and the Culture of the Heart.*

25. Arnold, *Reports,* 1880, 200–01.

26. Antony Harrison, "Victorian Culture Wars: Alexander Smith, Arthur Hugh Clough, and Matthew Arnold in 1853," argues that Arnold's concerns about "good poetry" are a "hugely important manifestation of class warfare" and that "everything Arnold has been constructed to cherish by his upper-class breeding and education" would have been threatened by poetry that did not adhere to Arnold's sense of "culture" (516).

27. *Cf.* Mangan, *Athleticism in the Victorian and Edwardian Public School.*

28. *Cf.* Heathorn, *For Home, Country, and Race;* Horn, *The Victorian and Edwardian Schoolchild;* Norman Mackenzie, *Imperialism and Popular Culture;* for an Edwardian era text from America on the disciplinary benefits of military drill, see Robert Tait Mackenzie, *Exercise in Education and Medicine.*

29. Lootens, "Victorian Poetry and Patriotism," 255–79.

30. Roberts, *A Nation in Arms,* 86–88..

31. "Kipling's Tribute to Lord Roberts: reproaches England for Refusing to hear His 'Pleading in the Marketplace,'" *The New York Times,* November 19, 1914.

32. Horn (*The Victorian and Edwardian Schoolchild*) describes how

the establishment of "Empire Day" owed much to the efforts of the Earl of Meath, who was determined that the nation's youth should be imbued with feelings of devotion to King and Empire. To this end in 1903, he founded the Empire Day Movement, and by the following year had persuaded a number of local education authorities to adopt 24 May, the anniversary of Queen Victoria's birth — as a day of celebration in their schools. . . . By 1907, over 12,500 elementary schools in England and Wales (well over 1/2 the total) were participating and the movement continued to expand thereafter (144).

33. Lootens, "Victorian Poetry and Patriotism." Lootens relies on Parry's 1992 *The Poetry of Rudyard Kipling* and Papajewski's 1983 "The Variety of Kipling," as her sources. Parry notes that "Recessional" was also performed by some 10,000 British soldiers in a Boer War victory ceremony outside the Parliament of the Transvall.

34. Horn, *The Victorian and Edwardian Schoolchild*, 45.

35. Though some reviewers did recognize Kipling's versification ("No measure is too intricate for him to master," said one anonymous reviewer in Blackwoods) most did not. But Kipling was aware of the national legacy of his versification. In a 1911 letter to Brander Matthews, who had just sent him his new book, Kipling engages with the prosodist on the subject of his rhymes: "Ever so much thanks for your 'Study of Versification.' It's useful to me in my job — like the rest of your books. . . . There isn't to my knowledge another set of workman's books like yours. By the way have you got Hood's '*How I taught a youngster to write verse?*' It was written serially ages ago for a boy's magazine in England and I remember reading it again and again . . . this yere poeting is a strange and baffling business. All the same I'm glad I wasn't born an Alexandrine Frenchman" (Kipling *The Letters of Rudyard Kipling*, 33–34).

36. Le Gallienne, *Rudyard Kipling: A Criticism*, 64.

37. "Kipling: Richard Le Gallienne's Volume Devoted to a Severe Criticism of Him."

38. Horn points out that military drill was first introduced in school curriculum as early as 1871, but that after the Boer War the *Model Course of Physical Training*, based largely on army training methods, was issued by the Board of Education in 1902 with the aim of "promoting discipline among the pupils" (*Victorian and Edwardian Schoolchild*, 56).

39. John Le Vay, "Kipling's Recessional," 153–54.

40. Barnett, *Teaching and Organisation*, 145.

41. In 1899, Edmond Holmes wrote that the main goals of National Education were "preparing children for the battle of life (a battle which will . . . be fought in *all* parts of the British Empire). *Report of the Board of Education for 1899–1900 vol. ix,* 256.

42. Newbolt, *My World as in My Time*, 8.

43. Fussell, *The Great War and Modern Memory*; Eby, *The Road to Armageddon*.

44. Pericles Lewis, *Cambridge Introduction to Modernism*; Margot Norris, *Writing War in the Twentieth Century*.

45. Michael Cohen, "Whittier, Ballad Reading, and the Culture of Nineteenth-Century Poetry"; Marsland, *The Nation's Cause: French, English, and German Poetry of the First World War*.

46. Elkin Mathews review of *Admirals All* by Henry Newbolt, 324.

47. *The Scotsman*, Poetry section, 3.

48. Cf. Eby, *Road to Armageddon*; Marsland, *The Nation's Cause*; Van Wyk Smith, *Drummer Hodge: The Poetry of the Anglo-Boer War (1899–1902)*.

49. Most notably in "Tommy": "it's 'Thin red line of 'eroes when the drums begin to roll'"; "Route Marchin'," in Kipling, *Barrack-Room Ballads and Other Verses*.

50. R.K.R. Thornton, *Poetry of the 1890s*, 6.

51. Vanessa Furse Jackson, *The Poetry of Henry Newbolt: Patriotism Is Not Enough*, 66.

52. In Newbolt's *My World as in My Time* he elaborates:

The Kaiser Wilhelm had made a threatening move, and it was announced that as proof of our readiness to meet a serious challenge, a Special Service Squadron would be sent to sea at once. I had in my drawer some verses which I had written with the title *Drake's Drum* more than a month before — early December, 1895. I posted them to the Editor, Sidney Low, as possibly appropriate to the present moment. . . . The sense of fatefulness was redoubled the next day, when we read that the Flying Squadron had gone to sea with the *Revenge* [also the name of Drake's ship] for flagship and Captain Drake as commander for her marines. (186)

53. See Eby, *The Road to Armageddon*, 90–106; Jackson, *The Poetry of Henry Newbolt*, 65–114.

54. See Mangan, *Athleticism in the Victorian and Edwardian Public School*, 183, 179–206.

55. Alfred Noyes published parts 1–3 of his twelve volume, "Drake: An English Epic" in 1906, and 4–12 in 1908 (see Tucker, *Epic: Britain's Heroic Muse 1750–1910*, 560–70). A poem of the same title published in 1918 by Norah Holland rhymes the drum's beat to "the chime of tramping feet," evoking not only Drake but Blake and Raleigh, to leave "the ports of Heaven" and join England in its national emergency (Holland, *Spun Yarn and Spindrift*, 88).

56. "Drake's Drum Heard in the German Surrender of 1918." Excerpt from *The Outlook*, April 26, 1919:

On the morning of November 21st, 1918, the British Navy awaited the enemy in a state of mind that is hard to describe. The surrender of the German fleet, they all know, had been demanded and granted; but at the last moment, our men thought, the unutterable disgrace must boil in the veins of those German sailors, and the guns of their great ships must speak their final word of fire before they sank beneath the water. . . . All the while the British fleet was closing round the German fleet, coming to anchor in a square about it, so that the German ships were hemmed in. And all the while that this was being done, the noise of the drum was heard at intervals, beating in rolls. All who heard it are convinced that is was no sound of flapping stays or any such accident. The ear of the naval officer is attuned to all the noises of his ship in fair weather and foul; it makes no mistakes. All who heard know that they heard the rolling of a drum. . . . At about 2 o'clock in the afternoon the German fleet was enclosed and helpless, and the British ships dropped anchor, some fifteen miles of the Firth of Forth. The utter, irrevocable ruin and disgrace of the German Navy were consummate. And at that moment the drum stopped beating and was no more heard. . . . But those who had heard it, Admiral, Captain, Commander, other officers and men of all ratings held then and hold now one belief as to that rolling music. They believe that the sound they heard was that of "Drake's Drum"; the audible manifestation of the spirit of the great sea captain, present at this hour of tremendous triumph of the British on the seas. This is the firm belief of them all.

57. Newbolt, *Poems, New and Old*, 9.
58. Newbolt, *Tales of the Great War*, 184.
59. Newbolt, *St. George's Day and Other Poems*, 28.

60. "Vitae Lampada's" refrain, "Play up and Play the Game," was picked up by war poetess Jessie Pope and is the reason behind most of the accusations of Newbolt's jingoism. But Newbolt wanted to distance himself from the poem. In 1923 he laments, after a lecture tour in Canada, that the poem became a "kind of a Frankenstein's Monster that I created thirty years ago and now I find it falling on my neck at every street corner! In vain do I explain what is poetry: they roar for 'Play up': they put it on their flags and their war memorials and on their tombstones: it's their National Anthem" (Margaret Newbolt, *The Later Life and Letters of Sir Henry Newbolt*, 300). Newbolt's frustration in 1923 echoes the popular sentiment that poetry and verse are distinct (Jackson, *Poetry of Henry Newbolt*, 52–53).

61. Newbolt, "The Future of English Verse," 367.

62. Newbolt is referring to the Reverend R. W. Evans, *Treatise on Versification*, 1852. Robert Wilson Evans also published *Daily Hymns* in 1860 and other religious works.

63. Robert Bridges to Henry Newbolt, letter 334, May 1, 1900:

> I am occupied today in revising my Milton's Prosody for the Clarendon Press. —It has sold out! The second edition is to have a long additional appendix on 'stress-prosody and the English accentual Hexameter'—and the delegates have consented to my proposal to print Stone's treatise on 'Classical Metres in English' with my 'Milton's Prosody.' Stone's tract is revised for the purpose, and will contain a full account of the true quantity of English syllables according to Latin and Greek prosody. He thinks that classical meters could be written. I don't quite agree with him, but it is certainly a most important thing for people to know about the true 'longs and shorts' on classical principles. I think that he is almost finally right about them, and no one yet has written any sense on the subject. The basis is of course phonetic, and some extraordinary results come from its application. It is all common sense, and convincing though revolutionary. (Stanford, *The Selected Letters of Robert Bridges*, vol. 1., 368–69)

Bridges's high opinion of Newbolt's poetry was important for Newbolt's confidence as a young poet. From a 1915 letter, Newbolt reminisces:

> One pleasure today has been a letter from Bridges, in his old style. He is at his anthology (*The Spirit of Man*), and has been going through my *New and Old*, where he says he finds 'a good many pieces that I should wish to include.' And at the end of the letter he says 'Your patriotic poems give me great pleasure, reading them again.' When R.B. is pleasant one feels 'There's an opinion worth having!' (Margaret Newbolt, Henry Newbolt, *The Later Life and Letters of Henry Newbolt*, 203)

And yet there are hints, as early as 1898, that Bridges finds some of the patriotic poems tiring. He writes, on October 28, 1898: "I have been reading in your book off and on since it came. I don't think it fair to read all those things at once, because one insensibly wears out one's enthusiasm in any given direction, and these poems mostly call for the same kind, and a good deal of it" (Stanford, *Selected letters*, 339). Indeed, Bridges predicts that the public will be "worn out" by this kind of patriotic verse by the end of the First World War.

64. Bridges even outlines his phantom piece on rhythm:

Part I. On the possible expression of 'poetic' Rhythm — demonstrating the Greek position to be the one logical method. Part II. Enquiry into Greek theory. Part III. Other methods in use. Part II exercises me much. I have come at last to see my way to explain their behavior so as to reconcile all the various things said about it by other writers. It is *amazing* to me to have to discover such things for myself. They are not in any book that I have found yet (Stanford, *Selected Letters*, 424).

In March 1903, he is stalling: "You say, 'Certainly I am hoping for a paper on rhythm from you.' This rhythm affair will come in due time. I am getting on" (428).

65. (Letter 416), 429.

66. In an unintentional irony, Bridges's letter to Newbolt on August 9, 1914 foreshadows the output of militaristic ballads that will result from the declaration of war: "I am much too excited to write. . . . I agree with you that this had to come — that is evident from William's conduct — and that the circumstances are particularly favorable to us, almost ominously favorable. . . . I pray heaven that the Battle of the North Sea, which will decide everything as far as one can guess probabilities, may be another theme for your nautical Ballads" (649–50).

67. Newbolt, *The Teaching of English in England*, 86.

68. Newbolt writes the history of linguistic change as one of conquest, in which other languages have been "subdued" by some mysterious power of Englishness, so that those languages that we might consider foreign are transformed into something "native"—"*become the native experience of men in our own race and culture*"—though clearly drawn from foreign influences. Newbolt performs a careful transformation, in which the philological complexity of English (the river and its tributaries) becomes its own stream ("sprung" naturally from English soil), "subduing" those traces that form an inherent part of it in order to achieve an (artificial) native purity.

The report continues:

> We believe that such an education based upon the English language and literature would have important social, as well as personal, results; it would have a unifying tendency. Two causes, both accidental and conventional rather than national, at present distinguish and divide one class from another in England. The first is a marked difference in their modes of speech. . . . The English people might learn as a whole to regard their own language, first with respect, and then with a genuine feeling of pride and affection. More than any mere symbol it is actually a part of England: to maltreat it or deliberately to debase it would be seen to be an outrage. Such a feeling for our own native language would be a bond of union between classes, and would beget the right kind of national pride (21).

69. *A New English Dictionary on Historical Principles* (1884–1928).

70. Spurgeon, *Poetry in the Light of War*, 1.

71. Esenwein and Roberts, *The Art of Versification*, 38.

72. Songs and sonnets for England in wartime: being a collection of lyrics by various authors inspired by the great war (v).

73. Esenwein and Roberts, *The Art of Versification*, 40.

74. Jessie Pope, *War Poems*, 38.

75. *The Times*, September 9, 1914. The "Masterman Group" was made up of well-known figures from a group of poets put together by Wellington House, the government propaganda office. Newbolt and Masterman encouraged the writers to compose occasional verses to boost national morale, as if to put the war solidly within the historical context of England's glorious literary heritage. Bridges, Hardy, Chesterton, Hewlett, and Kipling were among the members, and their poems were published as pamphlets and in *The Times*. [The contents: "Wake up, England," by Robert Bridges; "Song of the Soldiers" by Thomas Hardy; "For all we Have and Are" by Rudyard Kipling: "For the Fallen" by Laurence Binyon; "The Battle of the Bight" by William Watson; "Called Up" by Dudley Clark; "Gods of War" by A. E.; "Into Battle" by Julian Grenfell; "The Trumpet" by Rabindranath Tagore; "Resolve" by F. E. Maitland; "The Search-Lights" by Alfred Noyes; "The King's Highway" by Henry Newbolt; "Invocation" by Robert Nicols; "Happy England" by Walter de la Mare; "Expeditional" By C.W. Brodribb; and "August, 1914" 'by the author of *Charitessi*" (Robert Bridges's daughter Elizabeth Bridges, later Daryush)].

76. Clarke's anthology (*A Treasury of War Poetry*) also contained poems by Kipling: "For All We Have and Are," "The Choice," "The Mine-Sweepers," and Newbolt, "A Letter from the Front," "His Toy Band," "The Vigil." H. B. Elliott's anthology *Lest We Forget* contained "The War Shadow" by Hardy but did not contain Kipling's "Recessional." *The Fiery Cross: An Anthology of War Poems,* edited by Mabel C. Edwards, and Mary Booth, contained "The Farewell" by Newbolt and "The Knitting Song" and "The Lads of the Maple Leaf" by Jessie Pope. *Poems of the Great War*, edited by J. W. Cunliffe, contained Pope's poem "Socks" and Alice Meynell's poem "Summer in England, 1914." A more detailed analysis of these anthologies might produce an interesting study of the kinds of sympathies they hoped to produce, or the kinds of print communities the anthologies themselves formed.

77. Though I do not have time to explore or resituate Hardy's poetics in this narrative, his verses are famously difficult to scan. Indeed, when Herbert Tucker announced his new teaching website, "For Better or Verse," one of the first comments was a quibble about the scansion of Hardy's famous poem "The Voice." Dennis Taylor's excellent work on Hardy needs twentieth-century counterparts, particularly the much neglected war poems. *Cf.* Taylor, *Hardy's Literary Language and Victorian Philology*; *Hardy's Metres and Victorian Prosody*.

78. Mrs. Hardy explains:

In the reception of this [*Wessex Poems*] and later volumes of Hardy's poems there was, he said, as regards form, the inevitable ascription to ignorance of what was really choice after full knowledge. . . . He knew that in architecture cunning irregularity is of enormous worth, and it is obvious that he carried on into his verse . . . the principle of spontaneity . . . resulting in the "unforeseen" . . . character of his metres and stanzas, that of stress rather than of syllable, poetic texture rather than poetic veneer. . . . Among his papers were quantities of notes on rhythm and metre. . . . These verse skeletons were mostly blank, and only designated by the usual marks for long and short syllables, accentuations, etc., but they were occasionally made up of "nonsense verses" — such as, he said, were written when he was a boy by students of Latin prosody with the aid of a "Gradus"

(Florence Emily Hardy, *The Later Years of Thomas Hardy*, 78–80), quoted in Hynes *The Pattern of Hardy's Poetry*, 19.

79. Thomas, "War Poetry," 341–45. J. G. Fletcher disagreed (*Egoist,* Nov. 16, 1914), calling the poem "inane driveltry," and soldier poet Charles Sorley wrote in a letter of the same month that the poem was "arid" and "untrue to the sentiments of the ranks man going to war: "Victory crowns the just is the worst line he ever wrote — filched from a leading article in *The Morning Post*, and unworthy of him who had always previously disdained to insult Justice by offering it a material crown like Victory." Letter from Charles Hamilton Sorley, November 30, 1914. Quoted in Hibberd, *Poetry of the First World War: A Selection of Critical Essays*, 30.

80. Thomas, "War Poetry," 341–45.

81. Woolf, *To The Lighthouse*, 202.

82. Monro chose to read a Henry Newbolt poem at the opening of the famous bookshop in 1913.

83. Monro, "Varia," 251 (quoted in Samuel Hynes's excellent *A War Imagined*, 29).

84. Blenheim, "Song: In War-time," 446.

85. Thomas, "War Poetry," 333.

86. Gosse, "Some Soldier Poets," 296–316.

Chapter 5: The Trauma of Meter.

1. Ross, *The Georgian Revolt: Rise and Fall of a Poetic Ideal 1910–1922*, 22.

2. The English meter feminized by the modernists was also claimed and reclaimed as masculine by the military metrical complex before the war. Though the hysterical soldier was often characterized as feminine, the specifically female home-front communities were those from which the soldiers I describe felt alienated. This distaste for the women writers of the home front created a division between the illusion of stability that the home (that idea of England), provided, and the destabilized post-traumatic meter with which they reckoned.

3. Fussell, *The Great War and Modern Memory*, 167.

4. Hynes, *A War Imagined*, 28.

5. Winter, *Sites of Memory, Sites of Mourning*, 204.

6. Ford, *Parade's End*, 314.

7. Ibid. The completed sonnet, which does not appear in the text:

Now we affront the grinning chops of *Death*
And in between our carcass and the *moil*
Of marts and cities, toil and moil and *coil*
Old Spectre blows a cold protecting *breath*
Vanity of vanities, the preacher *saith.*   5
No more parades, Not any more. No *oil*
Unambergris'd our limbs in the naked *soil.*
No funeral statements cast before our *wraiths.*

"[H]e scribbled the rapid sestet to his sonnet which ought to make a little plainer what it all meant. Of course, the general idea was that, when you got into the line or near it, there was no room for swank, typified by expensive funerals. As you might say: No flowers by compulsion . . . No more parades!" (320).

8. Originally published in 1893, Owen's 1908 reprint included "a new and complete rhyming dictionary": Brewer, *The Art of Versification and the Technicalities of Poetry*. Owen's original copy can be found at the English Faculty Library at Oxford University.

9. *Cf.* Penn, *Targeting Schools: Drill, Militarism and Imperialism*; Lenox and Sturrock, *The Elements of Physical Education: A Teacher's Manual*; and Roberts, *A Nation in Arms*.

10. Owen and Bell, *Wilfred Owen, Collected Letters*, 175; Owen, *Journey From Obscurity, memoirs of the Owen family*; Stallworthy, *The Complete Poems and Fragments of Wilfred Owen*.

11. For Owen's relationship to Romanticism, see Breen, "Wilfred Owen, 'Greater Love' and Late Romanticism," 173–83 and Tomlinson, "Strange Meeting in a Strange Land: Wilfred Owen and Shelley," 75–95.

12. Stallworthy, *The Complete Poems*, 113.

13. In his 1917 poem, "The Schoolmistress," Owen critiques the pedagogical method of "stamping feet" to the rhythms of "brave days of old" recorded in the poetry chosen for the English language classroom, like Macaulay's "Horatius," from his *Lays of Ancient Rome*, a popular schoolroom text. Here, the octave of Owen's poem mocks the schoolmistress's methods of "stamping her feet" (presumably to an exaggerated conception of metrical form), her hands, imitating some naval officer's "swashing arabesque" wave, and how her voice "bleats" like an animal. From her lofty chair she listens to the schoolchildren memorize the poem by repeating it out loud, but she is distracted by the presence of soldiers. Her inability to acknowledge the soldiers is Owen's comment on the artificiality of these memorized "classic lines" in the context of modern conflict.

THE SCHOOLMISTRESS

Having, with bold Horatius, stamped her feet
And waved a final swashing arabesque
O'er the brave days of old, she ceased to bleat,
Slapped her Macaulay back upon the desk,
Resumed her calm gaze and her lofty seat.

There, while she heard the classic lines repeat,
Once more the teacher's face clenched stern;
For through the window, looking on the street,
Three soldiers hailed her. She made no return.
One was called 'Orace whom she would not greet. (Lewis edition, 141)

14. Owen and Bell, *Wilfred Owen, Collected Letters*, 250.

15. Reminiscent of Keats, himself: "I think I shall be among the English Poets after my death" (letter to George and Georgiana, 1818, *The Letters of John Keats*). I am grateful to Anne Jamison for this reference.

16. Owen, *Journey From Obscurity*, 144.

17. Robert Graves, *Goodbye to All That*, 22.

18. Graves, *Fairies and Fusiliers* (ll. 1–22), 14.

19. Specifically the erratic verse form of John Skelton, or "Skeltonics." Graves has two more poems in this meter, "Oh, and Oh" and "John Skelton" in *Over the Brazier.* As part of the prosody wars and general metrical discourse of the era, the late nineteenth and early twentieth century saw a resurgence in studies of Skelton's satires, especially around 1914–15. Day, in *Swifter than Reason*, has noted the Skeltonic influence on Graves's poems (6).

20. Graves, *Over the Brazier* (ll. 32–48), 14–15.

21. *Cf.* Cole, "The Poetry of Pain," 483–503, for a reading of Owen's "The Poet in Pain" along these lines.

22. Robert Graves, *Goodbye to All That*, 125.

23. In an unpublished 1917 poem written in twenty-three sections (each representing one mile of a sustained march), Graves himself writes: "Why are we marching? No one knows / Why are we marching? No one cares." "Night March" was first printed in Hibberd "'The Patchwork Flag' (1918) an Unrecorded Book by Graves" (1990).

24. http://www.oucs.ox.ac.uk/ww1lit/collections/document/1124/1070?REC=1 (last accessed June 5, 2011), The Robert Graves Collection: MS 141 Box 85, University Archives, University at Buffalo.

25. Owen, "The Poet in Pain," *The Complete Poems and Fragments of Wilfred Owen*, ll. 1–2.

26. Young, "W.H.R. Rivers and The War Neuroses," 368.

27. Rivers, *Conflict and Dream*, 93–94.

28. Young, "W.H.R. Rivers and The War Neuroses," 359.

29. Rivers, "The Repression of War Experience."

30. "Dreamers" (September 1917), "Wirers" (September 1917), "Thrushes" (November 1917), and "Break of Day" (December 1917) were all published in *The Hydra*.

31. Sassoon, *Sherston's Progress*, 84–85.

32. All quotations from Sassoon's poetry are taken from the collection, Hart-Davis, *Sassoon's War Poems*, 132–33. Sassoon objected to the publication of this letter in Robert Graves's 1929 edition of *Goodbye to All That*, and it was subsequently withdrawn.

33. Brock, "The Re-education of the Adult," 29; henceforth cited as *REA*.

34. Brock, *Health and Conduct*, 146. This idea of "outrance" previews Shoshana Felman's definition of testimony as the fragmentary product of a mind "overwhelmed by occurrences that have not settled into understanding or remembrance . . . events in excess of our frames of reference" (quoted in Gilbert and Gubar, *No Man's Land*, 187). Rivers's methods seem to coax the patient into renarrating his testimony into a new "frame of reference" or happier memory, whereas Brock's methods recognize the fragmentary nature of the patient's mind, seeing all forms of "speech" as "speech-acts," both expressing an experience and replicating that experience in the very fragmented act of speaking. In reference to Brock's characterization of "aboulia," it is interesting to recall that T. S. Eliot was diagnosed with "aboulie" by Dr. Roger Vittoz in Lausanne, Switzerland. Coincidentally, *The Waste Land* and the *Army Report to the War Office Committee Enquiry into "Shell Shock"* both appeared in 1922. Eliot composed *The Waste Land* while under psychiatric care in Lausanne.

35. Brock, *Health and Conduct*, 146.

36. Brock, *REA*, 35.

37. Owen and Bell, *Wilfred Owen, Collected Letters*, 497.

38. His complete medical board report is as follows:

In March 1917 he fell down a well at Bouchoir, and was momentarily stunned. He was under Medical treatment for 3 weeks, and then resumed duty. About the middle of April he was blown up by a shell explosion while he was asleep. On May 1st he was observed to be shaky and tremulous, and his conduct and manner were peculiar, and his memory was confused. The R.M.C. sent him to No. 41 Sty. Gailly where he was under observation and treatment by Capt. Brown, R.A.M.C., Neurological Specialist, for a month. On 7/6/17 he was transferred to No. 1. G. H. Etretat, and on 16/6/17 to the Welsh Hospital Netley. There is little abnormality to be observed but he seems to be of a highly strung temperament. He has slept well while here. He leaves Hospital today transferred to Craiglockhart War Hospital, Edinburgh, for special observation and treatment.

This report can be found at http://www.hcu.ox.ac.uk/jtap/images/misc/pro/ proceedings.jpg (last accessed June 5, 2011).

39. Box 3, Owen MSS, Oxford English Faculty Library (OEF), Fasc. BB Owen MSS OEF 427.

40. *The Hydra* (January 1918).

41. "Do Plants Think?" was the title of Owen's first field club presentation.

42. Owen and Bell, *Wilfred Owen, Collected Letters*, 475.

43. For detailed theories about Owen's pararhyme, see Welland, *Wilfred Owen: A Critical Study*; Hibberd, *Owen the Poet*; and Stallworthy, *Wilfred Owen*.

44. For a brief discussion of other hospital literary magazines, see Peter Leese, "'Why are They Not Cured?' British Shellshock Treatment During the Great War," 205–21. For more on Brock and shell-shock treatments, see Webb, "'Dottyville' — Craiglockhart War Hospital and shell-shock treatments in the First World War," 342–46; Crossman, "*The Hydra*, Captain A.J. Brock and the Treatment of Shell-Shock in Edinburgh,"119–23; Cantor "Between Galen, Geddes, and the Gael: Arthur Brock, Modernity, and Medical Humanism in Early Twentieth-Century Scotland," 1–41.

45. Owen and Bell, *Wilfred Owen, Collected Letters*, 508–9. He is not referring to Captain Rivers, here, but the military doctor stationed at Casualty Clearing, none other than Rivers's mentor, Captain William Brown.

46. Brock, *REA*, 28,

47. From Brophy and Partridge, *The Long Trail:*

Field Punishment was extremely harsh. Field Punishment Number One, for example, consisted of the offender being tied, like one crucified, to a gunwheel by the wrists and the ankles for one hour in the morning and one in the evening for as many days as were specified up to 28. This was meant to humiliate as well as to exhaust him, and his comrades were seemingly expected to jeer at him. It has been stated that some unfortunate men were so lashed to guns *in action*. (123)

48. See his manuscript pages, e.g. "An Imperial Elegy," available on the First World War Digital Archive: http://www.oucs.ox.ac.uk/ww1lit/collections/item/4614 (last accessed May 29, 2011).

49. Stallworthy, *The Complete Poems and Fragments of Wilfred Owen* vol. 2, 92; the fragment can also be viewed on the English Faculty Library website: *http:www.hcu .ox.ac.uk/jtap/warpoems.htm* (last accessed May 27th 2011).

50. Hibberd, *Owen the Poet*, 114; Hipp, "By Degrees Regain[ing] Cool Peaceful Air in Wonder": Wilfred Owen's War Poetry as Psychological Therapy," 25–49; Wordsworth, "Resolution and Independence," ll. 66–67, 167.

51. The visual beauty of the flares is an image that appears in many other war poems, including Apollinaire's *Caligrammes*. In "La nuit d'avril 1915," he writes: "The sky is starred by the Boche's shells / The marvelous forest where I live is giving a ball / The machine gun plays a tune in three-fourths time . . ." (Apollinaire, *Calligrammes*, 203).

52. Hipp, "By Degrees Regain[ing] Cool Peaceful Air in Wonder," 37.

53. Yeats, *Oxford Book of Modern Verse, 1892–1935*, xxxiv.

54. Graves, *Over the Brazier*, 595.

55. *The Sunday Times*, (December 18, 1920), OEF, 14:15.

56. *The Daily Herald,* (December 22, 1920), OEF, 14:17.

57. *The Daily News*, December 17, 1920, OEF, 14:13.

58. "Points to Note about my Sonnets" (sic) English Faculty Library, University of Oxford V.f404r, accessible here: http://www.oucs.ox.ac.uk/ww1lit/collections/ item/5017?CISOBOX=1&REC=4 date unknown (last accessed May 28, 2011).

59. "Poems of Wilfred Owen," *The Daily News*, 14:13.

60. *Times Literary Supplement* (January 6, 1921), OEF, 14:26.

61. Murry, "The Poet of the War," 705–7.

62. *Manchester Guardian* (December 29, 1920), OEF, 14:18.

63. December 26, 1936, *Letters on Poetry from W. B. Yeats to Dorothy Wellesley* (Oxford: Oxford University Press, 1940).

64. C. Day Lewis, *A Hope for Poetry*, 14.

Chapter 6: The Before- and Afterlife of Meter

1. Later collected as "Credo" in "A Retrospect" (Monro, *Poetry and Drama*; Pound, *The Literary Essays of Ezra Pound*, 9).

2. Pound, *The Literary Essays of Ezra Pound*, 3

3. Morrison, *The Public Face of Modernism*; Golston, *Rhythm and Race in Modernist Poetry and Science*; Preston, *Modernism's Mythic Pose*.

4. Pound, *The Literary Essays of Ezra Pound*, 12.

5. Pound, "A Retrospect," *The Literary Essays of Ezra Pound*, 6; "A Few Don'ts for an Imagist" first appeared in *Poetry* I, 6 (March 1913).

6. Pound, *The Literary Essays of Ezra Pound*, 13.

7. Pound *The Selected Letters of Ezra Pound*, 208.

8. Pound, "Robert Bridges' New Book," *Poetry Magazine*, 42. .

9. Bridges, "Letter to a Musician on English Prosody," 255–71.

10. T. S. Eliot, "Ezra Pound, His Metric and Poetry," *To Criticize the Critic*, 166 (originally published anonymously, in 1917, by Knopf).

11. Pound, *The Literary Essays of Ezra Pound*, 11.

12. *Cf.* Michael Golston's discussion of this essay in chapter 1 of his provocative *Rhythm and Race in Modernist Poetry and Science*.

13. "The linguistic mishmash of 'Speke Parrot'—English, Scots, Irish, Welsh, gibberish, Latin, Greek, French, Spanish, what not—finds a prosody not ill-fitted for it. The varieties of the Skeltonic itself are far from accidental, and very well worth study." Saintsbury, *A History of English Prosody*, 244.

14. Bridges, from the preface to *New Verse written in 1921*, xx.

15. Newbolt, *The Teaching of English in England*, 9, 10.

16. Bridges *New Verse written in 1921*, 4.

17. This metaphor of man's spirit like a caged bird calls to mind Hopkins's "The Caged Skylark," which was published in 1918. Other parallels between Bridges's and Hopkins's poems (six, to be exact) have been noted, but not this one. Hopkins writes: "As a dare-gale skylark scanted in a dull cage / Man's mounting spirit in his bonehouse, mean house, dwells."

18. From E. P. Coleridge's translation, *The Plays of Euripides, volume 1*. "Would to Heaven that the good ship Argo ne'er had sped its course to the Colchian land" (33).

19. Gerard Manley Hopkins makes this leap between disremember and dismember in "Spelt from Sybil's Leaves," "qúite / Disremembering, dísmémbering / áll now" (ll. 7–8, *The Poetical Works of Gerard Manley Hopkins*).

20. Ode XVI, *The Works of Horace*, 129.

21. For a fantastic discussion of alliteration, see Harmon, "English Versification: Fifteen Hundred Years of Continuity and Change."

22. *Cf.* Jackson and Prins, "Lyrical Studies," 521–30; Cavitch, "Stephen Crane's Refrain," 33–54; Jackson, "The Story of 'Boon' or The Poetess," 241–68; Michael Cohen, "Whittier, Ballad Reading, and the Culture of Nineteenth-Century Poetry," 1–29; Rudy, "Manifest Prosody"; Blair, *Victorian Poetry and the Culture of the Heart*.

23. In *The Realms of Verse*, Matthew Reynolds brilliantly shows the political implications and investments of nineteenth-century poets Tennyson, the Brownings, and Clough, and argues that "stylistic preference and political opinion belong together in a continuum of thought and feeling" (274), and he reads political implications in the exploitation of conflicts between "the law of the verse and the freedom of the language." In *Rhythm and Will in Victorian Poetry*, Matthew Campbell performs close readings of nineteenth-century poems to show the ways that the concept of "will" is allegorized as "freedom" through the formal quality of rhythm, so that the struggle between what is "free" and "bound" in formal poems is a way to read the struggle of individual agency. Both of these books are crucial in showing the broader historical contexts with which Victorian poets engaged with and manipulated poetic form, but neither questions the stability of metrical form itself, relying on accepted notions of iambs, trochees, and "meter" and "rhythm" in general so as to put forth arguments about expressive freedom and external stricture. Though I believe that this reading is necessary and important, my hope is to show that there are other ways to read metrical form, in addition to these evocative readings, that allow for even more insecurity and negotiation between poet and form, poem and reader, aesthetics and politics.

WORKS CITED

❧

Aarsleff, Hans. *The Study of Language in England, 1780–1860.* Minneapolis: University of Minnesota Press, 1983.

Abbott, Claude Colleer, ed. *Further Letters of Gerard Manley Hopkins.* Oxford: Oxford University Press, 1956.

———. ed. *The Letters of Gerard Manley Hopkins to Robert Bridges,* 2nd imp. rev. London: Oxford University Press, 1955.

———. ed. *The Correspondence of Gerard Manley Hopkins and Richard Watson Dixon.* Oxford: Oxford University Press, 1935.

Adams, R.J.Q. "The National Service League and Mandatory Service in Edwardian Britain." *Armed Forces and Society* 12, 1 (1985): 53–74.

Andrews, C. E. *The Reading and Writing of Verse.* New York/London: D. Appleton and Company, 1918.

Apollinaire, Guillaume. *Calligrammes.* Trans. Anne Hyde Greet. Berkeley/Los Angeles: University of California Press, 1980.

Armstrong, Isobel. *Victorian Poetry: Poetry, Poetics, Politics.* London/New York: Routledge, 1993.

Arnold, Matthew. *Reports on Elementary Schools General Report 1852–1882,* ed. F. S. Marvin, M.A. London: Wyman and Sons, Ltd., 1908.

———. *On the Study of Celtic Literature and On Translating Homer.* New York: Macmillan and Co., 1883.

Arnold, Thomas. *Introductory Lectures on Modern History.* London: Longmans, Green & Co. 1874.

———. *Miscellaneous Works of Thomas Arnold.* London: B. Fellowes, 1845.

Attridge, Derek. *The Rhythms of English Poetry.* London/New York: Longman, 1982.

August, Eugene R. "The Growth of 'The Windhover.'" *PMLA* 82, 5 (Oct. 1967): 465–68.

Baldick, Chris. *The Social Mission of English Studies 1848–1932.* Oxford: Clarendon Press, 1983.

Bar, Temple. "The Poems of Robert Bridges." *The Living Age* 199 (December 2, 1893).

Barbauld, Mrs. (Anna) *Poems.* London: Joseph Johnson, 1773.

Barnes, William. *An Outline of English Speech-Craft.* London: C.K. Paul, 1878.

———. *Poems of Rural Life in the Dorset Dialect.* London: John Russell Square, 1844.

Barnett, Percy Arthur. *Teaching and Organisation.* New York: Longmans, Green, and Co., 1897.

"Battle of the Scansionists," untitled review. *The Saturday Review,* April 12, 1902, 465–66.

Beasley, Rebecca. *Theorists of Modernist Poetry: T. S. Eliot, T. E. Hulme, Ezra Pound.* Oxford: Routledge, 2007.

Beeching, Henry, ed. *Lyra Sacra.* London: Methuen & Co, 1895.

———. ed. *Milton, Paradise Lost, Book I.* Oxford: Clarendon Press, 1887.

Beer, Gillian. *Open Fields: Science in Cultural Encounter.* Oxford/New York: Oxford University Press, 1999.

Berrington, Adrian. "Cover Design," cartoon. *The Hydra,* May 1918.

Blair, Hugh. *Lectures on Belles Lettres and Rhetoric.* Philadelphia: Matthew Carey, 1793.

Blair, Kirstie. *Victorian Poetry and the Culture of the Heart.* Oxford: Oxford University Press, 2006.

Blenheim, Herbert (pseud.). "Song: In War-time." *The Egoist* 1, 23 (Dec. 1, 1914): 446.

Bloom, Harold, ed. *Gerard Manley Hopkins: Modern Critical Views.* New York: Chelsea House Publishers, 1986.

Blunden, Edmund. *Undertones of War.* London: R. Cobden-Sanderson, 1928; Chicago: University of Chicago Press, 2007.

Bosworth, Joseph. *Elements of Anglo-Saxon Grammar: with Copious notes illustrating the structure of the Saxon and the formation of the English language, and alphabetic writing, with critical remarks.* London: Mavor and Lepard, 1823.

Bourne, Jane. *Granny's History of England in Rhyme.* London: Houston and Sons, 1871.

Bradbury, Malcolm, and James McFarlane. "The Name and Nature of Modernism." In *Modernism: A Guide to European Literature 1890–1930,* ed. Malcolm Bradbury and James McFarlane. New York: Penguin, 1976.

Breen, Jennifer. "Wilfred Owen, 'Greater Love' and Late Romanticism," *English Literature in Transition (1880–1914)* 17 (1974): 173–83.

Brégy, Katherine. A *Poet's Chantry.* London: Herbert and Daniel, 1912.

Brewer, R. F. *The Art of Versification and the Technicalities of Poetry.* London: William Deacon & Co., 1893; Edinburgh: John Grant, 1908.

Bridges, Robert. *Poetical Works of Robert Bridges Excluding the Eight Dramas.* London: Oxford University Press, 1970.

———. *Correspondence of Robert Bridges and Henry Bradley, 1900–1923.* Oxford: Clarendon Press, 1940.

———. *The Poetical Works of Robert Bridges.* London: Oxford University Press, 1936.

———. "Humdrum & Harum-Scarum: A Lecture on Free Verse." In *Collected Essays and Papers of Robert Bridges.* vol. 2. London: Oxford University Press, 1927.

———. *New Verse Written in 1921.* Oxford: Clarendon Press, 1926.

———. *Milton's Prosody with a Chapter on Accentual Verse.* Revised final edition. Oxford: Oxford University Press, 1921.

———. *Poems Written in the Year 1913.* Chelsea: Ashendone, 1914.

———. "Letter to a Musician on English Prosody," *Poetry and Drama* 2 (1914): 255–71.

———. *LXIX Sonnets.* London: Smith, Elder & Co. Vol. 1, 1898.

———. *Milton's Prosody.* Oxford: Clarendon Press, 1894.

———. *Shorter Poems.* Oxford: Daniel Press, 1894

———. *LXXIX Sonnets.* London: Oxford: Daniel Press, 1889.

———. *On the Prosody of Paradise Regained and Samson Agonistes: Being a Supplement to the paper On the Elements of Milton's Blank Verse in Paradise Lost, which is printed in the Rev. H. C. Beeching's edition of Paradise Lost, Bk. 1, Clarendon Press, Oxford.* London: Simpkin and Marshall, and Oxford: Blackwell, 1889.

————. *Milton's Prosody: An examination of the rules of the blank verse in Milton's later poems, with an Account of the Versification of Samson Agonistes*. Oxford: Clarendon Press, 1883.

————. *The Growth of Love: A Poem in 24 Sonnets*. London: Edward Bumpus, 1876.

————. ed. *The Spirit of Man*. London: Longmans, Green & Co, 1916.

Bridges, Robert, Robert Seymour, and William Johnson Stone. *Milton's Prosody; Classical Metres in English Verse*. Oxford: Oxford University Press, 1901.

Briggs, Asa. "Saxons, Normans, and Victorians." In *The Collected Essays of Asa Briggs*, vol. 2, 215–35. Urbana / Chicago: University of Illinois Press, 1985.

Brock, Arthur J. *Health and Conduct*. London: Williams and Norgate, 1923.

————. "The Re-education of the Adult," *The Sociological Review* 10 (Summer 1918): 25–40.

Brogan, T.V.F. *English Versification 1570–1980: A Reference Guide with Global Appendix*. Baltimore: Johns Hopkins University Press, 1981.

Brophy, John, and Eric Partridge, eds. *The Long Trail*. London: Andre Deutsch, 1965.

Brown, Daniel. *Hopkins' Idealism*. Oxford: Oxford University Press, 1997.

Brown, Goold. *The First Lines of Grammar*. New York: William Wood & Company, 1856, 1872, 1882, 1884.

————. *The Grammar of English Grammars*, 4th ed. New York: Samuel S. & William Wood, 1858.

Burt, Seymor. *A Metrical Epitome of the History of England Prior to the Reign of George the First*. London: Pelham, Richardson, 1852.

Campbell, Matthew. *Rhythm and Will in Victorian Poetry*. Cambridge: Cambridge University Press, 1999.

Cantor, David. "Between Galen, Geddes, and the Gael: Arthur Brock, Modernity, and Medical Humanism in Early Twentieth-Century Scotland," *Journal of the History of Medicine and Allied Sciences* 60, 1 (January 2005): 1–41.

Capell, Edward T. O. T. S. D. *Prolusions, Or, Select Pieces of Antient Poetry, compil'd with great care from their several Originals, and and offer'd to the Publick as Specimens of the Integrity that should be found in the Editions of Worthy Authors*. London: J. and R. Tonson, 1760.

Carlson, Julia. "Topographical Measures: Wordsworth's and Crosthwaite's Lines on the Lake District," *Romanticism* 16 (2010): 72–93.

Carroll, Lewis. *Memoria Technica*. Oxford: s.n, 1877, 1888.

"Cartoon of Captain Rivers." cartoon. *The Hydra*, September 15, 1917.

Cavitch, Max. "Stephen Crane's Refrain," *ESQ: A Journal of the American Renaissance* 54, 1–4 (2008): 33–54.

Chambers's Narrative Series of Standard Reading Books, specially adapted to the Requirements of the Revised Code including those in Writing, Arithmetic, and Dictation. London/Edinburgh: W. & R. Chambers, 1863–94.

Christie, William. "A Recent History of Poetic Difficulty," *ELH* 67, 2 (Summer 2000): 539–64.

Clarke, George Herbert, ed. *A Treasury of War Poetry, British and American Poems of the World War, 1914–1917; with introduction and notes, by George Herbert Clarke*. First Series. Boston: Houghton Mifflin, 1917.

Clutton-Brock, Arthur. Unsigned review. *Times Literary Supplement*, January 9, 1919, 19.

Cohen, Michael. "Whittier, Ballad Reading, and the Culture of Nineteenth-Century Poetry," *Arizona Quarterly* 64, 3 (2008): 1–29.

Cohen, William A. *Embodied: Victorian Literature and the Senses.* Minneapolis: University of Minnesota Press, 2009.

Cole, Sarah. "The Poetry of Pain." In *The Oxford Handbook of British and Irish War Poetry*, ed. Tim Kendall, 483–503. Oxford: Oxford University Press, 2007.

Coleridge, Edward P., trans. *The Plays of Euripides.* London: George Bell & Sons, 1891.

Collier, William Francis. *History of the British Empire.* London: 1870.

Collins, John Churton. *The Study of English Literature: A Plea for its Recognition and Organization at the Universities.* London/New York: Macmillan, 1891.

———. *Chapter of Kings.* London: J. Harris, Corner of St. Paul's Church Yard, 1818.

Collins, Philip. *Dickens and Education.* London: Macmillan, 1963.

Colls, Robert and Phillip Dodd, eds. *Englishness: Politics and Culture 1880–1920.* Dover, NH: Croom Helm, 1986.

Connell, W. F. *The Educational Thought and Influence of Matthew Arnold.* London: Routledge & Kegan Paul, Ltd., 1950.

Conybeare, John J. *Illustrations of Anglo-Saxon Poetry.* London: Hardy and Lepard, 1826.

———."English Paraphrase" of *Beowulf* contained in *Observations on the metre of the Anglo-Saxon poetry; further observations on the poetry of our Anglo-Saxon ancestors.* London: Archaeologia, 1814.

Cooke, John, ed., *The Dublin Book of Irish Verse 1728–1909.* Dublin: Hodges, Figgis & Co., Ltd.; London: Henry Frowde, Oxford University Press, 1900.

Coopers, Elizabeth. *The Muses Library.* London, 1737.

Coote, Charles. *Elements of English Grammar.* London: C. Dilly, 1798.

Court, Franklin E. *Institutionalizing English Literature: The Culture and Politics of Literary Study, 1750–1900.* Palo Alto: Stanford University Press, 1992.

"Coventry Patmore," *Atheneaum*, Dec. 5, 1896, 797.

Cowper, William. *The Didactic Poems of 1782, with selections from the minor pieces.* Ed. H. T. Griffith. Oxford: Clarendon Press, 1874.

Crossman, A. M. "*The Hydra*, Captain A. J. Brock and the Treatment of Shell-Shock in Edinburgh." *Journal of the Royal College of Physicians, Edinburgh* 33 (2003): 119–23.

Crowley, Tony. *Standard English and the Politics of Language.* New York: Palgrave, 1989.

Cunliffe, J. W., ed. *Poems of the Great War.* New York: Macmillan, 1919.

Cunningham, Valentine. *The Victorians: An Anthology of Poetry and Poetics.* Oxford/Malden, MA: Blackwell, 2000.

Cureton, Richard. "A Disciplinary Map for Verse Study," *Versification: An Interdisciplinary Journal of Literary Prosody* 1 (1997).

"Current Literature" (editorial). *The Western Antiquary: Or, Devon and Cornwall Notebook,* 11 (August–September 1891): 30.

Davis, Thomas Osbourne. *The Spirit of The Nation, Ballads and Songs by the Writers of "The Nation."* Dublin: James Duffy, 1845.

Davies, Anna Morpurgo. *History of Linguistics.* Vol. 4, *Nineteenth Century Linguistics.* London/New York: Longman, 1998.

Day, Douglas. *Swifter than Reason: The Poetry and Criticism of Robert Graves*. Chapel Hill: University of North Carolina Press, 1963.

Dean, Dennis R. *Tennyson and Geology*. Lincoln, UK: The Tennyson Soc., Tennyson Research Centre, 1985.

Devlin, Christopher, S. J., ed. *Sermons: The Sermons and Devotional Writings of Gerard Manley Hopkins*. London: Oxford University Press 1959.

Dickens, Charles. *A Child's History of England*. London: Chapman and Hall, 1880.

Dibdin, Thomas. *A Metrical History of England; or, Recollections in Rhyme of some of the most prominent Features in our National Chronology, from the Landing of Julius Caesar to the Commencement of the Regency in 1812 in two volumes*. London: Printed for the Proprietor, by Joseph Hartnell, Wine-Office-Court, Fleet Street, 1813.

Dowling, Linda. *Language and Decadence in the Victorian Fin de Siècle*. Princeton: Princeton University Press, 1986.

Doyle, Brian. *English and Englishness*. New York: Routledge, 1989.

"Drake's Drum Heard in the German Surrender of 1918." Excerpt from *The Outlook*, April 26, 1919.

Eaglesham, Eric. "Implementing the Education Act of 1902," *British Journal of Education Studies* 10, 2 (1962): 153–75.

Eagleton, Terry. *Literary Theory*, 2nd ed. Oxford: Blackwell, 1983.

Earle, John. *The Philology of the English Tongue*. Oxford: Clarendon, 1873.

Eby, Cecil B. *The Road to Armageddon: Popular Literature 1870–1914*. Durham: Duke University Press, 1988.

Edwards, Mabel C., and Mary Booth. *The Fiery Cross: An Anthology of War Poems*. London: Grant Richards Ltd., 1915.

Elfenbein, Andrew. *Romanticism and the Rise of English*. Palo Alto: Stanford University Press, 2008.

Eliot, T. S. *To Criticize the Critic: Eight Essays on Literature and Education*. New York: Farrar, Strauss & Giroux, 1965.

Eliot, T. S., and Valerie Eliot. *The Waste Land: A Facsimile and Transcript of the Orig. Drafts Including the Annotations of Ezra Pound*. London: Faber and Faber, 1971.

Elliott, H. B., ed. *Lest We Forget: A War Anthology*. London: Jarrold and Sons, 1915.

Emerson, Ralph Waldo. *Essays, Second Series*. Boston: J. Munroe and Co., 1844.

Empson, William. *Seven Types of Ambiguity*. New York: New Directions, 1947.

Enfield, William. *The Speaker*. Manchester: Thomas Johnson, 1792.

Engell, James. "The New Rhetoric and Romantic Poetics." In *Rhetorical Traditions and British Romantic Literature*, ed. Don H. Bialostosky and Lawrence Needham. Bloomington: Indiana University Press, 1995.

Esenwein, Joseph Berg, and Mary Eleanor Roberts. *The Art of Versification*. Springfield, MA: The Home Correspondence School, 1913.

Evans, Robert Wilson. *A Treatise on Versification*. London: Frances and John Rivington, 1852.

Fauvel-Gouraud, Francis, and Pliny Miles. *Phreno-mnemotechny*. London: Wiley and Putnam, 1845.

Feinaigle, M. Gregor von. *The New Art of Memory Founded on the Principles Taught by Gregor von Feinaigle*. London: R. Edwards, 1813.

Fletcher, J. G. *Egoist,* Nov. 16, 1914.

Ford, Ford Maddox. *Parade's End.* New York: Penguin Books, 2001, reprinted from *No More Parades.* London: Gerald Duckworth, 1925.

Fries, Charles C. "The Rules of Common School Grammars," *PMLA* 42, 1 (March 1927): 221–37.

Fuller, Henry. *The Art of Memory.* St. Paul: National Publishing Co., 1882.

Fussell, Paul. *The Great War and Modern Memory.* Oxford: Oxford University Press, 1975, 2000.

———. *Poetic Meter and Poetic Form.* New York: Random House, 1965.

———. *Theory of Prosody in Eighteenth-Century England.* New London: Connecticut College, 1954.

Gilbert, Sandra, and Susan Gubar. *No Man's Land.* New Haven: Yale University Press, 1988.

Gleig, G. R. *School History of England.* London: 1850.

Gliserman, Susan. "Early Victorian Science Writers and Tennyson's *In Memoriam:* A Study in Cultural Exchange," *Victorian Studies* 18 (1975): 277–308.

Golston, Michael. *Rhythm and Race in Modernist Poetry and Science.* New York: Columbia University Press, 2008.

Gordon, Peter, and Denis Lawton. *Curriculum Change in the Nineteenth and Twentieth Centuries.* London: Hodder and Stoughton, 1978.

Görlach, Manfred. *English in Nineteenth-Century England: An Introduction.* Cambridge: Cambridge University Press, 1999.

Gosse, Edmund. "Some Soldier Poets," *The Edinburgh Review, or Critical Journal* 226, 462 (October 1917): 296–316.

———. *Independent.* 52 (January 11, 1900).

———. "The Poetry of Mr. Robert Bridges," rev. of *Shorter Poems,* by Robert Bridges. *Academy* 53 (February 5, 1898).

Graff, Gerald. *Professing Literature: An Institutional History.* Chicago: Chicago University Press, 1987.

Graves, Robert. *Goodbye to All That.* London: Cassell, 1929.

———. *Fairies and Fusiliers* London: Heinemann, 1917.

———. *Over the Brazier.* London: Poetry Bookshop, 1916.

Green, Andrew Jackson. "Robert Bridges: Studies in His Work and Thought to 1904." Ph.D. diss., University of Michigan, 1940.

Grey, Richard. *First Thebaloi, or, Mnemonic Hexameters, after the Method of the Memoria Technica of Dr. Grey: Hellenic History.* London: J. W. Parker, 1855.

———. *Regdol or Mnemonic Hexameters after the Method of the Memoria Technica of Dr. Grey: Roman History.* London: J. W. Parker, 1855.

———. *Wilcongsau, or, Mnemonic Hexameters: after the Method of the Memoria Technica of Dr. Grey, English History.* London: J. W. Parker, 1850.

———. *Memoria Technica; or, a new method of artificial memory, applied to, and exemplified in chronology, history, geography, astronomy. Also Jewish, Grecian, and Roman coins, weights, and measures, &c. With tables proper to the respective sciences, and memorial lines adapted to each table.* London: Printed for John Stagg in Westminster Hall, 1737.

Grierson, H.J.C. *Lyrical Poetry of the Nineteenth Century.* New York: Harcourt, Brace and Company, 1929.

Griffiths, Eric. *The Printed Voice of Victorian Poetry*. Oxford: Oxford University Press, 1989.

Gross, John. *The Rise and Fall of the Man of Letters*. Chicago: Ivan R. Dee, 1969.

Guest, Edwin. *Origines Celticae: A History of Britain in Two Volumes*. London: Macmillan, 1883.

——. *A History of English Rhythms*. Ed. Walter Skeat, 2nd ed. London: George Bell, 1882.

——. *A History of English Rhythms*. London: W. Pickering, 1838.

Guillory, John. "Mute Inglorious Miltons." In *Cultural Capital*, 85–133. Chicago: University of Chicago Press, 1993.

Hall, Catherine. "At Home With History: Macaulay and *The History of England*." In *At Home with Empire: Metropolitan Culture and the Imperial World*, ed. Catherine Hall and Sonya O. Rose. Cambridge: Cambridge University Press, 2006.

Hall, Catherine, Keith McClelland, and Jane Rendall. *Defining the Victorian Nation: Class, Race, Gender and the British Reform Act of 1867*. Cambridge: Cambridge University Press, 2000.

Hall, Jason. "Popular Prosody: Spectacle and the Politics of Victorian Versification," *Nineteenth Century Literature* 62, 2 (September 2007): 222–49.

Hardison, O. B. *Prosody and Purpose in the English Renaissance*. Baltimore: Johns Hopkins University Press, 1989.

Hardy, Florence Emily. *The Later Years of Thomas Hardy*. London: Macmillan, 1930.

Hardy, Thomas. *Wessex Poems*. New York/London: Harper and Bros., 1898

——. *The Trumpet Major*. New York: Henry Holt, 1880

Harmon, William. "English Versification: Fifteen Hundred Years of Continuity and Change," *Studies in Philology* 94, 1 (Winter, 1997): 1–14.

Harrison, Antony. "Victorian Culture Wars: Alexander Smith, Arthur Hugh Clough, and Matthew Arnold in 1853," *Victorian Poetry* 42, 4 (2004): 509–20.

Harrison, Thomas P. "The Birds of Gerard Manley Hopkins," *Studies in Philology* 54, 3 (July 1957): 448–63.

Hart-Davis, Rupert. *Sassoon's War Poems*. London: Faber & Faber, 1983.

Hartman, Geoffrey. *The Unmediated Vision: An Interpretation of Wordsworth, Hopkins, Rilke, and Valéry*. New Haven: Yale University Press, 1954.

Haselwood, Joseph, William Baldwin, John Higgins, and Others. *Mirror for Magistrates, in Five Parts*. London: Lackington, Allen, and Co., 1815.

Heathorn, Stephen. *For Home, Country, and Race: Constructing Gender Class and Englishness in the Elementary School, 1880–1914*. Toronto: University of Toronto Press, 2000.

Hegel, G.W.F. *The Philosophy of Fine Art*. Trans. F.P.B. Osmaston. 4 vols. London: Bell, 1920.

Hendley, Matthew. "'Help us to Secure a Strong, Healthy, Prosperous and Peaceful Britain': The Social Arguments of the Campaign of Compulsory Military Service in Britain, 1899–1914," *Canadian Journal of History* (August 1995): 261–88.

Henry, and David S. E. Buchan. *The Metrical History of Sir William Wallace, Knight of Ellerslie*. Perth: Printed by R. Morison Junior for R. Morison, 1790.

Hibberd, Dominic. *Wilfred Owen: The Last Year, 1917–1918*. London: Constable, 1992.

———. *Owen the Poet*. Basingstoke: Macmillan, 1986.

———. ed. *Poetry of the First World War: A Selection of Critical Essays*. London: Macmillan, 1981.

———. "The Patchwork Flag' (1918) an Unrecorded Book by Robert Graves." *The Review of English Studies*, n.s., 41, 164 (Nov. 1990): 521–32.

Higgins, Lesley, ed. *The Collected Works of Gerard Manley Hopkins. Vol. 4, Oxford Essays and Notes*. Oxford: Oxford University Press, 2006.

Hipp, Daniel. "'By Degrees Regain[ing] Cool Peaceful Air in Wonder': Wilfred Owen's War Poetry as Psychological Therapy," *Midwest Modern Language Association* 35, 1 (Spring 2002): 25–49.

"A History of English Rhythms." *Academy* 22, Nov. 4. 1882, no. 548, July/Dec., 323.

Hodgson, Francis. Review of Dibdin, *A Metrical History of England*. *The Monthly Review* 71 (August 1813).

Holland, Norah M. *Spun Yarn and Spindrift*. London/Toronto: J. M. Dent & Sons; New York: E. P. Dutton & Co., 1918.

Hollander, John. *Vision and Resonance: Two Senses of Poetic Form*. 2nd ed. New Haven, CT: Yale University Press, 1985.

Holmes, Edmond. *Report of the Board of Education for 1899–1900*. Vol. 9. London: HMSO, 1900.

Holmes, John. "The Growth of *The Growth of Love*: Texts and Poems in Robert Bridges's Sonnet Sequence." *The Review of English Studies* 55, 221 (2004): 583–97.

Hopkins, Gerard Manley. "Carrion Comfort," l. 13, 1885–1887. In MacKenzie, Norman. *Poetical Works of Gerard Manley Hopkins*. Oxford: Clarendon Press, 1990.

Horace. *The Works of Horace*. New York: Harper and Row, 1863.

Horn, Pamela. *The Victorian and Edwardian Schoolchild*. Gloucester: Alan Sutton, 1989.

House, Humphry, ed. *The Journals and Papers of Gerard Manley Hopkins*. London: Oxford University Press, 1959.

Howat, G.M.D. "The Nineteenth-Century History Textbook," *British Journal of Educational Studies* 13, 2 (May 1965): 147–58.

Howlett, John Henry. *Metrical Chronology, in which most of the important dates in ancient and modern history are expressed by consonants used for numerals, and formed by aid of vowels into significant words: with historical notes, and questions for the exercise of young students*. London: Longman, Brown, Green, and Longmans, 1846.

Hughes, Linda K. *The Cambridge Introduction to Victorian Poetry*. Cambridge: Cambridge University Press, 2010.

Hughes, Tom. *Tom Brown's School Days*. Cambridge: Macmillan, 1857.

The Hydra. Edinburgh: Craiglockhart War Hospital, 1917–18.

Hynes, Samuel. *A War Imagined*. London: Pimlico, 1991.

———. *The Pattern of Hardy's Poetry*. Chapel Hill: University of North Carolina, 1961.

Ince, Henry. *An Outline of English History: Narrating, in a Methodical Form, the Principal Events of Each Reign; and Interspersed with a Variety of Instructive, and*

Pleasing Information, Relative to the Manners, Customs, Arts, Dresses, &c. of the Different Periods; Designed for the Use of Schools. London: James Gilbert, 1832

The Irish Monthly, 26, 299 (May 1898).

Jackson, Vanessa Furse. *The Poetry of Henry Newbolt: Patriotism Is Not Enough.* Greensboro, NC: ELT Press, 1994.

Jackson, Virginia. "The Story of 'Boon' or The Poetess," *ESQ: A Journal of the American Renaissance* 54, 1–4 (2008): 241–68.

Jackson, Virginia, and Yopie Prins. "Lyrical Studies," *Victorian Literature and Culture* 27 (1999): 521–30.

Jamison, Anne. *Poetics en Passant: Redefining the Relationship Between Victorian and Modern Poetry.* New York: Palgrave Macmillan, 2009.

Jespersen, Otto. *Language, Its Nature, Development, and Origin.* New York: Henry Holt, 1922.

Johnson, Samuel. *Dictionary,* 6th ed. (London, 1785).

———. *A Dictionary of the English Language: in which words are deduced from their originals, and illustrated in their different significations by examples from the best writers. To which are prefixed, a history of the language, and an English grammar.* London: W. Strahan; J. and P. Knapton; T. and T. Longman; C. Hitch and L. Hawes; A. Millar; and R. and J. Dodsley, 1755–56.

Jones, Dorothy Richardson. *King of Critics: George Saintsbury, 1845–1933.* Ann Arbor: University of Michigan Press, 1992.

Kay-Shuttleworth, James. *Sir James Kay-Shuttleworth on Popular Education.* With an introduction and notes by Trygve R. Tholfson, ed. New York: Teachers College Press, 1974.

Keats, John. *Letters of John Keats: A New Selection.* Ed. Robert Gittings. Oxford: Oxford University Press, 1970.

Kemble, J. M. *A Translation of the Anglo-Saxon Poem Beowulf.* London: Pickering, 1837.

Kennedy, Patrick John. *The Universal Irish Song Book.* New York: P. J. Kennedy, 1884, 1892, 1894, 1898.

Kerkering, John. *The Poetics of National and Racial Identity in Nineteenth-Century American Literature.* Cambridge: Cambridge University Press, 2003.

"King Alfred's Anglo-Saxon Version of the Metres of Boethius, with an English translation and notes," anonymous review. *A Gentleman's Magazine.* 158, 49.

Kipling, Rudyard. *Barrack-Room Ballads and Other Verses.* London: Methuen, 1872.

"Kipling: Richard Le Gallienne's Volume Devoted to a Severe Criticism of Him." *New York Times,* May 19, 1900.

"Kipling's Tribute to Lord Roberts: Reproaches England for Refusing to Hear His 'Pleading in the Marketplace.'" *New York Times,* November 19, 1914.

Lamborn, Arnold. *The Rudiments of Criticism.* Oxford: Clarendon Press, 1916.

Lawson, John, and Harold Silver. *A Social History of Education in England.* London: Methuen, 1973.

Layamon, Wace, Frederic Madden. *Layamon's Brut, or Chronicle of Britain; a poetical semi-Saxon paraphrase of the Brut of Wace.* London: Society of Antiquaries of London, 1847.

Le Gallienne, Richard. *Rudyard Kipling: A Criticism.* London: John Lane, 1900.

Le Vay John. "Kipling's Recessional," *The Explicator* 62, 3 (Spring 2004): 153–54.

Leese, Peter. "'Why are They Not Cured?' British Shellshock Treatment During the Great War." In *Traumatic Pasts: History, Psychiatry, and Trauma in the Modern Age, 1870–1930*, ed. Mark S. Micale and Paul Lerner. Cambridge: Cambridge University Press, 2001.

Leighton, Angela. *On Form: Poetry, Aestheticism, and the Legacy of a Word*. Oxford: Oxford University Press, 2008.

Lenox, David, and Alexander Sturrock. *The Elements of Physical Education: A Teacher's Manual* (with Original Musical Accompaniments to the Drill by Harry Everitt Loseby). Edinburgh: Blackwood, 1898.

Levine, Caroline. "Formal Pasts and Formal Possibilities in English Studies." *Literature Compass* 4, 4 (2007): 1241–56.

Lewis, C. Day. *The Collected Poems of Wilfred Owen with a Memoir by Edmund Blunden*. London: Chatto & Windus, 1963.

——. *A Hope for Poetry*. Oxford: Blackwell, 1934.

Lewis, C. S. *De Descriptione Temporum: An Inaugural Lecture*. Cambridge: Cambridge University Press, 1955.

Lewis, Pericles. *Cambridge Introduction to Modernism*. Cambridge: Cambridge University Press, 2007.

Lootens, Tricia. "Victorian Poetry and Patriotism." In *Victorian Poetry,* ed. Joseph Bristow. Cambridge: Cambridge University Press, 2000.

Loring, Andrew. *The Rhymer's Lexicon*. London: Routledge and Sons, 1905.

Lynch, Jack. *The Lexicographer's Dilemma*. New York: Walker & Company, 2009.

Macaulay, Thomas Babington, Baron. *Lays of Ancient Rome*. London: Longman, Brown, Green, and Longmans, 1842.

MacDougall, Hugh A. *Racial Myth in English History: Trojans, Teutons, and Anglo-Saxons*. Hanover, NH: University Press of New England, 1982.

Mack, Edward C. *Public Schools and British Opinion Since 1860*. New York: Columbia University Press, 1941.

Mackenzie, John M. *Imperialism and Popular Culture*. Manchester: Manchester University Press, 1986.

——. "Imperialism and the School Textbook." In *Propaganda and Empire: The Manipulation of British Public Opinion, 1880–1960*. Manchester: Manchester University Press, 1984.

MacKenzie, Norman. *The Early Poetic Manuscripts of Gerard Manley Hopkins in Facsimile*. New York: Garland, 1991.

——. *The Later Poetic Manuscripts of Gerard Manley Hopkins in Facsimile*. New York: Garland, 1991.

——. *Poetical Works of Gerard Manley Hopkins*. Oxford: Clarendon Press, 1990.

——. "Introduction to the Fourth Edition," *The Poems of Gerard Manley Hopkins*. W. H. Gardner and Norman MacKenzie, eds., 4th ed. Oxford: Oxford University Press, 1967.

Mackenzie, Robert Tait. *Exercise in Education and Medicine*. Philadelphia: Saunders, 1909.

Magnus, Laurie, and Cecil Headlam, eds. *Prayers of the Poets, A Calendar of Devotion*. Edinburgh: Blackwood, 1899.

Manchester Guardian, December 29, 1920, 14,18.

Mangan, J. A.. *Athleticism in the Victorian and Edwardian Public School*. London: Frank Cass, 2000.

Mangnall, Richmal. *Historical and Miscellaneous Questions for the Use of Young People*. London: Longmans, 1798.

Mann, Charles Wesley. *School Recreations and Amusements, Being a Companion Volume to King's School Interests and Duties, Prepared Especially for Teachers' Reading Circles*. New York: American Book Company, 1896.

Markley, A. A. *Stateliest Measures: Tennyson and the Literature of Greece and Rome*. Toronto: University of Toronto Press, 2004.

Marsland, Elizabeth. *The Nation's Cause: French, English, and German Poetry of the First World War*. London: Routledge, 1991.

Martin, Meredith and Yisrael Levin, eds. "Victorian Prosody," special issue *Victorian Poetry* 49, 1 (Summer 2012).

Mathews, Elkin. Review of *Admirals All*, by Henry Newbolt. *Literature* 1 (January 1, 1898): 324.

Mathieson, Margaret. *The Preachers of Culture: A Study of English and Its Teachers*. London: Allen and Unwin, 1992.

Maynard, Theodore. "The Artist as Hero." *New Witness*, January 24, 1919, 259–60.

Mayor, Joseph. *Chapters on English Metre*. London: C. J. Clay, 1886; 2nd edition, Cambridge: Cambridge University Press, 1901.

McKelvy, William. *The English Cult of Literature: Devoted Readers, 1774–1880*. Charlottesville: University of Virginia Press, 2007.

McPherson, Robert G. *Theory of Higher Education in Nineteenth-Century England*. Athens: University of Georgia Press, 1959.

Meynell, Alice. *The Rhythm of Life*. 5th ed. London/New York: The Bodley Head, 1896.

———. *The Last Poems of Alice Meynell*. London: Burns, Oates and Washbourne, Ltd., 1923

Michael, Ian. *The Teaching of English from the Sixteenth Century to 1870*. Cambridge: Cambridge University Press, 1987.

Miles, Alfred H., ed. "Gerard Hopkins." In *The Poets and Poetry of the Century*, vol. 8, "Bridges and Contemporaries." London: Hutchinson & Co., 10 vols. 1891–97; 12 vols. 1905–07.

Miles, Louis Wardlaw. "The Poetry of Robert Bridges," *Sewanee Review* 23 (April 1915): 129–40.

Miller, J. Hillis. *The Linguistic Moment: From Wordsworth to Stevens*. Princeton: Princeton University Press, 1985.

———. "The Univocal Chiming." In *Hopkins: A Collection of Critical Essays*, ed. Geoffrey H. Hartman. Englewood Cliffs, NJ: Prentice-Hall, Inc., 1966.

Milroy, James. *The Language of Gerard Manley Hopkins*. London: Andre Deutsch, 1977

Minto, William. "A History of English Rhythms," rev. of *A History of English Rhythms* by Edwin Guest, *Academy* 22, 548 (Nov. 4, 1882).

Monro, Harold. "Varia," *Poetry and Drama* 2 (September 1914): 251.

———. *The Poetry Review* 1 (January 1912)

Montefiore, J. Gompertz. *The History of England in Verse*. London: Ward, Lock, and Tyler, 1876.

Morley, Henry. *Shorter English Poems*. London: Cassell, 1883.

Morrisson, Mark S. *The Public Face of Modernism: Little Magazines, Audiences, and Reception, 1905–1920*. Madison: University of Wisconsin Press, 2001.

"Mr. Bridges and Metre," unsigned review in *The Academy and Literature* 62 (Jan./June 1902):85.

Mugglestone, Lynda. *Lost for Words: The Hidden History of the Oxford English Dictionary*. New Haven: Yale University Press, 2005.

Müller, F. Max, M.A. *Lectures on the Science of Language*. Vol. 1. London: Longmans, Green, and Co., 1871.

Murray, Lindley. *English Grammar Comprehending the Principles and Rules of the Language*. 6th ed., New York: Collins & Co., 1829; 58th ed., London: Longman, Hurst, 1867.

———. *English Grammar Adapted to the Different Classes of Learners*. 4th ed. York: Wilson, Spence and Mawman, 1798.

———. *English Grammar Adapted to the Different Classes of Learners. With an Appendix, Containing Rules and Observations for Promoting Perspicuity in Speaking and Writing*. York: Wilson, Spence and Mawman, 1795.

Murray, Lindley, and Abel Flint. *Murray's English Grammar, Abridged to Which is Added, Under the Head of Prosody, an Abridgement of Sheridan's Lectures on Elocution: Also, Murray's Treatise on Punctuation at Large: Together with a System of Exercises Adapted to the Several Rules of Syntax and Punctuation*. Hartford, CT: Lincoln & Gleason, 1807.

Murry, John Middleton. *Letters on Poetry from W. B. Yeats to Dorothy Wellesley*. Oxford: Oxford University Press, 1940.

———. "The Poet of the War," *Nation and Athenaeum* 28 (February 19, 1921): 705–07.

———. *The Muses Library; or a Series of English Poetry*. London: Printed for J. Wilcox; T. Green; J. Brindley; and T. Osborn, 1737.

N.J.G. "A Quartette of Irish Writers," *Irish Quarterly Review* 5, 20 (Dec. 1855): 697–731.

Nadel, Ira Bruce. *Cambridge Introduction to Ezra Pound*. Cambridge: Cambridge University Press, 2007.

Neuberg, Victor E. *Popular Education in Eighteenth Century England*. London: Woburn Press, 1971.

A New English Dictionary on Historical Principles. Oxford: Oxford University Press, 1884–1928.

Newbolt, Margaret, and Henry Newbolt. *The Later Life and Letters of Sir Henry Newbolt*. London: Faber & Faber, 1942.

Newbolt, Sir Henry. *My World as in My Time*. London: Faber & Faber, 1932.

———. *The Teaching of English in England*. London: HMSO, 1921.

———. *St. George's Day and Other Poems*. London: John Murray, 1918.

———. *Tales of the Great War*. London: Longmans, Green, 1916.

———. "British Ballads," *English Review* (1915): 452–61.

———. *Poems, New and Old*. London: John Murray, 1913, 1914, 1916, 1917.

———. "The Future of English Verse," *International Quarterly* 9 (Mar/June 1904): 366.

———. *The Island Race*. London: E. Matthews, 1898

———. *Admirals All: And Other Verses*. London: E. Mathews, 1897.

"No measure is too intricate for him to master," anonymous article in *Blackwood's Magazine,* 164 (October 1898): 470–82.

Norris, Margot. *Writing War in the Twentieth Century.* Charlottesville: University of Virginia Press, 2000.

"Notes and Correspondences," *Notes and Queries* 101 (January 20, 1900).

"Notes and News," *The Academy* 54, 25 (July 1898).

O'Brien, William. *The Ancient Rhythmical Art Recovered.* Dublin: Andrew Milliken, 1843.

Omond, T. S. *English Metrists of the Eighteenth and Nineteenth Centuries: Being a Sketch of English Prosodical Criticism During the Last Two Hundred Years.* New York/London: Oxford University Press, 1907.

———. *A Study of Metre.* London: G. Richards, 1903.

———. *English Metrists.* Turnbridge Wells: R. Pelton, 1903.

———. *English Hexameter Verse.* Edinburgh: David Douglas, 1897.

———. *English Verse-Structure (a prefatory study).* Edinbugh: David Douglas, 1897.

Owen, Harold. *Journey From Obscurity, Wilfred Owen, 1893–1918: Memoirs of the Owen Family.* London/New York: Oxford University Press, 1963–65.

Owen, Harold, and Clive Bell, eds. *Wilfred Owen, Collected Letters.* London: Oxford University Press, 1963.

Owen, Wilfred. "Outlook Tower," Box 3, Owen MSS, Oxford English Faculty Library (OEF), Fasc. BB Owen MSS OEF 427.

———. "Points to Note about my Sonnets" *(sic)* English Faculty Library, University of Oxford V.f404r, accessible here: http://www.oucs.ox.ac.uk/ww1lit/collections/item/5017?CISOBOX=1&REC=4 date unknown (last accessed May 28, 2011).

Owen Collection, "Early Press Cuttings 1914–1916" Box 14, English Faculty Library, University of Oxford *The Sunday Times,* (December 18, 1920), OEF, 14:15, *The Daily Herald,* (December 22, 1920), OEF, 14:17, *The Daily News,* December 17, 1920, OEF, 14:13. *Times Literary Supplement* (January 6, 1921), OEF, 14:26, *Manchester Guardian* (December 29, 1920), OEF, 14:18.

Palmer, D. J. *The Rise of English Studies: An Account of the Study of English Language and Literature from Its Origins to the Making of the Oxford English School.* London: Oxford University Press for the University of Hull, 1965.

Papajewski, Helmut. "The Variety of Kipling," *Kipling Journal* 56 (1983): 23.

Parker, Joanne. *England's Darling: The Victorian Cult of Alfred the Great.* Manchester: Manchester University Press, 2007.

Parry, Ann. *The Poetry of Rudyard Kipling.* Buckingham, UK/Philadelphia: Open University Press, 1992.

Patmore, Coventry. *Poems.* Volume 2, *The Unknown Eros, Amelia, Etc.* London: George Bell and Sons, 1890.

———. "Prefatory Study on English Metrical Law." In *Amelia, Tamerton, Church Tower, Etc.* London: George Bell and Sons, 1878.

———. "English Metrical Critics," *North British Review,* 1857.

———. and Mary Augustine Roth. *Coventry Patmore's "Essay on English Metrical Law": A Critical Edition with Commentary by Sister Mary Augustine Roth.* Washington, D.C.: Catholic University of America Press, 1961.

Patmore, Derek. "Three Poets Discuss New Verse Forms: The Correspondence of Gerard Manley Hopkins, Robert Bridges, and Coventry Patmore," *The Month*, n.s., 6, 2 (Aug. 1951): 69–78.

Penn, Alan. *Targeting Schools: Drill, Militarism and Imperialism*. London: Woburn Press, 1999.

Percy, Thomas. *Reliques of Ancient English Poetry: Consisting of Old Heroic Ballads, Songs, and other Pieces of our earlier Poets, (Chiefly of the Lyric kind.) Together with some few of later Date*, 2nd ed., 3 vols. London: J. Dodsley, 1767.

Perkins, David. *History of Modern Poetry: From the 1890s to the High Modernist Mode*. Cambridge: Harvard University Press, 1976.

Petheram, John. *A Historical Sketch of the Progress and Present State of Anglo-Saxon Literature in England*. London: E. Lumley, 1840.

Phillips, Catherine. *Gerard Manley Hopkins and the Victorian Visual World*. Oxford: Oxford University Press, 2007.

———. *Robert Bridges: A Biography*. Oxford: Oxford University Press, 1992.

Pinch, Adela. "Love Thinking." *Victorian Studies* 50, 3 (Spring 2008): 379–97.

Pinney, Thomas, ed. *The Letters of Rudyard Kipling: 1911–1919*. Vol. 4. Iowa City: University of Iowa Press, 1999.

Plotkin, Cary. *The Tenth Muse: Victorian Philology and the Genesis of the Poetic Language of Gerard Manley Hopkins*. Carbondale/Edwardsville: Southern Illinois University Press, 1989.

Poe, Edgar Allan. "Rationale of Verse," *Southern Literary Messenger* 14 (Oct.–Nov. 1848): 673–82.

"Poems of Wilfred Owen," *The Daily News*, December 17, 1920, 14:13. Box 14 "Early Press Cuttings 1914–1946" Wilfred Owen Collection, Oxford English Faculty Library.

"A Poet of Content," rev. of *Shorter Poems*, by Robert Bridges. *The Academy and Literature*, no. 1407. April 22, 1899, 454–55

Pope, Jessie. *War Poems*. London: Grant Richards, 1915.

———. *More War Poems*. London: Grant Richards, 1915.

———. *Simple Rhymes for Stirring Times*. London: C. Arthur Pearson, 1916.

Potter, Stephen. *The Muse in Chains: A Study in Education*. London: Jonathan Cape, 1937.

Pound, Ezra. *The Pisan Cantos*, ed. Richard Sieburth. New York: New Directions, 1948.

———. *Hugh Selwyn Mauberly*. London: Ovid Press, 1920.

———. *The Literary Essays of Ezra Pound*. New York: New Directions, 1918.

———. "Robert Bridges' New Book," *Poetry*, October 1915.

———. "A Few Don'ts for an Imagist," *Poetry* 1, 6 (March 1913).

———. "Prolegomena," *Poetry and Drama*, 1912.

———. *Ripostes of Ezra Pound*. London: S. Swift and Co, 1912.

Pound, Ezra, and D. D. Paige. *The Selected Letters of Ezra Pound, 1907–1941*. London: Faber and Faber Ltd., 1971.

Preston, Carrie J. *Modernism's Mythic Pose: Gender, Genre, Solo Performance*. New York: Oxford University Press, 201.

Priestley, Joseph. *The Rudiments of English Grammar*. London: P. Byrne, 1761.

Prins, Yopie. *Ladies' Greek*. Princeton, NJ: Princeton University Press, 2013.

————. "Nineteenth-Century Homers and the Hexameter Mania." In *Nation, Language, and the Ethics of Translation*, ed. Sandra Bermann and Michael Wood, 229–56. Princeton, NJ: Princeton University Press, 2005.

————. "Victorian Meters." In *The Cambridge Companion to Victorian Poetry*, ed. Joseph Bristow, 89–113. Cambridge: Cambridge University Press, 2000.

————. *Victorian Sappho.* Princeton, NJ: Princeton University Press, 1999.

Quiller-Couch, Arthur, ed. *Oxford Book of English Verse.* Oxford: Clarendon Press, 1912.

Quinn, William "Hopkins's Anglo-Saxon," *Hopkins Quarterly* 8 (1981).

Rask, Rasmus. *A Grammar of the Anglo-Saxon Tongue.* Translated from the Danish by Benjamin Thorpe. London: Trübner and Co., 1830; reprinted 1865.

Raymond, George. *Chronicles of England.* London: W. Smith, 1842, 1852.

Read, Allen Walker. "The Motivation of Lindley Murray's Grammatical Work." *The Journal of English and German Philology* 38, 4 (Oct. 1939): 525–39.

Read, Herbert. *Art Now: An Introduction to the Theory of Modern Painting and Sculpture.* London: Faber & Faber, 1933.

Report of the Commission on the State of Popular Education. Vol 1. London: HMSO, 1861.

Reynolds, Matthew. *The Realms of Verse.* Oxford: Oxford University Press, 2001.

Richards, I. A. *So Much Nearer: Essays Towards a World English.* New York: Harcourt, 1968.

————. *Basic English and Its Uses.* New York: Norton, 1943.

————. *Practical Criticism.* London: Kegan Paul, Trench, Trubner, 1929.

————. "Gerard Hopkins," *The Dial* 81, 3 (September 1926): 195.

Richards, James Brinsley. *Seven Years at Eton.* London: Richard Bentley and Sons, 1883.

Richardson, Alan. *Literature, Education, and Romanticism: Reading as Social Practice 1780–1832.* Cambridge: Cambridge University Press, 1994.

Ricks, Christopher. *Tennyson,* 2nd ed. Berkeley/Los Angeles: University of California Press, 1989.

Rivers, W.H.R. *Conflict and Dream.* London: Keegan Paul, 1923.

————. "'The Repression of War Experience': An Address Delivered before the Section of Psychiatry, Royal Society of Medicine, on Dec. 4th 1917." *The Lancet,* Feb. 2, 1918, 8.

Roberts, Field-Marshal Earl. *A Nation in Arms.* New York: E. P. Dutton, 1907.

Robson, Catherine. *Heart Beats: Everyday Life and the Memorized Poem.* Forthcoming, 2012.

————. "Standing on the Burning Deck: Poetry, Performance, History," *PMLA* 120, 1 (2005): 148–62.

Ross, Robert. *The Georgian Revolt: Rise and Fall of a Poetic Ideal 1910–1922.* Carbondale/Edwardsville: Southern Illinois University Press, 1965.

Rossendale, A. *History of the Kings and Queens of England in Verse; from King Egbert to Queen Victoria.* London: Souter and Law, 1846.

Rudy, Jason. *Electric Meters: Victorian Physiological Poetics.* Athens: Ohio University Press, 2009.

————. "Manifest Prosody." Special issue "Victorian Prosody," Meredith Martin and Yisrael Levin, ed., *Victorian Poetry* 49, 1 (Summer 2012).

Ruskin, John. *Modern Painters. Of Many Things. Part IV.* New York: Wiley and Halstad, 1859.

Saintsbury, George. *Last Vintage.* London: Methuen, 1950.

———. *Last Scrap Book.* London: Macmillan, 1924.

Saintsbury, George. *A History of Elizabethan Literature.* 2nd ed. New York: Macmillan, 1912.

———. *A History of English Prosody from the Twelfth Century to the Present Day.* Vols. 1–3. London: Macmillan, 1910.

———. *A History of English Criticism.* New York: Dodd, Mead, 1900.

———. *A History of English Criticism.* Edinburgh/London: W. Blackwood and Sons, 1901 (2nd edition 1902).

———. *A History of Nineteenth-Century Literature.* London: Macmillan, 1896, 1900, 1901.

———. *A Short History of English Literature.* London: Macmillan, 1898.

———. Review of Coventry Patmore's *English Metrical Law. Atheneaum* 2642 (June 15, 1878).

Sassoon, Siegfried. *Sherston's Progress.* London: Faber and Faber Ltd, 1936.

Saville, Julia. *A Queer Chivalry: The Homoerotic Asceticism of Gerard Manley Hopkins.* Charlottesville: University of Virginia Press, 2000.

Schipper, Jakob. *Englische Metrik, in three volumes.* Bonn: Verlag Von Emil Strauss, 1888. Trans. into English as *A History of English Versification.* Oxford: Clarendon Press, 1910. Abridged edition. *Grundriss der englischen metrik.* Vienna, 1895.

The Scotsman, Poetry section, October 18, 1897, 3.

Selleck, R.J.W. *The New Education: the English background 1870–1914.* Melbourne: Pitman, 1968.

Serl, Emma and William J. Pelo, comps. *American Ideals: Selected Patriotic Readings for Seventh and Eighth Grades and Junior High Schools.* New York/Chicago: Gregg, 1919.

Shaw, Bernard. "Preface: A Professor of Phonetics," *Androcles and the Lion, Overruled, Pygmalion.* New York: Brentano's, 1916.

Shayer, David. *The Teaching of English in Schools.* London/Boston: Routledge & Kegan Paul, 1972.

Sheridan, Thomas. *A General Dictionary of the English Language.* London: J. Dodsley, 1780.

———. *Lectures on The Art of Reading.* London: Printed for J. Dodsley, Pall-Mall; J. Wilkie, St. Paul's Church-Yard; E. and C. Dilly, in the Poultry; and T. Davies, Russell Street, Covent Garden, 1775.

———. *A Course of Lectures on Elocution Together with Two Dissertations on Language.* London: W. Strahan, 1762.

Shipley, Orby, ed. *Carmina Mariana.* London/New York: Burnes and Oak, 1893.

Silkin, Jon. *Out of Battle: The Poetry of the Great War.* Oxford: Oxford University Press, 1972.

Simmons, Clare. *Reversing the Conquest: History and Myth in Nineteenth-Century British Literature.* New Brunswick: Rutgers University Press, 1990.

Smith, M. Van Wyk. *Drummer Hodge: The Poetry of the Anglo-Boer War (1899–1902).* Oxford: Clarendon Press, 1978.

Society for the Purification of English Tracts. London: Clarendon Press, 1919.

Soffer, Reba N. *Discipline and Power: The University, History, & the Making of an English Elite 1870–1930.* Palo Alto: Stanford University Press, 1994.

Songs and Sonnets for England in War Time: Being a Collection of Lyrics by Various Authors Inspired by the Great War. London: John Lane, 1914.

The Spirit of The Nation, Ballads and Songs by the Writers of "The Nation." Dublin: James Duffy, 1845.

Spoel, Phillipa M. "Rereading the Elocutionists: The Rhetoric of Thomas Sheridan's 'A Course of Lectures on Elocution' and John Walker's 'Elements of Elocution.'" *Rhetorica,* 19, 1 (Winter 2001): 49–91.

Springhall, J. O. "Lord Meath, Youth, and Empire." *Journal of Contemporary History* 5, 4 (1970): 97–111.

Sprinker, Michael. "Gerard Manley Hopkins on the Origin of Language." *Journal of the History of Ideas* 41,1 (Jan.–Mar., 1980): 113–18.

———. *A Counterpoint of Dissonance.* Baltimore: Johns Hopkins University Press, 1980.

Spurgeon, Caroline Frances Eleanor. *Poetry in the Light of War.* London: English Association, 1917.

St. Clair, William. *The Reading Nation in the Romantic Period.* Cambridge: Cambridge University Press, 2004.

Stallworthy, Jon, ed. *The Complete Poems and Fragments of Wilfred Owen.* 2 volumes. Oxford: Oxford University Press, 1983.

———. *Wilfred Owen.* London: Oxford University Press, 1974.

Stanford, Donald. *In the Classic Mode: The Achievement of Robert Bridges.* Newark: University of Deleware Press, 1978.

———. ed. *Selected Letters of Robert Bridges. Volume 2.* Newark: University of Deleware Press, 1984.

Steele, Timothy. *Missing Measures: Modern Poetry and the Revolt Against Meter.* Fayetteville: University of Arkansas Press, 1990.

Steiner, George. "On Difficulty," *The Journal of Aesthetics and Art Criticism* 36, 3 (Spring 1978): 263–76.

Stewart, Susan. "Letter on Sound." In *Close Listening: Poetry and the Performed Word,* ed. Charles Bernstein. Oxford: Oxford University Press, 1988.

Stone, William Johnson. *On the Use of Classical Metres in English.* London: Henry Frowde, 1899.

Strabone, Jeff. "Samuel Johnson Standardizer of English, Preserver of Gaelic." *ELH* 77, 1 (Spring 2010): 327–65.

———. "Grammarians and Barbarians: How the Vernacular Revival Transformed British Literature and Identity in the Eighteenth and Nineteenth Centuries." Ph.D. Diss., New York University, 2008, *Dissertation Abstracts International.*

Stray, Christopher. *Classics Transformed.* Oxford: Clarendon Press, 1998.

———, and Gillian Sutherland. "Mass Markets: Education." In *The Cambridge History of Britain,* Volume 6, 1830–1914, ed. David McKitterick, Cambridge: Cambridge University Press, 2009.

Sweet, Henry. "On Germanic and English Philology." *Transactions of the Philological Society,* 1885, 115–20.

Swinnerton, Frank. *The Georgian Scene, A Literary Panorama.* New York: Farrar & Rinehart, 1934.

Symonds, John Addington. "Robert Bridges," *Monthly Review* 4 (July 1901): 114–27.

———. *Sketches and Studies of Southern Europe.* New York: Harper's, 1880.

———. "The Blank Verse of Milton," *The Fortnightly Review* 16 (December 1874): 767–81 (reprinted in *Blank Verse.* London: John C. Nimmo, 1895).

———. *Blank Verse.* London: John C. Nimmo 1895.

Taylor, Dennis. *Hardy's Language and Victorian Philology.* Oxford: Clarendon Press, 1993.

———. *Hardy's Metres and Victorian Prosody.* Oxford, Clarendon Press, 1988.

"Teachers and the Education Bill." *The Museum,* November 2, 1868, 296–301.

"Teaching by Versification," *Cyclopedia of Education.* 1913; London: Macmillan, 1911–13.

Thomas, Edward. "War Poetry," *Poetry and Drama* 2, 8 (December 1914).

Thornton, Robert Kelsey Rough (R.K.R.). *Poery of the 1890s.* Hammondsworth: Penguin Books, 1970.

T. M., Esq. "Poetical Chronology of the Kings of England." In "Poetical Essays." *Gentleman's Magazine* printed in serial, monthly between September 1773–January 1774.

Times Literary Supplement (January 6, 1921) 14: 26. Box 14 "Early Press Cuttings 1914–1946," Wilfred Owen Collection, Oxford English Faculty Library.

Tomlinson, Alan. "Strange Meeting in a Strange Land: Wilfred Owen and Shelley," *Studies in Romanticism* 32, 1 (Spring 1993): 75–95.

Trench, Richard Chevenix. *On the Study of Words (1851) and English Past and Present (1855).* London: J. M. Dent and Sons Ltd., 1927.

———. *On the Study of Words.* New York: Redfield, 1851.

Trilling, Lionel. *Matthew Arnold.* Cleveland: Meridian, 1939.

Tucker, Herbert F. *Epic: Britain's Heroic Muse 1790–1910.* Oxford/New York: Oxford University Press, 2008.

Turner, Sharon. *History of England: The History of Anglo-Saxons from the Earliest Period to the Norman Conquest.* 3rd ed. 3 vols. London: Longman, Orme, Brown, Green, and Longmans, 1820.

The Universal Irish Song Book. New York: P. J. Kennedy, 1898.

Valpy, Richard. *A Poetical Chronology of the Kings of England.* Reading: Printed by Smart and Cowslade. London: Sold by Elmsley, Pridden, Richardson, Robinson, and Williams, 1794.

Vandenhoff, George. *The Art of Elocution as an Essential Part of Rhetoric: With Instructions in Gesture and an Appendix of Oratorical, Poetical, and Dramatic Extracts.* London: S. Low, 1867.

Vandenhoff, George, and Edgar Allan Poe. *A Plain System of Elocution.* 2nd ed. New York: Shephard, 1845.

Vassey, Veronica. *Tiny Verses for Tiny Workers. Being a Series of Recitations and Games on Musical Drill & the Kindergarten Occupations.* London: Charles & Dible, 1898.

Vay, John Le. "Kipling's Recessional," *The Explicator* 62, 3 (Spring 2004): 153–54.

Vincent, David. *The Rise of Mass Literacy: Reading and Writing in Modern Europe.* Oxford: Blackwell, 2000.

———. *Literacy and Popular Culture in Britain, 1750–1914.* Cambridge: Cambridge University Press, 1989.

Viswanathan, Gauri. *Masks of Conquest: Literary Study and British Rule in India*. Oxford: Oxford University Press, 1989.

Walker, John, *Elements of Elocution*. London: Cooper and Wilson, 1781.

Wallcott, Fred G. *The Origins of Culture and Anarchy: Matthew Arnold and Popular Education in England*. Toronto: University of Toronto Press, 1970.

Ward, Thomas. *The English Poets*. London: Macmillan, 1881.

Ward, William. *A Grammar of the English Language*. York: A. Ward, 1767.

Warton, Thomas. *A History of English Poetry*. London: J. Dodiley, Pall-Mall, 1781.

Waterhouse, Elizabeth, ed. *Little Book of Life and Death*. London: Methuen & Co, 1902.

Webb, Thomas E. F. " 'Dottyville'—Craiglockhart War Hospital and Shell-shock Treatments in the First World War." *Journal of the Royal Society of Medicine* 99, 97 (July 2006): 342–46.

Welland, D.S.R. *Wilfred Owen: A Critical Study*. London: Chatto & Windus, 1960.

Wellesley, Dorothy. *Letters on Poetry from W. B. Yeats to Dorothy Wellesley*. Oxford: Oxford University Press, 1940.

Welsh, Charles, ed., *Golden Treasury of Irish Songs and Lyrics*. New York: Dodge Publishing Co., 1907.

Whitaker, Thomas. *Piers Plowman*. London: John Murray, 1813.

White, Norman. "Hopkins as the Crow of Maenefa." *Hopkins Quarterly* 23, 3–4 (Summer/Fall 1996): 113–20.

———. *Hopkins: A Literary Biography*. Oxford: Oxford University Press, 1992.

Wilson, J. Dover. Introduction to *Culture and Anarchy*, by Matthew Arnold, J. Dover Wilson, ed. Cambridge: Cambridge University Press, 1960.

———. "Poetry and the Child," *The English Association Pamphlet*, no. 34 (February, 1916).

Wimsatt, James I. *Hopkins's Poetics of Speech Sound: Sprung Rhythm, Lettering, Inscape*. Toronto: University of Toronto Press, 2006.

Winter, Jay. *Sites of Memory, Sites of Mourning*. Cambridge: Cambridge University Press, 1998.

Wolfson, Susan. *Formal Charges: The Shaping of Poetry in British Romanticism*. Palo Alto: Stanford University Press, 1999.

Woods, William F. "The Cultural Tradition of Nineteenth-Century 'Traditional' Grammar Teaching." *Rhetoric Society Quarterly* 15.1–2 (Winter–Spring 1985): 3–12.

Woolf, Virginia. *To The Lighthouse*. New York: Harcourt, Brace, and World, Inc., 1927.

Wordsworth, William. *Selected Poems and Prefaces,* ed. Jack Stillinger. Boston: Houghton Mifflin, 1965.

Yeats, W. B., ed. *Oxford Book of Modern Verse, 1892–1935*. Oxford: Oxford University Press, 1936.

———. *Letters on Poetry from W. B. Yeats to Dorothy Wellesley*. Oxford: Oxford University Press, 1930.

Young, Allan. "W.H.R. Rivers and The War Neuroses," *Journal of the History of the Behavioral Sciences* 35, 4 (Fall 1999): 359–78.

Zimmerman, Virginia. *Excavating Victorians*. Albany: State University of New York Press, 2008.

INDEX

❧

Page numbers in **bold** indicate illustrations.